EXPERIENCING GOD

EXPERIENCING GOD

A Theology of
Human Experience

by
Donald L. Gelpi, S.J.

PAULIST PRESS
New York/Ramsey/Toronto

Library of Congress
Catalog Card Number: 77-14854

ISBN: 0-8091-2061-5

Published by Paulist Press
Editorial Office: 1865 Broadway, New York, N.Y. 10023
Business Office: 545 Island Road, Ramsey, N.J. 07446

Printed and bound in the
·United States of America

Contents

Preface

This book needs a bit of explanation. It is chronologically the second of a series of essays in foundational theology. The third such essay is in process of preparation, and others lie sketched in the dust closet of my imagination.

The first essay published in this projected series was *Charism and Sacrament: A Theology of Christian Conversion*. But while it was chronologically the first, it is logically the second. Its first chapter is a culling of themes from the pages of the book you now hold.

My reasons for publishing *Charism and Sacrament* first were partly pastoral and partly pedagogical. Its scope goes beyond the interests and concerns of popular charismatic piety. I have myself become convinced, however, that unless the charismatic renewal can acquire a critical self-understanding and a theological sophistication it now too often lacks, it will end by "domesticating the Spirit." Already the renewal is growing institutional structures that are inbred and at times betray the absence of intellectual and moral conversion. Moreover, by focusing too narrowly on the gifts that grace human affectivity, the charismatic renewal seems to me on occasion to be popularizing a spirituality that is not integrally charismatic. Also lacking is a critical theology of conversion that is capable of relating a theology of the gifts to sacramental theology.

I attempted to address myself to many of these questions in *Charism and Sacrament*. But my deeper speculative intent was to elaborate a foundational theology that could interpret the experience of Christian worship in all of its social complexity. I realized at the time that such a theory can only be derivative. It presupposes a foundational anthropology and rests on very specific methodological postulates. *Experiencing God* is my attempt to articulate both with some clarity and, hopefully, with readability.

The two manuscripts took shape simultaneously. A good teacher tries, however, to capitalize on the interests of students and turn them to educational advantage. Whatever else it has done, the charismatic renewal has elicited considerable popular interest. Those involved in prayer groups have an insatiable demand for teaching, though not all enjoy the technicalities of foundational thought. And observers of the

1

movement feel a growing need to get some kind of theological handle on it. It made good teaching sense, therefore, to offer the public *Charism and Sacrament* first.

There were, I realized, some disadvantages to such an approach, as any reader of the first chapter of *Charism and Sacrament* will probably agree. Hopefully, its obscurities will be dissipated somewhat by the present study. My students, who are both critical and kind, assure me that they are.

There was in addition a less obvious disadvantage that the reader of both volumes will probably sense. *Experiencing God* is logically prior to *Charism and Sacrament*. In the present volume I argue that the archetype of the positive transformative anima is capable of yielding an appreciative insight into the reality of the Holy Spirit. Having exposed my argument, I refer subsequently to the Spirit as She. In *Charism and Sacrament* the Spirit is designated as He. The application of the feminine pronoun to the Spirit needs to be argued theologically. Since such an argument went beyond the scope of *Charism and Sacrament* I acquiesced in existing linguistic patterns rather than confuse or startle people unnecessarily.

Similarly, in the present volume I argue that the term "spirit" suffers from a number of misleading speculative connotations. I suggest that in the foundational problematic outlined here, the philosophical terms "spirit" and "matter" need not be employed. Having argued the point, I replace the traditional theological term "Holy Spirit" with the more Biblical term "Holy Breath." Here again the reader of both volumes will note stylistic discontinuity.

As I was engaged in the final revisions of the present manuscript, David Tracy's *Blessed Rage for Order* (New York: Seabury, 1975) came into my hands. I found myself sympathetic toward his revisionist approach to theology. But I discovered in his methodological postulates nothing to cause me to revise my own.

He is, I believe, correct when he suggests that two of the sources for Christian theological reflection are the principal texts of the Christian religion and human experience. If, however, theological speculation is to account for Christian hope as well as Christian faith and love, the term "text" must be interpreted broadly. It must be expanded to include both presentational and significant religious art. For the logic of hope is the logic of the Christian imagination, not the logic of inference.

Tracy is also correct to suggest that the task facing any theologian is to correlate the two sources of theology critically. The manner of correlation is one's theological method. I heartily agree with him that Paul Tillich's method of correlation must finally be abandoned as inadequate. But I continue to find the most practical overall approach to the doing of theology that suggested by Bernard Lonergan. I say so despite the fact that I find Lonergan's own method in need of some critical revision.

I find two aspects of Lonergan's approach to theological method especially appealing. His theory of functional specialties effects a practical division of theological labor. His operational approach forces any theologian to attempt to come to practical clarity concerning the kinds of operations that are appropriate to resolving the kind of question that defines the scope of inquiry proper to the theologian's own field of theological specialization. In other words, Lonergan's reflections on method make it clearer than Tracy's that there are at least eight different ways of correlating Christian texts and human experience.

Moreover, I am less sanguine than Tracy about discovering an implicit religious horizon already present in everyday and scientific experience and waiting only to be thematized by helpful theologians. Such a notion is dear to Maréchalean Neo-Thomists. It lies at the basis of Karl Rahner's supernatural existential. But the more I have examined the arguments for both the Maréchalean and Rahnerean positions the less convincing I have found them.

I have also become increasingly suspicious of the use some Neo-Thomists make of "transcendental method." The critique of one's own presuppositions is an unavoidable moment in any speculative process. But the elaboration of a philosophical set of "transcendental categories," i.e. of categories universally applicable in intent, is, I believe, a task for the creative imagination. And the attempt to derive such a set of categories by a Kantian or quasi-Kantian transcendental deduction a priori of the conditions for the possibility of knowing yields only an unverified hypothesis concerning the operations of the human mind. Like any hypothesis, it needs deductive clarification and inductive verification. This is a logical truth which defenders of "transcendental method" can all too easily overlook.

The approach to Christian morality suggested in the pages which follow is, moreover, convergent with that proposed by Bernard Häring in his new book, *The Sacraments and Your Everyday Life* (Ligouri, Missouri: Ligouri, 1976) pp. 59–64. The foundational anthropology I here propose suggests that the notion of "natural laws" can be rescued philosophically and theologically. But if the account of the Christian conscience proposed in Chapter VII is sound, those laws fail to provide us with an adequate norm of morality, although they condition moral development and need to be taken into account in reaching concrete moral decisions.

I am grateful to many good friends for criticising this book at various stages of the revision process. My students in the Graduate Theological Union and in the Institute for Spirituality and Worship have offered many helpful suggestions for improvement. Dorothy Donnelly C.S.J. read the manuscript in its roughest form and provided me with the key to a thorough recasting of the text. I am grateful to her and to Dan O'Hanlon, S.J. for suggesting an autobiographical approach to the problem raised in these pages and to the method I propose for resolving it. My sister-in-law, Barbara Charlesworth Gelpi, was of great help in critiquing the manuscript from a feminist and from a Jungean standpoint. John Stacer, S.J. helped me improve the handling of the Whiteheadean material. His careful combing of the manuscript has helped to improve both its argument and its style. I am very grateful to Paul Konkler, novice master of the Trappists at Vina, for his careful insights into the sections dealing with mystical experience. I also wish to thank Jerry Ryle, one of his novices, for reading and criticizing the semifinal version of the manuscript. Finally, I am grateful to Bernie Tyrrell, S.J., for his criticism and encouragement, to Michael Buckley, S.J., and to Robert Paskey, S.J. for their insightful suggestions. With friends such as these, I must take full blame for whatever is imperfect in the pages that follow.

Donald L. Gelpi, S.J.
Jesuit School of Theology at Berkeley
February 14, 1977

I. Toward an American Theology

Every theology is an attempt to decode a religious experience. The experience in question may be the theologian's own. It may be that of a significant religious figure. Or it may be the shared experience of a community or of a people. The decoding technique is the theologian's method. And the project is motivated by the hope of discovering within the decoded experience a word of life-giving truth worth sharing with others. This book is a book of theology. It is undertaken with the same hope.

The forces that shape a religious experience are often paradoxical and unpredictable. My own approach to theology is, for example, remotely influenced by the Mardi Gras. To be a child in New Orleans is to enter by enchantment every spring into a glittering, glowing world of fantasy. It is to know that on one magic day out of every year, one can become before the stupified eyes of all the city a cowboy, a prince, a pirate, a devil, a hero. It is to behold miraculous pageants rolling down the streets, swaying floats of exquisite beauty to which reeling maskers cling, and bands, and horsemen, and sirens, and at night dancing flambeau bearers.

Every spring in childhood, my brother and I let our fantasies feed on the Mardi Gras. During the rest of the year they fed on books. Daydreams led me to sketching, sketching to love of art. Fairy tales became novels, plays, poems, history. And these in time were transformed into the heady abstractions of philosophy and theology. But even as a thoroughly proper, celibate, male adult, no staid abstraction has dimmed the glittering wonder of the Mardi Gras. Nor has any argument ever convinced me for very long that feeling and fantasy are only illusions; or that the debunking argument itself, like the empassioned, careening discussions at our annual family reunions in New Orleans, is anything but a thin and fragile film on a bubbling sea of feeling.

I Become a Jesuit

In 1951 I entered the Jesuit novitiate at Grand Coteau, Louisiana. The building was a yellow, creaking, mildewed pile. But my time there was a season of grace. Beneath the moss-covered oaks and massive pines I resonated to the power of the Spiritual Exercises of Ignatius Loyola. I said yes (I thought) to the Standard of Christ and to the Third Degree of Humility, only to find that growth is more than saying yes. My novitiate was a searing, happy, bright, desolate time. I knew scruples, depression, ecstasy, growth. And I emerged from it all to discover C. J. McNaspy, S.J., and with him the whole of Western culture.

C. J. taught at our juniorate at Grand Coteau for over a decade. He now holds the position of University Professor at Loyola of New Orleans. Musician, musicologist, liturgist, historian, linguist, litterateur, art critic—he communicated with contagious enthusiasm a fascination with everything that is human. When I first met him he was well on his way to mastering all the romance languages, a project he has since completed. He was widely traveled in Europe and Mexico and has since put a girdle round the globe. Once for a week of mellow afternoons we listened our way through the Beethoven string quartets. I left Grand Coteau wanting to be like him in every way and longing to experience for myself some of the wonders he had seen.

In 1954 I was sent to St. Louis to begin my philosophical studies. And so it was that I cut my philosophical teeth on Missouri Valley Thomism. Our dean was George Klubertanz, S.J., a man of great kindness, insight, and scholarship. His philosophy texts were widely used in the fifties and early sixties. From him I learned to read philosophy in the light of psychology. In my university classes I learned from James Collins the meaning of meticulous, historical research. I was soon thoroughly at home in graduate studies.

Our seminary faculty were convinced, dedicated, and thorough teachers and scholars. I owe them much. Many had their degrees from Toronto; and in almost every systematic course, Etienne Gilson and the texts of St. Thomas loomed as our common masters. In fact so closely did the faculty agree on most questions that even we seminarians began to suspect in rare and tranquil moments our own philosophical indoctrination. But the truth of the matter was that our faculty had decided, not without wisdom, to introduce us to philosophy by teaching us a single system well.

Expanding Horizons
And for three or four years, Gilsonian Thomism seemed to fill most of my speculative needs. Not that I had much time for abstract speculation. In 1957 I was assigned to Jesuit High School in New Orleans to impart the rudiments of language, literature, religion, and speech to high school sophomores and juniors. I produced three plays

a year and taught in my spare time. But somehow I did steal moments for serious thinking. I retained a fascination with esthetic experience and was able to publish a somewhat strained and stilted scholastic tract on the relation of artistic and prudential judgment. The fruit of a summer of study with James Collins in St. Louis was another article, on Marxist aesthetic theory.

My master's thesis on Plotinus had reinforced a taste for mystical literature, and I had found that the works of St. John of the Cross spoke powerfully to my own religious experience. In St. Louis I had known a year of almost total darkness in prayer. I read the complete works of John of the Cross at least three times and have since reread his works more than once. Through John I discovered Teresa of Avila and found her a humane antidote to John's lapses into apophatic grimness.

My interest in psychology led me to William James. James led me to Josiah Royce and to John Dewey. The more I read, the more I liked. What they said about human experience carried conviction. I also began to read in Sigmund Freud and gestalt psychology. Thomism began to relax its grip on my mind.

An Innocent Abroad

In 1961, I was assigned to Collège St. Albert outside of Louvain, Belgium to begin my theological studies. The memory of Joseph Maréchal, S.J., was still alive there, and his kindly face smiled in benediction from one of the corridors. During my summers I saw as much of Europe as I could: southern England, northern France, Bavaria, northern Italy, Rome, Barcelona. Images emerge: the exploding light of Chartres; the delicate hues of Fra Angelico; the power of the David, of the Moses, of the Pietá; the linear grace of Botticelli; the mystery of Stonehenge; the immensity of St. Peter's; the vibrancy of the Flemish primitives; the eroded scratchings of Jesuits once imprisoned in the Tower of London; the majesty of the Alps; the poignancy of the catacombs; street dancing in Barcelona; the faded ecstasy of Assisi; the mélange of faith and superstition at Lourdes; the gardens at Dachau; the empty palace at Avignon.

In the summer of 1962 I spent a week with my brother in Venice. We both delighted in discovering the city but found even greater pleasure in discovering one another as friends. By different routes our lives had converged. I had fallen in love with American philosophy; he, with American poetry. And in the piazzas and alleyways of the sinking city we began a sharing of minds and hearts that has grown and deepened with the years.

At Louvain itself, I learned to explore a different landscape: the cliffs and valleys of my own heart. Culture shock quickly convinced me how thoroughly American I am and will remain. I realized to my dismay and loneliness that the gulf of feeling and expectation that divided me from most of the Belgian theologians was enormous. Some few became friends. Moreover, as the days stretched out into weeks and months, I understood with anger and with grief why Jansenius's tower stood crumbling in a corner of Louvain and why *The Imitation of Christ* had emerged from the mists of northern Europe. One of the chief differences between myself and the Belgian theologians seemed to be that they took quite seriously the manual asceticism I had studied in my novitiate but had never as an American Jesuit really been expected to live. Worse still, I was led with great pain to realize that I could never live such an ascetical vision and that in my heart of hearts I did not even want to try. An innocent abroad, I felt the truth of Dewey's embittered polemic against the destructive consequences of religious dualisms. I watched my physical and psychic energy gurgle down the drain. As I did so, I gradually realized that religious life in America, and indeed American Catholicism itself, had evolved into something very different from the patterns that informed the faith of the Church in Europe. And with that insight came the shattering knowledge that I had no personal rationale for being a vowed religious. Another truth I learned in the damp corridors of St. Albert's: my capacity for resentment and for rage.

I Am Ordained

In 1963 understanding superiors allowed me to complete my theology at St. Mary's College, St. Marys, Kansas. I was weakened in health and troubled at heart. I knew I could not remain a religious without a reason. I felt in a vague and uneasy way that the key to discovering a reason lay in self-understanding, and that to understand myself demanded critical reflection on the historical and cultural forces that had shaped me.

Our college was near Topeka, Kansas. The Menninger Clinic was nearby, and we had contact through lectures and workshops with some of the staff. As I began to face my own repressed anger and resentment, I discovered the truth in Neo-Freudian psychiatry. I began to read the books of Karl Menninger systematically. By 1964, I had found an island of peace within myself. I was ordained at Mobile, Alabama, on June 17, by Bishop Thomas Toolen in the chapel of Spring Hill College, not long after sunrise, before the stifling heat of the day.

I loved my two years at St. Marys: the clear skies, the villa shacks, the renewal of old friendships. I plunged into the study of Karl Rahner. Gerald Van Ackeren, S.J., our dean, gave the warmest encouragement to the project, and it eventually bore fruit in *Life and Light: A Guide to the Theology of Karl Rahner*. Cyrel Vollet, S.J., helped open me to the world of Teilhard de Chardin. My mother's ordination gift to me had been *The Collected Papers of Charles Sanders Peirce*. During the quiet winter afternoons, I began with kindling excitement to read systematically through the eight volumes. I resolved to pursue doctoral studies in philosophy at Fordham University. My superiors approved; and I began class work during the summers.

A summer course from John McNeil, S.J., on the sources of Maurice Blondel's *L'Action* gave new focus to my life and thought. Blondel's Christian polemic against the artificial separation of thought and action confirmed my own nascent instrumentalism. As I pondered Blondel's approach to apologetics, I began to see the possibility of applying pragmatic logic to theological questions. Studying Rahner had freed me to rethink my most basic religious beliefs; Blondel convinced me that no religious doctrine is worth holding that is not true to the dynamic thrust of life itself. My Christian faith was becoming a speculative wager that the self-revelation of God in Jesus could make sense out of every legitimate human value and aspiration. I began to read Henri Bergson and intensified my reading of Teilhard.

In 1965 I began my final year of official Jesuit training at our tertianship in Auriesville, New York. John McMahon, S.J., was our tertian instructor. Despite our difference of age, we became good friends. I explained to him my need to rethink my most basic religious commitment from the bottom up. He blessed the project enthusiastically. My thirty-day retreat bore fruit in *Functional Asceticism: A Guideline for American Religious*. It was an initial attempt to apply Peircean logic to the problems of religious living. But I realized on finishing the book that I had raised more questions than I had answered. In writing it, however, I had developed the habit of praying with a pencil, a practice I would continue during graduate residency at Fordham University. And my prayer at Fordham would eventually give shape to *Discerning the Spirit: Foundations and Futures of Religious Life*. I would look on the book as a personal religious credo and on its publication as an exercise in honesty.

Meanwhile, back at Auriesville I plunged into a systematic reading of Josiah Royce and of George Santayana. It was a winter of blizzards. But amid the searing winds, the pious clutter of the shrine

of the North American martyrs, near the place where Isaac Jogues
had been tortured and tomahawked and in the ravine that still hid
Réné Goupil's bones, I found a measure of healing and of peace.

Tap Roots

In 1965 my brother Al married in Cambridge, Massachusetts. He
was teaching American literature at Harvard. His wife had taught
Victorian literature at the University of California at Santa Barbara
and at Brandeis. Her maiden name was Barbara Charlesworth. She
has become not only a sister but a dear friend. I had been flattered and
pleased to assist at their wedding.

And as a tertian I served as an assistant chaplain at the Harvard
Newman Center. At the time Al and Barbara lived in a two-family
dwelling on Acacia Street, not far from the Newman Center and the
Harvard Yard. Through them I began to enter the Harvard scene. I
met the poet Adrienne Rich. One afternoon Al and I helped I. A.
Richards up to his apartment. He had sprained his back and needed
temporary support in negotiating the steep stairs.

One evening Al invited me to cocktails with Richards and his
wife. I listened as Ivor recalled being stuck for three hours in an
elevator with Alfred North Whitehead. The two men had done the
obvious and spent the time discussing Plato until rescue came. I left
the Gelpis and the Richardses for a counseling appointment at the
Newman Center. But I returned to Acacia Street later that evening to
find that Jack Kerouac had descended from out of the blue. I believe
my clerical presence intimidated him at first. But halfway through the
conversation, he strode across the room, touched his glass of scotch
to mine, and said, "The transubstantiation is complete." I do not
know what he meant; but I sensed acceptance.

As chaplain I learned to know the Harvard students. One desperate afternoon, I talked one of them out of suicide. I began to get a feel
for the Harvard Yard and for the people whose paths crossed within it.

Over the years, Al and Barbara have introduced me to other
things as well. They have led me into the scholarly world of Perry
Miller. They have sensitized me to the evocative power of archetypal
thinking. They have alerted me to the importance of Mircea Eliade
and of Joseph Campbell. They have helped me to empathize with the
struggle of women for equal rights. Through their delicate sensitivity
to others and immense respect for personal integrity, they have
forwarded in me the humanization in faith begun by my parents.
Through Al I have begun to understand the dialectical sweep of
American poetry.

I began graduate studies with enthusiasm. With William

Richardson, S.J., I did an intensive study of Martin Heidegger's *Being and Time*. Robert Roth, S.J., helped deepen my hold on American pragmatism. And the late Walter Stokes, S.J., introduced me to the world of Alfred North Whitehead. Wally had been a graduate student at St. Louis University when I was an undergraduate there. He had an all-too-rare appreciation for the strengths and weaknesses of both substance and process philosophy. As a lapsed Gilsonian and a student of Rahner, I resonated to his insights. Under his tutelage I began to understand the issues that divided the two traditions.

Pentecost

Toward the end of my graduate residency at Fordham, I underwent a religious experience that changed the course of my life. Since entering the novitiate I had been faithful to daily private prayer. But prayer had been more of a duty than a love.

One morning in the spring of 1968, I was late for breakfast. There was only one other member of the Jesuit community in the dining room: a New Englander named Jim Powers. As we talked I learned to my surprise that he was involved in the Catholic charismatic renewal. He witnessed to the difference charismatic prayer had made in his life. I felt profoundly moved.

After breakfast I was drawn almost physically to the chapel. As I prayed, I began to repeat a nonsense syllable: "la, la, la." There ensued a rapid movement of tongue and lips accompanied by a powerful sense of the power and presence of God. It was like being grasped, taken hold of. The Lord walked with me throughout the day. I seemed to move simultaneously on two levels of consciousness: one pragmatic and pedestrian; the other transcendent, ecstatic, and somewhat terrifying. By the end of the day I feared for my sanity. I withdrew from the grace and decided I would shelve the entire experience until my retreat two months later. During the interval, it was not repeated.

Since I was in transit to Cambridge, Massachusetts, where I hoped to write my dissertation, I made retreat in New Bedford at the Jesuit retreat house, Our Lady of Round Hill. It had once been the estate of Ned Green, the son of Hetty Green, the witch of Wall Street. MIT had subsequently used the estate as a weather research center, and a giant radar scope stood on a spit of land that jutted into Buzzards Bay. One evening during retreat I climbed the tower and sat in prayer gazing over the sea, looking up to the stars. I asked God that if my experience in the chapel at Fordham had indeed been a grace that I be open to it; but that if I were losing my mind, I would find courage to seek whatever professional help I needed. I resolved to lay the whole matter before my spiritual director once I had arrived at La

Farge House in Cambridge. I descended the radar tower and returned to the glittering manor house in peace.

Once settled in Cambridge I threw myself into the work of writing my dissertation. It was a study of Ralph Waldo Emerson's understanding of human religious experience. My director back at Fordham was Robert Neville. There was something uncanny about studying American Transcendentalism in New England in the late 1960s. As I poured over the musty manuscripts in the Houghton Library, I became convinced that most of the strident battle cries of the "new" radical left were in fact the faded clichés of nineteenth-century Transcendentalism. And I sensed the truth of Santayana's wry aphorism that those who live in ignorance of history are condemned to repeat it.

I began to sense that the myths and issues articulated by major American philosophers were far from dead. Instead they had been woven into the tapestry of American culture where they continued to function as hidden presuppositions. Studying Emerson was like turning the tapestry around.

My spiritual director had advised me to stay open in prayer to whatever graces God desired to give me. I subsequently found that in the concelebrated masses at La Farge House I would frequently be moved to pray silently in tongues. I began to take long walks in the crisp evenings praising God in tongues and thanking Him. Prayer was slowly transformed from a duty to a need.

Up to that time, I had never attended a charismatic prayer meeting. I resolved to go to the International Conference for the Catholic Charismatic Renewal at Notre Dame. There I met Harold Cohen, S.J. He was chaplain at Loyola University in New Orleans, where I was slated to teach the following year. He would be returning to New Orleans after the Notre Dame conference to begin a charismatic community.

I resolved to become involved in the charismatic community when I arrived at Loyola, but I felt the need to pray my way to an understanding of the terms on which I would become involved. The result of that prayer was *Pentecostalism: A Theological Viewpoint*. It was written at Bristol, Rhode Island, on the eastern shore of Narragansett Bay in a cottage I shared with C. J. McNaspy and three other Jesuits. It was a summer of great grace and beauty. We looked forward to the spectacle of each sunset and often sat on the porch in silence as the sky glowed and faded into grey dusk.

Glimmerings

At Loyola, I plunged into a systematic study of the American philosophical tradition. I read through the complete works of

Jonathan Edwards and absorbed as much secondary source criticism as I could get my hands on. I then returned to the primary sources and tried to pull together on paper my understanding of the man and of his thought. I did the same with the works of Benjamin Franklin, Thomas Paine, Thomas Jefferson, William Ellery Channing, Orestes Brownson, Francis Ellingwood Abbot, Charles S. Peirce, William James. In graduate school I had established a firm grip on Royce, Dewey, Santayana, and Whitehead. I now had the opportunity and stimulus in my courses to evaluate each of them.

As the work proceeded I became convinced that I could make the philosophical link between Edwardsean revivalism, Emersonian Transcendentalism, and Peircean pragmatism. And Peirce, I was convinced, provided the key to James, Royce, Dewey, and Santayana. I began to see the American philosophical tradition as an organic, evolving experience. I discovered clear lines of convergence, areas of consensus, problems in need of further clarification. As my grip on our common philosophical heritage tightened, I began to come to greater clarity about my own basic beliefs.

The classroom became a laboratory for testing my insights. I began to sense the extent to which all Americans are conditioned by the ideals and values articulated in American philosophical religion. Among my students I found Franklinsonian deists, Roycean loyalists, Jamesean psychologists, Deweyan naturalists, last Puritans, every shade of Transcendentalist. All resonated to Whitehead. The charismatics especially resonated to Jonathan Edwards. The more I studied American philosophy the more convinced I became that many of the confusions in the Catholic Church in America after Vatican II were linked to a failure to critique the motifs of American religious philosophy. At the same time, I also felt that one path to liberation for us all lay in a sympathetic but critical theological reassessment of American philosophical religion.

As I cast about for a method that would allow me to begin such an enterprise, I rediscovered the work of Bernard Lonergan. As a graduate student I had studied *Insight*. During the four years at Loyola I offered seminars on both *Insight* and *Method in Theology*. I began to glimpse with excitement the possibility of applying dialectical and foundational thinking to the problems raised by American philosophical religion. And with it was born the hope of creating an indigenous American theology.

As my work advanced, I began to sense my own inadequacies keenly. I needed the criticism and support of trained theologians as well as an ecumenical context for pursuing my work. In 1973 I accepted a position on the faculty of the Jesuit School of Theology at

Berkeley. I would be teaching systematic theology and working with James Empereur, S.J., in the Institute for Spirituality and Worship. Al and Barbara had by this time moved to the West Coast with their two children, Christopher and Adrienne. They were both teaching at Stanford University. My mother had also joined them in Stanford so that all of my immediate family lived in the Bay area.

Berkeley

My degree and my teaching had been in philosophy, not theology. I had a lot of catch-up work to do—much had happened in the theological world while I had rambled through the history of American thought. I had five new courses to prepare, all of them graduate courses. To make matters worse, I arrived at Berkeley exhausted from my many duties at Loyola. By the end of a summer of intensive reading and research, I felt ready to meet my classes. But I had in the process all but used up my psychic reserves. I turned to the Jesuit community and to the California landscape to help restore them. Several of the theologians and I took to camping together at regular intervals during the school year.

My initial discovery of natural beauty on Narragansett Bay had deepened in New Orleans. Joseph Tetlow, S.J., had joined the Loyola faculty the same year as I. We had worked together on many projects, he as dean of Arts and Sciences, I as a faculty member. Together we founded the Lewis and Clark Memorial Expedition—an annual foray into some national park far from any telephone. We had climbed the lush trails of the Smokies, stood stupified on the lip of the Grand Canyon, staggered under heavy packs into its desiccating depths. We had crawled through the ruins of Mesa Verde, descended into Carlsbad, contemplated the rugged splendor of Yosemite. Our trips together had been journeys into prayer. We had both found that one cannot pray on a mountain top without being brushed by the passage of God. With Joe I had seen the face of nature transformed with a touch of the divine glory. I had yet to experience its cruelty.

With my involvement in the charismatic renewal I had begun to have locutionary experiences in prayer with greater frequency. Once, for example, while typing in my office at Loyola, I received a sudden word from the Lord to go to the reception desk on St. Charles Avenue. When I arrived I found a young man desperate to see a priest. I ministered to him for over an hour.

De Profundis

Shortly after my arrival at Berkeley, a clear word came to me in prayer: "You must face your own death." I did not know what it meant, but I turned to the Lord for light. I prayed until I felt that I was ready to accept death if that was what the Lord was asking of me. Immediately a new word replaced the first: "You must be one with Jesus in His suffering." That word too I brought to prayer, but little light came.

During the spring break of 1974 I planned a river trip with two Jesuit theologians, Jerry McMahon and Mike Taylor. Jerry had spent whole summers in the wilderness and had himself organized and led a river trip for high school students. During the year we had become good friends. He studied the maps of the branch of the American River near our villa at Applegate and concluded that there would be no serious danger in attempting a trip. We made spot checks of the river before coming to a final decision. It seemed safe. We conferred with Mike and decided to set out the following morning.

Mike and I sat in the front of the raft. Jerry, the strongest and most experienced, steered. We had agreed to wear life jackets and to lash ourselves to the raft, just in case. . . . For about two hundred yards the river ran smoothly. Then it turned a sharp bend, and we were in the midst of white water. The raft was lethargic, intractable, uncontrollable. The water took us, spun us, dominated us. In an instant we were drenched. The inflated raft flooded with icy water. We paddled benumbed. A great mass of white water loomed ahead. After we had passed it, I looked back out of concern for Jerry. He was gone and his jacket trailed on a length of rope behind the raft. He had never put it on. The water was thundering, drowning all sound. "Oh God," I shouted, "where's Jerry? what happened to Jerry?" I glimpsed him for a moment on the far side of the river shooting the rapids feet first. Then the river took us.

We careened down the rapids and were swirled into a calm eddy. But the rock face was sheer. There was no way out. We could not hold the raft. The river claimed us again. Another wall of white water. We were thrown into it broadside and I was flipped from the raft. I struggled to the surface, buoyed up by my jacket. My jacket was tied to the seat of the raft, and with the aid of the rope I regained its side. I wrapped the rope that circled the raft several times around my wrist. Mike tried to help me in, but we were too benumbed to move. I felt that if the raft stayed afloat I could probably survive. We had lost all sense of time and space. The rapids seemed everything, unending. But at last we reached flat water, beached the raft, and began an agonizing climb for help. Mike's glasses were gone. We stopped for a moment and prayed for Jerry. We grappled with the steep slope, inched forward, slipped, began again.

At the police station, the bureaucratic ritual of filling out official forms and reports provided the illusion of sanity. Jesuits from the villa arrived, among them Carmichael Peters, a black student from the Graduate Theological Union who had applied to enter the Jesuit order the following year. He had lost both legs in an accident and walked with canes. Once they arrived I realized that in describing Jerry to the police I had been using the past tense. I was flooded with a torrent of unnamed, unnamable feelings. I realized Jerry's goodness and how much I had come to cherish his friendship and support. Then, as we stood at the door of the van, I began to sob. Carmichael held me in his arms until I stopped.

Jerry's body was buried in Denver in sight of majestic peaks. The funeral was an ordeal in anticipation and in fact, relieved by long periods of prayer. In the community chapel at Regis College I prayed for some kind of light. I opened my pocket New Testament and read:

> And when evening had come, since it was the day of Preparation, that is, the day before the sabbath, Joseph of Aramathea, a respected member of the council, who was also himself looking for the kingdom of God, took courage and went to Pilate, and asked for the body of Jesus. And Pilate wondered if he were already dead; and summoning the centurion he asked him whether he was already dead. And when he learned from the centurion that he was dead, he granted the body to Joseph. And he bought a linen shroud, and taking him down, wrapped him in the linen shroud, and laid him in a tomb which had been hewn out of rock; and he rolled a stone against the door of the tomb. Mary Magdalene and Mary the mother of Jesus saw where he was laid.[1]

With time and the support of my Jesuit brothers came healing and a measure of understanding. The meaning of the two words I had received in prayer was now clear. In the river the first word had sustained me: I had looked death in the face without fear. After the funeral, as I wrestled with my responsibility for the events that had led to Jerry's death, the second word took on new meaning. I knew a dying and a rising.

I had been there before. This pain was of a piece with other deaths, other resurrections: at Grand Coteau, at St. Louis, at Louvain, in New Orleans. Those smaller deaths had brought life. And with the passing of the months, I began to feel that once again I was being reborn.

In the meantime, the pressures of teaching, counselling, writing continued unabated. I had come to Berkeley determined to test the adequacy of Lonergan's theological method. His description of dialectical and foundational thinking was convergent with my own philosophical and theological beliefs. Dewey had convinced me that the test of a method is its use and that any method worth its salt will be self-corrective.

The most pressing doctrinal issues raised by the Catholic charismatic renewal were, I felt, the meaning of Christian conversion and the relation between charismatic and sacramental piety. I decided to attempt to use foundational thinking in order to elaborate a theology of Christian conversion that would provide an integrating context for discussing the relationship between the gifts of the Spirit and ritual sacramental worship. The result was *Charism and Sacrament: A Theology of Christian Conversion*. The book elaborated into a more systematic statement the germinal insights I had sketched in other articles and in *Pentecostal Piety*. I concluded that Lonergan's method gave some hope of resolving the issues raised by American philosophical religion but that the American philosophical tradition itself cast light on inadequacies that lay at the heart of Lonergan's own methodological presuppositions. Once again, the initial resolution of a problem had raised more questions than it had answered.

I had seen too that an "American" theology that aspired to be Catholic could not be narrowly conceived. I had absorbed Canadian influences from Lonergan. I resonated to the cry for human justice emanating from the Church in Latin America. An American theology, I realized, had to be sensitive to the soul of black religion and to the struggle of blacks and chicanos for their human dignity and rights. It should be sensitive to values that Christian faith derives from Hebrew piety. It should have a word to say to the aquarian religion of the sixties and to the fascination of American romantics with Oriental mysticism. And it should attempt to enter into dialogue with theological thought in Europe and in other parts of the Church. That I could accomplish all of these ideals equally well was of course doubtful in the extreme. But an ambitious failure would, I felt, be better than no attempt at all.

Note

1. Mk. 15:42-47.

II. In Search of a Method

The task I had set myself was the theological evaluation of two centuries of philosophical reflection. I had undertaken it not out of detached curiosity but as a way of reaching self-understanding. I realized that it was the work of a lifetime. In any single book, the best that I could ever do would be to dance around the problem like a Hollywood Indian. Perhaps a series of efforts would be more realistic and fruitful.

The American Philosophical Experience

As I pondered the result of the research I had done in the history of American religious philosophy, certain themes began to assume greater speculative importance than others. It seemed to me, for example, that the Augustinian caste of Calvinist theology had shaped American religious attitudes profoundly.[1] It had found a philosophical echo in a succession of Platonic or quasi-Platonic approaches to human religious experience: Edwards, Emerson, Brownson, Abbot, Santayana, Whitehead. And Platonic preoccupations had in turn endowed American religious experience with a penchant for individualism, subjectivism, personal mysticism.

I also realized, however, that Platonism was only one way of philosophizing in the American mode. Indeed, the more I pondered the development of American speculation, the more convinced I became that it had been given to Jonathan Edwards to strike the dominant chord in American religious philosophy: that of preoccupation with the structure of experience. From Edwards on, almost every major American thinker had wrestled with the question: What does it mean to experience anything? What does it mean to undergo a religious experience? Platonic solutions to both questions had, of course, been offered. But there were other solutions as well, solutions that provided important correctives to the inadequacies of Platonic theory. If my insight into the genius of the American speculative tradition was correct, any attempt to construct a systematic philosophy or theology in the American mode would have to adopt "experience" as its central category.

Moreover, I also saw that Edwards had first formulated the

18

problem of experience with considerable subtlety. His *History of Redemption* was a powerful, panoramic dramatization of the working of divine grace. In it Christ and Satan stood locked in mortal combat, while from age to age God's true saints were ravished by the unfolding spectacle of a divine, immutable, predestining justice and love.

Edwards's human complexity had, moreover, led him to describe the elements that shape religious experience with a corresponding theoretical complexity. His intense personal mysticism, his rapture in the face of natural beauty, and his metaphysical idealism had given intellectual sanction to American revivalism, and with revivalism to much of American popular religion.

His assimilation of the consent of faith to the experience of beauty had forced almost every subsequent American religious thinker to wrestle with the Edwardsean question: What is the place of affectivity in the human encounter with the Holy? Even today Edwards's definition of virtue as the "cordial consent of being to being in general" retains the ring of truth. Moreover, Edwards's thought had direct and profound influence on Emersonian Transcendentalism, and through Transcendentalism on American secular culture.[2]

American Deism, I perceived, had been born in large measure of the desire to escape the pitiless scrutiny of a predestining, Calvinist Jehovah. Benjamin Franklin was, I also saw, the historical, American anti-type to Edwards. In Franklin's religion, gracious affections were largely superfluous. Instead of myth, mystery, faith, and the Holy Spirit, he offered practical reason and the political and economic advantages of virtuous living; not creeds and sacraments but philosophy; not predestining grace but the patient cultivation of one's natural, human endowments; not conversion but civic spirit; not religious ecstasy but enlightened self-interest. And I sensed with considerable dismay that for too many contemporary American Christians, these options remain all too real.[3]

Nevertheless, the more I studied the founding fathers of the American republic, the more I felt the ghosts of Calvin, of Cromwell, and of Edwards presiding over their allegedly dispassionate philosophical debates. Our deistic founding fathers had preached a revolution that was divinely foreordained by the God of Reason. Their political rhetoric had transformed the Calvinist doctrine of divine predestination into a national sense of divine election. Edwards had, for example, in his preaching and writing prophesied the coming of a millennium, of a thousand years of peace and prosperity on earth that would precede the second coming of Christ. He had located the millennium in America, in the New World. The propagandists of the

Revolution promised Americans an idyllic era of peace and prosperity once not only popery but monarchy had been harried from American soil. Moreover, more than one of the founding fathers had secularized the Protestant "inner light" by transforming it into a natural, innate "moral sense" that gave each American intuitive, personal access within subjectivity to the immutable principles of moral conduct.

Indeed, I felt that the religious dilemma of American republican religion had come to be typified in the mad, deistic revivalism of the blind Elihu Palmer. In his futile battle to found a deistic Temple of Reason, Palmer had sought to vindicate the superiority of philosophical religion with arguments that appealed as unabashedly to pure emotion as any revivalistic circuit preacher.[4]

The first major spokesman for American Unitarianism had been William Ellery Channing. In his moral argument against Calvinism, he had challenged the total otherness of God proclaimed in classical Calvinist theology. He seems to have gained an important point. Every subsequent American theistic philosopher has to a man searched for analogies between human experience and the divine rather than acknowledge God's total metaphysical otherness.[5]

Romantic Speculation

As I pondered Emerson's speculative achievement, it seemed to me that he too had raised a complex set of perennial religious questions: the present experiential accessibility of God; the place of creativity within human religious experience; the realistic cognitive claims of mythic and poetic forms of thought; the relationship between artistic, literary, and scientific creative activity; the relationship between religion, morality, and poetry; the relationship between the individual genius and social reform. Emerson's various solutions to all of these questions had been naturalistic, pantheistic, dualistic, subjectivistic, mystical, and intuitionist. He had, however, been only the first major American naturalist. John Dewey, I realized, would raise many of the same questions in a different era and offer naturalistic solutions that were atheistic, wholistic, social, scientific, and instrumental. Santayana's naturalism seemed to me, by contrast, to fall between the two stools of Emersonian Transcendentalism and Deweyan instrumentalism: naturalistic and atheistic on the one hand, subjectivistic and intuitionist on the other. But Charles Sanders Peirce had, I felt, provided the speculative key that would unlock most of Emerson's puzzles.[6]

On more than one occasion, the late Perry Miller has called for a critical reassessment of the place of Orestes Brownson in the development of American thought and culture. But Miller's scholarly asides did not prepare me for the sweep of Brownson's intellectual achievement. Brownson, like Nathaniel Hawthorne, Edgar Allen Poe, and Herman Melville, was appalled at Emerson's naturalistic optimism. He had discovered a sense of guilt and fallenness in himself and in others that had reopened the pandora's box of original sin that the American enlightenment had (it thought) definitively closed. Brownson's speculative solution to the problem of sin and guilt was a social theory of redemption and a thoroughly incarnational sacramentalism. His autobiography. *The Convert*, is an incisive commentary on the development of American religious thought up to the mid-nineteenth century. His *American Republic* is a brilliant reworking of Edwardsean millennarian myths. And his synthetic philosophy marks a major turning point in American speculation about nature.

Prior to Brownson, there had been a tendency in American religious philosophers to locate the laws that govern the spatio-temporal process in the transcendent mind of God. Edwards, Emerson, and (in his own way) Theodore Parker had opted for such a solution. Brownson's robust incarnationalism could not, however, tolerate such a vision. In opposition to Emerson, he located the eternal Reason of God in material, sensible things.

The consequences of such a speculative option were for him enormous. For it meant that both God and the laws of nature could be grasped, not through some mystical ascent to an eternal realm of pure Spirit, but only through an incarnational encounter with concrete, sensible realities. Brownson's early Transcendental vision of a "Church of the future" had dimly foreshadowed his latter "synthetic" philosophical and theological vision. But it was the elder, Catholic Brownson, not the young, radical Brownson, who brought the germinal insights of his youth to systematic formulation.

I saw, moreover, that for a variety of speculative reason, which had nothing to do with Brownson's incarnationalism, no major American thinker subsequent to him would be able to see natural laws as anything but immanent within the spatio-temporal order. The fact of human fallenness, sacramentalism, incarnationalism, the relation of the political and the religious order of things, the presence of law and of God within the historical process—these are issues Brownson once posed and continues to pose for an American philosophical theology.[7]

Another forgotten American genius is Francis Ellingwood Abbot. His work, especially his *Scientific Theism* and his *Syllogistic Philosophy*, forms a crucial link between Transcendental and pragmatic forms of thought. More sensitive than Brownson to the claims of scientific method, he strove to reconcile a modified Emersonian vision of the cosmos with evolutionary theory and scientific logic. In the process he sharpened a number of basic philosophical questions: the meaning of universals and their place in human experience, the relational character of general laws and their objectivity in nature, the synthetic relationship between the rational and the empirical elements within cognition. These too are perennial philosophical issues, and they would exercise the brilliant mind of Charles Sanders Peirce.[8]

The Emergence of Process Speculation

Study of the American philosophical tradition had convinced me that Charles S. Peirce was and is its towering genius. I have an instinctive mistrust of humorless people. Peirce and Santayana were the only philosophers I could recall reading who had publicly satirized their own insights. Moreover, repeated perusal of the *Collected Papers* confirmed what I had sensed intuitively in Peirce. The range and depth of his interests and insights always brought new surprises.

In 1868 Peirce had, I saw, delivered the philosophical coup de grace to the Transcendentalism of Emerson and of Parker. He did so in a series of articles in which he demolished systematically the cognitive claims of philosophical "intuitionism." In the course of these articles he affirmed unambiguously the historical and environmentally conditioned character of all human knowing. He also formulated and explained for the first time his "pragmatic maxim": "Consider what effects that might conceivably have practical bearings we conceive the object of our conception to have. Then, our conception of these effects is the whole of our conception of the object." Inadequate as a definition of meaning, the maxim was subsequently reinterpreted by Peirce himself as a principle of hypothetical inference.

In elaborating his logical theory, Peirce had insisted on the fallible character of all systematic thinking. He had correctly distinguished three different kinds of inference. He had resonated to Abbot's philosophy of relation. And toward the end of his life he began to glimpse the possibility of transforming such a philosophy into an evolutionary cosmology and a subtle and complex metaphysics of symbol. Sensitive to the affective character of religious faith and mistrustful of the fallible abstractions of human reason, he laid the logical groundwork for the speculative fulfillment of that Edwardsean dream: an experimental approach to speculation about God. As I pondered the metaphysical and religious dimensions of his thought, I began to glimpse the possibility of fusing Edwards's religious experimentalism, Brownson's sacramentalism, and Peirce's philosophy of symbol and of embellishing all three with insights derived from Whitehead's account of the symbolic structure of experience.[9]

William James's pragmatic approach to God had, I perceived, focused on a different set of philosophical questions from those that preoccupied Peirce. His *Varieties of Religious Experience* had, I believed, established beyond question that personal emotional development conditions one's instinctive religious affirmations. I also saw, however, that Peirce had been correct to insist that all such instinctive religious beliefs must be subjected to deductive clarification and lived, inductive verification. Moreover, James, in his reflections on religious questions, had, I suspected, extricated himself only imperfectly from the individualism and the subjectivism present in his religious environment. He did attempt to transcend religious subjectivism by a generalization about the existence of God based on the scientific investigation of subjective religious experiences. His argument, while inadequate, was speculatively suggestive. But he was remarkably sensitive to the complexity of human experience. His insights into the psychology of conversion are richly suggestive even today. His ability to balance scientific data with vivid and sensitive descriptions of feelings and emotions held many rich insights. So too did his insistence on the irrational bases of many cherished human beliefs. His characterization of reason as a sentiment had once shocked my Thomistic sensibilities; but the more I pondered his position, the more convincing it became. It is a conviction that has since been reinforced by the study of Bernard Meland. An intuitive rather than a systematic effort, his *Pluralistic Universe* nevertheless contained many important theological and philosophical leads.

In the lifelong philosophical debate between William James and Josiah Royce, both men had, I felt, scored some important debating points. Their personal religious sensibilities were, I saw, both divergent and complementary. While James resonated to the felt, emotive basis of religious attitudes and beliefs, Royce was preoccupied with the ethical and intellectual dimensions of religious experience. Royce's attempt to ground morality in the ideal pole of human experience seemed to me to oppose fact and value too starkly; and his proof for the existence of God from the fact of error was, as both James and Santayana saw, ultimately inconclusive. But his voluntaristic idealism, while tinged with a certain subjectivism, was an interesting attempt to interrelate thought and action.

I felt that Royce had been quite correct to insist against James that society, reason, and suffering are all potential sources of religious insight. He had grasped with Emerson and Brownson that religious insight is in fact synthetic in character. His philosophy of loyalty and his reflections on the human search for salvation, while deistically tinged, were rich in theological suggestion. Finally, his use of Peirce's philosophy to probe the philosophical implications of a Pauline theology of the mystical body was fraught with theological consequences that Royce himself only vaguely glimpsed.

James, however, had correctly questioned the emotional adequacy of Royce's God. An all-knowing deity who does nothing to alleviate human suffering and misery is less than prepossessing. At the same time, James's critique of Royce's theism could, I also saw, be extended and deepened speculatively through philosophical and theological insight.[10]

John Dewey's educational theory seemed to me sound on the whole and true to the dynamics of human experiential development. Moreover, Dewey's sensitive, systematic exploration of the esthetic, logical, and ethical dimensions of experience was nuanced and suggestive. This theory of art was the only philosophical handling of esthetics I had found that seemed to speak directly to the experience of the artists I knew. Indeed, Dewey's central philosophical effort was, I realized, a systematic elaboration of Peirce's theory of the normative sciences. Dewey's reflections on the religious dimensions of human experience had, I believed, more to say to ethical theory than to religious understanding. And I was also convinced that his polemic against "supernaturalism" collapsed once one was willing to admit, as every good Jesuit and Edwardsean ought, that God functions as a discernible force within human religious experience.[11]

Having been raised in the sensuous south, I found Santayana's Latin temperament and humane style personally appealing. But his exploration of the realm of creative imagination was, I concluded with regret, tinged with the subjectivism that marred most of his thought. His later work, however, contained helpful flashes of brilliance and a fine sense of the affective continuity that pervades human experience. I resonated most strongly to his wry critique of American secular culture and of the uncriticized religious motives that cunningly transform the "universal American" into the "last puritan." At the same time, I sensed how Santayana himself had remained tragically caught in the grip of the "genteel tradition" he so bitterly and perceptively satirized. And I could not help but believe that in his attempt to reduce his life and thought to a beautiful esthetic vision devoid of any metaphysical or even realistic claims, he had brought the disillusioned, naturalistic mysticism of the mature Emerson to its logical conclusion.[12]

As I reflected on the collective achievement of American philosophers and their attempt to probe the complexities of human experience, I realized that they had gradually created a distinctive problematic within which religious questions could be addressed. That problematic accepts "experience" as its unifying category and attempts to clarify its meaning, much as the different varieties of Thomism accept "being" as a central category and attempt to clarify its meaning. An American religious problematic interprets experience as an emerging process. It rejects outright metaphysical certitude and affirms the affective, instinctive character of uncritical beliefs, whether religious or philosophical. It sees the religious mind as fallible, creative, developing. It lays great stress upon the role of creative imagination in religious reflection. It accepts an emergent, evolutionary account of the cosmic process. And it acknowledges the need to effect the wedding of religion with a scientific logic of consequences.[13]

Process Theology

As I pondered the issues raised by American religious philosophy, two conclusions came into focus. First, American religious thinkers had, I realized, raised a number of issues of perennial human significance. Second, it was also clear to me that no contemporary American theology that stood in dialogue with the past alone could lay even remote claim to speculative adequacy. Protestant process theology seemed to offer a contemporary point of entry into the historical issues that had over the decades shaped American religious attitudes.

For some the very term "process theology" may need nominal definition. By it I mean that loosely organized movement in Protestant theology that is characterized by the work of such diverse thinkers as Henry Nelson Wieman, Bernard Meland, Bernard Loomer, Schubert Ogden, W. Norman Pittenger, John C. Cobb, and Daniel Day Williams. Pittenger has been the chief spokesman for process theology in England, but the philosophical inspiration for his thought is the work of Alfred North Whitehead and of Charles Hartshorne. The writings of Pierre Teilhard de Chardin, S.J., together with the extensive commentary they generated are sometimes included under the umbrella of process theology. Among Catholic thinkers, both Bernard Lee and the late Walter Stokes are process thinkers in the

American mode. Process theologians working in the American tradition stand divided methodologically, philosophically, and creedally. But they are sensitive to one another and have attempted to engage one another in serious philosophical and theological discussion.[14]

I soon realized that contemporary process theology has not derived its philosophical inspiration from the American tradition as a whole. Dewey and James have significantly influenced this or that process theologian. But the presiding philosophical genius of the movement is Alfred North Whitehead, especially as creatively reinterpreted by Charles Hartshorne.[15]

As I reflected on the results of process theology, I realized that one could do worse than approach the American philosophical tradition through the eyes of Whitehead. In *Process and Reality* he states that his intention is to bring to systematic statement the philosophies of James and of Dewey. Santayana's Platonism is also a discernible influence on Whitehead's speculative system.[16] Moreover, through personal contact with William Ernest Hocking and the members of the Harvard philosophy faculty, Whitehead seems to have been able to tap many of the wellsprings of the American philosophical genius.[17]

Whitehead's early intellectual work was, however, done in England, not America. With Bertrand Russell, he coauthored *Principia Mathematica*, and he published some important essays in the philosophy of science.[18] Not until 1924, however, at the age of sixty-three did he come to Harvard. There he published in short order a remarkable philosophical trilogy: *Science and the Modern World, Process and Reality,* and *Adventures of Ideas.* In them he attempted to develop what he called a "philosophy of organism."

A major landmark in the history of thought, Whitehead's system recapitulates, systematizes, and transmutes many of the issues that have preoccupied American religious philosophy. Not unlike Edwards, Whitehead grounds the ongoing unification of religious experience in an esthetic consent to God and to the world. He adopts "experience" and "feeling" as basic metaphysical categories. With Channing, Whitehead repudiates a God who is essentially other than space-time entities and proclaims the deity to be the supreme exemplification of the laws that govern all spatio-temporal processing.

The cosmic lure of Platonic love that lay at the heart of Emersonian religion is transformed in Whitehead's scheme into the "lure for feeling." Like Emerson, Whitehead affirms the importance of creative imagination in religious belief and vindicates the synthetic character of religious insight.

With Peirce, Whitehead rejects the intuitionist claims of philosophical rationalism and acknowledges the need for the pragmatic testing of religious theories against the developing structure of experience. He espouses an evolutionary cosmology, and he envisages the self as an incremental harmonization of feelings. With Abbot he affirms the primacy of relationship. With James he affirms the finitude of God. Like Royce, Whitehead locates the essence of religion in world-loyalty, recognizes that historical and social experience is an important source of religious insight, and acknowledges the role of reason in leading religion to a synthetic interpretation of God and of the world.

Whitehead's system also has clear affinities with American naturalism. With Dewey, Whitehead affirms the interconnectedness of things, the dynamic relational continuity of the emergent subject and its environment. And he regards abstract logic as the conceptual illumination of the vaguer, felt, emotive pole of experience. Finally, as we have already noted, Whitehead's theory of experience was directly influenced by the Platonism of the elder Santayana.[19]

But I also saw quite clearly that the preoccupation of process theologians with Whitehead's philosophy could have negative consequences as well. I became convinced that the attempt to implement Whitehead's method within theology provided an important key to both the achievements and the oversights of more than one process theologian.

In *The Aims of Education*, Whitehead distinguishes, correctly I believe, three stages in the maturation of experience: the stage of romance, the stage of precision, the stage of generalization. The stage of romance is the stage of "first apprehension." The reality under study is endowed with novelty and vividness. And learning consists in the exploration of new possibilities of understanding. Study "holds within itself unexplored connexions with possibilities half-disclosed by glimpses and half-concealed by the wealth of material." The stage of precision enriches experience by endowing it with an exactness of formulation. Factual exploration ceases to be governed by whim and personal interest and is subjected to the exigencies of systematic thought. The stage of generalization marks the return to romantic experience with one's formulated system in order to enrich experience by systematic unification and to test the system's applicability and adequacy.[20]

Whitehead's philosophical trilogy was the attempt to implement his theory of the stages in the growth of understanding at the level of philosophical speculation. *Science and the Modern World* is the Whiteheadean system in the stage of romance; *Process and Reality* is the same system in the stage of precision; and *Adventures of Ideas*, his system in the stage of generalization. It is, then, in *Process and Reality* that one may expect to discover a precise rendering of Whiteheadean philosophical method.

Whiteheadean Method

In *Process and Reality* Whitehead describes speculative philosophy as "the endeavour to form a coherent, logical, necessary system of general ideas in terms of which every element of our experience can be interpreted." The system will be applicable to experience if there are some experiential variables it can interpret. It will be adequate to experience if there are no experiential variables it cannot interpret.[21]

The philosophical insight that Whiteheadean method attempts to yield is synthetic. It therefore seeks to render experience unified and coherent. As a result, it ambitions a categorial scheme in which the key categories are unintelligible apart from one another. In addition, it attempts to exclude internal inconsistency or logical contradiction from its account of reality.

There is much to commend in such a philosophical program. It is rooted and grounded in experience. It acknowledges concrete feelings as the creative matrix from which systems emerge and against which they might be tested. It seeks to lead one to a viable synthetic insight, one that integrates interpretatively one's speculative view of the world with one's search for self-understanding. It acknowledges the need for any philosophical insight to be true to the process of vital development. It distinguishes the adequacy of philosophical systems from the truth or falsity of individual propositions. It is epistemologically sophisticated and acknowledges the fallibility of philosophical insights. And it correctly construes the task of systematic philosophy as the construction of a theory of the whole that seeks to be faithful to every aspect of human experience.

Whitehead's method also envisages some sort of dialogic relation between philosophy and religion. "Religion," Whitehead writes,

> should connect the rational generality of philosophy with the emotions and purposes springing out of existence in a particular society, in a particular epoch, and conditioned by particular antecedents. Religion is the translation of general ideas into particular thoughts, particular emotions, and particular purposes; it is directed to the end of stretching individual interest beyond its self-defeating particularity.

Philosophy finds religion and modifies it; and conversely
religion is among the data of experience which philosophy
must weave into its own scheme.[22]

Whitehead was personally content to leave the relationship between religion and philosophy somewhat vague, although he did not
hesitate to pass philosophical judgment on traditional religious
creeds, a speculative stance that has been subsequently initiated, at
times cavilierly, by Charles Hartshorne. Hartshorne, for his part has
tended to accept the speculative adequacy of Whiteheadean methodology, although he has also sought to clarify in minor details what the
relationship between philosophy and religion ought to be in a
Whiteheadean universe.[23]

Here it is important for the student of theology to recall that
neither Hartshorne nor Whitehead lay personal claim to being professional theologians. Their academic *Fach* is philosophy. But both are
men interested in making a philosophical approach to God that is
rooted in a sound insight into the dynamic structure of human experience. They have sensed, quite correctly, that there are speculative
issues raised by belief in God that are purely logical and philosophical
in character. And they have correctly noted that such questions do
indeed demand philosophical competence in order to be understood
and resolved. Unfortunately they have also tended to presuppose that
only philosophy is ultimately competent to resolve speculative questions concerning God.

Hartshorne has, however, insisted more than Whitehead that
any philosophical understanding of God must be adequate to the
needs of worship. His definition of "worship" is, however, highly
abstract. He describes it as "integrating consciousness." He therefore
also allows for atheistic as well as theistic forms of worship.[24] Such a
re-definition of the term "worship" seems to me to be woefully
inadequate to experience as well as woefully vague. In some acts of
worship, its conscious integrating effect, if present, is so trivial as to
be speculatively negligible. Many prayers spring more from despera-
tion and a sense of personal disintegration than from any kind of
healing insight.

Moreover, to extend the term "worship" to every instance of
integrating consciousness is to do unwarranted violence to language.
A satisfying evening at the symphony or a clarifying philosophical
insight into logic or even into ethics or esthetics is not ordinarily
experienced as worship. Nor is "atheistic worship" a very illuminating concept, least of all for the atheist. The blaspheming revolutionary

exulting in a coup d'etat that he himself has engineered by dint of personal effort and suffering is not likely to see much relationship between such an experience and that of the cloistered contemplative. Nor should he.

By defining worship as any instance of "integrating consciousness," Hartshorne is in fact substituting metaphor for definition. Good definitions clarify the ordinary meaning of a term by so circumscribing its connotation that its denotative significance is made plain. Metaphors extend the connotation of a term in such a way as to render its denotative significance vague. By "defining" worship as any instance of integrating consciousness, Hartshorne has in effect simply extended the term "worship" metaphorically to experiences to which it does not literally apply.

But if, as Hartshorne insists, the adequacy of one's philosophical speculations about God is to be measured by their ability to interpret worship, then vagueness and inadequacy in one's understanding of worship means inadequacy in the criteria one invokes to judge the speculative sufficiency of one's theoretical insights into God.

At issue here is a deeper methodological question. Bernard Meland has chided American process theology for too often failing to ground its speculative generalizations in an adequate descriptive account of human religious experience. Meland has sensed, quite correctly, that much more is involved in an experiential approach to God than flights of the logical and metaphysical imagination. There is, to be specific, evidence of such a failure not only in Hartshorne's impoverished conception of worship but also in his cavalier assimilation of mystical experience to the experience of dogs and cats. It is, moreover, in the work of Schubert Ogden that the methodological inadequacies in Hartshorne's philosophical speculations have begun to take on theological significance.[25]

Ogden On Method

Ogden's first theological mentor was Rudolf Bultmann. Ogden has sensed, correctly I believe, the need to advance theologically beyond Bultmann himself. In *Christ Without Myth* Ogden dismisses New Testament mythology as irrelevant to the meaning of human existence. And he insists that "Christian faith is to be interpreted exhaustively and without remainder as man's original possibility of authentic existence as this is clarified and conceptualized by an appropriate philosophical analysis." He then assures his readers that the appropriate analysis of Christian religious experience has been supplied by Charles Hartshorne. This claim is all the more startling when it is viewed in the light of Hartshorne's own protestations that his and Whitehead's religious convictions are closer to Buddhism than to Christianity.[26]

What troubles Ogden most about Bultmann is not the latter's eighteenth-century rationalistic tendencies but the fact that his acquiescence in Heideggerian existential categories prevents him from being able to speak of God directly. (Paul Tillich's existential theology runs into a similar linguistic impasse.)

Ogden attempts to refurbish Bultmann's method by redefining what Bultmann had called the "existentiell" and "existential" structures of religious experience. He does so, moreover, in terms that conform to Hartshorne's discussion of the religious implications of Whitehead's philosophical method. It is not germane to our purpose to explain the meaning of these terms in Bultmann's writing. Our concern is with Ogden and American process theology, not with Bultmann.

Ogden suggests that Bultmann's attempt to describe the existentiell elements in experience is in fact only one way of talking about the human search for personal understanding. He also believes that the search for personal understanding can be better understood (with Hartshorne) as the elaboration of a notion of deity that is adequate to worship. He then correlates an analysis of the existential structures of experience with the search for philosophical rather than personal understanding. His motives in such a speculative strategy are, moreover, plainly stated: Hartshorne's philosophy allows him to speak analogically of God but Bultmann's does not. He therefore concludes that Hartshorne's method is a more sensitive theological instrument than Bultmann's.

For the theological layman all of this talk of analogical predication, of existentials and existentiells, is apt to be mystifying enough. What does it all mean? When the dust of theological jargon settles what it means is that, as far as Ogden is concerned, Hartshorne's elaboration of Whitehead's philosophical method is an adequate way of going about the task of theology. Let us reflect on what such a suggestion implies.

Bernard Lonergan has accurately described the basic task of theology as the attempt to mediate interpretatively between a culture and the place and function of a religion in that culture. He has also located the problem of method quite correctly at the level of operations. He correctly describes a method as "a normative pattern of recurrent and related operations yielding cumulative and progressive results."[28]

What Ogden has suggested is that Whitehead's philosophical

method (as embellished by Hartshorne) is adequate to the task of Christian theology. The question is: Is such a methodological position defensible or not? If, as Lonergan suggests, the best test of a method is pragmatic, what kind of theological results does Ogden's method yield?

Ogden has attempted to apply his method to two theological issues. He has tried to show that the statement "God acts in history" means that God's relation to the world is analogous to our relation to our bodies. He has also tried to show that the statement "God has acted decisively in Jesus" means that Jesus' life and death reveal God's transcendent love to us.[29]

To affirm an analogical resemblance between God's relation to the world and each individual's relation to his or her body is a basic tenet of Hartshorne's metaphysics. Nevertheless, as Robert Neville has correctly pointed out, that tenet has little or nothing to do with what is normally meant by divine activity. Moreover, Ogden's account of God's action in Jesus fails to differentiate it from God's action in Gandhi, in Martin Luther King, or in Dorothy Day. If Ogden is correct, God's action in Jesus is, then, something less than decisive.

Ogden himself seems to anticipate such an objection and offers a further "clarification" of what it means for a Christian to say "Jesus is Lord." It means, he suggests, that God has said nothing new in Jesus but that Jesus' human word is infinitely more than any other word of revelation because it has the power and authority to claim our ultimate allegiance. No other promise and demand can have the same divine significance.[30] But if, as Ogden insists, Jesus' word is only human, how is it infinite in its appeal? And if it is not infinite, why is it not surpassable by some other word? Moreover, does not the word of the Buddha or of Karl Marx give evidence of being able to claim ultimate human allegiance? One may object that the words of Buddha or of Marx do not seem to appeal to everyone. But, then, neither do the words of Jesus.

If, then, there is a way of integrating Whitehead's philosophical method into the theological enterprise, one may argue that there is solid evidence based on the results of Ogden's own speculations that he has yet to find it. For his own attempt to implement that method theologically yields a frank philosophical reductionism.

There are important methodological issues at stake here that lie at the basis of everything that follows in this book. Ogden's method is theologically inadequate because it yields a philosophical reductionism. That reductionism, however, has its roots in the inadequacies that mar Whitehead's own methodology. Whitehead's method acknowledges that there ought to be a dialogic relation between religion and philosophy. But his method fails to discover a speculative moment within religion itself. For Whitehead, religion is among the data the speculative philosopher must take into account. And religion has the task of rendering practical and concrete the insights of the philosophical genius. But religion furnishes no insights in its own right. It is this methodological oversight that (with hints from Hartshorne and Bultmann) inspires Ogden's philosophical reductionism. For if philosophy alone enlightens religion, then the theoretical meaning of religious affirmations must be derived exclusively from philosophical speculation.

One can, however, avoid Ogden's methodological impasse if one is willing to admit the presence of an autonomous speculative element within religion itself. In fact, every religious conversion has cognitive and even highly abstract speculative elements within it. It is, moreover, possible to establish within the theological enterprise a purely speculative dialogue between the insights born of conversion within a specific religious tradition and the insights born of the philosophical attempt to reflect on the most generic traits of experience. And the insights born of conversion can legitimately challenge those born of philosophical speculation, and vice versa.

Mythic Thinking

Not all of the cognitive elements that shape religious experience are abstract. Some are artistic, poetic, mythic. One reason Ogden seems to be unable to appreciate the speculatively autonomous character of religion is his deeper failure to appreciate the meaning and function of myth within human religious experience. In the pages that follow we will have occasion to reflect more than once on mythic elements that function within a Christian conversion experience. It will, then, repay us at this point to reflect on Ogden's theory of myth and to reach clarity concerning its inadequacies, if for no other reason than to arm ourselves methodologically against his oversights.

As Ogden's thought has developed he has shown a greater appreciation for mythic forms of thought than he did in *Christ Without Myth*. Rather than dismissing myth as irrelevant to contemporary experience he now seems ready to concede that truth in some form is made available through mythic thinking. He argues (without, however, presenting factual evidence for his position) that myths seek to interpret only internal experiences. He then locates the problem of mythic language in the fact that it derives its interpretative categories from external sensory perceptions. What is the point of this suggestion?

Ogden sees myths as seeking to assert a truth in the face of those "boundary situations" in human experience where rational categories break down. Such situations include experiences of death, chance, conflict, suffering, guilt, freedom, responsibility. So much he concedes to Langdon Gilkey. In the face of the mystery of human existence, Ogden argues, myths express our purely subjective feelings: (1) that life as we live it is somehow of ultimate worth and (2) that it is possible to understand ourselves and the world in their relation to totality so that this assurance of life's worth is itself assured.[31] For Ogden, however, the problem with myths is that by interpreting such purely subjective attitudes in objective, sense-derived categories, they commit the "category mistake," i.e., they mistake the objective categories employed by mythmakers for the subjective feelings they seek to interpret.

In his description of the place and function of myth in human religious experience, Ogden himself, however, falls victim to a fallacy of his own, one that can be appropriately termed the "patriarchal fallacy." Jungian psychology correctly distinguishes two types of human consciousness: one vague, concrete, emotive, archetypal; the other clear, abstract, logical, intellectual. Emotive consciousness yields a vague sense of the larger self of which clear, abstract, rational ego-consciousness is only an aspect. Jungian theory associates vague, emotive self-consciousness with the archetype of the feminine; clear, intellectual ego-awareness with the archetype of the masculine.[32] The former is, then, matriarchal in character; the latter, patriarchal. The patriarchal fallacy is the belief that only clear, abstract, rational conceptions give us cognitive access to the real world. In interpreting myths as the expression of purely subjective feelings Ogden commits just such a fallacy.

The scientific study of different mythic traditions, which his theory of myth largely ignores, has made it quite clear that myths seek to interpret much more than "purely subjective" emotions. Myths, as Ernst Cassirer, Mircea Eliade, and others have pointed out, are imaginative schematizations of environmental forces encountered within experience.[33]

The chief difference between myths and more abstract forms of thought is not that myths are more subjective but that they are vaguer. A vague conceptualization of the environmental forces that function in experience is, as Whitehead suggests, one in which many distinguishable forces count evaluatively as one. Joseph Campbell and Erich Neumann's reflections on the myth of the Hero are instructive here.[34]

Campbell offers the following schematic summary of the interpretative elements that function typically in heroic myths:

The mythological hero, setting forth from his common-day hut or castle, is lured, carried away, or else voluntarily proceeds, to the threshold of adventure. There he encounters a shadow presence that guards the passage. The hero may defeat or conciliate this power and go alive into the kingdom of the dark (brother-battle, dragon battle; offering, charm), or be slain by the opponent and descend in death (dismemberment, crucifixion). Beyond the threshold, then, the hero journeys through a world of unfamiliar yet strangely intimate forces, some of which severely threaten him (tests), some of which give magical aid (helpers). When he arrives at the nadir of the mythological round, he undergoes a supreme ordeal and gains his reward. The triumph may be represented as the hero's sexual union with the goddess-mother of the world (sacred marriage), his recognition by the father-creator (father atonement), his divinization (apotheosis), or again—if the powers have remained unfriendly to him—his theft of the boon he came to gain (bride-theft, fire-theft); intrinsically it is an expansion of consciousness and therewith of being (illumination, transfiguration, freedom). The final work is that of return. If the powers have blessed the hero, he now sets forth under their protection (emmissary); if not, he flees and is pursued (transformation flight, obstacle flight). At the return threshold the transcendental powers must remain behind; the hero re-emerges from the kingdom of dread (return, resurrection). The boon that he brings restores the world (elixir).[35]

Neumann, for his part, has argued persuasively that hero myths are interpretatively linked at an instinctive, emotional level with the emergence of ego-consciousness. In point of fact Neumann overstates his case. Hero myths are emotionally linked, not to the emergence of ego-consciousness in general, as he suggests, but to the development of masculine ego-consciousness in male-dominated societies. In societies in which women were not oppressed, there would seem to be no reason why Heroine myths could not emerge as imaginative interpretations of the development of feminine ego-awareness. Neumann links myths in which the Hero dies and is reborn with the disintegration and reconstruction of the ego. And he cites the Osiris myth as a clear example of a myth of transformation.[36]

We will reflect in greater detail on his suggestion in another context. Here it suffices to note that his citation is both correct and instructive. For if the Osiris myth was capable of interpreting for ancient Egyptians the complex biological, psychic, and social dynamics that govern male ego-development, the myth also interpreted for them their national sense of destiny as well as their feeling for God and for the ultimate meaning of human existence. In the myth, Osiris is simultaneously the personal embodiment of the best in Egyptian culture, the preceptor of all other nations, and the god whom loyal Egyptians worship. The myth of Osiris interpreted, therefore, a whole complex of social, psychological, and historical relationships and forces present in the environment of the ancient Egyptian. What is important for understanding the cognitive character of mythic thinking is that the myth interpreted all of these things at once. It was capable of this extraordinary interpretative feat because it eschewed the use of clear conceptual definition and employed instead metaphor and spontaneous archetypal categories that are heavy with feeling and rich with connotative significance.

It is connotative richness that renders any myth conceptually vague. Moreover, every myth, because it is conceptually vague, can be logically neither verified nor falsified until it is conceptually clarified. For, from a logical standpoint, a vague statement is one to which the principle of contradiction does not apply.

In order to verify logically the different levels of meaning present in any myth, one must attempt to reduce each level to propositional statements whose deductively clarified consequences can be tested against the data of experience. Such statements are not, however, themselves mythic in character. They are inferences in the strict sense and subject to the rules of logic. For example, the statement "The Osiris myth interprets the dynamics of male ego-development" is a proposition in psychology, not a myth. When deductively clarified it could, conceivably, be tested against the data of experience and pronounced either true or false, or at least assigned a degree of probability.

But if only propositions derived from mythic statements, not the myths themselves, are subject to logical verification or falsification, can the myths themselves be said to be either true or false? Clearly, if logical verification or falsification is the only criterion of truth, myths cannot be said to be true. But is logical verification or falsification the only criterion of truth? In point of fact, the rules of logic govern only one realm of evaluative response, that of inference in the strict sense. If, then, inference is not the only form of thought, neither is inferential truth the only form of truth. For art, literature, drama, myth, are forms of thinking. In what, then, does their truth or falsity consist? Susanne Langer is, I believe, correct to distinguish presentational from significant forms of artistic expression.[37] Presentational forms are nonlinguistic. They do not employ definable words and syntax. They are untranslatable. Painting, sculpture, dance music, are all examples of presentational art forms. Significant art forms are linguistic. They employ definable words and syntax, but they do so metaphorically rather than with abstract precision. Nevertheless, they do assert something linguistically and are translatable up to a point (as discursive prose is translatable only up to a point). The richer the metaphorical connotations of the work, of course, the more difficult will it be to translate it accurately. Poetry, drama, myth, are examples of significant art forms.

To translate a poem, one must be able to empathize cognitively with the feeling embodied in the poem. One must also understand at a concrete emotive level how the linguistic symbols used by the poet give cognitive shape to the feelings the poem conveys. And one must have sufficient mastery of another language to sense how similar feelings can be connoted (not defined) through the use of the linguistic symbols available in that language. Good translations of poetry are rare, not because they are impossible in principle, but because the necessary linguistic competence, the necessary poetic genius, and the motivation to undertake the translation rarely fuse in the same person.

Myths differ from poetry and drama in that they inform the lives of individuals and of peoples more profoundly. They give cognitive shape to the inchoate values that shape a culture. They lie closer to instinct than do the self-conscious creations of the artist. But like significant art forms, myths too are subject to a process of translation. In the case of myth, however, the process is more complex. When one nation or individual absorbs the myths of another, it is usually symptomatic of deep-seated emotional and cultural shifts that are only vaguely sensed as they occur. The changes in question may be either growth or decay. The Hellenization of native Roman deities subsequent to the Roman subjugation of Greece signaled, for example, the cultural coming of age of an emerging imperial power. The emergence of Gnostic myths at the dawn of the Christian era signaled the decay of that same culture.

In significant art forms (myth included), imagination, both archetypal and free-floating, replaces logic as the organizing principle of language. As a consequence the truth of a myth, like the truth of a poem or of a good drama, is connotative rather than logically verifiable. That is to say, a myth will be true if the imaginative symbols it employs are capable of connoting simultaneously all of the diverse environmental forces that the myth seeks more or less consciously to interpret. *Pace* Ogden, there is, then, no such category mistake in mythic thinking as he describes.

There is, moreover, a genuine irony in Ogden's insistence on the "subjective" character of mythic thinking. The clear (and fallacious) distinction between subjectivity and objectivity that infects our language is an unexorcised epistemological ghost born of substance philosophy. Subjectivity can exist only in a universe in which things exist "in themselves and not in anything else." For only in such a world do feelings and thoughts present for reflection events that occur inside each subject and not in anything else. If Ogden is willing to abandon the category of substance, as every good process philosopher should, then he should also be willing to let go the category of "subjectivity" as well. In Whitehead's "reformed subjectivist principle," for example, the subject is in fact consistently redefined to include its environment.[38]

Some Methodological Postulates

It is perhaps time to pause and summarize the conclusions to which the preceding reflections have led us. Our examination of the American tradition has yielded two important methodological postulates that ought to govern any attempt to theologize in the American mode:

(1) *Anyone attempting to do theology as an American must stand within the American tradition and attempt to speak to the kinds of religious issues it has raised.*

(2) *Anyone who stands within the American tradition in order to reflect on it theologically may legitimately adopt "experience" as an integrating speculative category.*

We decided, however, that a contemporary theological evaluation of the American philosophical tradition would have to stand in dialogue, not only with the American past, but with relevant and important issues being raised in contemporary American society. We discovered in process theology a contemporary point of access into American religious philosophy. We therefore examined process thought to see if it offered a method adequate to the task of evaluating systematically the theological implication of the American philosophical tradition. Our reflections on the methodological issues raised by process theology have, however, yielded several other important methodological postulates relevant to any attempt to create an American theology:

(3) *The basic task of any theology is interpretative mediation*

between a culture and the place and function of a religion in that culture.

(4) *To engage in theology effectively, one must recognize that religious conversion has the capacity to raise speculative issues in its own right.*

(5) *The philosophical theologian is one who seeks to mediate interpretatively between the philosophical issues raised by a given culture and the speculative issues raised autonomously by the religious conversion (s)he is attempting to understand.*

(6) *Since religious conversion is interpreted by artistic, poetic, and mythic categories as well as by abstract, speculative categories, a philosophical theologian must also seek to mediate between the philosophical issues raised by a given culture and the images that interpret the religious conversion experience (s)he is attempting to understand.*

(7) *The adequate interpretation of mythic religious categories demands that they be understood not merely as the expression of subjective feeling but as the attempt to grapple imaginatively with the forces that shape the self in its dynamic relationship to its environment.*

(8) *Since mythic imagery is connotatively rich but conceptually vague, any theological interpretation of a myth that presents a single set of speculative abstractions as an exhaustive explanation of the meaning of mythic thinking is methodologically unsound.*

(9) *In the pursuit of philosophical theology philosophical reductionism in all of its forms is to be scrupulously avoided for it fails to take into account the speculative issues autonomously raised by a religious conversion.*

The methodological insights I had derived from reflection on the procedures of process theologians seemed to me on reflection to be helpful but of themselves operationally inadequate. Moreover, I realized that apart from Ogden, Hartshorne, and Whitehead, no other process thinker had addressed himself in any extended way to the question of method. Was there, then, any other contemporary theological source to which I might turn for enlightenment concerning the kind of methodology that would be adequate to the task in hand—namely, to evaluate theologically the religious aspects of the American philosophical tradition?

The Method of Correlation

Neo-orthodox Protestant theology had, I felt, been correct to insist that theological thinking must transpire within faith. But by excluding philosophers from its theological republic, continental neo-orthodoxy had, I felt, dodged rather than faced the speculative challenge that philosophical reflection poses for the believer. Moreover, failure to integrate a philosophical critique of personal presuppositions into theological method had, I saw, all too often led neo-orthodox speculation to affirm in the name of religion a number of unexamined and destructive philosophical positions. Karl Barth's sacramental theology is a case in point, it rests on dualistic presuppositions that are both philosophically and theologically questionable.[39]

Since neo-orthodoxy offered little promise of methodological enlightenment, I turned to the work of Paul Tillich and Bernard Lonergan. Surely here were two thinkers who were sensitive to the speculative claims that philosophy makes upon the theological enterprise.

I began a detailed study of Tillich's *Systematic Theology*. But I was astonished to discover that the first postulate of the theological "method of correlation" that structures his system is a repudiation of philosophy and its insights. Surely, I reflected, if any man had used philosophical categories in the attempt to think theologically it had been Paul Tillich. Yet here was the same Tillich insisting that philosophical speculation has no place in theology. Here was a paradox I had to understand.

In his *Systematic Theology* Tillich describes philosophical thinking as detached and objective. It derives its categories from matter rather than from an "existential" analysis of human experience. Theology is by contrast depicted as personally involving and concerned with personal salvation.[40] These descriptions did considerable violence to my own philosophical and theological experience. The American philosophers I had studied were personally, even passionately involved in the search for religious meaning. They had wrestled with the problem of personal salvation. They had not derived their categories from "matter" alone; but neither were they "existentialist" in Tillich's sense of that term.

Moreover, as I watched Tillich's method do its work, I gradually came to realize that his repudiation of philosophy had a hidden and illegitimate purpose, namely, to endow his own use of philosophical categories with a fallacious aura of holiness that put them beyond the patient critique of other philosophical systems. The converted Tillichean had no choice but to take the existentialist category "Being" rather than the American category "experience" as the "unavoidable" starting point for all theological speculation. Tillich's method demanded that I identify "Being" with "infinite" and "a being" with "finite." It demanded that I oppose the grasp of "Being" to the grasp of "a being." As a consequence, it also demanded my willingness to deny that God is either a person or a self and that Jesus can be both God and man. It demanded in a word that I abandon both my American and my Catholic religious heritage in order to become a disciple of Paul Tillich. The more I reflected on the peace that surpasses understanding that I had discovered through a charismatic and sacramental encounter with a personal and incarnate God, the more loathe I was to join Paul Tillich in his endless circling flight around the abyss of Being.[41]

More to the point of the present argument, however, I saw that Tillich's exclusion of the philosophical critique of presuppositions from the theological enterprise had rendered his method of correlation incapable of dealing positively with speculative pluralism. His antiphilosophical stance had led him to employ existentialist philosophy dogmatically rather than critically. As a consequence any American religious philosopher who would be measured against the exigencies of Tillichean theological method would, I realized, suffer the same arbitrary speculative fate as the Christian doctrines of God and of the incarnation. Either their insights would be reduced to the categories that give shape to a Tillichean search for "new Being" or they must be dismissed as mere philosophers whose thought was bereft of "existential" significance and remained shackled to the earth from whence it had sprung.[42]

Functional Specialties

Bernard Lonergan's theological method, on the other hand, seemed to me on all these points clearly superior to Tillich's. Lonergan's method carefully distinguishes the tasks of philosophy and of theology. But he acknowledges an unavoidable philosophical moment within the experience of conversion. Moreover, by distinguishing intellectual from religious conversion, Lonergan's method had, I felt, done the one thing that Ogden, Tillich, and Protestant neoorthodoxy had been unable to do, namely, it created a methodological exigency for a speculative dialogue between philosophy and religion within the context of a theological reflection on human religious experience. Moreover, Lonergan's method, while formulated in the categories of a modified transcendental Thomism, explicitly allowed for a pluralism of philosophical approaches to the problem of religious experience, provided that they are methodologically sound.[43]

Lonergan's method also seemed to me to explicate the task of theology with greater subtlety than Tillich's. It divides the theological enterprise into eight "functional specialties." These specialties are an attempt to describe stages through which theological speculation must pass as it searches for a cumulative insight into a Christian religious experience. All eight specialties develop in simultaneous dialogic interdependence. Each may pose a question for another. Each specialty may find in another data and insights relevant to the resolution of one of its own questions. The functional specialties are: research, interpretation, history, dialectics, foundations, doctrines, systematics, and communications.[44]

In Lonergan's method, concern with collecting the factual data needed for theological reflection is the task of the research theologian. Research theology gives rise to religious archaeology, to the study of sacred languages, and to editing critical editions of theologically significant texts.[45] Interpretative theology seeks to explain what sacred artifacts and writings meant to the individuals who originally created them.[46] Historical theology seeks to describe the interaction of a religious community with the larger cultural environment from which it emerged. It traces its conflict and coalescence with other human communities as well as the internal tensions that marked its own development.[47]

So far, Lonergan's method and Tillich's manifest a certain superficial convergence. Both methods acknowledge the need for factual and historical research. But Lonergan's method is subtler than Tillich's in that it differentiates the tasks of research, interpretation, and history with greater operational clarity.

Lonergan's method introduces realms of reflection and discourse into the theological process that are unknown in Tillich's method of correlation. Lonergan insists, quite correctly, that responsible theological reflection must attempt to come to terms with the presuppositions that ground contradictory developments within any religious tradition. And he also insists correctly that such critical reflection must proceed in two stages. The first stage is the stage of dialectic. The second stage is called foundational thinking.

Dialectical thinking differs from the history of ideas in that it seeks to go beyond an accurate factual account of intellectual and cultural development to an evaluative assessment of the presuppositions that grounded the convergence, the disagreement, and the relative adequacy of diverse doctrinal pronouncements and positions. Moreover, the theological dialectician undertakes this evaluative assessment of the past with a view to foundational thinking. For where dialectic discovers internal contradictions and inadequacies in a given religious tradition, the foundational theologian must attempt to transcend and correct them. The dialectician does not, then, attempt to construct a coherent theory of conversion. But (s)he attempts to clarify those issues that will make the construction of such a theory possible.[48]

The work of theological reconstruction begins with foundational reflection. But it does not end there. The doctrinal theologian seeks to bring the insights of foundational thinking to the fruits of research, interpretation, history, and dialectics in order to evaluate which of the existing symbols of religious faith are truly expressive of an authentic conversion experience. The systematic theologian attempts to indicate the connections between authentic doctrines. And the communications theologian seeks to translate the fruits of technical theological thinking into terms that are intelligible to the community in which it occurs.[49]

When Tillich's systematic method of correlation is contrasted with Lonergan's method, its inadequacies become apparent. For what Tillich has attempted to do is to pass from the factual stages of theological research to systematic thinking without the mediation of dialectics, foundational theology, and doctrinal reevaluation. As a consequence, he has canonized a particular philosophical approach to theology—continental European existentialism—as normative for theological reflection without subjecting its presuppositions to rigorous dialectical and foundational criticism.

As I reflected on the implications of Lonergan's method, I realized that in his account of dialectics he had accurately described the operations I had spontaneously employed in my own researches into American religious philosophy. The dialectician, Lonergan suggests, must first assemble the historical materials pertinent to the resolution of a given theological question. The assembled materials must then be interpretatively "completed." That is to say, when viewed in the light of the question under examination they must be ranked initially according to their importance and relevance. The completed materials must then be compared and doctrinal similarities and differences noted. The presuppositions grounding those likenesses and differences must then be explicated. The reasons for irreconcilable opposition must be brought to light; the grounds of genuine consensus, laid bare. Finally, the dialectician must reach a personal judgment concerning the truth or falsity, adequacy or inadequacy, of the positions examined.[50]

I had, for example, noted that Edwards, Emerson, Brownson, Peirce, James, Dewey, Santayana, and Whitehead had all affirmed the importance of emotion in human religious experience. I had noted, however, that Edwards, Emerson, Brownson, James, and Santayana had all lacked the technical logical interest and competence needed to discuss the relation between religious inferences and religious emotions. Peirce and Whitehead had both enjoyed the needed logical competence. But of the two Peirce had, I felt, reflected in much more detail on the logic of religious faith than had Whitehead. Moreover, while their positions were convergent, Peirce's explanation of the genetic relation of thought to feeling within religious experience was, I felt, much more nuanced than Whitehead's. It was also more speculatively satisfying than the solutions offered by Edwards, Emerson, Brownson, James, and Santayana. Moreover, Peirce's approach to religious experience seemed to me to take into better account its potential complexity than either Whitehead's or Dewey's.

Moreover, as I had wrestled personally with the theological implications of the philosophical issues raised by American religious thinkers, I had found myself moving spontaneously toward a theology of religious conversion. And I realized with some excitement that the elaboration of a theology of conversion is the task that Lonergan assigns to the foundational theologian. My study of Lonergan was then both stimulating and clarifying because it named and raised to consciousness the very operations that had been spontaneously guiding my own philosophical and theological reflections. In other words, it yielded the kind of conscious self-appropriation Lonergan had said it would.

Completing Lonergan

But the more I studied Lonergan in the light of the American philosophical tradition, the more I sensed certain important lacunae in his thought. And I began to glimpse the possibility of using categories derived from the American philosophical tradition in order to complete and expand Lonergan's own theology of conversion. I also recognized that in the process of so doing I would have to subject to critique the philosophical underpinnings of Lonergan's own method. I found this realization reassuring, however; for Dewey had convinced me that any good method must be capable of self-criticism.

Lonergan describes conversion as any conscious act of self-appropriation that opens up a new evaluative horizon within which personal growth and commitment may subsequently transpire. He argues that one may undergo conversion at an intellectual, at a moral, or at a religious level. And he correctly insists that these three dimensions of conversion are interconnected but distinct. One who is intellectually converted may remain morally or religiously unconverted but should not. One morally converted may remain intellectually and religiously unconverted but should not. One religiously converted may remain intellectually and morally unconverted but should not. All of these suggestions seemed to me to be sound.[51]

What troubled me in Lonergan's theory of conversion was his almost total failure to take into account the emotive elements that shape human religious experience or to acknowledge their complex speculative claims. Symptomatic of that failure is his inability (reminiscent of Ogden's) to relate positively to mythic forms of thought.[52]

To make room in Lonergan's theology of conversion for emotions and their cognitive claims demanded, I realized, an expansion of the scope of foundational theology beyond that described by Lonergan himself. In his account of foundational thinking Lonergan distinguishes, correctly I believe, three "nests" of categories that ought to function in the elaboration of any theology of conversion: transcendental categories, general theological categories, and special theological categories.

Transcendental categories are those that seek universal applicability, that is to say, there ought to be nothing that a transcendental category cannot interpret. "Being" is such a category for the Thomist. "Experience" performs a similar function for more than one American philosopher. I had realized through my study of American philosophical religion that if I desired to stand within the American speculative tradition in order to reflect on its theological implications, I would have to adopt the term "experience" rather than "being" or some other category as central to my own thought. The shift offered a number of clear advantages. A foundational theology of experience could, I realized, accommodate an affective moment within conversion more easily than Lonergan's transcendental Thomism. More important still, the shift within foundational theology from a Neo-Thomistic "being" problematic to an American "experience" problematic opened the door to implementing within foundational theology the kind of philosophical enterprise Whitehead's system had envisioned—namely, the elaboration of a generalized theory of experience that is logical, coherent, applicable, and adequate. At the same time foundational theology provided a methodological context for establishing the kind of dialogue between philosophy and religion that process theology had in more than one instance failed to provide.

The shift to a problematic of "experience" demanded that I make other methodological shifts as well. In order to elaborate a set of "general theological categories," I would, I saw, have to address myself to the following kinds of questions: What does it mean to undergo a conversion experience? What facts, values, operations, forces, function within any experience of religious conversion? How do perceptions, emotions, inferences, doubts, questions, presuppositions, frames of reference, give structure to an experience of conversion? How do beliefs function within conversion? How does human speculation alter and illumine the experience of conversion? Are there levels of consciousness within conversion? If so, what distinguishes one level from another? What are the inauthenticities that can mar a conversion experience and undermine its healthy development? To resolve such questions would, I saw, be to construct a set of "general theological categories" applicable in intention to any authentic religious experience.[53]

The third problem facing an experiential foundational theology would, I realized, be to situate specific kinds of religious experiences normatively within one's theory of religious conversion in general. A Christian foundational theologian would, for example, have to face questions like the following: How ought the sacraments to function in an authentic Christian conversion? How ought grace, the gifts of the Spirit, to be experienced by the converted Christian? What is the normative function of the Christian community within an authentic Christian conversion? How within Christian conversion ought God, Jesus, the Holy Spirit, to come to experiential visibility? To resolve such questions would be to elaborate a theology of conversion that would be specifically Christian.[54]

It seemed to me, however, that one who stands in a Buddhist or a Hindu tradition could use the same methodology in order to elaborate a theory of authentic Buddhist or Hindu conversion. Foundational method could, then, provide an important theoretical basis for ecumenical dialogue, not only among Christians but among world religions as well, but not without the elaboration of a third "nest" of "special theological categories."

More Postulates

Critical reflection on neo-orthodox theological method and a comparison of Tillich's and of Lonergan's methodologies had, then, provided a second set of methodological postulates to complement those I had derived from process theology. Taken together these two sets of postulates seemed to me to provide the promise of advancing speculatively toward a systematic theological evaluation of the American philosophical tradition. The second set of postulates were the following:

(10) *Theological reflection must transpire in the context of faith; but any theology employing philosophical categories must make methodological room within the theological enterprise itself for a philosophical moment when those categories may be subjected to strict philosophical critique.*

(11) *Every speculative method may be described as "a normative pattern of operations yielding cumulative and progressive results."*

(12) *One may differentiate within theology at least eight distinct methods corresponding to eight functional specialties: research, interpretation, history, dialectics, foundations, doctrines, systematics, communications.*

(13) *Since the task of dialectics and foundations is the systematic critique of presuppositions, they provide a methodological context for integrating philosophy into the theological enterprise.*

(14) *The task of the dialectician is to clarify the issues relevant to the resolution of a theological question.*

(15) *Since theological issues arise out of the confrontation of a religion and a culture, the dialectician must be concerned both with issues that arise within religious conversion and with challenges and insights relevant to religious self-understanding that emerge in a given culture.*

(16) *The operations of the theological dialectician are the assembly and completion of relevant materials, a comparison of affinities and oppositions within them, explication of the roots of affinity and opposition, classification of problems, election of positions, reversal of counterpositions.*

(17) *The task of the foundational theologian is the elaboration of a normative and comprehensive theory of conversion.*

(18) *The operations of foundational theology are the creative elaboration of three nests of categories needed to interpret any conversion experience: (a) a set of general categories universally applicable in intent; (b) a set of categories that permit a normative description of conversion in general; (c) a set of categories that permit one to situate specific kinds of religious experience within one's general theory of conversion.*

(19) *Since any foundational theory must be logical and coherent, these three sets of categories must be elaborated in function of one another.*

(20) *The abstract, theoretical categories employed by the foundational theologian must also be capable of interpreting adequately the emotive elements that function cognitively within conversion.*

(21) *To engage in foundational thinking within the American tradition, one should raise and seek to answer the following questions: (a) What variables structure experience in general? (b) What variables structure an authentic religious experience? (c) What variables structure an authentic Christian conversion?*

As I reflected on these methodological guidelines, I felt that I was ready to begin a theological evaluation of American philosophical religion. But where was I to begin? I seemed to stand at the beginning of a stiff climb. I had broken through the thicket of methodology. My pack was settled snugly on my shoulders; my hip strap, comfortably adjusted. But I still hadn't found the trailhead.

Notes

1. Perry Miller, *The New England Mind* (2 vols.; Boston: Beacon, 1954), I, pp. 3–63; *Errand into the Wilderness* (Cambridge: Harvard, 1956), pp. 1–14, 48–98; see also: Ralph Barton Perry, *Puritanism and Democracy* (New York: Harper, 1944); Alan Heimert, *Religion and the American Mind* (Cambridge: Harvard, 1966); William Haller, *The Rise of Puritanism* (New York: Harper and Row, 1957).

2. Perry Miller, *Jonathan Edwards* (Toronto: Sloan, 1949); Conrad Cherry, *The Theology of Jonathan Edwards* (New York: Anchor, 1966); Roland Delattre, *Beauty and Sensibility in the Thought of Jonathan Edwards* (New Haven: Yale, 1968); John Gerstner, *Steps to Salvation: The Evangelical Message of Jonathan Edwards* (Philadelphia: Westminster, 1959); David Levin, ed., *Jonathan Edwards* (New York: Hill and Wang, 1969).

3. Adrienne Koch, ed., *The American Enlightenment* (New York: Braziller, 1965); G. A. Koch, *The Religion of the American Enlightenment* (New York: Thomas Y. Crowell, 1963); Alfred Aldridge, *Benjamin Franklin and Nature's God* (Durham: Duke, 1967); Paul Connor, *Poor Richard's Politics* (New York: Oxford, 1965); Henry Wilder Foote, *The Religion of Thomas Jefferson* (Boston: Beacon, 1947); Adrienne Koch, *The Philosophy of Thomas Jefferson* (New York: Columbia, 1943).

4. C. C. Goen, "Jonathan Edwards: A New Departure in Eschatology," *Church History*, XXVIII (March, 1959), pp. 25–40; Alan Heimert, *op. cit.*; Phillis Franklin, *Show Thyself a Man* (Paris: Mouton, 1969); G. A. Koch, *op. cit.*

5. David Edgell, *William Ellery Channing: An Intellectual Portrait* (Boston: Beacon, 1955); Octavius B. Frothingham, *Boston Unitarianism: 1820–1850* (New York: Putnam's, 1890); Conrad Wright, *The Beginnings of Unitarianism in America* (Boston: Beacon, 1955) and *The Liberal Christians* (Boston: Beacon, 1970).

6. There is no adequate intellectual portrait of Emerson in print; useful studies are: Jonathan Bishop, *Emerson on the Soul* (Cambridge: Harvard, 1964); Sherman Paul, *Emerson's Angle of Vision* (Cambridge: Harvard, 1952); Stephen Whicher, *Freedom and Fate: An Inner Biography of Ralph Waldo Emerson* (New York: Barnes and Co., 1961). Theodore Parker's Transcendentalism was of a different character from Emerson's: cf. John Edward Dirkes, *The Critical Theology of Theodore Parker* (New York: Columbia, 1948); H. S. Smith, "Was Theodore Parker a Transcendentalist?" *New England Quarterly*, XXIII (September, 1950), pp. 351–368.

7. Bertin Farrell, *Orestes Brownson's Approach to the Problem of God* (Washington: Catholic University Press, 1950); Arthur Schlesinger, *Orestes A. Brownson: A Pilgrim's Progress* (Boston: Little, Brown, & Co., 1939).

8. Francis Ellingwood Abbot, *Scientific Theism* (Boston: Little, Brown & Co., 1885); *The Syllogistic Philosophy* (Boston: Little, Brown & Co., 1906); D. D. O'Connor, "Peirce's Debt to F. E. Abbot," *Journal of the History of Ideas*, XXV (October, 1964), pp. 543–564.

9. T. A. Goudge, "The Conflict of Naturalism and Transcendentalism in Peirce," *Journal of Philosophy*, XLIV (July, 1947), pp. 365–375; Charles Hartshorne, "Charles Sanders Peirce, Pragmatic Transcendentalist," *New England Quarterly*, XIV (March, 1941), pp. 49–63; Murray G. Murphey, *The Development of Peirce's Philosophy* (Cambridge: Harvard, 1961); Vincent Potter, *Charles S. Peirce on Norms and Ideals* (Worchester: University of Massachusetts, 1967); Francis E. Reilly, *Charles Peirce's Theory of Scientific Method* (New York: Fordham, 1970); Edward Madden, *Chauncey Wright and the Foundations of Pragmatism* (Seattle: University of Washington, 1963); W. B. Gallie, *Peirce and Pragmatism* (Edinburgh: Penguin, 1952).

10. Alfred Ayer, *The Origins of Pragmatism: Studies in the Philosophy of Charles Peirce and William James* (San Francisco: Freeman and Cooper, 1968); Julius Seelye Bixler, *Religion in the Philosophy of William James* (Boston: Marshall Jones, 1926); Josiah Royce, *William James and Other Essays on the Philosophy of Life* (New York: Macmillan, 1911); Edward C. Moore, *American Pragmatism: Peirce, James, and Dewey* (New York: Columbia, 1961); *William James* (New York: Washington Square, 1966); James H. Cotton, *Royce on the Human Self* (Cambridge: Harvard, 1954); Gabriel Marcel, *Royce's Metaphysics*, trans. Virginia Ann Gordon Ringer, (Chicago: Regnery, 1956); John E. Smith, *Royce's Social Infinite: The Community of Interpretation* (New York: Liberal Arts Press, 1950); Mary B. Mahowald, *An Idealistic Pragmatism* (The Hague: Myhoff, 1972).

11. Thomas R. Maitland, *The Metaphysics of William James and John Dewey* (New York: Philosophical Library, 1955); George R. Geiger, *John Dewey in Perspective* (New York: Oxford, 1958).

12. William E. Arnett, *George Santayana* (New York: Washington Square, 1968); Richard Butler, *The Life and World of George Santayana* (Chicago: Regnery, 1960).

13. William Christian, *An Interpretation of Whitehead's Metaphysics* (New Haven: Yale, 1959); Nathaniel Lawrence, *Whitehead's Philosophical Development* (New York: Greenwood, 1968); Ivor Leclerc, *The Relevance of Whitehead* (London: Macmillan, 1961); *Whitehead's Metaphysics* (London: Macmillan, 1958); Victor Lowe, *Understanding Whitehead* (Baltimore:

John's Hopkins, 1962); Robert Palter, *Whitehead's Philosophy of Science* (Chicago: University of Chicago, 1960); Paul Arthur Schilpp, *The Philosophy of Alfred North Whitehead* (New York: Tudor, 1951).

14. For a good introductory anthology of process speculation and extensive bibliography, see: Ewert Cousins, *Process Theology* (New York: Newman, 1971).

15. Alan Gragg, *Charles Hartshorne* (Waco: Word, 1973); Ralph James, *The Concrete God* (Indianapolis: Bobbs-Merrill, 1967); Eugene Peters, *The Creative Advance* (St. Louis: Bethany, 1966); *Hartshorne and Neoclassical Metaphysics* (Lincoln: University of Nebraska, 1970).

16. Alfred North Whitehead, *Process and Reality* (New York: Free Press, 1929), pp. vii 165–166.

17. In the autobiographical notes that preface the Schilpp volume on Whitehead, the latter lapses into regrettable vagueness when he comes to discuss the Harvard influences on his thought; cf. Schilpp, *The Philosophy of Alfred North Whitehead*, pp. 3–14.

18. For a study of Whitehead's early intellectual development, see: Nathaniel Lawrence, *Whitehead's Philosophical Development* (New York: Greenwood, 1968).

19. Whitehead, *Process and Reality*, pp. 5–26, 76–99, 130–151, 165–166, 182–194, 256–326, 403–413.

20. A. N. Whitehead, *The Aims of Education* (New York: Macmillan, 1957), pp. 17–19.

21. Whitehead, *Process and Reality*, pp. 5–6.

22. *Ibid.*, p. 19.

23. Peters, *op. cit.*, pp. 113–124; Gragg, *op. cit.*, pp. 22–28; Charles Hartshorne, *Reality as Social Process* (Boston: Beacon, 1953), pp. 130–144, 153–176.

24. Charles Hartshorne, *A Natural Theology for Our Time* (La Salle: Open Court, 1967), pp. 1–6.

25. Bernard E. Meland, "Can Empirical Theology Learn Something from Phenomenology?" in *The Future of Empirical Theology* (Chicago: University of Chicago, 1969), pp. 283–305.

26. Schubert Ogden, *Christ Without Myth* (New York: Harper, 1961), pp. 146–151; cf. Charles Hartshorne, "The Buddhist-Whiteheadean View of the Self and the Religious Traditions," *Proceedings of the Ninth International Congress for the History of Religions* (Tokyo: 1960), pp. 298–302; "The Philosophy of Creative Synthesis," *Journal of Philosophy*, LV (October, 1958), pp. 944–953; *A Natural Theology for Our Time*, pp. 108–109.

27. Schubert Ogden, "Bultmann's Demythologizing and Hartshorne's Dipolar Theism," in *Process and Divinity*, ed. William S. Reese and Eugene Freeman (Lasalle: Open Court, 1964), pp. 491–513.

28. Bernard Lonergan, S.J., *Method in Theology* (New York: Herder and Herder, 1972), pp. xi, 5.

29. Schubert Ogden, *The Reality of God and Other Essays* (New York: Harper and Row, 1964), pp. 168–187; Robert Neville, "Neoclassical Metaphysics and Christianity: A Critical Study of Ogden's *Reality of God,*" *International Philosophical Quarterly*, IX (1969), pp. 605–624.

30. Ogden, *Reality of God*, pp. 192–204.

31. *Ibid.*, p. 116; Langdon Gilkey, *Naming the Whirlwind* (New York: Bobbs-Merill, 1969).

32. Cf. Erich Neumann, "On the Moon and Matriarchal Consciousness," trans. Hildegard Nagel, *Spring* (1954), pp. 83–90. See also Edward C. Whitmont, *The Symbolic Quest* (New York: Harper, 1969), pp. 170–215.

33. Ernst Cassirer, *The Philosophy of Symbolic Forms*, trans. Ralph Manheim (3 vols.: New Haven: Yale, 1955), II; Mircea Eliade, *Patterns in Comparative Religion* (New York: Meridian, 1968); *The Sacred and the Profane*, trans. Willard R. Trask (New York: Harcourt, Brace, and World, 1959).

34. Erich Neumann, *The Origins and History of Consciousness*, trans. R. F. C. Hull (Princeton: Billingen, 1954); Joseph Campbell, *The Hero With a Thousand Faces* (New York: Meridian, 1970).

35. Campbell, *op. cit.*, pp. 245–246.

36. Neumann, *op. cit.*, pp. 220–256, 315–444.

37. Susanne K. Langer, *Philosophy in a New Key* (New York: Mentor, 1942), pp. 75–94.

38. Whitehead, *Process and Reality*, pp. 182–194.

39. David Tracy's estimate of the method of neo-orthodox theology seems to me a sound one; cf. David Tracy, *Blessed Rage for Order* (New York: Seabury, 1975), pp. 27–31. Barth's sacramental theology presupposes a questionable philosophical distinction between subjectivity and objectivity. This allows him to characterize the sacramental ritual as purely "external" and faith as "internal" and "subjective." The same distinction underlies his conclusion that the sacramental ritual is "inefficacious." Cf. Karl Barth, *The Teaching of the Church Regarding Baptism*, trans. Ernst A. Payne (London: S.C.M. Press, 1965).

40. Paul Tillich, *Systematic Theology* (Chicago: University of Chicago, 1967), I, pp. 18–21.

41. *Ibid.*, I, pp. 163ff.; 202, 236–245; II, p. 94.

42. The key to Tillich's reductionism lies in the second and third phases of his method of correlation. In the first phase, one must correlate one's situation with that of the first Christians. In the second phase, one must correlate the gospel with uncriticized "existentialist" categories. In the third phase, one must equate the reality of the gospel with its "existential" correlates. *Ibid.*, I, p. 60.

43. Lonergan, *Method in Theology*, pp. 132, 238ff., 276–293. Cf. David Tracy, *The Achievement of Bernard Lonergan* (New York: Herder and Herder, 1970, pp. 232–269.

44. Lonergan, *op. cit.*, pp. 125–145.

45. *Ibid.*, pp. 149–151.

46. *Ibid.*, pp. 153–173.

47. *Ibid.*, pp. 175–234.

48. *Ibid.*, pp. 235–266.

49. *Ibid.*, pp. 267–368.

50. *Ibid.*, pp. 249–250.

51. *Ibid.*, pp. 237ff.

52. *Ibid.*, pp. 89–91, 122, 213–214, 238–243, 306; *Insight* (New York: Philosophical Library, 1958), pp. 530-549.

53. These questions transpose into an experiential problematic the problem areas in foundational thinking cryptically depicted in *Method in Theology*, pp. 286–287.

54. Lonergan, *Method in Theology*, pp. 288-293.

III. That They May Be One

The methodological postulates I had adopted demanded that if I were to achieve some measure of theological self-understanding I must stand within my own American religious tradition and probe the forces that had shaped both it and me.[1] I had begun to investigate some of the deeper religious aspects of the American secular tradition. But what of American Catholicism? It had shaped my earliest beliefs more profoundly than any philosophical abstraction.

The American Catholic Experience

I realized that American Catholic piety had derived its original shape and texture from the Counter-Reformation. It had rejected not only a Calvinist doctrine of predestination but also Lutheran belief in the "depravity of man." Protestant belief in human depravity inculcated a profound suspicion of any purely rational approach to any religious question. Catholic defense of the essential goodness of human nature despite its distortion by sin entailed, by contrast, a defense of the place of "natural" reason in religious speculation. One advantage of the Catholic position was that it made ample room for the development of a devout humanism, from the Renaissance scholarship of Erasmus to the exuberance of the Baroque, to the humanistic Catholicism of Jacques Maritain.

But the Catholic position also labored under a certain number of theological risks. The vindication of a place for natural reason in theological speculation rendered American Catholics extremely susceptible to the rationalistic blandishments of enlightened, eighteenth-century Deists. Catholics like Charles Carroll moved easily in revolutionary circles. The Catholic community as a whole identified strongly with Deistic suspicion and terror of both religious emotionalism and revivalistic enthusiasm. And with time such rationalistic tendencies would, I saw, reduce much popular Catholic piety to the same "corpse-cold" condition as early nineteenth-century Unitarianism.[2]

The colonial Catholic Church was a small missionary church surviving despite harassment and persecution in the heart of the American Protestant empire. But the massive influx of Catholic im-

migrants in the nineteenth century introduced radical changes into
the situation of the Catholic community. Many American Protestants
regarded the sudden expansion of the Roman Church in the United
States with mounting alarm. And alarm bred fear and even hostility.
As a result the expanding immigrant Catholic community found itself
in frequent need of articulate defenders. It found one of the best in the
person of Orestes Brownson.[3]

Brownson was a man of incredible energy and genius. But his
piety had all the exaggerated zeal of a convert. After his conversion
he had rejected out of hand his earlier Deistic creed as the speculative
dead-end of Protestantism. He assaulted Protestant faith as atheism
in religious garb. And he insisted that outside the Catholic Church
there is no salvation. His simplistic interpretation of Church membership and its salvific consequences would, of course, be further dis-
torted into a twentieth-century heresy by Leonard Feeney.[4]

Disillusionment with populist political movements had also left
Brownson suspicious of any social group that refuses the yoke of
authority. Catholics, he insisted, are willing to submit to nonpolitical
religious authority. Hence, they are better prepared to participate in
the processes of democratic government than most Protestants. The
latter fall easy victim to the subjectivism and antinomianism of "inner
light" piety. Such tendencies, untempered by the restraints of authority, can easily transform democracy into mob rule, or so Brownson
feared.

Brownson's polemic was an accurate reflection of the religious
consciousness of nineteenth-century Catholicism. The immigrant
Church had to deal with two distinguishable adversaries: Nativism
and Know-Nothingism. The former was anti-immigrant; the latter,
anti-Catholic. As Brownson's rhetoric suggested, the American
Catholic community tended to draw two different lines of defense in
the face of this two-pronged attack.[5]

It responded to Protestant anti-Catholicism with an equally
militant contempt for all things Protestant. The residue of that embittered and prolonged conflict is still the greatest obstacle to meaningful
ecumenical dialogue and to eventual reunion between American
Catholics and Protestants.

But to the anti-immigrant Nativist, the Catholic community set
out to prove that it could out-American any Yankee. As a consequence, by the end of the nineteenth century, American Catholics
were doing more than acquiescing in secular values; they were em-
bracing and defending them militantly. The ossified, contemporary
product of this sad process is the "America-love-it-or-leave-it" Cath-

olic. It took longer, however, for Catholic immigrant laborers to help transform the labor movement into an effective arm of the established economic power structure.[6]

After Modernism

By the end of the nineteenth century, American Catholicism had become so thoroughly domesticated that it had begun to engender something like a Catholic intellectual and cultural renaissance. One of the most depressing chapters in the history of the Catholic Church in America is the mindless, bureaucratic suppression of that creative impetus in the wake of the modernist crisis.[7]

The speculative alternative legislated to replace indigenous creative thinking was the sterile codification of truth enshrined in nineteenth-century, European scholastic manuals. Manual theology inculcated the blindest kind of intellectual assent to authority, studied obtuseness to the historical character of revelation and of faith, and insensitivity to the different contexts that give meaning to biblical and doctrinal statements. Generations of American clergy and religious warped their minds to the nominalistic methods of manual "thought." And they dutifully taught "the faithful" to do the same.

When the attitudes engendered by manual theology fused with frenetic, anti-Protestant vindication of simplistic theories of papal infallibility, the result was a phenomenon that can only be described as creeping infallibility. Creeping infallibility is the tendency to endow unreflectively any aspect of Catholic life that enjoys any degree of bureaucratic or ecclesiastical sanction with a false aura of immutable truth.

The combined forces of institutional inertia, militant anti-Protestantism, and anticontraceptive morality kept the American Catholic community growing, complacent, and fixed unswervingly in a collision course with the new European theology that came to be officially sanctioned at Vatican II. By the middle of the twentieth century, the immigrant Catholic Church had, however, already "arrived." It had accomplished most of the conscious goals it had set itself. And it celebrated its arrival by constructing an immense shrine to the Virgin in Washington. But beneath the uniform rubrical worship, the canned theology, and the scripted piety of American Catholics, forces were secretly and subtly reshaping religious attitudes.

The unthinking assimilation of the values of American secular culture had combined with rote religion to produce an inordinate number of compartmentalized Catholics. These good but often complacent people managed to keep most of their lives uncontaminated by important religious values. And they were quick to resent any suggestion that religion might demand more sacrifice than the weekly substitution of fish for meat and the dutiful but often passive and perfunctory attendance at unintelligible Sunday liturgies. At the same time the Catholic intelligensia were smouldering under the galling, anti-Modernist restraints that continued to shackle them. To both of these groups, Vatican II dawned with apocalyptic power: a judgment to the one, a liberation to the other.

It did not take me long to realize that the contemporary Catholic offspring of this tangled and not always bright religious history are for the most part ill equipped to cope with the intellectual challenge of American philosophical religion. In American Catholic circles, scholastic epistemological naiveté often combined with the authoritarian attitudes engendered by generations of training in nominalistic manual theology to create the mistaken belief that religious truth can be handed one objectively on a platter. One of the persistent fallacies of American Catholic thought is, I saw, the ontic fallacy: the naive assumption that one can fix one's religious (or secular) beliefs with pure objectivity and without being either personally creative, personally responsible, or personally transformed in the process.

Moreover, while the majority of American Catholics are thoroughly secularized in many ways, they have on the whole dutifully attempted to keep most of their traditional religious beliefs from contaminating secular influences. They have as a result developed an amazing capacity for double-think: a facility in approaching "secular" problems with "secular" categories and evaluations in order to reach "secular" solutions, and "sacred" problems with "sacred" categories to reach ·"sacred" solutions. The magical dividing line between the "secular" and the "sacred" tends to be drawn arbitrarily by an appeal to religious authority. This disjunction between the "secular" and the "sacred" helps ground the extreme forms of religious schizophrenia that one tends not infrequently to encounter in contemporary American Catholic circles.

For while the American secular tradition is oriented toward process, toward scientific logic, toward the repudiation of metaphysical certitude, toward epistemological fallibilism, toward imagination, creativity, and novelty, toward evolution and the future, the American Catholic traditionalist is in religious matters oriented toward a static substance philosophy, toward the vindication of immutable metaphysical insights and revealed propositional certitudes, toward tradition and the past, toward the defense of a simplistic theory of infallibility, and toward rationalistic suspicion of novelty, feeling, and the imagination. Is it, then, any wonder that "the faithful" feel the need to compartmentalize their religion?

State of the Question

These insights into the historical forces that have helped to shape the American Catholic tradition yielded a final methodological postulate:

(22) *A contemporary American Catholic attempt to elaborate a foundational theology of conversion must rest upon a dialectical insight into the issues that divide substance philosophy and theology from process philosophy and theology.* The reasons for such a postulate should by now be clear. Foundational method has a philosophical moment: the critical attempt to elaborate a set of transcendental categories, i.e., a set of categories that are universally applicable in intent. The elaboration of a set of transcendental categories is the fruit of a dialectical insight into the speculative issues that define the relationship between a specific religious tradition and the culture in which it develops. Until relatively recently, American Catholicism has, for a variety of historical reasons, defended a metaphysics of substance. American secular culture in its philosophically critical representatives has tended over the decades to espouse some form of evolutionary, process metaphysics. These two traditions stand, then, in irreconcilable opposition on a number of key issues. Hence, any contemporary American Catholic attempt to engage in foundational theology must, in its "transcendental" moment, take account of the dialectical issues that divide these two philosophical traditions. Moreover, as we shall see, both traditions offer some valid insights into the structure of human experience.

This final methodological insight also provided me with the speculative starting point for which I had been searching. One of the most fundamental problems facing both myself and every other living American Catholic is the problem of religio-cultural schizophrenia. Religio-cultural schizophrenia is the more or less conscious attempt to live out of contradictory value systems derived independently from one's religious heritage and from the cultural matrix that informs one's thought and life. American Catholic values and the values inculcated by American secular society do in fact stand at loggerheads on more than one issue: in their understanding of change, of psychological processes, of freedom, of conscience, of God. My investigation into the historical forces that had helped shape my own religious attitudes had, then, raised an important theological question whose correct resolution would seem to have implications, not only for myself, but for the Church in America.

My question was the following: What are the speculative terms under which the contemporary American Catholic can move toward religio-cultural integration? Moreover, as I pondered the implications of such a question, it seemed to be fraught with ecumenical significance as well. The contemporary American Protestant needs to come to terms with the contradictions that divide his or her secular and religious heritage. Perhaps, then, a foundational theological evaluation of secular values could provide a common ground for fruitful theological discussion among the different Christian churches.

I realized with some excitement that I had found the trailhead I sought and was now ready to begin my speculative ascent. But anyone who has ventured into an unfamiliar wilderness knows the utility of consulting a topological map before attempting a climb. The trail that lies immediately before us has been charted by the methodological postulates of the preceding chapter. It begins with a gradual ascent through the perennial images that have shaped human and Christian aspiration for salvific integration. From these images we will derive a specific set of theological questions that demand a foundational response.

The trail will then dip sharply into a deep philosophical crevasse. Both the descent and the climb out promise to be taxing. For before we can engage in foundational thinking we must, if we are to be faithful to our method, formulate a set of transcendental categories universally applicable in intent. Our method also demands that those categories be derived from a dialectical insight into the issues that divide substance and process philosophy. We will suggest four such categories: "experience," "quality," "fact," "law." An initial definition of their meaning will bring us to the bottom of our philosophical trench.

The ascent back to the level of theological thinking will be mediated by an attempt to use our four transcendental categories to elaborate a working model for dealing with human experience. We shall attempt to give a preliminary account of how human experience grows, without, however, attempting as yet the empirical verification of our hypothetical model.

Once we have regained the theological rim of our crevasse, we will pause to look back at our original path of ascent. We will reflect in the light of our foundational model for dealing with human experience on the implications of the images that shape the religious search for integration. We will attempt an initial foundational response to the questions those images suggest. In the process, we hope to clarify some of the theological implications of our model of human experience. But we will also be forced to formulate a new set of questions whose resolution will preoccupy us in the remaining chapters of this book. The trail invites us. Let us begin our ascent.

Images of Wholeness

The search for salvific integration at a personal and social level is not, of course, a new problem. It would seem to be a driving motive in every human religious quest. The method I had adopted demanded that I begin reflection on this or any other foundational problem by an initial investigation of those mythic images that would seem to be relevant to its resolution. For as we have seen, mythic thinking gives promise of disclosing how any given problem is initially and concretely felt before theologians bring it to abstract and theoretical formulation.

The comparative study of world religions reveals that the personal search for salvific integration has bred at least three clusters of related mythic images. At the center of the first cluster is the image of light. Salvific integration is commonly felt as a kind of personal enlightenment. The enlightenment that saves is associated in turn with spatial images of personal ascent to the heavenly source of light. Saving revelation is accordingly imagined as reflected light, as an illumination that endows our present darkness with an integrating clarity. Moreover, it is significant that religious light imagery is also associated with the development both of personal ego-consciousness and of integrating self-awareness.[8]

The second cluster of images is concerned with the deity who radiates the light that saves. The enlightening God is like fire, like the sun, like a flashing ray. At the same time, because the enlightening action of the deity is felt as salvifically integrating, mythic thinking presents it as a force that reconciles all things in itself. Primitive bisexual gods and deified demonic powers would seem to express the groping of the mythic imagination toward the vision of a divine reality that is, in Mircea Eliade's phrase, the *coincidentia oppositorum*, the still point at which all opposing forces coincide.

The reconciliation of all things in God through salvific enlightenment breeds a third cluster of images that are cosmic in scope and connotation. Utopian myths that predict the coming of an enlightened age of universal peace and happiness, myths of humankind's collective return to a lost state of innocent enlightenment, myths of common resurrection and of the collective return of the dead from the world of shadows, express in concrete images the religionist's felt sense that the personal achievement of integrating, salvific enlightenment is a function of a larger social and cosmic process of which each individual is a part.[9]

The use of images of integrating, salvific enlightenment in different mythic accounts of the origin and end of all things inserts them into an inchoate doctrinal context. Moreover, as religious thinkers have explicated the doctrinal implications of different mythic traditions, they have come to recognize that those traditions can stand in irreconcilable opposition.[10]

Paul Ricoeur is correct to distinguish prephilosophical from postphilosophical myths. Postphilosophical myths eschew philosophical reflection but are nevertheless shaped by philosophical abstractions and arguments. The Gnostic religion, on whose myths we will reflect in greater detail in the following chapter, abounded in postphilosophical mythic thinking. Prephilosophical myths, on the other hand, betray no such speculative influences. Rather they provide the imaginative matrix out of which more abstract philosophical reflections emerge.[11]

There is, of course, still a third kind of myth, namely, the philosophical myth. The use of myth as a vehicle for philosophical reflection is perhaps best exemplified in the works of Plato. But it has recurred in the reflections of philosophers whenever, like Plato, they wish to suggest a probable account of dimensions of human experience that elude strict logical analysis or to concretize an abstract insight.

The mythic patterns of thought that originally gave imaginative shape to the Christian tradition were on the whole prephilosophical. Moreover, Mircea Eliade has argued convincingly that the uniqueness of the Judeo-Christian mythic tradition lies in its attitude toward history. Greek mythology and philosophy, like the mysticism of the Orient, acquiesced in a cyclic view of time. Both portrayed the temporal process as the eternal unfolding of a pattern of events that return within time itself to their original point of generative origin.

Belief in cyclic time is linked imaginatively with a soteriology either of nostalgia or of escape. A soteriology of nostalgia seeks through ritual reenactment to return within time to the creative moment that lies at the source of religious life and enlightenment. A soteriology of escape seeks to liberate one from involvement in a meaningless repetition of the same cycle of temporal existence.

But for the Hebrew, and therefore for the Christian as well, history does not turn back upon itself. It moves forward toward the salvific goal set for it by the Lord of history. This belief did not prevent Hebrew thinkers from employing religious images found in other traditions: enlightenment, ascent, resurrection, the return to primordial innocence. And Hebrew cult responded to the cycles of the seasons. But the people who shaped the Hebrew tradition endowed such spontaneous images and archetypes with new religious meaning by inserting them into an eschatological doctrinal context. Hebrew cult transformed seasonal feasts into occasions for recalling the eschatological promise revealed in the saving deeds of the Lord of history.[12]

Hebrew religion thus manifested a different feeling for the religious significance of spatio-temporal events. In a cyclic religious cosmology, personal salvation tends either to be sacrificed to the exigencies of cosmic and tribal renewal or to be accomplished by escape from the meaningless repetition of an endless cycle of temporal deaths and rebirths. But in a biblical, eschatological account of the salvific process, personal salvation is achieved through a commitment to transform the temporal process itself by shaping it creatively to God's salvific ends. As a consequence, biblical men and women can reach integrating, personal salvation and enlightenment, not by escaping from history, but only through transforming immersion in history. As a consequence the converted Jew and Christian stand consciously coresponsible with and before God for the creative renewal and advancement of the spatio-temporal process.

The Christian Search for Wholeness

Like many other deities, the Christian God is experienced in faith as the *coincidentia oppositorum*. The goal of Jesus' mission is the reconciliation of the members of the human family with one another and with the Father through His own ministry and the mediation of the Holy Spirit. His prayer is that all may be one. He comes to restore the innocence lost by Adam and to create a new heaven and earth by bringing about cosmic enlightenment and peace. But once again, the eschatological thrust of Judaeo-Christian religious experience endows these images with specific doctrinal connotations.[13]

In the Old Testament, one of the vivid images of personal and social disintegration was the tower of Babel. God's dispersion of the nations in a chaos of different languages was the culminating sociopolitical effect of Adam and Eve's eschatological deviation from God's salvific command. Yahweh's redemptive response to personal and social disintegration was in the first instance His covenant: an unambiguous summons to His people to find reconciliation with Him by putting right order into their social dealings with one another. But in prophetic teaching, hope for salvific reconciliation was increasingly focused upon the Messiah. When the Anointed One would come, he would gather all the nations under Israel in the worship of the one, true God. A new David, he would bring peace and reconciliation to God's chosen people; and as Son of Man (*ben Adam*), his reign would extend to all peoples.[14]

The first Christians found in Jesus, the Spirit-baptizer, the fulfillment of these prophetic images. By His atoning death and His sending of the Spirit, Jesus unites those He calls into a single social body. The Davidic shepherd of the new Israel, He reconciles all people to the Father by freeing them in the Spirit to be reconciled with one another. He thus seals in their hearts the new covenant promised by Jeremiah. Moreover, as Son of Man, He conquers the forces unleashed at Babel by confounding the tongues of humankind anew at Pentecost through the gift of the Holy Spirit. For through the gift of tongues on Pentecost day, the Spirit is revealed as the one who comes to teach the people of all nations to unite in praising the name of the Lord. As the new Adam, Jesus stands at the head of a new race of men and women, reborn of water and the Holy Spirit.[15]

Moreover, in the symbolic theology of John the Evangelist, the notion of integrating, salvific enlightenment was consciously reshaped to meet the need of an incarnational, eschatological faith. The light that saves is not to be found by escaping history in an ascent to some Neo-Gnostic or Platonic heaven. It is the glory of God that shines in the human face and in the historical words and deeds of Jesus. The same glory is revealed in the Spirit-led words and deeds of those who believe in Him. The enlightenment that saves does not, then, take one out of this world. It commits the true believer to the pneumatic transformation of this world and of human history with the same unshakeable love as Jesus himself. Moreover, the light of God made visible in Jesus reveals the historical forces of darkness to be not only anti-God but Anti-Christ.[16]

Clearly, then, reflection on some of the important religious images that have shaped the Christian search for a personally integrating salvific enlightenment yields some important initial insights into the Christian solution to this perennial religious problem. First, since Christianity is an eschatological religion, the enlightenment it promises is a consequence of an encounter with God that occurs within history, not in some transcendent realm of eternal and immutable being. Second, in covenant religion integrating enlightenment is a function of commitment. As the seal of the covenant, the Spirit frees one to make an integral personal assent to the saving word of God historically spoken in Jesus. The response to God's call demands commitment in faith and love to the person of Jesus, to His teachings, and to the pneumatic community that proceeds from Him. It is this commitment that yields the enlightenment that saves. As a consequence, Christian enlightenment can never be adequately interpreted as a purely intellectual process. It is an enlightenment mediated by a religious love that is both healing and integrating. Third, in new covenant religion, integrating enlightenment is a function of the evaluative stance one chooses to take toward God, toward others, toward history, and ultimately toward the whole of creation. For to be committed to God in the image of Jesus is to be committed to one's sisters and brothers and to the world with the same atoning, forgiving love as Jesus Himself. Finally to be committed thus to God is to stand opposed to Anti-Christ, i.e., to those historical forces that seek to frustrate God's saving action within history. Moreover, by that committed opposition one opens one's heart to the saving transformation of the Spirit of Jesus, who shapes one into God's instrument for the salvific transformation of the world. As a consequence, Christianity stands opposed to any religion that preaches a soteriology either of nostalgia or of escape from the burdens and responsibilities of historical involvement and action.

What are the foundational implications of the four preceding propositions? To answer that question we must first formulate a set of transcendental categories. We must do so in the light of the issues that divide substance and process speculation. A philosophical crevasse yawns before us. There is no bypassing it. It is time to begin our descent.

Substance or Process

For the substance philosopher and theologian, the practical search for personal religious integration must be understood in the context of a much larger and more basic metaphysical question, namely, how are we to understand the unity of each human person? Substance philosophy holds that each person is essentially and substantially one. In other words, as a person I am one by the very exigencies of human nature itself.

Moreover, for the substance philosopher, the fact that personal substantial unity is a metaphysical given implies not only the presence of fixed essences in things but also a certain theoretical model for interpreting change. Let us reflect on what this means. In a universe of substances, the "substantial essence" of any reality remains unaffected by any "accidental modification" it undergoes. Through all the vicissitudes of life I remain essentially and substantially human. My human essence is, of course, different from that of a dog, a tree, a rock. But their substantial essences too remain unchanged despite every accidental modification that befalls them. Because every substantial essence perdures through accidental mutation, it is conceived as in some sense "underlying" the changes it undergoes. Moreover, since the underlying essential subject of every accidental change is conceived as a "substance," it is also affirmed to "exist in itself and not in anything else," for such existence characterizes every substance by definition.

In the world of substance philosophy, every human "essence" is, then, divided into its substance and its accidental modifications. Since, moreover, accidents like quality, quantity, motion, habit, specify a substance, they are related to that substance as "act" to "potency." "Act" and "potency" are, moreover, regarded as the most basic principles of being. All of reality may be divided into either act or potency. Act specifies; potency is the principle specified.

The human substance too is divided into act and potency. A human person's substantial potency is "matter"; his or her substantial act is a spiritual soul. A body is a material substantial principle accidentally quantified.

Most of the accidental powers of a human substance are organic and material. But intellect and will are two spiritual accidents which inhere in the human soul alone. Moreover, the whole of each human essence is potency to the act of being that gives it existence.[17] The metaphysical structure of every human person proposed by substance philosophy may, then, be schematized in the following diagram:

Diagram 1
The Human Person: A Substance View
(⟶ indicates relation of act to potency)

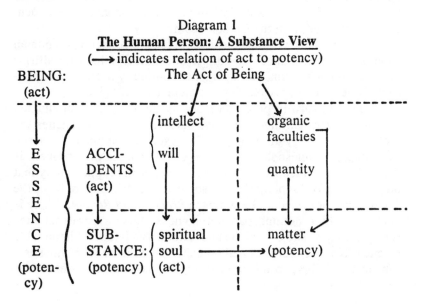

At this point the reader may be asking: What do these metaphysical flights have to do with the human search for personal religious integration? But if taken seriously, the highest level of abstraction can have some astonishing practical consequences. And a substance account of human nature is no exception.

It is a basic maxim of substance metaphysics that action must follow being (*agere sequitur esse*). That is to say, since action proceeds from an immutable substantial essence, it ought finally to be conformed to that essence. In a world of substances this abstract principle rules human action as well. As a consequence, in a strict metaphysics of substance, the problem of personal integration can be solved only by positing actions that conform to one's fixed substantial essence. Salvific integration in a universe of substances can then only consist in actions that conform to one's essential nature once it has been elevated by the gift of grace.[18]

Moreover, in a substance problematic, one must look upon all people as sharing the same substantial essence. Individual differences are as a consequence only "accidental." As a consequence, the legislation of uniform religious and moral activity is not only possible but desirable. Uniform fidelity to fixed moral and canonical laws is, then, the only sound practical basis for religious and ethical living. The Roman Catholic hierarchy has over the years taken substance metaphysics very seriously indeed. As a consequence that philosophy has provided speculative justification not only for Catholic natural law theory but for the essentialistic legalism that has too long characterized Catholic religious practice. Nor have such tendencies disappeared from the Catholic community.

There is, however, one clear advantage to reflecting on human experience in substance categories. Substance philosophy affirms unambiguously the unity and personal continuity present in experience. Indeed, it believes both to be metaphysical "givens."

When we turn to process theory for an account of the human search for personal integration, we discover that it approaches the problem with a very different set of categories from those proposed by substance philosophy. The dean of all process philosophers is Alfred North Whitehead. It is a basic principle in his philosophy that all of reality is "experience" in some form: ". . . apart from the experiences of subjects," he writes in *Process and Reality*, "there is nothing, nothing, nothing, bare nothingness." Since every experience is in process, no subject can be understood as a fixed and immutable essence. Nor are there act and potency. There is no such thing as a substance. Rather, to understand any occasion of experience one must come to an insight into the different kinds of variables that function within it.

Whitehead distinguishes five such interrelated variables: (1) the "subject" that emerges from change, (2) the "initial datum" from which it emerges, (3) its "objective datum," (4) its "negative prehensions," (5) its "subjective form." The initial datum from which any subject emerges is the state of the universe at the beginning of its processing. For in a Whiteheadean problematic, every subject must in the course of its development constitute itself to be what it is in a relation of opposition to the rest of the cosmos. As a subject emerges from its initial datum, it must define its "objective datum," i.e., its peculiar perspective on the universe. It must decide which environmental and evaluative variables will function positively within it and which are to be excluded. The decision of exclusion establishes the emerging subject's "negative prehensions," i.e., its negative relations that distinguish it from every other entity. The emerging subject's evaluative stance toward the actual data that function objectively within it is its "subjective form." The subjective form of any emerging subject is the way in which it experiences the universe emotively, conceptually, evaluatively.[19] Subjective aims are elements within the subjective form of experience and endow it with purpose.

Using these five basic categories, Whiteheadean theory attempts to provide a descriptive analysis of emerging subjects as concrescent unifications of feeling. It designates as "physical feelings" the actual, concrete, spatio-temporal variables that function in human experience. It designates as "conceptual" feelings of pure abstract possibility. And it designates as "propositional" those feelings that interrelate physical and conceptual feelings in the same emergent subject. Propositional feelings are subdivided into imaginative and perceptual feelings; perceptual, into "authentic" and "unauthentic," "authentic," into "direct" and "indirect." Whitehead also speaks of feelings of "physical purpose," of "comparative feelings." He calls his analysis of experience his theory of prehension.[20] It may be roughly schematized as shown on the following page.

Evaluating the Issues

There is no need at this point to enter into a critical analysis of the details of a Whiteheadean theory of prehension. My present purpose is simply to provide the reader with an initial felt sense of the differences that characterize a Whiteheadean evaluative response to human experience and that of a traditional substance metaphysics. A more detailed dialectical analysis of the two systems does, however,

Diagram 2
Whitehead's Anatomy of Feeling

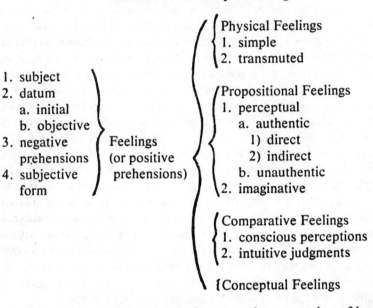

1. subject
2. datum
   a. initial
   b. objective
3. negative prehensions
4. subjective form

Feelings (or positive prehensions)

Physical Feelings
1. simple
2. transmuted

Propositional Feelings
1. perceptual
   a. authentic
      1) direct
      2) indirect
   b. unauthentic
2. imaginative

Comparative Feelings
1. conscious perceptions
2. intuitive judgments

{Conceptual Feelings

reveal that they stand speculatively opposed on a number of basic issues. It is to these issues that a foundational analysis of religious experience must address itself. If then the reader desires a fuller introduction to Whitehead's terminology, (s)he may explore the existing commentaries on his thought. It is for us to saddle our Rocinante, and have at the issues.

a. The substance philosopher sees the space-time universe as constituted by fixed and essentially immutable principles of being. The Whiteheadean sees the world as comprised of self-creative, concrescent "drops" of feeling. The term "concrescent" is a technical Whiteheadean term. It implies both the organic "growing together" of the realities that function in experience as well as the fact that by growth every subject moves to concreteness.

b. The substance philosopher believes that action follows being: What a thing does is an accidental expression of its fixed, essential nature. For the Whiteheadean, the opposite is true: Every entity is a self-defining, creative process. Hence, what an entity is, is the result of the evaluative stance it decides to take toward the physical variables that function efficaciously in it as an experience. In this sense, for the Whiteheadean "being," or what a thing is, follows "action," i.e., decision.

c. The substance philosopher believes that the ultimate subject of change is a fixed substantial essence that underlies the change. The Whiteheadean believes that the spatio-temporal subject of change is a reality that emerges from a concrete datum. In the process of emerging it defines itself evaluatively to be what it is from one moment to the next.

d. The substance philosopher believes that what things are can be defined "essentially," by genus and specific difference. The Whiteheadean holds that what a thing is, is the result of its total history and of all the concrete and evaluative variables that have functioned in its development. The process philosopher is, therefore, contemptuous of any attempt to reduce the "essence" of anything to its alleged "metaphysical" genus and specific difference.

e. The substance philosopher holds that relations are either "predicamental" (i.e., accidental) or "transcendental" (i.e., the relation between act and potency). The Whiteheadean rejects the idea of transcendental relations. And (s)he regards the kinds of relations the substance philosopher calls "predicamental" as more primordial in experience than the defining characteristics of any emerging subject. For in a process universe relationship grounds the possibility of concrescent development. It is because things stand in relationship to one another that they can define themselves to be concretely what they are from one moment to the next.

f. The substance philosopher looks upon things as existing in themselves and not in anything else. The Whiteheadean sees everything as "objectified" either positively or negatively in everything else.

g. In substance philosophy the principle of individuation is quantified matter. In Whiteheadean theory, the principle of individuation is decision. The term "decision" is not, however, conceived as the act of the accidental faculty of the will, as it is in substance philosophy. For Whitehead decision is the creative act of the emerging subject by which it integrates into itself certain potentials for process and excludes others. In a Whiteheadean optic, therefore, individuality is more fundamentally a question of the "quality" of an experience than of mere "quantity." An actual entity is individualized by becoming a concrete way of experiencing the universe.

h. In substance philosophy something "is" to the extent that it is fixed and unchangeable. Hence, the central preoccupation of substance thinking is to discover the stable reality underlying change that renders an entity intelligible in the midst of flux and development. In a Whiteheadean optic, an entity is to the extent that it is in process. The moment a subject ceases to be in process, it perishes as a subject and passes into the "objective immortality" of realized fact. Hence, a major preoccupation of Whiteheadean process theory is to affirm that every subject is concretely what it is here and now.

i. In a substance problematic, it is the underlying subject that grounds the unity and continuity present in experience. That unity is, moreover, conceived as an immutable substantial essence that remains unchanged beneath accidental mutations. As a consequence, for the substance philosopher, in each human person as in other created entities, the substantial form, or soul, is not only the source of intelligible unity but also the ultimate ground of essential specification. It makes a person to be essentially what (s)he is. For Whitehead, however, a person is not a perduring substance but a society, or nexus, of many actual occasions.

To speak of an individual person as a "society" is at best paradoxical. But in Whitehead's philosophical scheme it is an unavoidable consequence of his insistence on the atomic structure of experience. Whitehead began his speculative career as a mathematician and a theoretical physicist. In his approach to experience, he therefore presupposed its atomic structure as a speculative given. As a consequence, he felt the need to provide an account of what would seem to be the illusory character of continuity as experience advances from one atomically discrete moment to the next. A substance philosopher, by contrast, presupposes the presence of continuity within change and asks how the former is in principle possible.

In a Whiteheadean universe, every emerging subject is, then, a "drop" of experience that atomizes the extensive, space-time continuum of relationships that form the matrix of all concrescent development. Whitehead conceived of spatio-temporal processes as enduring only a fraction of a second. As each new subject achieves concreteness it perishes, and a new subject must be creatively evoked if the cosmic process is to advance beyond what is given.

Some subjects in a nexus of actual occasions are capable of little more than reaffirming themselves from one moment to the next. Others are capable not only of self-reaffirmation but of incorporating novel possibilities into the data supplied by their immediate past. The latter we call "living." In both cases, some element of the subjective form of each atomic drop of experience is passed on from one subject to the next as the nexus of atomic occasions of experience unfolds.

A society of actual occasions is, therefore, a genetically linked series of concrescent drops of experience that enjoy a common element of subjective form, an element that is imposed on each emerging subject by its prehension of the other members of the nexus. A society of actual occasions has "personal order" when the transmission of form is all from one side of an imagined cut in the nexus of occasions.[21]

As a common element of form is transferred from one occasion to the next, it can create the illusion of motion, much as the blinking bulbs of a theatre marquee create the illusion of moving light. But in a Whiteheadean universe, motion in the strict sense is impossible. Motion presupposes an enduring subject that is capable of being transported from one place to the next. In a Whiteheadean cosmology there are no such enduring subjects, only emerging ones that perish in a fraction of a second. Each emerging subject atomizes the space-time continuum where and when it is. What we call motion is the successive transferral of a common element of form from one atomic occasion of experience to the next. But atomicity remains the ultimate metaphysical actuality.[22]

I do not intend to suggest that Whitehead makes no attempt to account for continuity in experience. He postulates the existence of an "extensive continuum," a unified relational structure at the basis of the space-time universe that is atomized by each emerging occasion of experience. As each occasion of experience atomizes the extensive continuum it must establish a perspective on the universe. The continuum insures that those perspectives will overlap. It thus endows experience with perceptual continuity. The universe that I perceive from my angle of vision is the same universe that you view from a somewhat different angle.

Moreover, each occasion of experience in atomizing the extensive continuum must become localized. To do so it must take into itself elements from the occasion of experience that is its immediate predecessor. This transfer of physical elements from occasion to occasion is somewhat less than perfect physical continuity. But it does insure that in a nexus of occasions with temporal thickness some of the same physical variables will function from one moment to the next.

Finally, the subjective aim that endows each occasion of experience with purpose and direction grounds evaluative continuity within the occasion within which it functions.[23]

Nevertheless, for Whitehead atomicity is the ultimate fact of facts. And the physical atoms that structure experience and fragment the continuum are the only things that are finally real. Hence, on strict Whiteheadean principles the continuities that shape experience are ideal and possible rather than completely and ultimately real. As the reader shall soon discover, in the account of experience presented in these pages I suggest with Charles Peirce that our understanding of what is finally real within human experience be expanded to include laws that are different from both facts and values. These laws are evolving, habitual tendencies to act and value in specific ways. And, among other things, they endow the realm of the "finally real" with a degree of continuity that is absent from orthodox Whiteheadeanism.

The speculative inadequacies latent in Whitehead's atomism seem to me to be reflected in his philosophy of "person." For Whitehead a "person" is a nexus of many actual occasions with a certain kind of serial order. To the best of my knowledge no Whiteheadean has ever challenged this definition of "person," despite the fact that it would seem to preclude any unified understanding of a person as a person. In order to think "my mother" as a Whiteheadean, I must, for example, distinguish between "my mother" as the subjective form common to several occasions of experience, "my mother" as a nexus of atomic occasions, and "my mother" as any single occasion in that nexus. I must then decide to which of these "mothers" I refer. But in a Whiteheadean cosmos, there would seem to be no single unified reality in experience to which the term "my mother" is applied.[24] Moreover, the only way a strict Whiteheadean may encounter another person is as an objectified datum. There would, then, seem to be no place in Whitehead's scheme for the mystery of personal encounter so eloquently described by Martin Buber and by other existentialists. Clearly, then, Whitehead's system suffers from inadequacy in its attempt to account for the unity and continuity in personal experience and, by its own methodological presuppositions, needs revision in this matter. On the other hand, substance philosophy would seem to be better able to account for personal unity and continuity.

At the same time, all of Whitehead's negative criticisms of substance philosophy would seem to be sound. Substance metaphysics rests on a form of the "essence fallacy." Its account of change does reflect the structure of language more than the structure of experience. In a substance universe of fixed essences, it is difficult, if not impossible, to account adequately for the dynamics of personal growth or for cosmic evolution. Whitehead's redefinition of the subject of change as an emerging, self-defining reality would seem to be truer to experience than substance theory. Such a view of the subject of change implies, however, in opposition to substance philosophy, the primacy of relationship over essence.

A dialectical analysis of the issues dividing substance from process philosophy leads then to a speculative impasse,. But that very impasse gives rise to an important foundational conclusion: *To pose the foundational question of personal, salvific integration in either substance categories alone or in the categories of Whiteheadean process theory alone is to acquiesce in a false speculative option. For neither problematic is adequate to interpret human experience in all of its complexity. Hence a sound foundational analysis of religious experience must seek to move speculatively beyond both traditions by seeking to incorporate into its categorial scheme the insights that are valuable in each.* In other words, the position assumed in these pages is in fundamental agreement with the suggestion of Nels Ferré that the time has come to move beyond both process and substance philosophy. It also stands in sympathy with the suggestion of Roy Wood Sellars that the needs of contemporary philosophy are better served by a refurbished Aristotelianism rather than by a refurbished Neo-Platonism.[25] The theory I will propose will be called a theory of emergence.

Positions and Counterpositions

There is a hint of the form such a theory might take in the dynamic Scotism of Charles Sanders Peirce. When viewed from the standpoint of Peirce's later philosophy, Whiteheadean theory seems to acknowledge the presence within experience of only two basic variables: qualities (or eternal objects) and facts (or actual occasions). For in a Whiteheadean scheme, the conceptual feeling of an eternal object endows experience with its qualitative dimension. The physical feeling of an actual occasion renders it factual. Propositional feelings and comparative feelings bring together conceptual and physical feelings.[26]

But in the final form of his philosophy, Peirce insisted quite correctly on the need to acknowledge a third kind of variable in experience, the variable of law. Whitehead's own handling of the notion of law leaves something to be desired. In *Adventures of Ideas* Whitehead distinguishes four theories of law that have emerged in the development of Western thought: (1) law as immanent in nature; (2) law as imposed upon nature; (3) law as observed order of succession, (4) law as conventional interpretation. He associates the first theory with scientific rationalism, the second with religious belief and substance philosophy, the third with scientific positivism, and the fourth with contemporary theoretical physics.[27]

Although Whitehead's intent remains somewhat obscure, he seems to be suggesting that there is a partial truth coming to expression in all of these theories. With the immanentists, he acknowledges that science is the search for an explanation of natural phenomena and not merely for a descriptive account of them. Although he rejects the notions of "extrinsic relationship" and of "substance" that he finds implicit in the idea of "extrinsic law," he does acknowledge with religious thinkers the primordial nature of God as a transcendent source of order in the space-time process and as an enduring guarantee against the universe ever lapsing into absolute and lawless chaos. With the positivists, he acknowledges that facts measure theories and that there is an observable dynamism concretely immanent to each atomic occasion of experience. Finally, with those who equate law with the conventional interpretation of observed phenomena, he acknowledges the finite, abstract, fallible, developmental character of different speculative accounts of the laws operative in the cosmos.

But while it is clear that Whitehead would like to give an adequate account of the laws in nature, it is not clear that his categorial scheme allows him to do so self-consistently. For in a universe composed finally only of facts and qualities, one is forced to confound the notion of "quality" with the notion of "law." Thus, for Whitehead, the "laws" of a given cosmic epoch are the eternal objects concretely ingredient within it. But it is difficult to see how eternal objects can account for the dynamic, developmental character with which laws endow human experience. Laws ground efficacious impact; but of themselves, Whiteheadean eternal objects are devoid of efficacy.

Whitehead actually ascribes the dynamic, efficacious movement of experience to its physical pole. But once again it is difficult to discover in the physical pole of experience as he describes it a basis for efficacious dynamism. For in a Whiteheadean universe the physical pole of experience loses its internal dynamism when a subject achieves satisfaction. Once satisfaction is achieved, the subject of that experience perishes and with it its processing. For a new subject to emerge, it must somehow prehend God in his "primordial nature." But God in his primordial nature is finally a concatenation of inefficacious eternal objects. It would seem, then, that on Whiteheadean principles, one must explain the origination and development of each atomic occasion of experience by the juxtaposition within experience of a fixed and determinate fact and an inefficacious possibility. Why dynamic change and development ought to emerge from such a juxtaposition is somewhat less than self-evident.

At this point a convinced Whiteheadean might be inclined to interpose: Just one moment, my friend. Aren't you forgetting the power of eternal objects to lure experience? And haven't you overlooked all that Whitehead says about the function of subjective aims within experience? Doesn't Whitehead make it quite clear that the subjective aim of experience endows it with a purpose, a "why," just as subjective form endows it with a modality, a "how"? Doesn't he point out that the subjective aim controls the becoming of each emerging subject by orienting it to a specific kind of satisfaction? Doesn't the subjective aim organize the occasion of experience in which it functions, give shape to its evaluative form, draw it forward to decision and to the objective immortality of a past fact? Doesn't the subjective aim endow each occasion of experience with unity and continuity? Do not all these elements in Whitehead's thought adequately interpret the experience of change and development?[28]

I would be personally dishonest and unfair to Whitehead were I not to say yes to all of the above questions save the last. Even more, I am willing to concede that on the whole aims function in experience in the way in which Whitehead describes them, although I would prefer personally to call aims "personal" or "individual" rather than "subjective." But having done so, I remain troubled by the question: What endows any given aim with its power over experience? Why should it have the capacity to change stubborn facts? I have yet to find a satisfying response to either question in Whitehead.

The more I have pondered these issues, the more convinced I have become of the revolutionary implication of Charles Peirce's analysis of the act of perception. Peirce argues that in the conscious perceptions that shape human experience the laws within experience are actually perceived. But they are perceived inferentially. He also argues that laws are generalized tendencies that are irreducible to either fact or value. On all of these points his position seems to me to be sound.[29] The aims that lure experience with such power do so because they present within experience the developing laws or habitual tendencies that shape it. They endow those laws with what Whitehead calls "presentational immediacy." That is to say, through their evaluative disclosure, the laws themselves become present to me within experience. As we shall see, the laws that shape experience may be so presented either affectively or inferentially. But we anticipate ourselves.

For if the preceding suggestions are sound, then it is false to suggest, as Whitehead does, that facts are what is "finally real" in experience. Beyond facts and qualities, beyond actualities and eternal objects, there are the laws in which both are grounded and by which both are explained. Instead of being dipolar as Whitehead suggests, experience is tripolar as Peirce suggests.

Whiteheadean method envisages the possible revision of his categorial scheme. But in a system that ambitions a logical and coherent account of experience, such revisions should not be undertaken lightly. Major adjustments may well entail rebuilding the system from the bottom up.

Nor should one be philosophically naive about grafting one thinker's insights upon another. Peirce elaborated his philosophy under the shadow of scientific mechanism and determinism. And his understanding of law reflects in part the scientific preoccupations of his day. He looked upon the legal variables in experience as grounding mathematically predictable patterns of operation. He therefore associated "law" with the notion of "mechanical repetition." He was as a consequence forced to postulate chance as a factor distinct from law in order to account for spontaneous development.[30]

But while Peirce at times associates the notion of law with mechanical activity, other elements of his thought suggest a certain organic plasticity in the laws of nature. Laws are habits; and habits grow and develop, are acquired and lost. Is it possible to reconcile the regularity of legal processes with their plasticity?

Peirce suggests correctly that the legal variables in experience are the ground of its continuity as it changes and develops. In a world of organic processes, continuity has, then, a double dimension: It implies (1) the sustaining of a process but (2) as the basis for subsequent growth and development. The notion of law can, therefore, imply not only regularity in activity but regularity as the condition for the possibility for further growth and development. It is in this sense that the term "law" will be used in the pages that follow. Laws endow experience with regularity and continuity *in growth*.

Growth is organic, developmental change. Growth is self-transcendence, and self-transcendence is moving creatively into the future beyond the limiting factors that function in experience. Self-transcendence is, then, an aspect of the open-endedness of experience in general. It is not, as Transcendental Thomism seems at times to suggest, a characteristic of human spiritual faculties alone. What is distinctive of human experience, however, is that this thrust toward self-transcendence can not only become conscious but is also capable of self-direction through inferential processes.

As the simultaneous ground of growth and regularity in experience, laws can never be adequately understood as purely mechanical. They are dynamisms, not mechanisms. Moreover, the more complex the physical basis of a process, the greater the potential plasticity it manifests. Teilhard was, then, correct in characterizing pre-protoplasmic structures, not as "non-living," but as "pre-life."[31]

One may use the preceding conception of law in order to revise one's understanding of the emerging subject in Whiteheadean theory. An emergent subject should not be understood as comprised of physical, conceptual, propositional, and comparative feelings alone. It is more basically a vectoral feeling, a legal entity, relationally distinct from physical, conceptual, and propositional feelings. Its specific character is progressively defined by the physical limits from which it emerges and by the evaluative stance it finally decides to assume toward both the factural variables and the values and aims that shape it as a process. Vectoral feelings ground the continuity in each emerging self. Facts, by contrast, provide the concrete links among different selves. Vectoral feelings are disclosed within experience by affectivity and by inference.

The preceding description of the vectoral elements that shape experience is a radical departure from Whitehead's own use of the same term. Its introduction demands other revisions in Whitehead's categorial scheme as well. It is time, then, to pass from dialectical to foundational thinking. In the process we will attempt to formulate our own model for dealing with experience, one that attempts to incorporate the valid insights of both substance and process thought. Our model will attempt to explain the dynamics of experiential growth in terms of three basic variables: "qualities," "facts," and "laws." Together with "experience" these three categories will function as the "transcendental" categories that structure our foundational theory.

Some Transcendental Categories

"Experience" may be defined initially as a process in which three kinds of variables function: qualitative, factual, and legal. A process is the growing together of different kinds of feelings. A feeling is a relational element within experience. The kinds of feelings correspond to the kinds of variables that structure experience. "Experience" is the most generic of our four transcendental categories. To provide an adequate descriptive account of experience in general lies outside the scope of the present study. Our concern is with human experience and the kinds of qualitative, factual, and legal variables that shape it.

"Qualities" may be defined as instances of particular suchness. They may be called "conceptual" provided one does not limit the term "concept" to the kinds of feelings that substance philosophy labels as "intellectual," i.e., to abstract predicates. The experiential realm of quality embraces a broad spectrum of evaluative responses, many of them thoroughly concrete. It includes taste, touch, sight, smell, sound, visceral perceptions, emotions, moods, and images as well as abstract predicates. A conceptual feeling is, then, any qualitative variable in experience that endows it with an evaluative modality or form. Aims are specific kinds of evaluation. They are a "how" become a "why."

Facts belong to the realm of physical interaction rather than to the realm of conceptual evaluation. Factual interaction renders relationships concrete. Facts terminate definitively the abstract, evaluative, conceptual moment in experience, and they seek to effect the mutation of one's environment. As one entity has factual impact upon another, it is transformed in the latter's experience into what we shall hereafter call a "conformal feeling." For the acting entity becomes an efficacious, limiting reality to which the other must conform initially if it is to grow and develop realistically. The heat of the sun not only warms; it sometimes blisters. Swallowed cyanide will kill me unless I take action. A healthy, growing body must be nourished.

Facts are, then, irreducibly relational. They do not exist "in themselves and in nothing else." They are the brute operational impact of one entity upon another, the situational interplay of action and reaction. Paradoxically, then, to grasp a "pure fact" one must engage in a high-level abstraction. For one must abstract the dynamic relationship present in factual activity from the conceptual variables that interpret it and from the laws that ground it.

The abandonment of a substance problematic for an experiential one also allows for the reinterpretation of the cognitive status of facts. In a world of substances where everything exists "in itself and not in anything else," facts must be seen as somehow extrinsic to my "subjective" experience of them. As a consequence, substance philosophy is hard put to explain how cognitive union with a fact is possible. For how can something exist only in itself and yet be cognitively present in something else? But once one ceases to understand entities as "substances" and "supposits" and sees them instead as emerging experiences, then it becomes possible to interpret them, not as metaphysically extrinsic to one another, but as mutually inexistent.

The term "inexistence" does not imply nonexistence but "existence in" something else. It is a technical term derived from trinitarian theology. In classical trinitarian theology Father, Son, and Spirit are understood as "mutually inexistent." That is to say, they are dynamically interrelated yet relationally distinct.

An emergent account of experience affirms the principles of

inexistence and of mutual inexistence. The principle of inexistence asserts that one entity exists in another to the extent that it functions in the other as an experience. The principle of mutual inexistence affirms that two entities exist in one another to the extent that they function in one another as experiences. To function is to endow experience with new specificity.

The third variable that shapes experience is law. Laws are dynamic tendencies to react efficaciously and evaluatively in a specific way. Legal variables have specific characteristics. They are emergent entities; they develop and decay. They derive their ongoing definition, not from some scholastic formal object or metaphysical essence, but from the conformal feelings out of which they develop and from the character of the total evaluative and decisive response they ground.

They are organic realities in that their complexity may wax or wane. The complexity of a law is measured by the number of processes it can coordinate simultaneously. Its plasticity is a function of its complexity.

Laws are habitual realities. They ground continuity in experience by being tendencies to act and react in a certain way and by grounding the vectoral thrust of experience beyond achieved satisfactions.

Laws also ground reactive autonomy in experience. For they are the causal principles from which both actions and evaluations proceed. As reactive principles endowed with autonomy, laws exist in their own right. But as the relational ground of action and evaluation, they too are governed by the principles of inexistence and of mutual inexistence.

Facts are dyadic relationships: the brute impact and reaction of one thing upon another in abstraction from any mediating principle of intelligibility. Laws, however, endow experience with a triadic structure both because they introduce a third kind of variable into experiential development and because they are habits of activity that link one fact to another in intelligible relationships. The law operative in water explains, for example, why it boils at one temperature and freezes at another. Laws differ from facts: Facts are concrete, while laws are generalized tendencies to certain kinds of reaction and growth. Laws also differ from qualities: Qualities are inefficacious, while laws are the efficacious ground of action and evaluation. Qualities, facts, and laws all function simultaneously in experience but can be distinguished analytically.

"Quality," "fact," "law," "experience": these, then, are the basic "transcendental categories" in our foundational theory of emergence. If that theory is to be adequate, those categories must be applicable in some sense to the whole of reality. Whatever exists must be conceivable as an experience composed of factual, conceptual, and legal variables. To test the total adequacy of these categories would take us far beyond the scope of this work. To demonstrate their applicability to nature and to God would, for example, demand extensive argumentation. Our concern in the present pages is more modest, namely, their ability to interpret human experience.

We have reached the bottom of our philosophical trench. It is time to reascend. We must use our four transcendental categories to elaborate a working model for dealing with human experience. We have descended into a thickening gloom. But our reascent to a theological plateau will demand an explication of the descriptive possibilities latent in our four categories. By the time we emerge from this philosophical crevasse, the light may not be brilliant but it will be adequate for us to find our way. In bringing our four transcendental categories to bear on human experience, the first thing we notice is that they demand an adjustment in our understanding of the term "environment."

Environment Revisioned

Perhaps no American thinker has insisted more than John Dewey on the importance of environmental factors in the shaping of human experience. At the heart of his educational theory is concern for and control of the student's learning environment. Artificial environmental restrictions that fail to foster growth are censured. The learning process itself is conceived as the disciplined expansion and mastery of the environmental stimuli that shape the student's experience. Moreover, for Dewey, the purpose of education is to equip the student to create adult environments in which human society can be brought collectively to shared consummatory experiences.[32]

A sense of environment also lies at the heart of Dewey's theory of knowledge. Deweyan instrumentalism insists that the clarification of both feeling and thought is accomplished through dynamic interaction with one's environment, and especially with those symbolic elements in that environment that serve as the tools of artistic expression and of abstract logical reflection.[33]

These insights are on the whole sound, although Dewey's naturalism prevented him from doing full speculative justice to the religious events and symbols that shape human social environments. His theory of art is, moreover, subject to qualification at more than one point.

The very term "environment" is, however, a vague one and needs initial clarification. Process theory has correctly insisted that the grammatical structure of our language conditions and is conditioned by the presuppositions of substance philosophy. The term "environment" is no exception. In ordinary parlance, it is, for example, opposed to one's physical body. That is to say, in ordinary usage, my environment consists of the sustaining, disintegrating forces that lie outside my skin. The speculative warranty for such a notion of environment is, of course, the belief that things are substances existing only in themselves and that their quantity is their principle of individuation. Once it is properly quantified, a substance can then be slipped into its surrounding world, like a letter into an envelope. The surrounding world thus becomes its environment.

The shift from substance theory to an emergent, experiential problematic demands, however, a concomitant shift in the notion of environment. In a world in which quality and decision, not quantity, function jointly as a principle of individuation, in a world governed by the principles of inexistence and of mutual inexistence, any attempt to distinguish absolutely between my body and its surrounding environment collapses. My bodily processes are in fact penetrated by forces they do not originate: heat, light, moisture, radiation, gravity, injections, food, microbes. My body is itself, not an inert thing, but a complex set of coordinated processes, of decisive actions that shape me in my ongoing transaction with the forces that impinge on me. Indeed, it is the dynamic interaction of my bodily processes with those in its immediate vicinity that makes personal growth possible. For my body is nothing else than that portion of the spatio-temporal process that I have successfully subjugated to the exigencies of self-development. It is, in other words, the spatio-temporal environment from which I personally emerge. Moreover, the decisions, whether conscious or unconscious, that shape my bodily processes constitute my immediate personal past.

The self that I am is not, however, simply identical with my body. For each self is an emerging legal entity relationally distinct from its evaluative responses and from its physical, factual activity, although it shapes both and is shaped by them. In an emergent universe it is not, then, proper to restrict the term "environment" to those forces that lie outside my skin. Rather, the fact that my body exists in relational continuity with the forces that surround it and is the environment from which I personally emerge demands that I affirm the presence in experience of two kinds of environment: One sustaining, the other sustained. My sustained environment is my body processes. But their survival as a personal basis for growth demands their successful coordination with those forces that impinge upon them. The latter constitute my sustaining environment.

But not every impinging environmental influence serves the interests of growth and development. My bodily processes may be overwhelmed by forces of dissolution. I may be crushed, roasted, lacerated, invaded by parasites, devoured. My own decisions may set my body working at cross purposes: I can destroy myself with drink, drugs, overwork. I can terminate my bodily processes through suicide. My impinging environment must, then, be described as either sustaining or disintegrating; my body, as either sustained or disintegrated.

Finally, as Whitehead saw clearly, I can distinguish in my environment two kinds of facts.[34] Initial facts are alien forces that impinge on me and to which I must respond realistically if I am to grow and develop personally. They define the realm of conformal feelings. Final facts are the personal decisions I take in reaction to my impinging environment. Such decisions are more or less conscious. Some, like most visceral processes, are wholly unconscious. But conscious or unconscious, each decision is the act of the whole self. The dynamic interplay of initial and final facts constitutes the shifting web of relationships that links me to my world.

My link to the cosmos as a whole is, then, a mediated one. It is mediated by those realities with which I am in direct, dynamic, factual relationship. In an emergent universe, therefore, facts are the forged and dissolving links in the cosmic chain, not, as in the case of Whitehead's "extensive continuum," a reified geometrical abstraction.

Dative Feelings

One of the important philosophical contributions of process theory has been its attempt to create a new language for describing the unfolding of experience as a genetic spatio-temporal process. So many of the words we use for describing experience are colored by misleading philosophical or psychological presuppositions: by subjectivism, objectivism, faculty theory, atomistic empiricism, spiritualistic dualism, materialistic mechanism. The catalogue could be extended. Forging a new language to describe the growth of experience demands, then, the discovery or creation of terms that are free of the potentially misleading connotations that mar standard psychological and philosophical vocabulary. Such new terms must also be capable of describing the unfolding of experience as a process.

One of the most suggestive new terms created by Whitehead in his attempt to describe the symbolic structure of experience is the term "presentational immediacy."[35] It attempts to imply the genetic function that quality plays in the growth of experience. Qualitative responses are, as we have seen, evaluative and conceptual. The term "presentational immediacy" suggests that my evaluative responses to the environmental forces that shape experience have a twofold function: (1) They present those forces to me for further evaluation and (2) in the process they ground simultaneously my experience of the present moment. The nail that pierces my shoe is initially presented within conscious experience by a sense of localized pain. The pain that presents the nail mediates a feeling of what is happening to me now.

Here three points should be noted: (1) The conformal feelings (or initial facts) that shape experience are not simply identical with the qualitative perceptual responses that present them to me. If my foot is anesthetized, the intruding nail will not be presented to me as a conscious evaluation, but it will nevertheless lacerate my skin. (2) When perceptual qualities do function in experience, what they present to me is, as Maurice Merleau-Ponty has correctly insisted, not merely a sense of quality, but an impinging factual reality. They therefore resist direct volitional control. (3) The introduction of perceptual qualities into the factual experience of environmental forces transmutes that experience.

The term "transmutation" is employed here and elsewhere in a technical sense. An experience is transmuted: (1) when it develops in real continuity with a prior experience; (2) when it includes a qualitatively distinguishable variable not present in the prior experience; and (3) when the novel variable is integrated into the subsequent experience in such a way as to reduce the latter's constitutive relational structure, more or less successfully, to a mutually reinforcing unity. By changing the constitutive relational structure of the subsequent experience, transmutation transforms it into a new kind of experience analogous to the one out of which it developed. Hence, transmutation grounds the analogy of experience.

What has been traditionally called "sense perception" transmutes the conformal feelings that shape experience by endowing them with "presentational immediacy." When the nail thrusting into the ball of my foot becomes present to me as localized, effected pain, it, the nail, is perceived. Here, two more points should be noted. First, in every conformal feeling, my past becomes actual, i.e., concrete. For the conformal elements of any experience define the concrete factual limits that condition the process of transmutation. In the

example just cited, the thrust of the nail into my flesh is an actual
limiting factor in my immediate personal past to which I must respond
appropriately if I am to walk on without further injury and pain.
Second, when, through the dynamics of presentational immediacy
the conformal feelings that shape me as an experience come to be
illumined by sense qualities, my actual personal past becomes my
experienced present. Thus the thrusting nail enters into my experienced present through the sense of pain in the ball of my foot. In other
words "sense perception" endows experience with an initial, overt
temporal structure.

More recent philosophical studies of the act of perception, like
those undertaken by Maurice Merleau-Ponty and by Charles
Hartshorne, have only dramatized the inadequacy of the language
traditionally used to describe such perceptual experiences.[36] Past
philosophical and psychological descriptions of perception have, for
example, been marred by the futile efforts of empiricist psychology to
describe perceived objects as discrete sense qualities, as atomic
conceptual units linked by association to form complete perceptual
experiences. Discourse about perception has also been marred by a
fallacious philosophical concern to characterize perceptions as either
subjective or objective, or by an exaggerated intellectualism that
ignores more primitive forms of bodily awareness.

In an attempt to move beyond these and other linguistic confusions, we will henceforth abandon the term "perception" altogether
and will speak instead of "dative feelings." This term too was coined
by Whitehead and is derived from the Latin verb *do, dare* (I give, I
present). As here employed it is intended to suggest the way in which
presentational immediacy initially transmutes the conformal variables that function in experience by presenting them for further
evaluative response.

Here it is perhaps important to remind ourselves once again that
what the dative moments of a developing experience present is not
some inert object or thing existing in itself. It is not my body alone,
nor its impinging environment alone. Rather it is the first phase of a
transaction between my bodily processes and their sustaining, disintegrating environment. The language of pure subjectivity or of pure
objectivity will, then, never be adequate to describe what such an
experience presents. As my dative response takes on differentiation, I
may, of course, focus my evaluative response more or less exclusively on this or that aspect of my environment. As I step on the nail,
the pain in my foot may, for instance, momentarily absorb my attention. I may as a consequence be led to say: "There is a nail in my foot."

The statement would be true. But much more is being presented to me datively at that moment than such a statement expresses. Sight, sound, taste, smell, touch, visceral feelings, are in fact combining with the experience of localized pain to give shape to what I feel now.

Moreover, what is presented more or less vaguely, more or less consciously in any dative experience is the whole of my initial bodily transaction with my impinging environment. A dative feeling is vague when qualitatively distinguishable variables present within it function evaluatively as one. All sense experiences are, for example, hopelessly vague. The radiation of light from a rose, its impact on the rods and cones in my eye, and the complex physiological processes that mediate my visual response are all presented to me vaguely and simultaneously in the experience of localized color. Moreover, not all the scientific studies of perception have to date been able to explain fully why perceptual responses happen precisely the way they do.

The Developing Ego

The development of consciousness is in part a function of evaluative differentiation, as Whitehead and Lonergan have both realized. As ego-consciousness grows it dispels vagueness. For example, as I learn to identify trees by their different kinds of leaf, bark, and shape, my consciousness of them is most certainly sharpened. But not every form of evaluative differentiation is conscious. Dream experiences, for example, are differentiated, evaluative adjustments to events in my immediate past. But they are most frequently unconscious. Similarly, sleepwalkers and automatic writers give evidence of responding to unconscious impulses and evaluations.

Individual ego-consciousness would seem to enter dative experience with the capacity to differentiate, however vaguely at first, bodily responses from impinging environmental stimuli. Body-consciousness is, then, as Jungian psychiatry suggests, ego-consciousness in its most primitive form.[37] But even body-consciousness is relational, environmental, and transactional, not substantial. That is to say, body-consciousness is not the awareness of my body as a thing-in-itself. Rather it is an element in a felt contrast between "me" and "not-me." In its first apperception, therefore, the body is felt as a relational element in a total dynamic transaction with an impinging environment.

Consciousness that is the result of evaluative differentiation and of the interrelation of what has been evaluatively differentiated will be hereafter termed "ego-consciousness." The term "ego-consciousness" was originally popularized by Freudian psychology.

But the ego depicted by Freud is too limited in its psychic functions. Its chief purpose is to mediate between the irrational impulses of the Id and the coercive taboos imposed by the Super-ego. Indeed, the dilemma of the Freudian ego has been compared with some justification to that of the matador who must deftly avoid the horns of a charging bull, while driven to the task by the shouts of "Olé!" from the crowd. The bull is the Id; the shouting crowd, the Super-ego; the matador, the beleaguered ego.

As psychological theory has developed, however, a Freudian account of the ego has been subjected to considerable criticism and its psychic functions gradually expanded. Logotherapy has, for example, insisted that the ego is more than just a coping device. Human beings need to find meaning in their lives. The conscious search for meaning is, then, another important aspect of developing ego-awareness. Abraham Maslow has also correctly criticized Freud for deriving his understanding of psychic processes almost exclusively from a study of the mentally ill. In his own studies of mentally healthy, self-actualizing individuals, Maslow has discovered within human consciousness a thrust toward self-transcendence. In Maslow's theory, the healthy ego has fairly regular conscious access to ecstatic "peak experiences." Jungian personality theory, on the other hand, discovers three stages in the development of ego-awareness: body consciousness, genital awareness, and the higher forms of rational thought and abstract speculation.[38]

These four psychological accounts of the ego are convergent and complementary, not contradictory. Ego-awareness does emerge from primitive forms of body-consciousness. Sexual maturation brings with it new forms of social and intellectual awakening. When ego-consciousness is weak, it can, as Freud realized, serve largely as a coping device. But in the balanced personality, ego-awareness moves beyond mere coping, beyond the romantic fantasies and speculative awakening of adolescence, to the more or less systematic search for meaning and purpose in one's world, in oneself. And in the course of that search, the healthy ego knows ecstatic moments of conscious self-transcendence through insight.

The most primitive form of ego-awareness is, however, dative: the vague evaluative differentiation of one's body functions from one's impinging environment. It is difficult to say exactly when such consciousness emerges in living organisms. The oyster's experience of the forces that impinge on it is probably no more vivid than my stomach's perception of the food that enters from the esophagus. Both react unconsciously, but both know how to react. One of the surest signs of conscious, differentiated bodily awareness is, of course, the development of a sensory apparatus for dealing with the impinging environment.

In adult human experience, body-consciousness contrasts clearly with awareness of one's impinging environment. I can turn away from this or that impinging stimulus, but I cannot turn from my own body. My consciousness of impinging stimuli comes and goes, but body consciousness perdures. I can explore my impinging environment by moving through it; my body defies such exploration: it is always presented to me from the same angle. Moreover, it is through such experiences that my body is presented datively to me as uniquely and intimately mine.

Dative awareness of one's own body is fairly vague, but it does not lack all evaluative differentiation. It includes, for example, a vague sense of bodily states: of well-being, of exhaustion, of oncoming illness. It also includes kenetic and kinesthetic sensations, awareness of posture and of movement. Most moods have a strong dative element.

As ego-consciousness grows, the more primitive forms of body-consciousness are transmuted into more complex instances of bodily awareness and response. Movement becomes gesture. Gesture becomes coordinated body skills. Coordinated body skills become games, sports. Sexual awakening opens new possibilities for tactile, emotional, and personal satisfaction and frustration. Gesture is shaped by imagination and becomes dance, pantomine, drama. Abstract insight into movement creates the instruments of transportation and eventually of technology. It is, then, time to begin an initial descriptive exploration of these more complex forms of ego-awareness.

The Affective Continuum

In his study of perceptual experience, Charles Hartshorne develops a concept that is important for understanding the transition from dative feelings to more complex forms of ego-consciousness. Hartshorne affirms the presence in sensory experience of what he calls an "affective continuum."[39] He argues not only that different forms of sense perception blend evaluatively into one another but also that sensory responses are in fact already emotive in character. Among human dative responses, visual experiences are, for example, by far the sharpest and most vivid. Not only do the colors that structure our visual responses blend into a continuous spectrum, but we also discover that the experience of color itself blends spontaneously with other forms of sensory experience. We instinctively describe certain colors as "sharp" or "light," others as "heavy" or "dull." Sounds are felt as "bright" or "dark."

It is, moreover, impossible to draw a clear line between the dative presentations of environmental forces and our emotional reaction to them. Indeed, the transactional character of the conformal feelings that dative experience discloses is revealed by the double fact that dative perceptions are not only localized but emotively charged. In other words, in dative experiences environmental forces are presented to me only in and through my initial evaluative response to them. Moreover, as my evaluative response to environmental stimuli is prolonged beyond dative feelings, it grows in evaluative complexity. There is, for example, evidence that the primary colors scarlet, buttercup-yellow, violet, and blue-green are regularly linked in the affective continuum to specific attitudinal orientations: scarlet, to warmth and activity; buttercup-yellow, to brightness and joyousness; sea-green, to coldness and passivity; violet to dullness and sorrow. Sounds too evoke a broad spectrum of emotional responses: surprise, fear, anticipation. The sudden application of a pointed object to the back of one's neck is transformed from a sense of sharpless, to pain, to fear, without any clear line of demarcation in these stages of emotional response. Similarly, smells and tastes are imperceptibly transformed into revulsion and craving.

Contemporary psychology has explored a fairly wide spectrum of theories concerning the nature of human emotional response. William James and C. G. Lange initiated the debate by attempting to depict emotional responses as a species of visceral sensation. In effect, they tried to reduce emotions to dative feelings. The refutation of the James-Lange theory by A. Lehmann and W. B. Cannon opened the door to other theoretical explanations of human affective response. An attempt to correlate specific emotional reactions with specific bodily drives proved to be inadequate. As psychiatry evolved, it cast important light on the place emotions play in personality development; but psychiatry has failed so far to provide a truly comprehensive theory of human emotion. Some psychologists have interpreted emotions as charged with significance; others, as disorganized and disorienting; others still, as organizing and motivating different forms of behavior.[40]

There is, of course, an element of insight in many of these theories. Emotional attitudes do have a physiological basis. They do modify behavior. Some emotions are disorienting; others, integrating. Both kinds shape personality development. In the course of scientific and philosophical debate about human affectivity, the term "emotion" has, however, all too often been depicted as "purely subjective." Behaviorists especially are inclined to such a linguistic blunder. In point of fact, however, emotional responses, like dative feelings, are as we shall soon see both situational and transactional in character. In order, then, to avoid any misleading subjectivist connotations in our own discussion of emotion we will speak hereafter, not of "emotions," but of "physical purposes."

Physical Purposes

The term "physical purpose" is also derived from Whitehead, but it is used here in a sense quite different from his.[41] The advantage of the term is threefold. First, it is neutral with regard to the alleged "subjective" or "objective" character of affective responses. Second, the term "physical" links affectivity to concrete biological processes, while the term "purpose" links it to a felt sense of the legal, vectoral, telic dimensions of experience. Third, the term aptly suggests an important function of emotional response: the concrete, evaluative readjustment of vital responses.

The scientific refutation of the James-Lange theory of emotion gives clear evidence that more is disclosed evaluatively in the physical purposes that shape experience than in its dative moments. Dative feelings, as we have already seen, transmute conformal, factual feelings into a feeling of one's actual past as present. They thus endow experience with an initial temporal character. Physical purposes, on the other hand, lend experience a vague sense of growth and development. They do so by expanding the temporal thickness of presentational immediacy. In so doing, physical purposes lead experience to greater evaluative differentiation and complexity.

The problem with any descriptive analysis of the realm of physical purpose is that it includes a fairly broad spectrum of distinguishable kinds of experience. Some affective adjustments have, for example, very little temporal thickness. Stimulus evokes an all-but-instantaneous response. Instantaneous affective adjustments engage deep, subconscious motives as well as physiological processes that resist direct volitional control. The sight of mutilation may, for example, cause me to vomit on the spot. An offensive word may trigger deep-seated resentments that cause me to lash out against my antagonist with a mindless blow. Such reactions approximate reflex reactions. And reflex reactions would seem to be among the most primitive instances of physical purpose.

As physical purposes grow in temporal thickness, they may also grow in evaluative differentiation and consciousness as well; but they need not do so. I may, for example, spend days, even weeks or months, in a state of depression or of euphoria without gaining any clarifying insight into its causes and motives. But as the affective continuum acquires a measure of evaluative adjustment, it begins to exhibit a broad spectrum of developing human tendencies. Our most basic affective responses seem to be linked with feelings of pleasure and of pain. Pleasure gives rise to the sympathetic feelings: feelings of desire, delight, enjoyment. If the reality that excites a sympathetic response is felt to be attainable, it breeds hope. If it is felt to be unattainable, it breeds discouragement. Pain gives rise to negative responses: aversion and depression, anger and daring, fear and flight.

As they grow in complexity, the sympathetic affections embrace an enormous range of distinguishable feelings: calmness, serenity, pleasure, happiness, joy, ecstasy, acceptance, attentiveness, anticipation, sympathy, compassion, affection, appreciation, friendship, craving, love, orgasm. Negative feelings too develop into an expanding spectrum of aversions and hostilities. Dislike may become resentment, disgust, loathing. Timidity may breed apprehension, fear, terror, panic. Pensiveness may give way to gloom, dejection, grief, regret, remorse, despair. Resentment may become anger, rage, violence. Unexpected stimuli may produce surprise, amazement, astonishment. And these in turn may evoke a melange of sympathetic or negative attitudes.

Dream and Archetype

Dream images bring affective adjustment to a still higher level of evaluative differentiation. Dreams transmute positive and negative affective responses just as the latter transmute more primitive feelings of satisfaction, pain, and surprise. When first subjected to analysis, however, dream images appear to be a shifting and undecipherable pattern of concrete personal feelings that defy any kind of generalization. Jungian psychology has, however, documented the existence within dreams of imaginative patterns that are distinctive enough to be termed "archetypal." Jung's own account of these patterns is not, however, beyond qualification and question. Nevertheless, the recurrence of similar imaginative patterns in different individuals who live in different epochs and cultures provides a basis for theoretical generalization about the morphology of developed human affectivity.

Throughout his life, Jung groped for an adequate descriptive definition of an archetype. Some of his attempts and those of his followers betray a questionable subjectivism or a bias toward

Platonism. This is not the place for a detailed discussion of a Jungian theory of archetypes. In the present essay, we therefore accept the fact that human physical purposes are shaped by distinguishable archetypal patterns; but at the same time we intend to dissociate the notion of archetype from Jung's theory of an "objective psyche" and from his theory of "instinct." We define the term "archetype" to mean: "a spontaneous image that recurs in a variety of individuals, epochs, and cultures, that is heavy with affective significance and therefore connotatively rich, and that is endowed with a central core of meaning that is linked by free association with images and attitudes of varying degrees of conscious or unconscious evaluative differentiation."

The emergence of an archetypal image is, as Jung suggests, a spontaneous occurrence. It is neither controlled nor contrived. When it happens, it unleashes a flood of associated feelings and images. As a consequence, it grips the heart with power. Moreover, its link with vague unconscious motives endows it with an awesome sense of mystery.

Jungian psychology has discovered five archetypes of special importance in the development of human affectivity: the persona, the shadow, the animus, the anima, the self. There is no reason to regard this list as exhaustive. The persona is an archetypal symbol for personal social adaptation. It is exemplified most obviously by a mask worn in the presence of others; but in dreams it may take other forms, like clothes—a uniform perhaps, a clown suit, or a religious habit. As an archetype it symbolizes the felt demands society makes upon the dreamer. The shadow is a dark and menacing figure, always of the same sex as the dreamer. It symbolizes the repressed, unpleasant aspects of the dreamer's personality, either undeveloped potential or dangerous and shameful feelings and attitudes. The anima is the archetype of the eternal feminine; it finds exemplification in a variety of images: the Great Mother, the Terrible Mother, the Hetaira, the Amazon, the Witch, the Woman of Wisdom. The animus is the archetype of the eternal masculine; it is exemplified in images of the Father-god, the Man-child, the Trickster, the Hero, the Wise Old Man, the Wizard. The self is the archetype of transcendent and purposive wholeness. It has a negative aspect (exemplified in demonic and satanic images) as well as a positive dimension (exemplified by images like the mandala or the *hieros gamos*).[42]

Archetypal dream images never occur in a vacuum. They lie at the heart of a complex of interrelated images and attitudes derived from the personal experience of the dreamer. Not long ago, for example, I had a shadow dream. I dreamed that I had escaped with several other Jesuits from the high school I had attended in New Orleans and was driving around the city in a van that belonged to the Jesuit School of Theology at Berkeley. The reason for our escape was a male sniper with a rifle lurking on the roof. We suddenly found to our dismay that we had to return to the school. We parked at the Banks Street entrance to the Jesuit residence. As I descended from the van to enter the house, I looked up to the roof of the building. The dark and menacing figure of the sniper appeared over the parapet. I stood transfixed in terror expecting to be shot. But instead, the sniper threw me a sleeping bag. As my terror began to fade, I awoke.

There is no need to attempt a detailed analysis of the dream here. Three things only need be noted. First, around the figure of the sniper/shadow were clustered a host of spontaneous images derived from my remote and immediate past. Second, not these peripheral images, but the archetypal shadow struck terror into my heart, a terror that proved to be unwarranted. Third, the dream was a prelude to a healing of memories, many of which had strong associations with my high school career.

If the preceding analysis is sound, physical purposes effect at least four distinguishable transmutations of dative feelings. (1) They endow the evaluative element in dative presentations with a greater or lesser temporal thickness that yields a vague, felt sense of transition beyond the past as datively presented. (2) Sympathetic and negative feelings endow the vectoral thrust of experience with a measure of conceptual clarity absent from dative presentations. (3) Archetypal patterns cast still more evaluative light on the emotional significance of the vectoral tendencies that shape me as an experience. (4) Peripheral images derived from my personal past link dream archetypes to specific situations and influences I have known.

The Affective Disclosure of Meaning

Clearly, the physical purposes that shape experience disclose much more than the dative feelings they transmute. But what do they disclose? The refutation of the James-Lange theory of emotions has made it clear that affective response is more than the "perception of one's body." Dative feelings are predominantly factual in focus, the initial evaluative disclosure of environmental impact. Those forces are, however, grounded in laws, or dynamic, vectoral tendencies, as are my evaluative and decisive responses to them. What physical purposes bring to more or less vague, initial, evaluative disclosure are, then, the laws, the vectoral tendencies, that are shaping both the emerging self and the environmental vectors with which it stands dynamically engaged.

Laws, as we have seen, ground continuity in experience. It is for this reason that the evaluative disclosure of legal tendencies demands that the conceptual variables in experience acquire greater temporal thickness. The disclosure of continuity presupposes an evaluative continuum. Moreover, the differentiation of the laws that shape experience begun by physical purposes eventually culminates, as we shall see, in inference and logical argument.

Here, however, it is important to insist that physical purposes are never purely subjective experiences. Like dative feelings, they are always situational responses. In them, the vectoral tendencies that shape both the emerging self and its environment are simultaneously and, more or less vaguely, disclosed. For every physical purpose is the evaluative anticipation of or adjustment to an environmental stimulus. Reflex adjustments are, for example, clearly situational in character. When I swoon at the sight of blood, it is because the sight of blood has emotional significance for me. Anger, fear, surprise, desire, love—almost any affective response one can name reveals the way in which the living organism is gearing itself to deal with forces whose action it anticipates. In other words, the way in which the organism gears itself affectively to deal with diverse situations reveals the way in which the dynamic, legal tendencies in both the self and its environment are presented initially and vaguely within experience. Similarly, archetypes function as symbols, not of subjective processes, but of different forms of situational involvement. And peripheral dream images reveal how past experiences condition my present capacity to respond emotionally to the situation in which I live. Too often the language we use to describe affectivity confounds the vagueness or personal character of evaluative response with "subjectivity."

Appreciative Consciousness

Most of the physical purposes that shape experience are, of course, unconscious. It takes an effort to recall dreams, though we spend a good part of our lives simply dreaming. It takes an effort to become attuned in the present moment to each succeeding affective response. Negative feelings pose a special problem: anger, guilt, and fear—these are the affections we suppress and that stand guard at the threshold of the unconscious. But physical purposes can with effort become conscious. And when they do, they give rise to what Bernard Meland has called "appreciative consciousness." Meland describes appreciative consciousness as "an orientation of the mind which makes for a maximum degree of receptivity to the datum under consideration on the principle that what is given may be more than what is immediately perceived, or more than one can think." It is the conscious act of "feeling into a situation."

In the search for appreciative understanding, I rely more on affective cognition, on heart knowledge, than on the rules of abstract logic. I assume a more passive, contemplative stance in the face of persons and situations than is possible in the search for insight through logical inference. In moments of appreciative understanding, I seek to allow my situation to present itself to me in all its significant complexity. Appreciative understanding is, however, realistic: it does not ignore dative facts but attends to them only as limiting elements in a total situation. At the same time it preserves an even livelier sense of the intimations of meaning that transcend both dative fact and abstract inference. Appreciative consciousness thus endows experience with "aspirational outreach," with emotional perspective, and with a sense of mystery. It is the seed bed of conscious human hope. When it is informed by religious faith, it becomes a "nisus toward deity."[43]

The interpretative exploration of appreciative consciousness is the task of ritual, of myth, and of art. Prephilosophical and post-philosophical myths tend to be linked with ritual expression. Both transmute unconscious archetypal feelings by lifting them to shared consciousness. Philosophical myths are the tools of abstract, speculative thought. As a consequence they are normally sundered from spontaneous ritual expression by the restraints of logical thinking.

Art uses the creative mastery of some potentially significant medium to explore the realm of appreciative understanding.[44] In art the human heart brings to expression an appreciative insight into the human situation; but the insight *is* situational rather than merely subjective or pure illusion. We may, then, conclude that the emergence of appreciative consciousness and its expression and transformation through ritual, myth, and art effects a final transmutation of human affectivity. For the artistic idea is itself an affect, not a theory in the strict sense, though literary art forms may also express personal beliefs. The symbolic transformation of human appreciative understanding in art and literature thus brings human evaluative response to the threshold of abstract inferential forms of understanding.

Clearly, then, our physical purposes are not only situational but cumulative. Hence, as different physical purposes transmute one another they create, as William James saw, a particular kind of evaluative perspective, a temperament, an affective bias toward the universe that corresponds more or less adequately to the laws that shape our impinging environments. There is, then, a truth in James Hillman's suggestion that affective development is a species of "soul building."[45]

Understanding Affectivity

This insight casts some light on the scientific debate over the nature of human affectivity. Affectivity is rooted in dative presentations and grows from them, although it cannot, as James and Lange once thought, be reduced to dative feelings. Physical purposes may be perceived as "disorienting" for two possible reasons. Repressed negative feelings of anger, fear, and guilt may in fact effect either the temporary or the pathological disintegration of ego-consciousness. Or the vagueness of affective evaluations may lead me to inappropriate attempts to deal with dative stimuli. I may, for example, respond to a cold sharp object pressed to the back of my neck by wounding my supposed aggressor, only to find that it was a friend playing a practical joke. The pathological patient for a variety of reasons finds it difficult to respond with affective appropriateness to environmental stimuli. In both instances, however, the evaluative response is better described as "situationally inadequate" rather than "subjective." Moreover, in both cases the inadequacy is rooted in a failure to bring vaguely felt purposes to the degree of conceptual clarification that will ensure smooth adaptive control. Healthy emotional responses are situationally adequate. They not only do not disorient experience, they lead it forward to new appreciation and motivating insight.

The realm of physical purpose is ruled by metaphor and by the law of synchronicity,[46] not by logic. It develops by free imaginative association, not by controlled inferential processes. Human inferences, on the other hand, whether scholarly, philosophical, theological, or scientific, attempt to endow human evaluative responses with conscious control and with conceptual accuracy and adequacy. They seek to do so by replacing archetype and metaphor with precise definition and free imaginative association with the governing principles of logic. Indeed, accurate definition breeds logic. Language grows initially from metaphor. But as connoted meanings are excluded from the formal definition of a term in the interests of its precision and accuracy, its correct use is correspondingly circumscribed. Logic is born of the attempt to come to a careful understanding of the correct interrelation of precisely defined terms.

Thus, language is the link between literature and logic; and logical inference opens the door to the most abstract forms of ego-awareness. Moreover, the development of precise definition and of logical control transmutes appreciative consciousness into a different kind of experience. But in its initial phase, inference develops in continuity with emotive forms of knowing. There are no rules for coming up with the correct hypothesis to explain unexplained phenomena. Initial hypotheses emerge from a matrix of appreciative understanding. They emerge spontaneously. Moreover, when properly conducted, inference seeks to lend clarity and precision to our evaluative grasp of realities vaguely grasped in appreciative insight. It does not seek to usurp or abolish appreciative forms of knowing. It is in order to insist on the genetic continuity between affectivity and inference and on the sympathy that ought to reign between these two forms of knowing that we hereafter characterize logical processes as "propositional feelings."

The Forms of Inference

There are, as Peirce has suggested, three basic forms of inference: abductive, deductive, and inductive. Abductive inference classifies a fact on the basis of a rule, or principle, assumed to be true. Deductive inference clarifies the meaning of that rule by predicting further facts that ought to follow from it. Inductive inference uses the verification or falsification of the predicted facts as a basis for inferring that the assumed rule, or principle, actually obtains in reality. Any inference may, then, be described as the logical interrelation of a rule, a case, and a result. A result is some fact in need of explanation. A case is the classification of the fact as an instance of some rule. The rule is the general principle that seeks to disclose the law that renders the fact intelligible.[47]

Abductive inference concludes to a case from a result and a rule. An abduction is the formulation of an hypothesis. It infers that if a specific rule holds true in experience, then a given fact may be interpreted as an instance, or case, of that rule. After a dinner with friends, I may, for example, be filled with euphoria and affirm: "This was a great meal!" In the back of my mind is a general understanding of what constitutes a "great meal." And on the basis of that understanding and of the more or less vague feelings the meal has produced, I classify it as an instance of a "great meal." My judgment on the meal is a common sense abduction. Relativity theory would be an example of a complex scientific abduction. But mathematicians, scholars, philosophers, and theologians also engage in more technical kinds of abductive reasoning.

Deductive inference concludes to a result from a rule and a case. It infers that a certain result ought to follow if a concrete fact is indeed a case of a specific rule. Deductive inference seeks to clarify the theoretical or practical consequences of an abductive hypothesis. If, for instance, I am challenged as to the truth of my evaluation of the meal I have just enjoyed, I must clarify in my own mind just what I meant when I said: "This was a great meal." I must set up specific criteria for evaluating a meal. I will reason that a "great meal" should be nourishing, non-toxic, not hazardous to one's health, imaginatively prepared from superior ingredients, and served according to certain standards of taste and decor. And I will infer that if the meal I just finished was truly "great," it will meet all of these evaluative standards. I reason, therefore, that because a general rule holds true for a particular case, specific factual results can be verified in the case in question. Similarly, the conclusion of Sir Arthur Eddington and Sir Frank Dyson that if Albert Einstein's theory of relativity was in fact correct, one would be able to observe the "bending" of light in the solar eclipse of 1914 is an example of a complex scientific deduction.

Inductive inference concludes to a rule from a case and a result. It is the verification of a deductively clarified hypothesis. I may, for example, investigate the restaurant whose meal I pronounced "great" and discover that it meets none of the standards of "greatness" I had established deductively and that my original abductive assumption was a false one. Or I may verify it and conclude that my clarified rule for evaluating "greatness" holds in the present instance. Similarly Eddington's and Dyson's observation of the "bending of light" gave warranty to Einstein's original hypothesis and was an example of a complex scientific induction.

Of the three forms of inference, only the second is endowed with logical necessity. No abduction has any guarantee of automatic verification. Nor is a completed verification beyond challenge by a new and unexplained fact or by the creation of a more adequate theoretical context for explaining the facts of experience. Moreover, the necessity that attends deductive inference is a logical characteristic of the argument itself, not a psychological trait of the mind that constructs it. My mind may blunder in explaining a geometrical proof because I am tired, distracted, bored. Moreover, deductive necessity obtains only in historically conditioned frames of reference.

Indeed, the historically conditioned character of human inferential activity means that there are in the last analysis two distinguishable kinds of human beliefs. A belief is a proposition for whose consequences I am willing to assume personal responsibility. There are beliefs held as a consequence of a personal insight into their abductive, deductive, and inductive grounds as well as into their contextual and emotive presuppositions. And there are beliefs held uncritically and in ignorance of those same presuppositions and grounds.

The abductive interpretation of a sense perception transforms it into a perceptual judgment. In his analysis of the perceptual act, Peirce correctly distinguished between the concrete sense percept, the abductive inference that classifies it, and the "percipuum," or the abductively clarified percept. In the present analysis the "percept" includes the dative feelings and physical purposes that present in a vague way the facts and dynamic tendencies that shape experience. And the "percipuum" is the transmutation of such experiences through abductive inference.[48]

Appreciative consciousness becomes propositional, then, through inference. Inferential feelings are propositional because they always refer to a factual result as the case of some rule. There are three forms of propositional feelings corresponding to the three forms of inference. Hence, one may distinguish in the ongoing transmutation of experience abductive propositional feelings, deductive propositional feelings, and inductive propositional feelings.

Inference and Time

As they transmute experience evaluatively, propositional feelings illumine its temporal structure with greater clarity. Physical purposes, as we have seen, expand the temporal thickness of dative feelings and endow experience with a vague sense of transition beyond the dative present. In dative feelings my actual past becomes more or less vaguely, more or less consciously, or even unconsciously present to me within experience. But when, by the mediation of conscious and unconscious physical purposes, dative experiences are transmuted into an abductive propositional feeling, my actual past becomes more vividly present to me. It is one thing, for example, to feel malaise at the presence of a vague pain in the stomach. It is quite another to know that there is a cancer gnawing at my vitals.

As I clarify the consequences of abductive beliefs, I anticipate my future. Once my stomach cancer has been diagnosed, I know that I must either undergo an operation or suffer the consequences. And I can anticipate what the further consequences of a successful or unsuccessful operation will be. Through deductive inference, then, my vivid abductive sense of my present predicament begins to breed a more or less vivid sense of future alternatives.

Finally, when, through inductive inference, I verify or falsify my deduced expectations, my anticipated future becomes vividly and factually present. A successful operation may in fact prolong my life as the doctor predicted. Or it may fail and confront me with a different future than the one I had anticipated. Thus, in deductive inference my present becomes a future. In inductive inference my future becomes my present.

But it is the emerging self that endows experience with a sense of the future as future. For each emerging self is a vectoral feeling, a legal entity, habitual in structure, that thrusts beyond conformal or dative feelings, beyond any specific physical purpose, beyond any inferential process, beyond any decision that terminates evaluative processes and effects the reactive transformation of environmental forces. When disclosed to ego-consciousness, the future as future is felt as an indeterminate horizon of vaguely felt and unrealized possibility. On strict Whiteheadean principles, such an experience of the future as future is, however, impossible. The emerging Whiteheadean subject knows a physical past and a conceptual present. But as soon as it achieves satisfaction, it perishes. It has no abiding future to be felt. This deficiency in Whitehead's scheme dooms it as we shall see to inadequacy in any theological discussion of Christian eschatology.

We have reflected on the dynamics of experiential development and on the evaluative disclosure of time as ego-consciousness develops. But there is one final characteristic of the inferential phases of ego-awareness that should be noted before we bring this analysis to a close. Lonergan is, I believe, correct to distinguish two possible phases in the development of inferential understanding, although we characterize those phases in slightly different terms than his.[49] The first phase is "classicist." The classicist mind is preoccupied exclusively with questions of truth or falsity. Truth or falsity is the characteristic of specific inferences. Inferential understanding ceases to be "classicist" and becomes "critical" when in addition to questions of truth and falsity it attends to questions of adequacy or inadequacy. Adequacy or inadequacy is the property, not of inferences, but of the evaluative frames of reference, or contexts, within which inferences are made. A frame of reference, or evaluative context, is neither true nor false because it is never affirmed or denied as such; it is presupposed as the matrix of inferential affirmations and denials.

Vista Point

We have climbed out of our philosophical trench. We have formulated a working foundational model for dealing with human experience. It is schematized in Diagram 3. From our present vantage point we can see clearly our initial path of ascent. It led through the images that have shaped the human search for integration in God. Reflection on those images led us to formulate four conclusions concerning Christian religious experience whose foundational significance was obscure. Implicit in those four propositions are six interrelated questions we are now in a position to address. They are: (1) Why do human beings search for integration? (2) How does the human search for integration acquire a religious character? (3) Why is the religious search for integration felt to be cosmic in its scope? (4) Why is the religious search for salvific integration experienced as enlightenment? (5) When does the religious search for integration through enlightenment become Christian? (6) Why must saving enlightenment be mediated by the historical process? If one adopts the emergent model for experience just sketched, how ought one to respond to the preceding set of questions?

(1) *Why do human beings search for integration?* An emergent account of experience contrasts with substance philosophy in the way in which it conceives the problem of self-integration. In a world of substances self-integration becomes a problem only at the level of accidental change. In a substance universe, I can make decisions that fail to conform to my substantial essence and thus introduce an element of discord into experience. But whatever the accidental differences my decisions make, I remain substantially intact.

In an emergent problematic there are no substances. Hence, the "substantial unity" of experience is in no sense a metaphysical given. Experiential integration is an ideal to be achieved. It must be maintained from one moment to the next. And it depends concretely on the kinds of decisions that shape the vectoral thrust of experience. Contradictory decisions divide the emerging self. They have the capacity to set me at odds with myself, to tear me quite literally apart. Since the Christian God is experienced as the *coincidentia oppositorum*, the source of all reconciliation and healing integration, decisions that set me at odds with myself are also decisions that set me at odds with God and with those realities God bids me love. They are, therefore, sin. For sin is wrongdoing before God.

The sinful forces of disintegration that mar experience are presented to the Christian believer at the level of conscious physical purpose under the image of the "powers of darkness." In the gospel of John, these dark powers are forced to reveal themselves through their confrontation with Jesus.[50] For as the light of God grows it not only illumines the hearts of believers, but it also brings to light the hypocrisy and the murderous violence of the forces of Anti-Christ. The

Diagram 3
The Dynamics of Experience
The Realm of QUALITY: evaluative response

The laws of nature: the emergent, dynamic ground of spatio-temporal, environmental impact

Conformal Feelings: initial realm of FACT: environmental impact on the emerging self; sense of past as actual	*Dative Feelings*: initial conceptual illumination of environmental impact; sense of actual past as present	*Physical Purposes*: more or less vague sense of the legal tendencies that shape experience; a sense of transition beyond the dative present: reflex reactions; all but instantaneous affective adjustments; differentiated affections both negative and sympathetic; archetypal images; freely associated images; myth, art: abstracted feelings of what affective responses would be like	*Abductive Propositional Feelings*: classification of a fact as instance of a rule; vivid sense of past as present	*Deductive Propositional Feelings*: clarification of factual consequences of a rule; vivid sense of the present becoming future	*Inductive Propositional Feelings*: verification or falsification of deductively clarified rule; vivid sense of future becoming present	*Decision*: initial: the termination of conscious evaluative response; final: reactive impact on the environment; subsequent realm of FACT

The Self: emergent legal ground of evaluative response and decision

Vectoral Feelings: the realm of LAW: vague sense of future as future

lifting up of Jesus in glory through His death, resurrection, and mediation of the Spirit is, then, the illumination that allows the Christian to name the powers of darkness and know them for what they are. Chief among them are violence, oppression, and the pharisaical conscience. The hour of Jesus reveals the murder that rankles in the hearts of Jesus' enemies. Their accomplices in murder are the rulers of this world. And their intransigence is the fruit of religious hypocrisy. An emergent account of human experience allows us to see the threads that bind together these three forces into a web of darkness.

Personality Dysfunction

Neo-Freudian psychology has cast dramatic light on the subconscious roots of overt human violence. Violent actions tend to express repressed negative emotions: unacknowledged fear, anger, and guilt. Moreover, Neo-Freudian psychology has also provided us with a fairly detailed descriptive account of the stages of self-disintegration such repression breeds.

The "well-balanced" individual is a person who is able to deal with pain, anger, guilt, and fear through the ordinary coping devices of everyday living. For the "normal" person the reassurances of touch, of basic life rhythms, of sound, of speech are enough to restore smooth adaptive response to common emotional challenges. A good meal, drinking, gum-chewing, smoking, sleep, self-discipline, laughing, crying, cursing, boasting, can all perform a similar psychic function. Dreaming and fantasizing together with conscious rational processes, like talking problems out or thinking them through, usually enable the balanced person to cope. Sometimes activity is a coping device: it may be relatively pointless, or counterphobic dynamisms may lead one to seek out the source of difficulty or of fear. Slips of the tongue, minor accidents or mismanagements, or other forms of symbolic substitution may provide a normal and healthy release of tension. So may sneezing, itching, coughing, scratching, pacing.[51]

When such ordinary coping devices fail, individuals begin to manifest symptoms of "nervousness": of a slight but definite impairment of smooth adaptive control. Self-control begins to demand conscious effort. Unwanted feelings are repressed and breed a variety of emotional inhibitions. Hypersensitivity to sounds, smells, or other dative stimuli emerge. Emotional releases assume exaggerated expression in tearfulness, over-gaiety, or emotional volatility. Restlessness, worry, exaggerated negative attitudes, may emerge. "Nervousness" may also breed minor bodily or sexual dysfunctions.[52]

When these coping devices fail, an individual moves to a second level of personality dysfunction. At this second level, coping devices begin to take a more serious toll of human growth and development. Unwanted feelings of anger, fear, and guilt may be blocked from consciousness by a variety of psychic dynamisms: dissociative withdrawal, fainting, costly forgetting, sleepwalking, phobic or counterphobic states. Aggressive feelings may also be directed to one's own body in exaggerated ascetical practices, in acts of self-mutilation, in martyr complexes, in drunkenness or drug abuse. Fear, guilt, and violence may be symbolically discharged in a variety of ways: in public and private rituals, in compulsions, obsessional thinking, in deviant sexual activity such as promiscuity or homosexuality. Or aggressive-destructive tendencies may breed frozen emergency reactions: the miser, the bully, the sissy, the worrywart, the fuss-budget, the liar, the con-artist, the overgrown infant, the schizoid personality, the selfish narcissist, the unstable personality, the pessimist.[53]

The third level of personality dysfunction is marked by the escape of dangerous, destructive impulses. One begins to disregard customs, social regulations, laws, and other reality structures with little or no disturbance of conscience. Destructive impulses either elude or ignore concealment. Prior to aggressive activity, impairments of perception, judgment, or consciousness are apt to occur. Following violent activity there is a noticeable reduction of tension that is reflected in the temporary disappearance of symptoms that characterize earlier stages of personality disintegration. At the third stage, explosions of violent emotion tend to be either minor but frequent or major but relatively infrequent. The latter may, however, take the form of homicidal assaultiveness, periods of extreme demoralization, delirium, or manic states. Violence may also be vented in physical symptoms like convulsions or brain-damage syndromes.[54]

The fourth order of personality dysfunction is marked by the loss of emotional control and ego-identity. Emotional reactions are inappropriate, increasingly exaggerated, unrelated to environmental stimuli. Productive activity ceases. One retreats into an autistic, solipsistic world and gives way to bizarre, chaotic behavior. Often the afflicted individual requires hospitalization and prolonged treatment.[55]

The final stage of personality disintegration is suicide. It is the ultimate and total collapse of conscious control in an act of self-hatred and self-destruction.[56] We will consider the healing of the violent heart in Chapter IV.

The Authoritarian Personality

Repressed negative feelings are also the seed bed of oppression.

In the city of Munich there is an ancient triumphal arch partially destroyed by bombs during the Second World War. The shattered portions have been rebuilt with rough and unadorned stones that contrast starkly with the decorations of the original classical structure. On the restored stones there is a simple inscription: "Constructed in victory, destroyed by war, warning for peace."

The Second World War stands in history as a grisly reminder of the viciousness and destructiveness of which the human heart is capable. Blitzkrieg, total war, saturation bombing, Dresden, Hiroshima, Nagasaki, Auschwitz, Dachau—the scope of the horror is all but incomprehensible. How could so many of the German people have been hoodwinked by Hitler into becoming the instruments of his psychotic schemes? The attempt to answer that question produced an illuminating insight into the reason why human beings seek to oppress one another.

Persons with a strong authoritarian bent manifest a certain number of stable emotional tendencies: (1) The authoritarian personality is strongly inclined to conventionalism, to blind, rigid adherence to accepted values. (2) The authoritarian submits easily to moral authorities in the groups to which (s)he belongs and idealizes them beyond measure. (3) The authoritarian assumes an aggressive attitude toward those who violate the conventional values (s)he upholds. Such a person desires to see the violators condemned and punished for their deviations. (4) The authoritarian is suspicious and fearful of subjectivity, imagination, the more tender human emotions. (5) The authoritarian is inclined to be superstitious and to imagine that his or her life is ruled by some inexorable fate. (6) The authoritarian thinks of members of other groups in rigid stereotypes. (7) The authoritarian is preoccupied with the pursuit of power and admires powerful leaders, their strength and toughness. (8) The authoritarian is inclined to believe that wild and dangerous things go on in the world and that one must always be on one's guard against lurking enemies.[57]

Human beings must be trained to authoritarian attitudes. Individuals of authoritarian bent tend to emerge from households in which a relatively harsh and threatening home discipline prevails. The children of such households tend to relate to their parents with fearful subservience. They think of them as distant and forbidding figures and find exacting parental discipline arbitrary.[58]

Parents who breed authoritarian offspring tend to manifest a high level of anxiety concerning their own scio-economic status and that of their family. And they tolerate no behavior in their children that deviates from status-anxious goals. Rigid conformity to parental goals engenders in children a diminished sense of personal identity.[59]

In such families the free-flowing exchange of affection is replaced by the faithful execution of roles and duties. Human relationships tend to be opportunistic, manipulative, and exploitative. Good behavior on the part of the child is enforced with only meager rewards. Since the child's growing fear, anger, and resentment can find no legitimate outlet within the family, it is redirected against other social groups: other families, neighborhoods, races, classes. The child's inability to find a legitimate family outlet for its growing sense of rage and frustration bears fruit in a negative identification with the weak and in a positive though superficial identification with the strong. Within the family circle, the child identifies with the stronger of the two parents.[60]

The person shaped by such an upbringing tends to repress fear, weakness, passivity, personal sexual impulses, and aggressive feelings against authority figures. Fearful of facing a felt lack of personal identity and of unacknowledged feelings of rage, the emerging authoritarian repudiates both introspection and threatening novel insights. (S)he has a low capacity for entering into tender human relationships or for the enjoyment of sensual or passive pleasures. Appreciation for companionship, affection, art, music, is also low. The authoritarian is personally rootless, inclined to mobility. (S)he craves material security. The authoritarian's life is ruled by a tissue of ethical clichés. There is a deeply felt need for simple, firm, stereotyped social categories and structures in order to cope. The authoritarian reacts violently to those who question his or her rigid moral code by their nonconformity, although the violence may take subtle forms.[61]

The authoritarian person tends to import these emotionally rigid attitudes into the religious sphere as well. (S)he approaches religion with conformist attitudes. Submission to religious authority is often a way of simply ingratiating oneself with others. The authoritarian subordinates religious values to nonreligious goals, like personal achievement or mental hygiene. (S)he is firmly loyal to "official Christianity," but retains a stereotyped, simplistic understanding of the meaning of creedal statements.[62]

Clearly, the authoritarian personality is in full flight from personal freedom. Low in ego strength, the authoritarian needs to identify with somebody or something outside his or her own self in order to feel personal individual worth. Unable to say "I want" or "I am," the authoritarian's subservient submission to authority is self-accusing and self-critical. At the same time, relationship with weaker individuals or groups is marked by a desire for control and domination, even though such domineering, manipulative tendencies are not infrequently rationalized as an expression of "true concern" for those who are too foolish to realize what is good for them.

Erich Fromm summarizes succinctly the dilemma of the authoritarian personality. "As long as I struggle," he writes,

> between my desire to be independent and strong and my feeling of insignificance or powerlessness, I am caught in a tormenting conflict. If I succeed in reducing my individual self to nothing, if I can overcome my awareness of separateness as an individual, I may save myself from the conflict.[63]

Such a person will, then, seek to be submerged into a larger social reality with which (s)he can identify while craving the kind of domination over others that yields a sense of security. (S)he will be an easy prey to political and religious demagogues who share a felt need to wield power over others and who know how to channel the bigoted aggressions of the masses against the weak and defenseless.[64]

Hitler's sadistic craving for power, his creation of a ruling "elite," his persecution of racial minorities as a sop to the sadism of the masses, his Social Darwinism, his love of power and contempt for the powerless, his demand that individuals sacrifice their very lives in the interests of national conquest—all of these mad visions are the expression of the authoritarian impulse in its starkest form. And they stand in continuity with every despot and martinet who has trampled on the defenseless.

For wherever authoritarianism is found it breeds bigotry and social oppression in the family, in economic society, in politics, in the Church. It splinters the human community into a Babel of in-groups and out-groups, divided by fear but locked in conflict. It deprives the black race of the means of growth and then stigmatizes all blacks as inferior. It excludes women from access to power and then oppresses them as the weaker sex. It creates the social and political structures that breed poverty and then condemns the poor for their laziness and lack of initiative. It calls oppression the will of God.

The Pharisaical Conscience

Violence breeds oppression, and oppression breeds violence. But both conspired with a third force to nail the Son of God to the cross: the pious rationalizations of the pharisaical conscience. Not every Pharisee at the time of Jesus was a religious villain, as the figure of Nicodemus in the gospel of John is intended to remind us. The "pharisaical conscience" is not a person or class but the incarnation of a complex set of perennial religious attitudes to which Jesus stood unalterably opposed.

Paul Ricoeur has argued that religious consciousness of evil develops through at least three distinguishable phases: the sense of defilement, the sense of sin, and the sense of guilt. There is a truth in his suggestion but we must postpone critical reflection on it until Chapter VII. The sense of defilement is the most primitive expression of a religious awareness of evil. It bespeaks a low level of ego-consciousness, for it makes no clear distinction between conscious and unconscious fault. A taboo violated indeliberately warrants the same punishment as one deliberately broken.

The sense of sin emerges when indeliberate and deliberate fault come to be evaluatively discriminated. "Sin" is conscious, personal transgression of the divine will. Among the Greeks it fed a sense of social and political responsibility. Among the Hebrews it helped inspire prophetic preaching. The sense of sin bespeaks a more highly developed religious ego than the sense of defilement, for it holds each individual responsible before God for personal decisions.

The sense of guilt distinguishes degrees of moral culpability before God. It recognizes that some faults are more serious than others and attempts to rank sins in order of gravity. A nuanced sense of guilt demands close reasoning and presupposes a highly developed ego.[65]

The "pharisaical conscience" is another name for the scrupulous conscience. It marks an advanced stage in the development of guilt consciousness. Scrupulosity emerges when rational differentiation of the manifold ways in which guilt before God can be incurred combines with an intense revulsion for any transgression of the divine will in order to produce an equally intense desire to free oneself from all defilement, sin, and guilt. The scrupulous conscience thus bespeaks not only a developed ego but an ego in a high state of inflation.[66]

The term "ego-inflation" is Jungian in origin. It attempts to describe a peculiar phenomenon in the development of ego-consciousness. As ego-consciousness becomes inferential, it grows in clarity, in abstractness, and in its capacity to control its own growth. These three traits are interrelated. Conceptual clarity is the fruit of evaluative differentiation. Evaluative differentiation focuses conscious attention. As conscious attention becomes focused, it excludes from consideration more and more potential objects of interest. It thus renders human evaluations increasingly abstract.

Almost inevitably, then, as the rational ego advances in self-control through evaluative differentiation and abstraction, it becomes by its own proper dynamic increasingly oblivious of those forces within experience that lie outside the gamut of its own abstract and increasingly specialized interests. In the case of the inflated ego, such oblivion has reached an advanced stage of development. The inflated ego is riding high, sure of itself and of its insights, confident of firm rational control, negligent of the existence and importance of realities and forces that are irrelevant to its immediate abstract concerns.[67]

The person in a high state of ego-inflation is, then, potentially quite dangerous. The inflated ego is all too prone to deal cavalierly with realities and values that do not fit easily into the narrow focus of its own abstract preoccupations. Moreover, ego-inflation becomes doubly dangerous when it is subconsciously motivated by a failure to confront one's own shadow. The shadow is the archetype for the undeveloped and shameful aspects of one's own personality. It symbolizes the violence, the fear, and the guilt that paralyze my heart and that I am terrified of facing.

The pharisaical conscience betrays its inflated character in its decision to rid itself of all guilt by dint of meticulous self-control. Scrupulous self-conquest is the expression of an emotional inability to face one's shadow. It breeds self-righteous contempt for those less pure and upright than oneself.

Failure to face the shadow breeds shadow possession. The violence, the terror, and the unacknowledged guilt festering in the heart will out. But if they are to surface in activity guided by a self-righteous conscience they need to be explained and justified by hypocritically pious rationalizations. But for one practiced in abstract forms of ethical reflection, the manufacture of such rationalizations is easy enough. And so it is decided once again that it is morally and religiously better for one person, one family, one people to die rather than that I and others like me should perish.

The message of the fourth gospel is, then, clear: one possessed by the dark powers is incapable of faith in the God who has come to self-revelation in Jesus and the Spirit. Such a one will confront the love of God made visible in Jesus and the Spirit either with mocking skepticism or with pious rationalizations that mask inner violence and unbelief.

What, then, motivates the human search for integration? The answer should be clear. The powers of darkness are powers of dissolution, misery, and death. They suffuse human existence with a pain that is intolerable.

(2) *When does the human search for integration take on a religi-*

ous character? Not every search for integration and for life is a religious search. Nor is every human experience a religious experience. Transcendental Thomism has tended to obscure this basic truth by attempting to demonstrate that God is the transcendent object of the human intellect and that the divine Being is implicitly affirmed in every intellectual act. The proofs offered in support of this position lack conviction for at least two reasons. First, they rest on an untenable faculty psychology. (We will reflect in more detail on some of the implications of such a psychology in Chapter IV.) Second, transcendental Thomism presupposes a questionable metaphysics of God. Ogden has correctly criticized the early work of Lonergan on this second point, although his own arguments presuppose, incorrectly I believe, the theological adequacy of Whitehead's philosophy of God. Ogden's critique also ignores the shifts that have occurred in Lonergan's later thought.[68] We will reflect on the problem of God in Chapter VI.

In an emergent problematic, the immediate problem confronting any developing experience is not the search for God but the search for satisfaction. "Satisfaction" is used here as a technical term. It is defined as the transmuted state of experience effected by decision.

Decision performs a threefold function within experience. It terminates the evaluative processes that shape reaction. Those evaluative processes are both conscious and unconscious. Preliminary decision terminates conscious processes. For example, after wrestling with a vocational decision. I may decide that I will stop thinking about the problem and become a doctor rather than a teacher. Final decisions reshape the impinging environment and have consequences there. In applying for admission to medical school, I act to insert myself into a new environment that will have significant impact on my future growth. But unconscious evaluations may reshape final decisions in ways that may on occasion modify or reverse preliminary ones. When I am accepted into medical school, I may be surprised to discover that my prior decision to apply runs counter to my deeper feelings and that a medical vocation is simply not for me. Such realizations are not the fruit of conscious thinking; they rise spontaneously from the subconscious. The specific character of any given decision is, of course, in part a function of the impinging forces to which it seeks to respond and of the kinds of evaluative processes it terminates.

But decision does more than terminate evaluative response. It reshapes one's environment and it reshapes the emerging self. Preliminary decisions prepare the body for reactive impact on the impinging environment. Final decisions exert that impact. Reactive impact gives new shape to my total environment, both impinging and bodily.

Decisions, however, also redefine the emerging self. Through decision, both preliminary and final, the dynamic tendencies that shape me as an experience acquire ongoing definition. Here it is important to note that decision brings about these three effects simultaneously. That is to say, through decision the factual, qualitative, and legal variables that shape experience are reharmonized in a new dynamic synthesis. This dynamic reharmonization is an instance of "satisfaction."

Human satisfactions are more or less successful. Minimally successful satisfactions sustain existing life processes. As the success of a satisfaction increases it incorporates into experience new forms of life and growth. The success of a satisfaction is, then, measured by its intensity; i.e., by the capacity of a decision to reduce the greatest number of factual, evaluative, and legal variables to the greatest degree of structural unity. Structural unity is measured by the mutual relational interdependence of the variables that shape a satisfaction. There are three kinds of relation: conceptual, factual, and legal.

Spatio-temporal satisfactions are always only partially successful. The world in which we live is, as William James suggested, a pluralistic universe.[69] Human satisfactions must, then, be reached pluralistically. And pluralism combines with the forces of darkness to deprive any given satisfaction of ultimacy. The powers of darkness deprive satisfaction of ultimacy by suffusing it with pain, physical and mental. Pain is the initial evaluative disclosure of discord and contradiction. At the level of satisfaction, discord and contradiction are identical with dissent.

Where dissent is not mediated by the powers of darkness, it is mediated by the finitude that is the necessary concomitant of pluralism. How often do well-intentioned persons find themselves pitted against one another in meaningless and theoretically avoidable conflicts that are the fruit of human limitation rather than of malice? Such conflicts are bred of an ignorance and a myopia that are in turn the inevitable by-product of the increasingly abstract character of ego-consciousness. Lack of information; apathy; fatigue; emotional, intellectual, moral, and religious irresponsibility—all these forces combine to make mutual consent vacillating and haphazard.[70]

The dynamic structure of experience also prevents any concrete satisfaction from becoming ultimate. For, as Emerson saw clearly, there is a restlessness in experience that is born of its thrust into the future.[71] Every successful satisfaction breeds new capacities for life and growth. Every unsuccessful satisfaction breeds the desire for deliverance from violence, oppression, hypocrisy, dissent, limitation. Neither experience can be ultimately satisfying. For ultimate satisfaction would not only leave nothing to be desired but it would have to exclude all disintegrating forms of dissent.

Human experience takes on a religious dimension when the experience of the nonultimacy of each and every satisfaction raises the religious question. The religious question asks: Does human life have any ultimate meaning and purpose?[72] Or to put the same question differently: Does human experience move toward ultimate satisfaction? One may react to such a question in a variety of ways. One may choose to ignore it. If so, one's experience remains devoid of personal religious meaning, although impinging religious stimuli may raise the question again at some future date. Or one may repudiate religious meaning altogether and align oneself less ambiguously with the powers of darkness. But a positive answer to the religious question endows all one's subsequent experience with a religious character, although the religious intensity of one's personal satisfactions will, of course, be a function of the extent to which religious realities and values lie at the integrating center of one's decisions and unify all the other elements in experience.

(3) *Why is the religious search for integration felt to be cosmic in its scope?* All evolving life, all spatio-temporal experience is, as we have seen, shaped by the environment out of which it grows. Life, Teilhard observed, emerged only to swarm.[73] And the swarming of life means that living things are brought to cohabitation. Through cohabitation they become for one another both the condition for further growth and the source of dissolution and death. The delicate ecological balances that sustain living species are maintained in large measure by the presence of checks and balances in the food chain.

There is, then, an element of dissent built into any experience whose evaluative form is merely natural. Living things are natural predators. And the predatory impulse demands that some things perish in order that others might survive. We find no moral blame in natural predation. We acquiesce in it as a "law of nature," though gentle folk do so somewhat uneasily. For the predatory impulse in nature serves as a grim reminder that human beings have the capacity to prey on one another. *Homo homini lupus.*

Religious experience is experience in search of ultimate satisfaction. Such a satisfaction would leave nothing to be desired. It would have, therefore, to exclude all contradiction, all dissent. The presence of dissent at the heart of natural processes demands the reshaping of the cosmos in the interests of ultimate satisfaction. The religious vision of a world thus transformed is the vision that Edward Hicks never tired of painting: that of the peaceable kingdom.

> The wolf shall dwell with the lamb,
>> and the leopard shall die down with the kid,
> and the calf and the lion and the fatling together
>> and a little child shall lead them.
> The cow and the bear shall feed; their young shall
>> lie down together;
>> and the lion shall eat straw like the ox.
> The sucking child shall play over the hole of the asp,
>> and the weaned child shall put his hand on the
>> adder's den.
> They shall not hurt or destroy in all my holy mountain;
>> for the earth shall be full of the knowledge of
>> the Lord
>> as the waters cover the sea.[74]

The realization of such a vision would seem to demand two things: not only the present reshaping of our environment into an expression of mutual consent in love but the transcendence of those very environmental limitations that make mutual predation inevitable. In Chapters VII and VIII we shall return to a reflection on some of the ethical and religious implications of these two germinal insights.

Here, however, three other preliminary points need to be noted: (1) To redirect a dissenting, pluralistic world marred by the disintegration of the powers of darkness to the goal of ultimate satisfaction demands a cosmic consent of atoning love. (2) The world as we know it is incapable of eliciting such a consent. (3) If ultimate satisfaction is possible, its ground would, then, have to be both real and transcendent.

Atoning Love

Love is consent. As consent is evaluatively transformed, it gives rise to different kinds of love. The child's love is born in large measure of need, but as it matures it becomes affection, friendship, romance, contemplation, self-sacrifice. Atoning love is a form of self-sacrificing gift love. It is sustained in the absence of reciprocating consent. Perfect atoning love is unrestricted in its scope, in its conditions, in its consequences. It is unrestricted in its scope if it excludes no person or life-giving value from its consent. It is unrestricted in its conditions if it is simply there irrespective of the merits of the beloved and before any sign of response. It is unrestricted in its consequences if it is sustained before, during, and after its refusal.[75]

Atoning love is creative and gratuitous. It is creative for it seeks and sometimes succeeds in evoking the consent of love where before only dissent and disintegration prevailed. It is a consent that is simply there. In his great and seminal work *Agape and Eros*, Anders Nygren argues that the gratuity of divine love can be preserved only by denying all intrinsic value to God's beloved. For Nygren, gratuitous, agapastic love must be unmotivated. His position is untenable. Unmotivated love is a contradiction in terms, for it could have no object. At the same time, the denial of motivation is not the only speculative justification of the possibility of gift love in God. God's love for the world would in fact be gratuitous if two conditions would obtain in reality: (1) that the divine reality be identical with love and (2) that the divine reality be capable of meaningful description as prior to the reality of the world. Both affirmations are basic New Testament beliefs. If both obtain in reality, God's love of the world would not be a function of the world's merits or response. Such a love would be prior to any capacity on the part of the world to respond. Such a love would be doubly gratuitous if sustained in the face of cosmic dissent in all its forms.

In his sensitive reflections on the meaning of Christian love, Daniel Day Williams argues, correctly I believe, that both an Augustinian model for understanding Christian love and Nygren's evangelical model suffer from serious speculative inadequacies.[76] Williams correctly insists that a critique of the dualistic philosophical presuppositions that mar an Augustinian theology of God demands a corresponding speculative transformation of an Augustinian theology of love.

> To love another in God does depersonalize, *if we make God's eternity the key to his perfection in contrast to the creatures*. Then another person can only be a pointer toward the eternal which is superior to all temporality. But in process doctrine the meaning of God's being is his creative communion with the creatures. God values each person in himself, and as a participant in the creative history of the world. Thus to love another in God is to acknowledge in the divine love that which affirms the unique value of the person. Once we break through the traditional deification of

timelessness for its own sake, the meaning of the *imago dei* takes on a new dimension.[77]

Williams also acknowledges the atoning character of the divine love revealed in Jesus. And he correctly finds a suggestive philosophical analysis of the meaning of Christian love in Josiah Royce's philosophy of loyalty:

> In this philosophy of loyalty, Royce is interpreting the meaning of love so that the power of love's dealing with guilt is brought to the fore. Atonement is that working of love in which the meaning of being human is made plain. Thus the idealist philosopher illuminates the doctrine of atonement. He has gone beyond the traditional doctrines by drawing his metaphor from within the action of loyalty when it deals with the broken community. He has described the human process of reconciliation.[78]

Williams's book is an impressive theological achievement; its chief defect is its failure to subject the inadequacies in a Whiteheadean conception of God to a rigorous philosophical critique. But his endorsement of Royce is suggestive and on the whole sound. We shall return to this question in Chapter VI.

The purpose of divine atoning love is the creation of a community of mutual consent in which every betrayal is forgiven in advance because the love of each member of the community for each other imitates the scope and quality of divine love. That love in its historical self-revelation in Jesus and the Spirit is experienced as simply and gratuitously there.

The world without God could never elicit a consent of atoning love adequate to effect a reconciliation so cosmic in its scope that its fruit would be ultimate satisfaction. The reasons should be clear. Spatio-temporal activity is pluralistic. Every spatio-temporal reality is finite; and no finite reality is capable of impact that is cosmic in its scope. Moreover, ultimate satisfaction demands the abolition of all dissent, but dissent is woven into the very texture of both natural and sinful satisfactions. A satisfaction is natural when its evaluative form consists of values that are not opposed to the will of God but that remain untouched by religious faith. It is personally sinful when its evaluative form stands in conscious opposition to the moral exigencies of faith in the God who is self-revealed in Jesus and the Spirit.

If, then, God is a fiction only and not real, then all satisfactions are at best natural and marred in part by predation. At worst they are violent, oppressive, hypocritical. If God is to be the source of a realistic search for ultimate satisfaction and therefore a force of atoning love capable of triumphing over the dissent that is born of natural limitation and of sinful submission to the powers of darkness, then God must not only be real but transcend and encompass this dissenting world. If there is no such God, the religious search for ultimate satisfaction must, as Freud suggested, be dismissed as finally an illusion.

(4) *Why is the religious search for salvific integration experienced as enlightenment?* The religious search for salvific integration is the search for ultimate satisfaction. The powers of darkness breed the disintegration of ego-consciousness and the dissociation of rational processes from the affective matrix out of which they spring. Both diminish the presentational immediacy operative in any given experience and, with it, certain forms of consciousness. The disintegrating ego is less and less capable of inferential insight. The inflated ego is blind to large areas of appreciative understanding and inferential response.

By the same token the consent of atoning love creates the social context in which ego-consciousness may develop in healthy ways. Loving transition from subjection to the powers of darkness to mutual reconciliation in a community of faith that lives open to a saving God creates the matrix in which conceptual enlightenment may grow. Moreover, that very transition can only be itself enlightening; for it demands the repudiation of the pharisaical conscience, confrontation with the shadow, and belief in the reality and power of divine love. It is, therefore, mediated by conscious disclosure of one's sinfulness and conscious assent to the revelation of divine atoning love. Finally, the integrating consent of atoning love mediates enlightenment, for, as we shall see in Chapter VIII, as it intensifies, it becomes a form of knowing.

(5) *When does the religious search for integration become Christian?* The Christianization of a religious experience is effected when one is led to affirm Jesus as the normative historical embodiment of divine atoning love and the Spirit of Jesus as the source and agent of such love in the redeemed. Belief in the normative character of God's self-revelation in Jesus is, as Karl Rahner has correctly insisted,[79] inseparable from belief in the hypostatic union. That belief may be formulated in a variety of ways; but it demands that one affirm that the human reality of Jesus gave those who knew Him conscious

access to a person whose divinity was on a par with the God He proclaimed. Cognitive access to the divine reality made manifest in Jesus is mediated through the power and illumination of the Spirit of love who proceeds from him.

(6) *Why must saving enlightenment be mediated by the historical process?* One may respond to such a question in several ways. It may, then, be clarifying to contrast the response presented here with that offered by another contemporary theologian: Karl Rahner.

Rahner is a transcendental Thomist. He accepts a metaphysics of Being and the whole cumbersome apparatus of Thomistic faculty psychology. With Joseph Maréchal, he believes that it is possible to ground a strict metaphysics of Being in an analysis of the conditions for the possibility of human knowledge. He locates the dynamic thrust of the human mind toward Being in the agent intellect, a spiritual faculty of the spiritual soul that moves the possible intellect to act by deriving an intellectual species from the phantasm present in the imaginative faculty.

Rahner argues that, because the human spiritual soul is the form of a corporeal, material body, the human intellect can grasp Being only by deriving intelligibility from the phantasm. If, then, the human mind is to grasp the universal and the transcendental, it must discover them in the concrete and the sensible. In the world of transcendental Thomism, moreover, the goal of human transcendence can only be God. At the same time, any divine act of self-revelation must be initially conformed to the capacity of the human mind to grasp it. If, then, God is to reveal Himself to human beings, it must be by becoming concrete, enfleshed, incarnate. Since, however, the realm of matter is the realm of space and time, God's self-revelation must be historical.[80]

The position taken in these pages also affirms the irreducibly historical character of divine revelation, but for very different reasons. We have opted here for a foundational problematic that takes "experience" rather than "being" as its central, unifying category. We have replaced medieval faculty psychology with a theory of the transmutation of experience. As we have seen, in such a problematic, human ego-consciousness must be conceived as irreducibly temporal in its defining structure. In an emergent universe there is, then, no need to demonstrate the historical character of human experience despite the static, a-historical principles that give shape to reality. The relational structure of human experience demands that it be spatio-temporal in origin. It must arise from an environmental past and move through the development of ego-consciousness toward some kind of future. If, then, God is to be encountered within ego-consciousness, that experience must have an historical, spatio-temporal structure. We shall explore the implications of this insight in Chapter VIII.

But the kind of future toward which I am moving is not the result of some postulated, subjective, a priori structure of consciousness. It is the result of the kind of past out of which I emerge and of the evaluative stance I choose to take to that past. On emergent principles, then, God will become my future only to the extent that God is a force that shapes my past. But the God who is my past must be integrated into the fabric of my present evaluative response if He is to become my future. To be the Omega of my faith God must be its Alpha as well.

For the believing Christian, the normative, factual revelation of God is Jesus. The only adequate evaluative response to that normative revelation is the hope and faith inspired by the Holy Spirit. The Spirit is, then, the abiding, interpretative link between the God who is my past and the God who is my future. By the same token, divine salvation enters the past of the non-Christian by each charismatic impulse of the Spirit that prepares the heart for assent to the divine incarnate fact of Jesus.

Our foundational analysis of the Christian search for saving enlightenment and integration has given rise to three interrelated questions. (1) If it is the Spirit who gives abiding cognitive access to the mystery of God incarnate and thus reorients human experience to the God who desires to become our future, then what does it mean to speak of the transformation of experience in the power of the Spirit? (2) What initial conditions must be met if such a transformation is to be possible? (3) What is the locus of initial, present, experiential access to God? (4) What are the practical consequences of consent to Jesus as the revelation of God and source of the Spirit?[81] In the chapters that follow, we will attempt to respond to each of these questions in order.

Notes

1. The best one-volume study of the development of American religion is, of course, Sydney E. Ahlstrom, *A Religious History of the American People* (New Haven: Yale, 1972). Also useful are: Martin E. Marty, *Righteous Empire* (New York: Dial, 1970); John Tracy Ellis, *American Catholicism* (Chicago: University of Chicago, 1969); Frederick Sontag and John K.

Roth, *The American Religious Experience* (New York: Harper and Row, 1972).

2. Ellis, *American Catholicism*, pp. 37–40; Ahlstrom, *op. cit.*, pp. 330–342; Charles H. Metzger, *Catholics and the American Revolution* (Chicago: Loyola University, 1962).

3. Ahlstrom, *op. cit.*, pp. 527–568; Gustavus Myers, *A History of Bigotry in the United States*, ed. with additional material by Henry M. Christman (New York: Capricorn, 1960).

4. Orestes Brownson, *Works*, ed. Henry F. Brownson (20 vols.; Detroit: Nourse, 1884–1904), X, pp. 20–22, 488–489; XVII, pp. 282–293, 300–379; DS 3866–3876.

5. Orestes Brownson, *The American Republic* (Clifton: Kelly, 1972), pp. 348–439.

6. Ellis, *op. cit.*, pp. 84–123; Ahlstrom, *op. cit.*, pp. 998–1018.

7. Michael V. Gannon, "Before and after Modernism: The Intellectual Isolation of the American Priest," in *The Catholic Priest in the United States*, ed. John Tracy Ellis (Collegeville: St. John's University, 1971), pp. 293–383.

8. Mircea Eliade, *The Two and the One* (New York: Harper, 1962), pp. 19–77.

9. *Ibid.*, pp. 78–124.

10. *Ibid.*, pp. 125–159.

11. Paul Ricoeur, *The Symbolism of Evil*, trans. Emerson Buchanan (Boston: Beacon, 1969), pp. 282–283.

12. Mircea Eliade, *Cosmos and History: The Myth of the Eternal Return*, trans. William R. Trask (New York: Harper and Row, 1959); Ricoeur, *op. cit.*, pp. 232–278.

13. Jn. 4:16, 17: 21ff.; Rm. 5:12–21; Rev. 21:1ff.

14. Gn. 11:1–9; Ex. 19:1ff.; Is. 52:13–53:12; Dn. 7:13–28; Ez. 34:23ff.; 37:21–24.

15. 1 Co. 12:1–30; Lk. 1:31–38; Jr. 31:31–34; Act 2:1ff.; Rm. 5:12–8:39.

16. Jn. 1:9–14, 5:17–24, 8:12, 12:23–28; 14:10–13, 15:8, 16:13–15, 17:5–6, 21–24.

17. *Summa Theologiae*, I. QQ. 75–77.

18. *Ibid.*, I–II, QQ. 90–97.

19. Whitehead, *Process and Reality*, pp. 26–27, 182–194, 240–275.

20. *Ibid.*, pp. 276–326.

21. *Ibid.*, pp. 39–42.

22. *Ibid.*, p. 94.

23. *Ibid.*, pp. 76-99, 105, 150, 194, 262, 274, 285, 334, 333-353.

24. A. N. Whitehead, *Symbolism* (New York: Capricorn, 1927), pp. 27–28. Whitehead's most explicit treatment of the notion of "person" occurs in *Adventures of Ideas*. There he associates the idea with the dominant nexus in a monarchically ordered nexus of actual occasions and indicates that "person" need not imply "living." Cf. *Adventures of Ideas* (New York: Mentor, 1933), pp. 205–207. In the emergent problematic here adopted, "person" is defined as a relational reality subsisting in its own right (i.e., as a center of reactive response) but not like a substance, "in itself and not in anything else," with the capacity (either developing or realized) for conscious self-understanding as such. In an emergent problematic, then, every person

is a living reality. And human persons achieve full personhood through conversion.

25. Roy Wood Sellars, "Philosophy of Organism and Physical Realism," in *The Philosophy of Alfred North Whitehead*, pp. 407–433; Nels F. S. Ferré, "Beyond Substance and Process," *Theology Today*, XXIV (1967), pp. 160–171.

26. C. S. Peirce, *Collected Papers*, ed. Charles Hartshorne and Paul Weiss (8 vols.; Cambridge: Harvard, 1931–1958), 1.15–34, 300–416.

27. Whitehead, *Adventures of Ideas*, pp. 107–416.

28. Whitehead, *Process and Reality*, pp. 24, 29–30, 61, 86, 105, 150, 194, 243, 261–262, 274, 282, 285, 320, 323, 334, 407–409.

29. Peirce, *Collected Papers*, 7. 642–687, 5. 180–212.

30. *Ibid.*, 1. 337–353, 5. 59–119, 6. 238–271, 287–317.

31. Pierre Teilhard de Chardin, *The Phenomenon of Man*, trans. Bernard Wall (New York: Harper, 1961), pp. 67ff.

32. John Dewey, *Democracy and Education* (New York: Macmillan, 1944), pp. 41–206, 291–360; cf. R. Archambault, *Dewey on Education* (New York: Random House, 1966); Melvin Baker, *Foundations of Dewey's Educational Theory* (New York: Atherton, 1966).

33. John Dewey, *Experience and Nature* (New York: Dover, 1958).

34. Whitehead, *Process and Reality*, pp. 52–75.

35. Whitehead, *Symbolism*, pp. 13–16.

36. Maurice Merleau-Ponty, *Phenomenology of Perception*, trans. Colin Smith (London: Routledge and Kegan Paul, 1962); Charles Hartshorne, *The Philosophy and Psychology of Sensation* (Chicago: University of Chicago, 1945).

37. Neumann, *op. cit.*, pp. 293–312.

38. Victor Frankl, *Man's Search for Meaning* (New York: Washington Square, 1965); Abraham Maslow, *Toward a Psychology of Being* (New York: Van Nostrand, 1962); Neumann, *loc. cit.* The definition of ego-consciousness here proposed is "logical" rather than psychological, although it expands the notion of "logic" to include appreciative insight. Ego-functions are those based on evaluative differentiation and evaluative synthesis. In addition, they mediate a form of knowing that may or may not be loving. There are, as we shall see, several advantages to such an approach to ego-processes. First, it calls attention to the continuity that links conscious and unconscious ego-functions. Unlike psychological theory that opposes the ego to the unconscious, an emergent theory of experience expands ego-functions to include unconscious processes as well. One may, then, speak of conscious and unconscious ego-cognition. When we come to discuss mystical forms of knowing, the advantages of such an approach will become more evident.

39. Hartshorne, *Philosophy and Psychology of Perception*, pp. 9ff.

40. Magda B. Arnold, ed., *The Nature of Emotion* (New York: Penguin, 1969).

41. Whitehead uses the term to designate a feeling in which the subjective form has acquired a special appetition—adversion or aversion—in respect to an eternal object as a realized element of definiteness in some physical datum; cf. *Process and Reality*, pp. 213–214. In an emergent problematic, the term designates the vague evaluative presentation of the legal variables that shape experience. Physical purposes are, then, rendered more

precise by inference. In an emergent problematic, then, the term "physical purpose" presupposes the validity of Peirce's analysis of the inferential presentation of vectoral feelings within perception and affirms in addition the vague anticipation of inferential processes in the experience of appreciative insight.

42. Whitmont, *The Symbolic Quest*, pp. 156ff.; see also: C. G. Jung et al., *Man and His Symbols* (New York: Laurel, 1964).

43. Bernard E. Meland, *Higher Education and the Human Spirit* (Chicago: University of Chicago, 1953), pp. 50–182.

44. Susanne K. Langer, *Feeling and Form* (New York: Scribner's, 1953), pp. 34–37, 69ff. Despite these qualifications, Dewey's esthetic theory remains on the whole sound. The rhythms of artistic creation foreshadow at a vaguer level of ego-cognition the logical dialogue between thinker and environment. The creative interaction between both artist and thinker, on the one hand, and the environmental forces that shape and are shaped by their evaluative responses are symbolically mediated primarily by concrete images in the case of the artist, primarily by abstract inference in the case of the thinker.

45. James Hillman, *Revisioning Psychology* (New York: Harper and Row, 1975).

46. C. G. Jung, *Synchronicity: An Acausal Connecting Principle* (Princeton: Billingen, 1973). The law of synchronicity was first formulated by Jung. It is the law governing the meaningful coincidence. As Jung saw, its "logic" is not inferential. It involves, therefore, a form of knowing other than the causal explanations of science. He felt, quite correctly, the presence of archetypal influences in meaningful coincidences. The archetype draws to itself by connotation and free association an increasingly complex cluster of related images. It is, therefore, capable of casting light through connotation on two events that strictly speaking have no logical connection. Thus, by the mediation of the archetypes, a chance occurrence may illumine a personal psychic state or vice versa. The same law can endow a chance experience with predictive power. Synchronicity provides, then, the key to the "logic" of predictive prophecy.

47. Cf. Reilly, *Charles Peirce's Theory of Scientific Method*, pp. 23–77; Peirce, *Collected Works*, 2. 623–635. One of the serious inadequacies of Whitehead's system is its failure to account for a sense of the future as future. Having shattered experience into a series of atomic moments that grow and perish in a fraction of a second, the philosophy of organism is forced to explain the temporal structure of experience as a past illumined by a present and instantly transformed into another past. The "future" becomes the "eternal," the transcendent realm of unrealized possibilities in God's mind; cf. Alfred North Whitehead, *Adventures of Ideas*, pp. 193–201. C. S. Peirce had a clearer sense of the continuities that undergird the factural and evaluative elements in experience. He accordingly was more interested in constructing his metaphysics out of a logic of inference rather than on the model of a subject-predicate proposition, although he did believe that every subject-predicate proposition was syntactical shorthand for an inference. In the model for experience I have here proposed, I have used Peirce's logic to correct and embellish Whitehead's theory of propositional feelings. And I have used Whitehead's initial insights into the temporal structure of experi-

ence to explicitate the temporal aspects of Peirce's inferential processes. Finally, I have used Peirce's notion of thirdness to ground the reality of experiential access to the future as future. An emergent account of experience thus draws freely but critically on both thinkers and can be reduced finally to neither.

48. Peirce, *Collected Papers*, 5. 180–212, 6. 238–271, 7. 615–635; Whitehead, *Symbolism*, pp. 6–29; *Process and Reality*, pp. 195–248. A comparative reading of the above passages is an interesting exercise. Both Peirce and Whitehead affirmed the symbolic structure of experience, but on very different grounds: Whitehead by appealing to "symbolic reference," Peirce by appealing to "synechism" and to the inferential perception of thirdness. Peirce's theory seems to me to be the more adequate. It is used here and in *Charism and Sacrament* to ground a foundational theory of natural symbolism and to endow the notion of primordial sacramentality with greater philosophical precision than it enjoys in the thought of Rahner and Schillebeeckx.

49. Lonergan, *Method in Theology*, pp. xi–xii.

50. Jn. 19:4–16.

51. Karl Menninger, Martin Mayman, and Paul Pruyser, *The Vital Balance* (New York: Viking, 1963), pp. 125–152.

52. *Ibid.*, pp. 153–173.

53. *Ibid.*, pp. 174–212.

54. *Ibid.*, pp. 213–249.

55. *Ibid.*, pp. 250–262.

56. *Ibid.*, pp. 262–270.

57. T. W. Adorno, Else Frenkel-Brunswick, Daniel J. Levinson, R. Nevitt Sanford, et al., *The Authoritarian Personality* (New York: Harper, 1950), pp. 222–287; see also, Gordon W. Allport, *The Nature of Prejudice* (Garden City: Doubleday, 1954), pp. 371–397.

58. *Ibid.*, pp. 384.

59. *Ibid.*, pp. 385, 480–481.

60. *Ibid.*, p. 386.

61. *Ibid.*, pp. 386–387.

62. *Ibid.*, pp. 733–734; Allport, *Nature of Prejudice*, pp. 413–426.

63. Erich Fromm, *The Fear of Freedom* (London: Routledge and Kegan Paul, 1942), p. 131.

64. *Ibid.*, pp. 122–222.

65. Ricoeur, *Symbolism of Evil*, pp. 25–118.

66. *Ibid.*, pp. 118–159.

67. Edward F. Edinger, *Ego and Archetype* (Baltimore: Penguin, 1973), pp. 37–61.

68. Schubert M. Ogden, "Lonergan and the Subjectivist Principle," *Journal of Religion*, LX (1971), pp. 155–172.

69. William James, *Pluralistic Universe* (New York: Longmans, Green, 1909), pp. 60–68; cf. 1–40, 301–331. James was, I believe, quite correct to protest against Royce's automatic grounding of all finite reality in that of the All-Knower. In an emergent problematic, God can become the integrating cosmic ground of socialization but need not. The failure of any human self to achieve grounding in the divine reality is the descent into hell.

70. In *Process and Reality*, Whitehead speaks of evil (1) as the conflict

born of finite, creative processes whose subjective aims are irreconcilable and (2) as the perpetual perishing of things; *Process and Reality*, pp. 400–402. An emergent problematic goes beyond his refurbished Neo-Platonism and affirms evil as a positive force in the world. There is more to evil than just the absence of good or the conflicts born of finitude. The force of evil is finally the force of sin: those vectoral feelings that set reality in opposition to God, to Christ, and to the Holy Breath.

71. This is a common theme in Emerson. For typical expressions of it, see: Ralph Waldo Emerson, *Collected Works*, ed. Edward Emerson (14 vols.; Boston: Houghton Mifflin, 1903–1904), I, pp. 66–77, 227–244; II. pp. 3–41, 267–322.

72. This insight constitutes the only major debt to Tillich's system owed by a theology of human emergence; cf. Tillich, *Systematic Theology*, I, p. 53.

73. Teilhard de Chardin, *Phenomenon of Man*, pp. 77–160.

74. Is. 11:6–9; cf. Elanore Price Mather, *A Peaceable Season* (Princeton: Pyne, 1973).

75. Donald L. Gelpi, *Discerning the Spirit* (New York: Sheed and Ward, 1968), pp. 57–107; *Charism and Sacrament* (New York: Paulist, 1976), pp. 157–186; Otto Bird, "The Complexity of Love," *Thought*, XXXIX (June, 1964), pp. 210-220.

76. Daniel Day Williams, *The Spirit and Forms of Love* (New York: Harper and Row, 1968), pp. 1–89; see also: Anders Nygren, *Agape and Eros*, trans. Philip S. Watson (New York: Harper and Row, 1969), pp. 1–80; Martin C. D'Arcy, S.J., *The Mind and Heart of Love* (New York: Meridian, 1960).

77. Williams, *op. cit.*, p. 140.

78. *Ibid.*, p. 181.

79. Rahner, *Theological Investigations*, I, pp. 149–200; III, pp. 35–46; IV, pp. 105–120.

80. Karl Rahner, *Spirit in the World*, trans. William Dych, S.J. (Montreal: Palm, 1949); *Hearers of the Word*, trans. Michael Richards (New York: Herder and Herder, 1969).

81. Before we proceed to a consideration of these questions, it will perhaps be clarifying to note the analogies between the position just sketched and Jonathan Edwards's theology of true virtue. For that theology and the spirituality of Ignatius Loyola it resembles have in part inspired the preceding analysis and will color much of what follows.

Edwards defined "true virtue" as "the cordial consent of being to Being-in-general." His definition implied several basic beliefs: (1) that virtuous activity is unintelligible outside of a religious context; (2) that consent to God incarnate engages one totally: affectively, intellectually, practically; (3) that an authentic human experience of God is psychologically akin to esthetic experience; (4) that authentic cordial consent to God is always a response to a prior divine initiative. With all these positions, an emergent view of human experience stands in substantial agreement, although as we shall see authentic consent to "Being-in-general" may in fact begin to emerge in experience only with the higher stages of mystical prayer. For only then does the human self give evidence of beginning to transcend the crochets and neuroses of ego-consciousness. Still, virtuous consent to God is possible within ego-consciousness.

An emergent anthropology attempts, however, to defend the above

theses on different grounds from Edwards himself. It eschews his predestina-
tionist theology and the idealistic metaphysics that subtend his vision. Edwards, like Berkeley, sought to construct the world out of substantial spirits
and their ideas. Despite his fascination with Lockean psychology, or perhaps
because of it, he sought to subsume the realm of fact into the realm of quality.
Like most scholastic thinkers he accepted "being," not "experience," as his
central, unifying metaphysical concept. He never questioned the legitimacy
of the traditional Greek distinction between matter and spirit. An emergent
problematic rejects all of these speculative stances as inadequate and misleading. Cf. Jonathan Edwards, *The Nature of True Virtue* (Ann Arbor:
University of Michigan, 1969); Delattre, *Beauty and Sensibility in the
Thought of Jonathan Edwards* (New Haven: Yale, 1962).

IV. The Breath of God

Our initial foundational analysis of the Christian search for salvific integration has disclosed a nest of interrelated questions. At the close of the last chapter we were able to formulate the first question in the following terms: "If it is the Spirit of Jesus who gives present cognitive access to the mystery of God incarnate, then what does it mean to speak of the transformation of experience in the power of the Spirit?"

A glance at our topos indicates that the trail before us meanders for some time in the realm of religious imagery. We will reflect on the Biblical images that surround the Christian experience of Spirit. Then we will contrast those images with those that shaped a Gnostic sense of "spirit." We will reflect on the irreconcilable religious visions implicit in these two image clusters. Finally, we will suggest how Christian Neo-Platonism mediated the theological assimilation of a modified Gnostic iconography of "spirit." On the basis of these reflections, we will conclude to the necessity of redefining our theological understanding of "spirit" in abstract, conceptual terms that better conform to the original Biblical experience of "spirit."

Our trail will then double back over some of the material discussed at the end of the preceding chapter but at a higher elevation. We will begin an examination of the conflict between the Spirit of Christ and the first of the dark powers described at the end of the last chapter. We will suggest that the healing of personality dysfunctions in faith lies at the heart of what St. John of the Cross means by the "dark night of sense." At the close of this analysis we will find ourselves standing almost directly above the trailhead, but at a considerable elevation. For our insights will have led us to the realization that the integration of human experience in Christian faith is its healing through the power of the Spirit in conversion. The trail before us is clearly marked. Let us, then, begin to climb.

Images of Spirit

For a variety of historical reasons the contemporary Christian spontaneously opposes the notion of "spirit" to that of "matter." "Spirit" means what is immaterial, incorporeal, removed from sen-

122

sory experience. But the people who wrote the Bible thought of "spirit" in very different terms. For them "spirit" was like wind. It was force doing work. Though invisible like the wind, "spirit" nevertheless impinged upon experience. Its effects were felt, qualitatively recognizable, concrete.

Biblical imagery acknowledged both the creative and the destructive power of pneumatic energy. It could be the gentle breeze that brings peace, or the refreshing wind that brings the rains to renew the face of the land. But pneumatic power could also be the destructive force in the raging storm, or the desiccating blast of the desert sirocco that dries up all life in its passage.[1]

In the Jewish and Christian scriptures, pneumatic force is also "breath," the life source in things that moves and enlivens them. The breath of life in human beings is, therefore, diversified in the different "spirits" that move the heart: pride, anger, joy, fear. Since these "spirits" may also be either creative or destructive, they must be subjected to the discernment of wisdom and of faith.[2]

Not every "spirit" is, then, from God. The "Holy Spirit" is that pneumatic impulse that shapes human acts to God's salvific ends and thus transforms individuals into conscious visible instruments of divine, saving action. It raised up the leaders and teachers of the Hebrew religion: the judges, the prophets, the wise men, those anointed kings who were true servants of the Lord. It was present in Moses, the archetypal charismatic leader.[3]

Messianic expectation in post-exilic Judaism bred the popular hope for the coming of a religious hero in whom the Divine Breath would dwell with such power that he would be the compendium of all the great Jewish leaders of old.[4] It was also hoped that in the last age, a faithful God would bring into being a new Israel, covenanted heart and soul to God. Then each member of the people of God would have the kind of personal access to the Spirit of Yahweh that in an earlier age had been the prerogative of isolated charismatic leaders alone.

The first Christians had no doubt but that Jesus was the fulfillment of both of these hopes. The Breath of God dwelt in Him with a personal power that came to expression in His anointed teaching and in His miracles of healing. But the final proof that He was the Anointed of God was that as risen Lord He breathed His own Pentecostal Spirit into the hearts of His followers. For on Pentecost the Spirit had, through the outpouring of the charismatic gifts, begun to effect the same kind of visible transformation of the Christian community as had been effected in Jesus after His pneumatic anointing on the banks of the Jordan.[5]

In the New Testament, the experience of Spirit is, of course, associated with other images than "wind" and "breath." In the synoptic gospels the Spirit descends at Jesus' baptism under the sign of a dove in order to inaugurate His manifestation as the beloved Son of God, the beginning of a New Israel. In the Acts of the Apostles, the Spirit descends under the sign of "tongues like fire" to unite the world in the praise of God and to send the apostles forth to proclaim the good news. Fire is a standard biblical symbol for divine holiness. As fire, the Spirit purifies the hearts of believers while consuming in judgment those who stand opposed to the divine saving plan. In the gospel of John, the Spirit is compared to "living water," a sustaining source of refreshment, purification, and eternal life that springs up in the heart of each believer. Johannine theology also describes the Spirit as "another defense attorney" like Jesus, who vindicates the authenticity of Jesus' mission. Needless to say, such images explicate the first Christian community's felt sense of the scope of the Holy Spirit's saving action.[6]

The theological transition from the Biblical experience of "Spirit" as a divine force doing work in the world to the contemporary speculative equation of the "spiritual" with the "immaterial," the "incorporeal," and the "eternal" is an instructive chapter in the history of Christian thought. And an initial insight into some of its technicalities is important for the reflections that follow. The transition begins in the first century with the conflict between Christianity and Gnosticism.

The Gnostic Sense of "Spirit"

Gnosticism was a syncretistic mystical religion that flourished during the first four centuries of the Christian era. It expressed a profound revulsion against the growing decadence of Greco-Roman civilization. And it offered men and women a saving enlightenment that freed them from the corrupting influences of this world.[7]

Gnosticism gave rise to a bewildering variety of mythologies. But, as Hans Jonas has shown, they all tended to be dominated by a recurring cluster of interrelated images: images of alienation and of transcendence, images of the demonic and of the struggle of light and darkness, images of fallenness, of imprisonment, of dread, of forlornness, of homesickness, of numbness, of sleep. The Gnostic believer experienced existence in space and time as an "exile" from the soul's "true spiritual home." The world of matter and of the body was imagined as the soul's "prison." An "alien" in a strange land, the converted Gnostic felt keenly out of step with the corruption, the tedium, and the decadence of everyday human existence. The true

Gnostic longed, therefore, to return to the immutable realm of "light" and of "truth" from which the soul had "fallen," a realm totally removed from the violence, tawdriness, and corruption of "this world." This sense of alienation also shaped the Gnostic feeling for God. The God of Gnostic faith was conceived as "wholly other," for a true God could have nothing in common with the corrupt, "demonic" world of matter.[8]

Gnostic faith condemned human reason as corrupt; it repudiated philosophy as false wisdom. But Gnosticism was in fact a post-philosophical religion. And its myths contained a number of unacknowledged dualistic philosophical presuppositions, most of them Platonic.

Ego-consciousness grows through evaluative differentiation, and philosophy is an advanced, inferential form of ego-awareness. Philosophers must, then, distinguish the variables that shape experience. The dualistic philosophical mind, however, differentiates interrelated realities in such a way that their relationship to one another cannot thereafter be affectively or speculatively grasped or affirmed. Platonism, for example, portrayed the human person as composed of two distinct substances whose essential natures were so opposed that they could share nothing in common: the spiritual, immaterial soul and the physical, corporeal body.

Similarly, in its imaginative vision of the cosmos, Platonism proclaimed an essential and irreconcilable difference between the eternal and the temporal. It correlated the realm of eternity with the realm of spirit, and it found there the real, the true, the good, the essential, the intelligible. It equated the corporeal realm of the body with the illusory, the deceptive, the mutable, the sensory, the surd. And it challenged the seeker after wisdom to choose between these irreconcilable opposites.

In its account of human knowledge, Platonism distinguished sharply between the inner, spiritual enlightenment available to the soul in its solitary ascent to the eternal realm of truth, on the one hand, and external sensory awareness, on the other. It therefore sought the truth by withdrawing from external sensory illusions into the solitude of subjectivity.

Born during the twilight of the Athenian polis, Platonic thought stood in profound suspicion of existing social and political structures and located the perception of moral value in the subjective enlightenment of the individual conscience. It was an illumination that promised escape from enslavement to the body and from the corrupting influences of society.

In the lingering twilight of Greco-Roman civilization, Gnostic mythologies transformed the Platonic realm of matter into a mythic realm of evil and corruption created and controlled by personal demonic forces. These malignant powers, called aeons, kept the human spirit imprisoned in an alien and corrupt body, which darkened the mind by its passion and lust. The Gnostic was, then, even more convinced than the Platonist that neither truth nor reality could be found in sensory experience. Hence, the Gnostic search for religious enlightenment also led away from the material, sensory universe and from corrupt and sensual social structures. As in the case of Platonism, Gnostic enlightenment was, then, irreducibly individualistic and subjectivistic.

Gnosticism and Christianity in Conflict

The Christian gospel too offered a salvific enlightenment, but Christian faith understood both "salvation" and "enlightenment" in terms very different from Gnostic piety. The Gnostic religious mind acquiesced in the same cyclic conception of history as Neo-Platonism. But the Christian imagination was dominated by an eschatological view of the salvific process. In contrast to the Gnostic, therefore, the Christian saw history itself as instinct with religious meaning and as moving forward to conscious fulfillment in Christ. For the Gnostic, saving enlightenment could be achieved only by present disengagement from an endlessly repetitious historical circle of material corruption and defilement.

Similarly, both Christianity and Gnosticism affirmed that God is one. But Gnosticism projected a unity into God that was beyond all multiplicity whatever. The wholly other God of Gnosticism was, as a consequence, shrouded in a wordless silence that transcended all sensation, emotion, and rational comprehension. The Christian, on the other hand, believed that the one God had been historically revealed in the law and the prophets, and in the last age in the Word of God made flesh and in the mission of the Holy Spirit. As a consequence, the Christian God could be neither completely ineffable nor absolute one.

Gnostic belief that the body is evil and matter demonic also made the notion of an incarnate God blasphemous. In the world of Gnostic dualism, God could never enter into contaminating contact with. matter.

It is no wonder then that the two religions originally conceived of enlightenment in very different terms. Gnostic enlightenment was individualistic and subjectivistic, and it sundered salvific illumination from love of this-worldly realities. Christianity, on the other hand,

offered an enlightenment that is incarnational, charismatic, and ecclesial. The God whose face was revealed in the physical face of Jesus
is the same God whose glory is revealed in the charismatically inspired words and deeds of the community that was born on Pentecost
day. Moreover, true Christian enlightenment is not, as the first letter
of John insists, divorced from love. It is in the final analysis the
knowing that is loving. Christian faith, therefore, provides no excuse
for spitting in contempt either upon the sensible, material universe or
upon human values and social institutions. Instead, it binds one
irrevocably and absolutely to serve in this world as God's chosen
instrument for the salvific transformation of the physical universe and
of human society as well.

Gnostic subjectivism combined with its suspicion of human
reason to cause its devotees to veer unpredictably between
sadomasochistic rigorism and a destructive, licentious antinomianism. The Gnostic rigorist demonstrated an enlightened
superiority to the corruptions of sense experience by subjecting his or
her body to an exaggerated ascetical discipline. Or (s)he ridiculed
accepted social mores as corrupt and rational insight into moral
obligation as unspiritual. To "prove" that true spiritual enlightenment
placed one beyond all sensible taint, the Gnostic was not above
indulging in morally licentious acts or justifying violence in the name
of religious enlightenment. Christian enlightenment, however, brings
no such liberation from moral restraint. It demands all that the
decalogue demanded and more.

For the Gnostic, to sin was to fall from a purely spiritual existence to a state of bondage to the body and to the demonic forces that
rule the material sensible universe. But for the Christian, "sin" is not
a fall from some preexistent state of immaterial, spiritual enlightenment. Sin is deviation from the salvific goal that God has set for the
historical process. Gnostic mysticism, moreover, promised escape
from sin through a mystical insight into the soul's essential divinity.
The Christian sought enlightenment through recommitment to the
God of history in a repentance and covenanted love that bound the
believer to seek the salvific transformation of this world.

The Affective Significance of Gnosticism

The mythic caste of Gnostic thought links it to the realm of
physical purpose. There are three clues to the sources of its affective
power: the dualistic caste of Gnostic thought, its repudiation of inferential forms of knowing, and the negative caste of its dominant mythic images. The Gnostic imagination was dominated by

images of fallenness, numbness, dread, alienation. Its dualistic vision of the world was the imaginative projection of personal fragmentation. Its anti-intellectualism set inference at odds with affectivity. All of these symptoms suggest an ego in a state of deflation and disintegration.

The Greeks had a name for ego-inflation. They called it *hybris*, pride. And they saw that life itself conspires with nature to bring the inflated ego down, like Icarus in the tangle of his wings. When it overextends itself, the ego posits what Jung has called "the inflated act." The inflated act is some deed done in the expectation of success that wreaks havoc for oneself or for others. It reveals to the inflated ego the narrowness of its self-infatuated vision and the folly of its complacent self-assurance. It discloses the dark, unconscious purposes that often hide beneath conscious rationalizations. And by precipitating failure and rejection, it forces the ego to confront its shadow self. Faced with the collapse of its familiar world, the deflated ego feels fragmented, disoriented, oppressed by forces it can no longer dominate and control. Its mood is one of alienation.[9]

The healthy ego is able to survive such setbacks. Recognition of its folly motivates a change of heart and the realistic adjustment of conscious expectations. Acknowledgment of the shadow brings repentance; and, in a healthy environment, repentance bears fruit in renewed acceptance by others and the initial restoration of self-confidence. Before long, the ego is once again riding high, ready for another fall. The healthy ego repeats this cycle again and again.

But ego-consciousness develops in a social matrix. A supportive social matrix tends to reinforce the self-confidence that breeds inflation. And it provides comfort and rehabilitation in moments of deflation and depression. A decadent and disintegrating social milieu breeds the evaluative disintegration of the self.

The Gnostic religion developed in a society that was in an advanced stage of decadence. It was a society that bred deflation and disillusionment. Gnostic affectivity was as a result suffused with a sense of futility and fallenness; with feelings of paralysis and of impotence; with a sense of meaninglessness, of isolation, and of rejection; with a dread of facing the demons within that bar one's way to wholeness and peace of heart; with the need to reconstruct one's world in solipsistic issolation.

Once the affective significance of many Gnostic images is grasped, the perennial appeal of Gnostic patterns of thought becomes more intelligible. Gnostic imagery informs the more radical expressions of Romanticism, just as it interprets the perennial crisis of adolescence. It resurfaces whenever human and religious idealism has been shattered against the forces of corruption and decadence. Gnostic patterns of thinking have helped to shape every movement of divisive mysticism: Montanism, Circumcellianism, Catharism, Spiritualism, Albigensianism, Waldensianism, Anabaptism, Jansenism, Quietism, classical Calvinism, "inner light" Quakerism, Moravianism, "new light" revivalism, classical Pentecostalism. Secularized Gnostic tendencies can be discerned in Cartesian rationalism, in the "enlightened" ethical religions of the eighteenth century, in twentieth-century existentialism, in aquarian mysticism.

But Gnostic solutions to the human religious dilemma do more than interpret the sense of alienation that is born of ego-disintegration. The Gnostic religion is filled with images of saving light. But Gnostic enlightenment does not yield reconciliation with this world in atoning love. Rather it yields the self-righteous conviction of one's elevation above the common herd. It gives religious justification to its own sense of alienation by characterizing the world as essentially demonic. As a consequence, Gnostic enlightenment eschews responsibility for the decadent state of things. It breeds religious snobbery and contempt for others. And in affirming the soul's essential divinity it refuses to deal honestly with the unacknowledged fear, anger, and guilt that lie at the heart of its alleged conversion. In other words, Gnostic imagery interprets and reinforces the physical purposes that the pharisaical conscience reduces to inferential clarity and precision.

It was, then, inevitable that Christianity and Gnosticism should collide. For in the last analysis, the two religions offered solutions to the religious question that were at the level of appreciative consciousness diametrically and irreconcilably opposed. It is, then, truly ironic that Christian theology gradually acquiesced in a dualistic vision of the world not that far removed from the dualism that dominated so much of Gnostic piety. That acquiescence was, of course, effected by the speculative alliance of Christian theology with Neo-Platonic mysticism and metaphysics. This improbable alliance becomes more intelligible, however, once one understands that Neo-Platonism and Gnosticism themselves stood dialectically opposed on three important issues.

Gnosticism vs. Neo-Platonism

The Neo-Platonist was as much of a dualist as the devout Gnostic. But the Neo-Platonist repudiated the Gnostic attempt to portray matter as evil. In Neo-Platonic mysticism, physical shapes and forms are illusory but not corrupt, an imperfect reflection of an eternal, spiritual beauty.

Neo-Platonism also rejected the antinomianism that characterized Gnostic ethical teaching. Gnostic enlightenment regarded every product of human reason as decadent and corrupt. Nor could the Gnostic find a principle of morality within nature itself; for in a Gnostic universe nature is the creation of malignant, demonic powers. Neo-Platonism, by contrast, affirmed with the Stoics the existence of an immutable natural law. It located this natural principle of right conduct in a transcendent divine intelligence, or *Nous*. And it affirmed that each individual has personal subjective access to this eternal principle of right reason.

Finally the Gnostic attributed the fall of each soul into matter to some forgotten moral fault. It is some primordial sin that exiles the Gnostic soul from the eternal realm of spirit and imprisons it in a body darkened by passion and by lust. But for the Neo-Platonist, the fall of the soul was a regrettable metaphysical necessity, not the expression of personal guilt.[10]

The Theological Impact of Neo-Platonism

But while Neo-Platonism rejected three basic tenets of Gnostic piety, on many other issues the Gnostic and the Neo-Platonist were in complete accord. Both were cosmic and psychological dualists. Both preached a form of salvific enlightenment that was individualistic and subjectivistic. Both located the true essence of each person in his or her spiritual soul. Both acknowledged the need to free the soul from the fleshy trammels of the body. Both preached the possibility of a salvific escape to an eternal, immutable realm of truth and of pure spiritual light. Both acquiesced in a cyclic view of time and believed that salvation could only lie in the escape from history, from the ceaseless repetition of temporal acts devoid of salvific meaning and purpose.

One of the ironies of Western theology is, then, that despite the initial confrontation between Christian faith and Gnostic enlightenment, by the high Middle Ages many of the Platonic dualisms present in exaggerated form in Gnostic piety had impregnated large areas of Christian belief and ascetical practice. Under the inspiration of Augustine and of Pseudo Dionysus,[11] Christian theological speculation had acquired a dualistic bent in its approach to human nature, to human knowledge, and to the cosmos. Monasticism had over the centuries attenuated somewhat the Gnostic individualism that sometimes marred the piety of the Christian hermits. But all too often Christian prayer was depicted, not as the communal sharing of the gifts of the Spirit, but as withdrawal from the body and from the senses in order to ascend within subjectivity to the eternal source of

light and truth. The rigorism and antinomianism that Gnostic subjectivism breeds, its suspicion of the body and of sex, its chiliastic desire
to escape the corruptions of this world and to rest in an eternal,
immutable vision of God—religious impulses such as these emerged
in medieval piety with disconcerting regularity, often to be futilely
condemned by Church authorities. Moreover, in the wake of the
Black Death and in the face of the growing decadence of late medieval
culture, the dualistic vision popularized by Christian Platonism was
readily transformed into an angry disillusioned denunciation of the
decadence and demonic inspiration of social and ecclesiastical structures. Indeed, such denunciations would form the stock in trade of the
Protestant Reformation.

The Glories and the Woes of Thomism

The Thomistic revolution in the thirteenth century offered an
important speculative alternative to Platonized Christianity. It would
offer important qualifications to an Augustinian philosophy of
"spirit," qualifications that still affect contemporary theological
thinking. For Thomism was a partial repudiation of the epistemological and anthropological dualism popularized in academic circles by
Christian Platonism. Its occasion was the rediscovery of the texts of
Aristotle in the West, and with them of the Aristotelian critique of
Platonic theory. Immersion in Aristolelian logic, metaphysics, and
cosmology convinced Aquinas that the human mind discovers intelligibility in sensible, material things, not in some transcendent realm
of Platonic ideas. He therefore repudiated a Platonic theory of knowledge. He also denied the substantial dualism that characterizes a
Platonic view of the human person.

But Aquinas remained in many ways an Augustinian. With Augustine, he equated "Being as such" with "eternity" and "immutability." He therefore acquiesced in the cosmic dualism of time and
eternity that is one of the hallmarks of Platonic philosophy. The
divine *Ipsum Esse Subsistens* of Aquinas was in His own way as
immaterial and immutable as any Platonic idea, even though the
Thomistic God was conceived, not as a Platonic essence, but as the
metaphysical principle "act" expanded to infinity. Moreover, while
Aquinas denied direct access within subjectivity to the eternal ideas
of God, he imagined the divine mind in terms that were not too far
removed from the *Nous* of Neo-Platonic metaphysics.

In elaborating his revised anthropology, Aquinas remained extremely sensitive to the objections of Christian Platonists that the
application of Aristotelian hylemorphic theory to human nature

would lead inevitably to a denial of human immortality. But he proposed a complex and ingenious antidote to the philosophical hesitations of his adversaries.

He used an Aristotelian formal object analysis of the human faculties to argue that the substantial vital principle in each person, the soul, is possessed of two immaterial, inorganic powers: an intellectual power of conceptual abstraction and judgment and a volitional power of free choice and decision. Since in substance philosophy, activity follows being, Aquinas was able to argue against the Christian Platonists that the presence of purely spiritual, inorganic activities in the human soul was philosophical proof of the fact that it is immaterial and therefore capable of subsistence after death, even though it is by nature the form of the body. [12]

But ingenious as Aquinas's argument was, it labored under some serious tensions that continue to color our contemporary theological understanding of "spirit." Thomistic faculty psychology assumed that human actions (and therefore the faculties that ground them) can be defined by their formal objects. The material object of an action or faculty is the reality to which it is operationally ordered. Its formal object is the aspect under which it attains the object to which it is ordered. The faculty of sight, for example, perceives extended, material objects under the aspect of color.

Differences in the formal objects of two faculties render them really distinct. But really distinct faculties must have really distinct activities. Sensible activity must be really distinct from spiritual activity; cognitive activity, really distinct from appetitive; the action of the intellect, really distinct from the action of the will. Hence, for the human experience to grow and develop in a Thomistic psyche, the different faculties must somehow "move" one another to act. The external senses must somehow "move" the internal senses. The internal senses must "move" the intellect. The intellect must "move" the will.

Contemporary psychology has long since abandoned the language of faculty theory as inadequate to describe the growth of human experience. But even within the context of Thomistic philosophy, faculty theory labors under serious speculative tensions. The most basic problem of Thomistic faculty psychology is to reconcile this complex apparatus of faculties with the Aristotelian epistemological postulate that intelligibility is somehow derived from material, sensible things. For if the sensible faculties give one cognitive access to the intelligibility present within material substances, then they must somehow be able to "move" the spiritual intellect. Unfortunately, however, the human intellect, being immaterial, lies by definition beyond the operational scope of any sensible faculty.

To bridge the gulf between spiritual, intellectual knowledge and material, sensible knowledge, Thomistic psychology postulated, without proving, the existence of two distinct intellects in the human soul: one passive, the other active. The former was called the "possible intellect"; the latter, "the agent intellect." The unique function of the "agent intellect" was to use the material phantasm in the sensible imagination in order to "move" the possible intellect to act. Since in faculty psychology the phantasm is derived from the external senses, the theory seemed to account for the derivation of intelligibility from material, sensible reality, while appeal to the agent intellect seemed to explain why a lower faculty could produce an effect upon a higher faculty that exceeded the scope of the former's formal object.

When contrasted with other medieval accounts of the "agent intellect" Aquinas's position is at one level a forthright and admirable affirmation that the human mind has all that it needs in order to reach insight and understanding. What is questionable are the speculative terms in which the affirmation is made. Aquinas suggested that the action of the agent intellect was not unlike the action of a person using a pen to make intelligible marks upon a page. Of itself the pen could make only marks. But its use by a human being endowed it with the power to write not only marks but intelligible words. The analogy, of course, limped. For while a pen writes on an essentially corporeal reality like paper, the sensible phantasm was supposed to "write" not on paper but on the immaterial possible intellect. For the immaterial agent intellect to use the sensible phantasm to move the immaterial possible intellect to act would, then, be closer to one Thomistic angel using a slide projector in order to project, not an image, but an idea onto another Thomistic angel. In other words, it is finally impossible within the operational dualism espoused by faculty theory to provide a convincing account of how the lower, sensible faculties may be meaningfully said to move the higher spiritual faculties to act. Nor does elaborate rhetoric about the "spiritualizing power" of the agent intellect finally resolve the dilemma.

The Impact of Thomism

It is, of course, all too easy to fault Thomistic faculty theory from the standpoint of contemporary philosophy and psychology. Our purpose here is not to mount a detailed critique of Aquinas but only to call attention to questionable aspects of a Thomistic philosophy of "spirit." For as in the case of Christian Platonism the impact of

Thomism on Christian doctrine has over the ages been profound.

In 1312 the Council of Vienne repudiated a Platonic theory of the human soul and proclaimed that the "substance" of the rational principle in each human person is truly, of itself, and essentially the "form of the body." The decree was a condemnation of the Platonizing theories of Peter John Olivi. And while its language is not technically Thomistic, its intent is clearly convergent with the vision of Aquinas.[13]

Moreover, through the Thomistic revival in the nineteenth and early twentieth centuries, faculty theory continues to exert a profound influence on contemporary Catholic theology. Some of the most popular theological theories of Karl Rahner are predicated on the dubious existence of a Thomistic "agent intellect" in each human soul. The early work of Bernard Lonergan also acquiesced in Thomistic faculty theory as do the more recent statements issuing from the Vatican on human sexual morality.

On the other hand, more recent Catholic thought gives evidence of a growing theological malaise over the continued credibility of medieval faculty theory. In his more recent writings Lonergan has in fact repudiated faculty psychology outright. Other theologians, like Joseph Powers, S.J., have attempted under the influence of horizon analysis to redefine "spirit" in terms that prescind from faculty theory as such.[14] The emergent theory of human experience proposed in these pages concurs in that malaise, and it seeks to press the Thomistic critique of Platonic dualism beyond positions possible to Aquinas in the thirteenth century.

Beyond Thomism

An emergent account of human experience abolishes substantial, epistemological, social, and operational dualism. Substantial dualism shatters the world into things that exist in themselves but not in anything else. Epistemological dualism sunders subjectivity from objectivity. Social dualism isolates the individual from society. Operational dualism divides human faculties into those that are essentially spiritual and those that are essentially material. A discussion of cosmic dualism, which divides the universe into two essentially different realms, the temporal and the eternal, lies outside the scope of a foundational anthropology and must be postponed for another study.

That an emergent view of experience rejects substantial dualism should by now be clear. An emergent anthropology is wholly convergent with the teaching of the Council of Vienne concerning the relation of "soul" and "body." But unlike Vienne it attempts to describe human unity in terms not employed by substance philosophy. An emergent anthropology speaks of the relational unity of the "self" and its "sustained environment" rather than of the unity of the "substance of the soul" and the "body." Implicit in that terminological shift is, of course, the abandonment of the very category "substance."

The negation of the notion of substance entails the principles of inexistence and of mutual inexistence. Those principles prohibit any hard-and-fast distinction between subjectivity and objectivity. They therefore exclude dualistic theories of human knowing. The same principles also forbid any attempt to understand individuals in abstraction from the natural, social, political, and religious environments that shape them and that they in turn transform.

An emergent anthropology also rejects operational dualism. It speaks instead of the self as a developing, habitual principle for the ongoing harmonization of different kinds of feeling. In the process an emergent account of human activity replaces "essential" distinctions among faculties with a theory of the ongoing transmutation of feeling. As a consequence an emergent hypothesis neither affirms nor denies the "spiritual" character of intellectual and volitional activity in the sense intended by Thomistic faculty theory. Nor does it characterize them as "material." Instead, it abandons both categories as speculatively misleading and foundationally inadequate.

Pneumatic Transformation

The abandonment of "spirit-matter" language in one's account of the human opens the door to a foundational reevaluation of the biblical images of "spirit" noted at the beginning of this chapter. The different "winds," or "spirits," described in the Bible are the laws that give experience purpose and direction. Those dynamic tendencies may be creative or destructive. They may also be either spatio-temporal or divine. For among them is the experience of the "Holy Breath" of Jesus, that pneumatic force whom Paul aptly described as the "law" that replaces the written Mosaic code.

This foundational redefinition of the "spirits" described in Sacred Scripture as legal, vectoral feelings has some important speculative consequences. As long as Christian theology attempted to move within the technical parameters set by Platonic or Thomistic vocabulary, it had to equate the term "spirit" with a certain kind of immutable "essence." In an emergent problematic, the laws that shape experience are not essences. They are evolving principles of evaluation and reactive decision. Their character is defined by their history and consequences: by the facts, evaluations, and decisions that shape them cumulatively and by their capacity to reshape the world through evaluative and decisive activity.

In such a universe, the "Spirit of God and of Jesus" is also interpreted, not as an essence, but as a force at work in the world. In what touches the development of a Christian faith experience, we can, then, speak of its "pneumatic transformation" in terms not far removed from those used by the apostle Paul in his account of the activity of the Spirit of Jesus. The "Holy Breath" of Jesus is a life-force functioning in the midst of other vectoral feelings that shape experience. The history of the Breath's influence upon human experience can be described; its future consequences anticipated.

The pneumatic transformation of experience, its transmutation in the power of the Breath of Jesus, becomes then the present enterprise of salvation and redemption. In such an enterprise, the stakes are frighteningly high. For even now God stands locked in a cosmic struggle with the powers of darkness. At any moment it is possible for any individual to exclude the saving impulses of the Breath of Jesus from experience and thus thwart God by joining forces with the powers of violence, oppression, hypocrisy, and complacency. William James has suggested that the only kind of God who satisfies human affectivity is one who needs the world, needs me in order to accomplish His divine aims. In an emergent universe, God's involvement with the world is a result of God's free and gracious choice. But once involved God needs the world, not in order to become God (as Whitehead and Hartshorne suggest), but in order to accomplish His salvific ends.[15] For having created a world instinct with freedom and having chosen in His dealings with us to enhance rather than abolish freedom, God cannot save us without our cooperation.

If, then, the pneumatic transformation of experience lies at the heart of the salvific enterprise, in what does it consist? Those with the greatest insight into the dynamics of pneumatic transformation are those who have advanced furthest in holiness: the Christian saints and mystics. They all assure us that the salvific transmutation of experience proceeds in distinguishable stages but that it must begin with what St. John of the Cross has called "the dark night of sense."

The Meaning of the "Dark Night of Sense"

Most people dread the "dark nights" described by John as times of intense personal suffering. The fear is in part justified. The "dark night" is a season of purification through suffering. But the "dark nights" celebrated by John in his poetry are first of all and above all nights of love, nights of assignation when the Divine Lover and the beloved escape, meet, are betrothed, and finally united in the mystical marriage.

O guiding night!
O night more lovely than the dawn!
O night that has united
The Lover with His beloved,
Transforming the beloved in her Lover.

Upon His flowering breast
Which I kept wholly for Him alone,
There He lay sleeping,
And I caressing Him
There in a breeze from the fanning cedars. . . .

I abandoned and forgot myself,
Laying my face on my Beloved;
All things ceased; I went out from myself,
Leaving my cares
Forgotten among the lilies.[16]

The "dark night of sense" is the first of four such nights. It is a period in which disordered affectivity that obstructs divine union is brought to a preliminary healing in faith. The affections in question are described by John as those that "weary, darken, defile, torment, and weaken" the self. They are, in other words, the first of the "dark powers" described in the preceding chapter: the repressed fear, anger, shame, and guilt that motivate personality disintegration.[17]

Such affections weary and torment, for they set one at odds with oneself: at the second level of personality dysfunction they bear fruit in destructive attitudes and activities, in frozen personalities and in costly psychosomatic illnesses. Repressed negative affections darken and confuse the human heart; at the third level of dysfunction, they give rise to sexual aberrations and moral callousness. At the fourth level they induce autistic, solipsistic withdrawal from reality. Such disordered feelings are defiling, for they enslave the self to irrational feelings of guilt and to destructive taboos; but, as Paul Ricoeur has noted, the most primitive form of religious awareness of evil is a vague sense of defilement. Repressed negative feelings debilitate and weaken by undermining healthy ego-strength and by prohibiting balanced personality development.

If the account of human experience proposed in these pages is sound, these disordered affections can be healed in faith only when the physical purposes that shape experience are transformed in the power of the Holy Breath. The pneumatic transformation of physical purpose has two dimensions: one environmental, the other personal and attitudinal.

When anger, fear, and guilt lie buried in the heart they still shape behavior in destructive ways; and behavior in turn shapes environments. Behavior born of unhealed anger, fear, and guilt creates environments infected with violence, bigotry, and oppression, environments in which the pharisaical conscience spawns plausible rationalizations for irrational deeds of violence.

To the extent that human environments lie under the shadow of the dark powers, they may be legitimately characterized as "diabolic" and "demonic." These two terms are related, but not synonymous. The "diabolic" is opposed to the "symbolic." Anything may be legitimately called "symbolic" that mediates the creation and evaluative grasp of meaning. The "diabolic" by contrast shatters, thwarts, and counterfeits meaning. It is violence, hypocrisy, and falsehood blandly masquerading as wisdom, sanity, and enlightenment.

The "demonic" on the other hand designates an aspect of what Rollo May has called the "daimonic."[18] The term "daimon" is Greek in origin. Daimonic tendencies force themselves upon us and were for that reason associated in Greek imagination with the idea of "fate." They resist clear inferential analysis and decisive, rational control. Traditionally, the "daimonic" has been associated with dreams, with creativity, with ecstasy, with frenzy, with madness. The "daimonic" is, in other words, a term for the unexpected surge of powerful physical purposes into consciousness.

Daimonic physical purposes may embody either sympathetic or negative affections. They may be good, not evil, yet religiously neutral. The daimonic comes to conscious expression in art and poetry, in the excitement of novel speculative insight, in erotic passion, in bigotry, in the sado-masochism of authoritarian forces, in psychotic acts of violence and suicide.

The term "demonic" designates the destructive power of the daimonic. But demonic power encompasses two distinguishable forces: the eruption of repressed anger, fear, and guilt, on the one hand; and, on the other, demonic harassment, obsession, and possession. In the case of the latter, the demonic gives some (though often ambiguous) evidence of manipulation by preternatural forces of evil.

As we shall also see, the "Satanic" is the demonic masquerading as the "divine."

The "demonic" lies at the basis of the "diabolic." For the negative daimonic powers either shatter or counterfeit meaning and purpose. If, then, the "symbolic" stands opposed to the "diabolic," the irreconcilable antagonist of the demonic is the Holy Breath of God. For transformation in the Breath of God is creative not only of meaning but of ultimate meaning and purpose.

The pneumatic transformation of experience imbues positive daimonic forces with authentic religious meaning. It creates environments that breathe of religious faith, hope, and love. Experience is, as we have seen, irreducibly social. As the power of the Holy Breath interweaves with the developing fabric of experience, communities are born in which the influence of the dark powers can be disclosed, healed, and banished. Human affectivity is transformed into gracious affections; poetry, into prophecy; art, into liturgy; appreciative consciousness, into adoration, petition, thanksgiving, praise. As the physical purposes that shape experience are reshaped to the Spirit's own ends, Christian hope is born in the human heart, for religious hope becomes possible as repressed negative feelings are named and channeled in faith and love to creative ends.

Negative affections lie at the root of conservatism. The stronger they are, the more entrenched the conservatism they breed. It is for this reason that embittered conservatives are such sad, pitiful creatures, clinging in fear to a fading past while lashing out against the creative forces that challenge them to a realistic hope in the future.

If, then, the healing of affectivity breeds hope, deliverance and exorcism manifest the power of the Breath over preternatural, demonic influences which harass individuals.

Entering the Dark Night of Sense

We began our reflections on the pneumatic transformation of experience by distinguishing two conditions for entering into the dark night of sense: the creation of pneumatic, Breath-filled environments and the healing of disordered affectivity. Clearly, in an emergent problematic the two must go hand in hand.

The dark nights are shadow worlds in which the heart learns to acknowledge and forgive its own lovelessness by being forgiven in Jesus' name. My capacity to forgive others and be reconciled with others is, moreover, in part a function of my capacity to forgive myself. For as long as I flee the shadow, I am all too apt to be shadow-possessed and to lash out at those who reflect back to me aspects of myself that I fear and am unable to face.

But to face the shadow self in authentic Christian repentance is not to indulge in do-it-yourself salvation. The healing that takes place in the dark night is the work of the Breath. It must begin and end in faith. As a consequence entry into the dark night is through the narrow gate of prayer. Human psychopomps will always be helpful, of course: counsellors who are wise in the ways of the heart and of the Breath. But their function is in the last analysis catalytic.

But if the healing that occurs during the dark night of sense is the work of the Breath, it will not occur without an active response to the Breath's promptings. Especially important is constant, prayerful reflection on the life and teachings of Jesus and on the action of the Breath in Him, in His saints, and in the historical development of the Christian community over the ages.

As one passes into the dark night of sense, the first gift to be sought from God in prayer is, as Ignatius Loyola saw, an initial insight into the demands of the conversion process itself. I must find the freedom to acknowledge in the presence of the Lord that I am created for the divine praise, reverence, and service and that all things else are given me as means to that end. As a consequence, I must be willing to seek freedom of mind and of heart from bondage to anything that is not Breath-inspired, Breath-led. To seek such freedom is to set oneself in initial opposition to the dark powers.[19]

But no individual can conquer the dark powers without divine assistance. Before I confront them in my own life, therefore, I must seek from God a second gift: heartfelt conviction of His mercy and forgiveness. For only with the graced realization that there truly is nothing that can separate me from the love of God made visible in Jesus will I ultimately find the freedom I need to face and forgive my shadow self.[20]

The third gift to be sought from God in prayer is insight into my sinfulness. It is the Lord who must reveal to me my need for healing. It is the Lord who must grant me spontaneous repugnance for anything that leads away from Him. It is the Lord who must uncover to me the historical roots of the disorders that darken my life. It is the Lord who must grant me freedom of heart to eradicate them without fear insofar as it lies in my power to do so. All these graces must, then, be sought through petitionary prayer.[21]

Moreover, in the normal providence of God, it is only after all these graces have been granted in significant measure that I should begin to contemplate what it would be like to confront the dark powers alone, naked and stripped of the grace and love of God. For to contemplate such a prospect is to meditate the descent into hell. And if that imaginative descent is to be a healing one, it cannot, as Dante saw, be made alone. Nor should it be made prior to repentance and the heartfelt assurance of divine forgiveness.[22]

The Divine Beauty

But if the night of sense is a time of painful purification in fire and the Breath, it is also a night in which love is born. For it bears fruit, as both Edwards and Loyola saw, in a growing sensitivity to the divine beauty incarnate in Jesus and in those Breath-led persons whose lives are in some way like His.

Appreciative consciousness assumes many forms, and the sense of beauty is only one of them. Remorse, agitation, anxiety, terror, frustration, hostility, disgust, are all ways of feeling one's way toward an appreciative sense of the forces that shape situations. But such feelings yield no awareness of beauty. Indeed, beauty is always absent from the evaluative form of any experience whose affective elements are dominated by negative attitudes. The comic, for example, gives evidence of engaging the aggressive destructive drives. Their sublimation in laughter is enjoyable but not beautiful.[23]

The sense of beauty always engages the sympathetic emotions. The beautiful is the poignant, the tragic, the inspiring, the ecstatic. As repressed negative feelings find healing in faith and through the ministry of others, the capacity to respond sympathetically is correspondingly enhanced.[24] Once again, studies of the authoritarian personality cast some important light on the dynamics of emotional development. The typical authoritarian has no taste for art, poetry, literature, and is contemptuous of the tender human emotions. Authoritarians are inclined to despise and oppress women whom they regard as the human embodiment of emotional softness.[25]

At the same time, not every instance of esthetic appreciation is religious. Esthetic insight too can be marred by ego-inflation. When it is, it degenerates all to easily into a fatuous dilettantism or an effete academicism. Moreover, even the evaluative form of an authentic esthetic experience may be untouched by any sense of faith in God.

On the other hand, as both Edwards and Loyola realized, authentic openness in faith to the beauty of God revealed in Jesus nourishes sensitivity to beauty in all of its natural and human manifestations. In his *Personal Narrative* Edwards describes the affective transformation of heart wrought by his own cordial conversion to Christ.

I began to have a new kind of apprehensions and ideas

of Christ, and the work of redemption, and the glorious way
of salvation by him. An inward, sweet sense of these things,
at times, came into my heart; and my soul was led away in
pleasant views and contemplations of them. And my mind
was greatly engaged to spend my time in reading and
meditating on Christ, on the beauty and excellency of his
person, and the lovely way of salvation by free grace in him.
I found no books so delightful to me, as those that treated of
these subjects.

Not long after I first began to experience these things,
. . . I walked abroad alone, in a solitary place in my father's
pasture, for contemplation. And as I was walking there, and
looking up on the sky and clouds, there came into my mind
so sweet a sense of the glorious *majesty* and *grace* of God,
that I know not how to express. I seemed to see them both in
a sweet conjunction; majesty and meekness joined together;
it was a sweet, and gentle, and holy majesty; and also a
majestic meekness; an awful sweetness; a high, and great,
and holy gentleness.

After this my sense of divine things gradually increased,
and became more and more lively, and had more of that
inward sweetness. The appearance of every thing was altered; there seemed to be, as it were, a calm, sweet cast, or
appearance of divine glory, in almost every thing. God's
excellency, his wisdom, his purity and love, seemed to
appear in every thing; in the sun, moon, and stars; in the
clouds, and blue sky; in the grass, flowers, trees; in the
water, and all nature; which used greatly to fix my mind. I
often used to sit and view the moon for continuance; and in
the day, spent much time in viewing the clouds and sky, to
behold the sweet glory of God in these things; in the mean
time, singing forth, with a low voice my contemplations of
the Creator and Redeemer. And scarce any thing, among all
the works of nature, was so sweet to me as thunder and
lightning; formerly, nothing had been so terrible to me. . . .
While thus engaged, it always seemed natural to me to sing,
or chant for my meditations; or, to speak my thoughts in
soliloquies with a singing voice.[26]

Confrontation with the shadow self is emotionally deflating. But
contemplation of the divine beauty is healing and integrating. Its fruit
is praise and an assent of faith instinct with enthusiasm. Esthetic

appreciation of the ethical traits incarnate in Jesus motivates, as Edwards saw, the works of Christian virtue; it inspires deeds of mercy, forgiveness, compassion, tenderness, love. Moreover, whenever religious assent lacks an esthetic dimension, it degenerates, as Hans Urs von Balthasar observes, into the sterile repetition of creedal formulas and wearisome fidelity to increasingly repugnant religious obligations.

Clearly, then, the pneumatic transformation of physical purpose lies at the heart of the earliest stages of religious growth. Moreover, as sensitivity to the divine beauty waxes, it yields new insight into unhealed corners of the heart where the light of Christ has yet to penetrate. As they are exposed to the Breath's healing touch, the emerging self is confirmed in a stable orientation toward God in expectant hope and love. At the same time, a deepening sense of the healing presence of God in prayer creates a heartfelt conviction of the divine reality and truth that lies deeper than any abstract inferential formulation of belief or philosophical proof of God's existence.

The Morphology of Christian Hope

Hopelessness describes the impact of the dark powers upon human affectivity. The hopeless, as William Lynch has correctly noted, are overwhelmed with a sense of helplessness. The environmental forces that assault them and the confusions born of past suffering, frustration, and failure are more than they can understand, control, and endure.[27]

As one sinks into hopelessness, imagination dies. The reason is not far to seek. Anger, fear, and guilt are notoriously conservative in their impact on personality development. Their repression, as we have already seen, breeds rigidity of heart and mind: frozen personality reactions, bigotry, and authoritarianism. Refusal to face negative feelings can, then, lead to painful entrapment in neurotic complexes. Hopelessness becomes a gladiator's net; struggle achieves only further entanglement.[28] Abraham Maslow describes the dynamic:

> Complete neurotic dependence implies expectations that must be thwarted. This necessary thwarting creates anger additional to that probably already involved by the admission of weakness and helplessness implicit in complete dependence. This anger, however, tends to be directed against the very person on whom one is dependent and through whose help one hopes to avoid catastrophe, and such anger feelings immediately lead to guilt, anxiety, fear of

retaliation, etc. But these states are among the very factors that produced need for complete dependence in the first place. Examination of such a patient will show *at any one moment* most of these factors coexisting in continual flux and mutual re-enforcement. While a genetic analysis may show priority of one over another in time, a dynamic analysis will never show this. All the factors will be equally causes and effects.[29]

Hope is born with the capacity to wish for something better. As repressed negative feelings are with help and support named and brought to conscious healing, the rigidity of mind and heart they inspire begins to dissolve. Negative feelings can begin to be either sublimated in harmless ways or channeled to creative ends. New imaginative vistas of sympathetic feeling, thought, and action begin to be disclosed. The possibility of re-creating one's world begins to be believable.[30]

Hopelessness isolates one from reality. It breeds personality disintegration, autistic withdrawal, and eventually suicide. The hopeful, by contrast, grapple with life and reality. They are alert to factual limits and concerned to organize life forces for creative purposes. Hence, true hope, no matter how idealistic its ultimate goals, never diminishes the capacity to deal realistically with short-term objectives. At the same time hope is incompatible with cynicism. It searches for the laws and purposes behind factual limitation that give them meaning and potential plasticity. Hope is the force behind every creative use of the imagination.[31]

If human hope inspires the creative search for meaning, religious hope inspires the creative search for ultimate meaning. Christian hope discovers that meaning in the incarnate Word and in those events of salvation history shaped by the action of the divine Breath. It affirms the abiding legal tendency that inspires its vision to be none other than the Breath of the Living God.

Eschatology is, then, Christian hope moving toward an ever greater consciousness of the new and exciting possibilities created by the pneumatic transformation of experience. It aspires to the total transformation of experience in God. But it envisages short-term objectives that are concrete and wholly historical in character. Christian hope is not then confined, as both Mircea Eliade and Jürgen Moltmann have insisted, to some eternal future that will be revealed when time is at an end.[32] On the contrary, while Christian hope longs for the final and full establishment of God's reign, it is also thoroughly realistic. It yields insight into the present possibilities of transformation in God.

Indeed, authentic Christian hope encompasses both the past and the future in its present longing and aspiration. For it discovers in God's past fidelity to His promises assurance of His present and future faithfulness. Needless to say, for the Christian Jesus' resurrection, His total transformation in the power of the Spirit, provides the ultimate realistic basis for all religious hope. Hope allows us to imagine and believe that the Breath who raised Jesus from the dead can do the same for all who believe. We will return to this insight in the final chapter.[33]

At the same time, belief in the saving promises of God implies that the salvation promised does not yet exist in its fullness. Who hopes for what is seen? But Christian hope also finds present evidence that that salvation is even now in process of accomplishment. Hope then sets the Christian, as Moltmann correctly insists, in creative tension with the world as (s)he finds it. It binds one to oppose the powers of darkness in the name of Jesus and in the power of His Breath; and it demands the creative transformation of any merely human value in faith and through the anointing of that same Breath.

The Shape of the Christian Imagination

In the *Varieties of Religious Experience*, William James argues, correctly I believe, that "temperament," by which he means vague affective attitudes, conditions the ways in which we imagine our worlds and think of them. He attempts to describe three distinguishable kinds of religiously significant temperament: the healthy-minded individual, the sick soul, and the convert.[34] Healthy minded persons have yet to cross the "pain-threshold." Their vision of the world is optimistic. For a variety of affective reasons, they tend to ignore or deny the forces of disintegration, destruction, and death. They are, in a word, ego-inflated. Their imaginations will, as a consequence, tend to be what William Lynch has called either "exploitative" or "rebounding."[35]

The exploitative imagination does not value dative presentations of fact in their own right but regards the realm of the concrete as a pure instrumentality. It is the kind of imagination that would transform a giant sequoia into newspaper pulp. It is the imagination of the ego-inflated extravert.

The rebounding imagination also touches dative values only superficially. It does not manipulate the factual but recoils from it into solitary, and vaguely narcissicistic contemplation. It is the imagina-

tion of the naive, impractical idealist, i.e., of the ego-inflated introvert.

"Sick souls," on the other hand, have crossed the pain threshold
and done so with a vengeance. They have known the anguish of
subjection to the "dark powers" and are as a consequence oversen-
sitized to the presence of evil and of pain. They betray, in other
words, the symptoms either of ego-deflation or of more serious forms
of personality dysfunction. Their imagination will, as a consequence,
tend to what Lynch has called the imagination of the "double-
vacuum" or of the "pure fact."

Like the rebounding imagination, the imagination of the double
vacuum is introverted. It recoils from the factual and the finite but it
does so in disgust, boredom, and anger. And it finds "within" a chaos
of unintelligible feelings. It is the imagination of the hopeless. The
imagination of the pure fact is, by contrast, extraverted. It confronts
the world of the concrete but finds no meaning there. Appreciative
and inferential insight is blocked. The discovery of religious meaning
in the concrete and factual is even further from question. It is the
imagination of the sceptic, the cynic.[36]

The convert, on the other hand, strikes a middle ground between
healthy-mindedness and soul-sickness. Converts pass through the
pain of ego-deflation and the subsequent re-construction of meaning.
It is the only kind of imagination adequate to the Christian experience. The workings of the ego-inflated imagination are incompatible
with the Christian word "repent." The workings of the soul-sick
imagination are incompatible with the Christian word "believe the
good news."

James himself, who survived a period of emotional collapse by
his "will to believe," seems to have felt that conversion provides the
only emotionally adequate response to the complexities of human
experience. An emergent anthropology concurs in that judgment.

Christian hope is born of conversion. It is the fruit, not of a
Promethean attempt to create meaning self-reliantly, but of a relationship of faith-dependence on Jesus, the Breath-baptizer. Because
it transcends the follies of ego-inflation, the Christian imagination is
neither exploitative nor rebounding. Because it transcends ego-
deflation and disintegration, it transcends the imagination of the
double vacuum and of pure fact. The Christian imagination gives,
therefore, full value to dative presentations of value and seeks to
enhance them. It does not recoil from the concrete nor is it
checkmated by facts. Rather it plunges into the world of the concrete
in search of meaning and of divine beauty incarnate.

Lynch, drawing his inspiration from medieval exegesis, has suggested that the Christian imagination moves progressively through four distinguishable realms of meaning.[37] They correspond to the four stages in growth of consciousness described in the preceding chapter. Literal meaning corresponds to dative feeling and to the early phases of physical purpose; both yield a more or less vague sense of facts and their corresponding relationships. Allegorical meaning structures appreciative understanding and corresponds to the realm of archetypal and imagistic thought. It grows through metaphor, free association and synchronicity. Anagogical meaning is found in the inferential grasp of truth. Tropological meaning is ethical insight into the conditions and consequences of responsible decision.

To bypass the dative presentation of fact is to become the prisoner of one's own fantasies. To bypass the allegorical is to fall victim to the inflated rational ego. To bypass the anagogical is to deprive decision of clear and adequate motivation. To bypass the tropological is to blind oneself to personal moral responsibilities. To say so much is to say that the authentic Christian imagination ought to be both healthy and thoroughly human. It is to say that the Christian imagination acknowledges God, the emerging self, and its spatio-temporal environment as interrelated but autonomous realms of value.

But Christian hope demands that the workings of the imagination be more than just healthy and human. It demands that they be pneumatically transformed. As repressed negative feelings are named and lifted up to God in repentance and prayer for healing in faith, the sympathetic affections become sensitized to divine beauty incarnate. But sensitivity to concrete manifestations of divine beauty engages archetypal patterns of thinking. An example may illustrate the interpretative processes involved.

Hero myths occur in every major culture. The Hero archetype reveals an aspect of the animus, of the perennial male. His various adventures yield appreciative insight into the different phases of the development of ego-consciousness. Even a rapid perusal of the images that cluster spontaneously around the archetype of the Hero reveals that they have been selectively employed not only by the authors of the New Testament but also by Christians throughout the ages in order to achieve an appreciative (or allegorical) insight into the divine mystery revealed in the Word made flesh: Jesus' miraculous birth; His struggle with Satan, the serpentine tempter; His combat with demonic powers; His authority over the angelic hosts of His Father; His symbolic dismemberment through crucifixion; His descent through death into the kingdom of darkness; His triumphant return in risen glory—all these archetypal categories yield to Christian hope an appreciative sense of the noumenal forces at work in the pneumatic transformation of Jesus' human experience.

Since in Jungian theory the Hero is a symbol of the developing ego, it is no surprise to discover a Jungian psychologist like Edward F. Edinger suggesting that in the Christian gospels, Jesus is presented for Christian contemplation as a symbol of ego-development.[38] A more accurate statement of his thesis would be that the historical figure of Jesus interpreted by a selective use of archetypal, heroic imagery functions in the allegorical Christian imagination as a symbol of the graced transformation of ego-consciousness. We will return to this point in Chapter VI.

Jung himself, on the other hand, has suggested that the risen Christ functions in the Christian imagination as a symbol of the self.[39] Once again theological qualification is needed. The risen Christ is presented to Christian hope as a symbol of the graced transformation of the human self. We will return to this question in Chapter VIII.

In addition to the archetypal images that structure the imagination, there are personal images. They are of two sorts: cultural and uniquely personal. Cultural images are the common historical heritage of the members of the same human community. Such images may be sexual, familial, regional, civic, national, creedal. Uniquely personal images are those proper to an individual as a consequence of viewing the world from a unique spatio-temporal perspective.

Personal images, whether cultural or uniquely personal, relate archetypal images to the emerging self and to its concrete situation. The pneumatic transformation of personal imagination emerges as a more or less vague sense in prayer of the relevance of graced archetypal understanding to the emerging self and its specific salvific situation.

The Theology of Hope

Hans Urs von Balthasar is, I believe, quite correct in suggesting that the Christian imagination has a unique gestalt born of the action of the Breath. Since hope resides at the level of appreciative understanding, however, that gestalt is better described as a gestalt of hope rather than one of faith.[40]

For in an emergent anthropology, the relationship between Christian hope and the creedal profession of belief in God must be conceived in very different terms from those suggested by Thomistic faculty psychology. In Thomistic faculty theory, the spiritual faculties of intellect and will are those that orient the soul to an immaterial

Deity. As a consequence, the theological virtues of faith, hope, and charity are all located in the spiritual intellect and will. Infused supernatural faith lifts the intellect to God. Hope and charity are supernatural virtues of the will. Through charity the will is ordered to a supernatural end. Through hope it aspires to complete union with God in love.

In a Thomistic account of the theological virtues, the operational order between the intellect and will determines the relationship among faith, hope, and charity. In faculty theory, the will is blind and must follow the intellect. As a habit of the intellect, the supernatural virtue of faith, then, takes causal precedence over Christian hope and love.[41]

The Christian mystical tradition, however, offers a very different account of the relationship between faith and hope. John of the Cross, for example, following Augustine, associates hope, not with the will, but with memory. Without the graced healing of the memory, of the deep-seated disorders and anxieties that cause me to absolutize the familiar, hope is impossible.[42]

An emergent account of human experience endorses the latter position. Hope is born of the healing of affectivity. Moreover, in an emergent anthropology, the transmutation of feeling replaces faculty theory. Hence, the genetic order of feelings as they undergo pneumatic transmutation defines the relationship within experience between hope and faith. Christian hope is born of the pneumatic transformation of the realm of physical purpose. Since the realm of physical purpose is the affective matrix of abductive beliefs, Christian hope must be seen as the affective matrix from which creedal assent emerges under the promptings of the Holy Breath.

Moreover, the specific gestalt of Christian hope excludes many possible creedal positions as incompatible with the dynamic structure of Christian aspiration. Since, for example, Christian hope is appreciative insight pneumatically transformed, any demythologizing exclusion of appreciative understanding from the realm of faith is false and misleading. It is in fact an ego-inflated assault upon Christian hope.

Similarly, the conflict between Christianity and Gnostic thinking provides some important insights into the gestalt of hope. Any creed that is true to Christian aspiration excludes belief in a God who bears no analogical resemblance to human experience or whose unity excludes a trinity of divine persons within the Godhead. The exigencies of Christian hope require that the physical universe be conceived in such terms that the incarnation of the eternal Word of God and the indwelling of the Breath be speculatively conceivable. They demand that consent in faith to God encompass consent in atoning love to the pneumatic transformation of this world. They demand that sin be understood not as fall but as deviation. They demand that history be conceived eschatologically, i.e., as the medium of divine self-revelation and as the locus of any saving encounter with God.

The gestalt of Christian hope also excludes ego-inflated or soul-sick solutions to the religious question. As R. C. Zaehner, William Johnston, and Henri Bergson have all severally suggested,[43] Christian hope rests dissatisfied with any form of mysticism but a mysticism of graced encounter. A mysticism of encounter excludes the religious use of drugs to the extent that it is an ego-inflated attempt to manipulate the divine. It excludes religious psychosis as the working of the dark powers. It deems inadequate any merely natural mysticism, whether solipsistic or self-annihilating. For a self-induced lapse into wordless solitude or mystical evaporation into the cosmos bear no signs of the Spirit's guiding presence. We shall return to a reflection on Christian mysticism in Chapter VIII.

We must also postpone detailed consideration of the genesis and development of Christian creedal affirmations until we have laid the proper speculative foundations. But if Christian creeds involve the inferential clarification of realities vaguely and appreciatively understood in hope, we can anticipate at this point the kind of insight that will be adequate to Christian aspiration.

The dark night of sense effects the birth of Christian hope. It heals repressed negative feelings and sensitizes the human heart to divine beauty incarnate. The insights of the heart are, however, as Emerson saw, synthetic,[44] although the dualistic caste of his mind prevented him from experiencing that truth fully and from explaining why it is so. Reflection on the evaluative structure of the realm of physical purpose, however, casts light on the question. It reveals, for example, that the archetypal images that lend interpretative structure to Christian hope gather spontaneously to themselves a rich panoply of connoted images and meanings that recede from consciousness into vague and mysterious depths. Within this cluster of images, the archetype itself is a glowing center of meaning haloed by a fading penumbra of connotative significance.[45]

Christian hope is born of an appreciative insight into the beauty of God made visible in Jesus and in the action of His Breath. That perception is experienced as both integrated and integrating. It is integrated because it proceeds from an affectivity that is in process of being healed. Negative feelings have begun to be named before God and channeled in faith to creative purposes. The sympathetic affections have been allowed fuller scope to emerge and function within experience. Christian hope is integrating because the symbolic functioning of archetype and metaphor within esthetic experience endows sympathetic feelings with a complex unified relational structure.

Clearly, then, any inferential interpretation of a Christian religious experience that is true to the dynamic thrust of Christian hope must also be integrated and integrating. That is to say, it must be not merely analytic but synthetic. Orestes Brownson knew this truth and cherished it, while Josiah Royce glimpsed it philosophically.[46] We shall reflect in greater detail on the implications of this germinal insight in Chapter VI.

Faith, Hope, and Love

The realm of decision is, of course, pneumatically transformed through faith and through love. Let us reflect why this is so. An emergent theory of experience distinguishes two moments in the development of decision. Preliminary decisions terminate conscious evaluative processes and prepare one to respond through activity to environmental impulses. Christian faith effects the pneumatic transformation of preliminary decision. The termination of conscious inferential processes effects the ongoing fixation of belief. The initial assent of faith is a decision made under the prompting of the Spirit, which fixes religious beliefs about a self-revealing God. But faith involves more than the fixation of belief. For while faith is motivated by developing insight into the meaning of divine revelation, faith lives at the level of commitment rather than of thought. It is the decision to look to God as the ultimate source of light and of salvation. That commitment can be sustained even as the beliefs that originally motivated it are revised. Indeed, not infrequently, those beliefs, because inadequate, must be revised, if faith is to be sustained.

The pneumatic transformation of final decision is effected by Christian love. Final decision is reactive impact on one's environment. Final human decisions are words and deeds. Love that is not incarnate in words and deeds is a sham. Christian love is a certain kind, or quality, of love. It is atoning love in the image of Jesus. Its quality is derived from Christian faith and hope. The latter effect the pneumatic transformation of the evaluative form of experience; and the evaluative form of experience defines the quality of decision.

Hope, then, helps supply the contemplative element that inspires Christian love. Otto Bird has suggested, quite correctly, I believe, that Christian charity is a synthesis of three forms of love: gift love, need love, and appreciative love.[47] Gift love is kenotic, atoning love. It creates love and value in the beloved and forgives in advance any fault or offense. In its purest form it is God's saving love for us. Need love is concupiscent love. It is motivated by dependence on others for life and growth. Appreciative love is contemplative love. It is motivated by the beauty already present in the beloved.

Christian charity blends these three forms of love. Contemplation of the beauty of the divine gift love incarnate in Jesus and in the mission of the Spirit frees me to acknowledge my own need for God and for reconciliation with others in God's name. It also motivates me to enter actively into Jesus' own atoning sacrifice by ministering to others and being ministered to by them with a self-emptying gift love that imitates God's own love for me. If, then, the preceding analysis has been sound, growth in hope through the pneumatic transformation of affectivity is the key to growth in appreciative love of God and of others in Jesus' name.

Notes

1. Ez. 13:13, 27:26; 1K. 19:12; Ex. 14:21.

2. Gn. 2:7, 6:3, 41:8, 45:27; Jb. 33:4, 34:14ff.; Qo. 12:7; Ws. 15:11; Jg. 8:3, 9:23; Nm. 5:14-30; Ho. 4:12; Ze. 12:10, 13:2; Is. 11:2; 28:6; Ez. 36:26ff.; 1S. 19:9; 1K. 22:23.

3. Nm. 11:24-30; Jg. 16:14; 1S. 16:13; Si. 24:3.

4. Is. 11:1-9.

5. Mt. 3:13-17; Mk. 1:12-13; Lk. 4:1-13; Jn. 1:32-34; Ac. 1:6-11, 2:1ff.; 1 Co. 12:1-15:40.

6. George T. Montague, S.M., *The Holy Spirit* (New York: Paulist, 1970), pp. 237-310; cf. Raymond E. Brown, "The Paraclete in the Fourth Gospel," *New Testament Studies*, XIII (1967), pp. 113-132; C. K. Barrett, *The Holy Spirit and the Gospel Tradition* (London: S.P.C.K., 1947); James D. G. Dunn, *Jesus and the Spirit* (Philadelphia: Westminster, 1975); G. W. H. Lampe, "The Holy Spirit in the Writings of St. Luke," in *Studies in the Gospels*, ed. D. E. Nineham (Oxford: Blackwell, 1955), pp. 159-200.

7. Hans Jonas, *The Gnostic Religion* (Boston: Beacon, 1967), pp. 3-47. See also: R. Wilson, *Gnosis and the New Testament* (Philadelphia: Fortress, 1968); Hans Leisgang, *Die Gnosis* (Stuttgart: Kroner, 1955); G. Quispel, *Gnosis als Weltreligion* (Zurich: Origo, 1951); Gilbert Murray, *Five Stages of Greek Religion* (New York: Oxford, 1925); M. Grant, "The Gods of Light and Darkness," *History Today*, XVIII (April, 1968), pp. 268-276; A. Nock, "Gnosticism," *Harvard Theological Review*, LVII (October, 1964), pp. 255-279.

8. Jonas, *Gnostic Religion*, pp. 48-99.

9. Edinger, *Ego and Archetype*, pp. 37-61.

10. Jonas, *op. cit.*, pp. 241-289, 320-340.

11. Etienne Gilson, *The Christian Philosophy of St. Augustine*, trans. L.E.M. Lynch (New York: Random House, 1960); Nygren, *op. cit.*, pp. 576–593; Hans Urs von Balthasar, *Die Herrlichkeit: eine theologische Aesthetik* (2 vols.; Einseideln: Johannes Verlag, 1961), II, pp. 152–207.

12. Etienne Gilson, *The Christian Philosophy of St. Thomas Aquinas*, trans. L. K. Shook (New York: Random House, 1956). The same set of questionable philosophical presuppositions structure Karl Rahner's *Geist in Welt*.

13. DS 902.

14. Joseph Powers, S.J., *Spirit and Sacrament* (New York: Seabury, 1973), pp. 31–61.

15. Whitehead, *Process and Reality*, pp. 403–413; Charles Hartshorne, *The Divine Relativity* (New Haven: Yale, 1948).

16. John of the Cross, *Collected Works*, trans. Kieran Kavanaugh, O.C.D., and Otilio Rodriguez, O.C.D. (Washington: ICS Publications, 1964), p. 69.

17. *Ibid.*, pp. 73–101.

18. Rollo May, *Love and Will* (New York: Dell, 1969), pp. 121–178.

19. Louis J. Puhl, S.J., trans., *The Spiritual Exercises of St. Ignatius* (Chicago: Loyola, 1951),#23; cf. William A. M. Peters, S.J., *The Spiritual Exercises of St. Ignatius: Exposition and Interpretation* (Jersey City: Program to Adapt the Spiritual Exercises, 1967), pp. 43–55.

20. Puhl, *op. cit.*,#45–54; Peters, *op. cit.*, pp. 57–60.

21. Puhl, *op. cit.*,#55–64; Peters, *op. cit.*, pp. 61–65.

22. Puhl, *op. cit.*,#65–71; Peters, *op. cit.*, pp. 68–70.

23. Arthur Koestler, *The Act of Creation* (New York: Dell, 1967), pp. 27–97.

24. *Ibid.*, pp. 271–409.

25. Adorno et al., *op. cit.*, pp. 387, 475.

26. Clarence H. Faust and Thomas H. Johnson, eds., *Jonathan Edwards* (New York: Hill and Wang, 1962), pp. 60–61.

27. William Lynch's insights into the dynamics of hopelessness are poignant and helpful; see William Lynch, *Images of Hope* (Notre Dame: University of Notre Dame, 1974), pp. 47–62.

28. *Ibid.*, pp. 63–125.

29. Abraham Maslow, *Motivation and Personality* (New York: Harper, 1954), p. 38.

30. Lynch, *op. cit.*, pp. 189–210.

31. *Ibid.*, pp. 211–256.

32. Mircea Eliade, *Cosmos and History*, pp. 102–112; Jürgen Moltmann, *The Theology of Hope*, trans. James W. Leitch (New York: Harper and Row, 1965), pp. 46–91.

33. Moltmann, *op. cit.*, pp. 103ff.

34. William James, *The Varieties of Religious Experience* (New York: Macmillan, 1969), pp. 78–210.

35. William Lynch, *Christ and Apollo* (New York: Mentor, 1960), pp. 23–25.

36. *Ibid.*, pp. 25–27.

37. *Ibid.*, pp. 183–192.

38. Edinger, *Ego and Archetype*, pp. 131–156.

39. C. G. Jung, *Aion: Researches into the Phenomenology of the Self* (Princeton: Bollingen, 1959), pp. 36–71.

40. Von Balthasar, *op. cit.*, I, pp. 30–34, 137–146.

41. *Summa Theologiae*, I–II, QQ. lxii, a. 4.

42. John of the Cross, *op. cit.*, pp. 213–237.

43. R. C. Zaehner, *Mysticism, Sacred and Profane* (New York: Oxford, 1957), pp. 175–207; William Johnston, *Christian Zen* (New York: Harper and Row, 1971); *The Still Point* (New York: Fordham, 1970); Henri Bergson, *The Two Sources of Morality and Religion*, trans. R. Ashley Andra (New York: Doubleday, 1935), pp. 228–260.

44. Sherman Paul, *Emerson's Angle of Vision* (Cambridge: Harvard, 1952).

45. Erich Neumann, *The Great Mother*, trans. Ralph Manheim (Princeton: Bollinger, 1955).

46. Brownson, *Works*, I, pp. 58–129, III, pp. 543–560; Josiah Royce, *The Sources of Religious Insight* (New York: Scribner's, 1912) pp. 80–102.

47. Bird, *op. cit.*; cf. Gelpi, *Charism and Sacrament*, pp. 168–171.

V. Exodus

The attempt to engage in systematic thinking is like climbing switchbacks. Only regular pauses make it endurable. Pausing at vista points allows the eye to expand. It can absorb the landscape and with it the very path of ascent.

We are attempting a Christian foundational theology of the human. The gateway to foundational thought is critical understanding of the historical forces that have shaped one's own experience of religious conversion. But mere autobiography is not an explanatory, foundational theory. For as in the case of Brownson's *The Convert*, it yields only an initial insight into the kinds of theoretical issues that must be addressed if one is to reach theological self-understanding.

My own autobiographical reflections suggested the need for a theological method that could set the American and the Catholic traditions in serious speculative dialogue. The method we finally adopted ambitioned a dialectical analysis of the anthropological issues raised by substance and process theory. We soon realized that the very attempt to understand tensions and contradictions in one's cultural and religious heritage raised an important problem for foundational thinking, namely, what does it mean for human beings to search for conscious salvific integration? After examining both perennial and Christian images of integrating enlightenment we began to address ourselves to the task of formulating an account of the human search for religious wholeness.

Foundational method demands the elaboration of an initial set of integrating categories that are universally applicable in intent. We proposed and attempted to clarify four such categories: "experience," "quality," "fact," and "law." Application of these categories to human experience led to a preliminary descriptive account of the kinds of feelings that function within human growth and development. On the basis of these insights we were able to envisage the growth of ego-consciousness from environmental and bodily modes of awareness, through appreciative forms of understanding, into inferential, propositional insights. These preliminary conclusions paved the way for a theoretical reinterpretation of the images that help motivate the Christian search for salvific, integrating enlightenment.

As a consequence, we were able to name and to describe three of the dark powers that fragment human experience: violence, oppression, and the pharisaical conscience.

These preliminary insights left us with four interrelated questions. The first concerned the meaning of "spirit." Accordingly, in the course of the last chapter we achieved a measure of insight into some of the misleading mythic, philosophical, and theological interpretations of the term "spirit." We redefined "spirit" to mean "any legal, vectoral feeling." And we began to reflect on the conflict between the Breath of Jesus and the other dark powers that harass the human heart. Initial insight into the pneumatic healing of the heart accomplished during the dark night of sense lent foundational clarification to the meaning of Christian hope and cast light on its genetic relation to Christian faith and love.

Having paused in retrospect, let us look forward to the next stage of our climb. It is time to turn our attention to the second question raised at the close of Chapter III: "What personal conditions must be met if conscious, integrating transformation in the power of the Holy Breath is to be possible?" What, in other words, are the most basic human prerequisites for entering into an authentic Christian conversion?

Our topos indicates that the path leading to the resolution of such questions is a long and winding one. From the first, Christian conversion has been experienced as a kind of exodus. We will, then, begin our reflections by examining exodus imagery and some of the ways it illumines the conversion process. The ascent here will be a gentle one.

Every hiker knows, however, that a successful climb is punctuated by frequent rest stops with much nibbling. Before we begin the taxing portion of our ascent we will make another pause to clarify a number of key terms. Without that clarification, much of what follows would, I fear, be unintelligible.

We will then begin to climb in earnest. The trail mounts steadily in three sets of switchbacks. As we shall see, there can be no serious question of conversion to God in the strict sense prior to adolescence. To understand the conditions that must be fulfilled before conversion to God is humanly possible we must, then, examine the speculative, moral, and affective stages of human growth that culminate in the adolescent crisis. In the process, we will provide empirical grounding for the philosophical model of human experience elaborated in Chapter III.

On the basis of this preliminary analysis, we will then describe the stages of growth that ought ideally to give dynamic structure to the experience of natural conversion itself, at an affective, speculative, and moral level.

Finally, we will extend the account of the pneumatic transformation of human affectivity begun in the last chapter beyond primitive affective responses into the realm of archetypal thinking. And on the basis of this analysis we will draw some conclusions concerning the socio-political consequences of growth in Christian hope. The path is clearly marked. Let us begin to climb.

Exodus and Redemption

In Hebrew faith, the exodus was more than the liberation of an oppressed minority from tyrannical task masters. It was that. But it was also the prelude to the sealing of the Sinai covenant with its assurance of divine blessing to God's faithful in the land He had promised.[1]

Fidelity to the covenant was inculcated by the Torah itself, by prophetic preaching, and by post-exilic piety. As a consequence, Passover was recognized as the greatest feast of obligation in the Hebrew liturgical calendar. For at Passover time, the devout Israelite remembered the mighty deed of God that had founded the Jewish nation and (s)he blessed Yahweh.[2]

Jesus' violent death and glorification at the time of Passover and His use of covenant imagery at the Last Supper to explain their meaning to His disciples linked these two events permanently in Christian faith and aspiration. The blood of Jesus replaced the blood of the paschal lamb as the sign of the divine promise of liberation. In being lifted up in suffering and in glory, Jesus, the Breath-baptizer of the new Israel, had passed through the waters of chaos and of death to the bosom of the Father. As a consequence, Christian baptism into the death and resurrection of the Lord came to be experienced affectively and ritually as a Passover event. The Lord's supper replaced the paschal meal as the ritual recall of those saving events by which God had finally and definitively liberated His people and bound them to Himself in a new, pneumatic covenant. Moreover, Jesus in passing over to the Father revealed to the people of God reborn in His image that their true "promised land" was in fact His Father's home, the "heavenly Jerusalem" of the Apocalypse.[3]

For the twice-born Christian, Jesus was then the new Moses who leads His people from bondage. He mediates to them the new and everlasting covenant and feeds them with the eucharistic manna. He refreshes them with the living water of His Holy Breath as they wander in pilgrimage through this desert of trial and testing to the heavenly city.[4]

For the Christian as for the Hebrew, therefore, liberation is also a covenant event. It brings freedom from the forces of oppression, sin, and death by healing the pharisaical heart to consent in hope to a covenanting God on the terms that God Himself has set. For the integrally converted Christian, therefore, human oppression is the second of the dark powers.[5]

A Pause for Clarification

What light do these images throw on a foundational theology of human freedom? In any sound theology of Christian conversion, "conversion" and "liberation" should be interpreted as two sides of the same coin. One passes to freedom through a conversion whose abiding fruit is covenanted commitment to the God who stands revealed in Jesus and in the Holy Breath.[6] Moreover, as we shall see again in greater detail, that commitment demands dedication to others in the name and image of God. But if liberation is the fruit of conversion, it must also be the result of integrating, salvific enlightenment. And that enlightenment must be the fruit of the ongoing pneumatic transformation of experience.

Authentic religious conversion brings with it certain kinds of freedom. But there are other kinds as well. Indeed, experience testifies that the growth of human freedom is linked inseparably to the natural development of ego-consciousness.

Freedom has been traditionally and correctly described as the ability to act or not to act, to do one thing rather than another. Freedom is a character, or quality, of a decision. Since, however, the character of a decision is derived from the kinds of evaluative processes it terminates, freedom may aptly be described as an aspect of the qualitative, or conceptual, form of an emerging experience. The ability to act or not to act, to do one thing rather than another, presupposes that either action or inaction, either this practical course rather than that, have both been evaluatively discriminated and evaluatively compared. Ego-consciousness, as we have seen, grows through evaluative differentiation and evaluative synthesis. The greater the number of discriminated possibilities presented for decision, the greater the freedom attending the choice ultimately made.

In the course of this chapter and of the two that follow, we will, then, attempt to establish the following theses: (1) The natural human conquest of freedom culminates in the growth and consolidation of ego-consciousness. (2) In the course of natural human development, ego-consciousness ought to culminate in affective, intellectual, and moral conversion. (3) Christian conversion effects the pneumatic transformation of natural human conversion by transvaluing the values that give the latter conceptual shape.[7]

In an emergent problematic, the terms "nature," "grace," and "sin" are not substantives but adverbs. Like freedom they describe aspects of the evaluative form of a developing human experience. One acts sinfully, graciously, naturally. And natural, graced, or sinful acts give cumulative definition to the emerging self by shaping the character of its dynamic orientation toward environmental forces with which it interacts.

The term "nature" designates that aspect of the evaluative form of an experience that is motivated by the choice of values that are not opposed to the historical self-revelation of God but that remain untouched by overt religious faith.

The term "grace" designates that aspect of the evaluative form of an experience that is shaped by positive faith-dependence on the Breath of Jesus.

"Sin," viewed as a personal, human response, designates that aspect of the evaluative form of an experience that stands in conscious opposition to the moral exigencies of faith in the God who stands self-revealed in Jesus and the Spirit.

Freedom can, then, develop either naturally or graciously. Natural and gracious freedom differ in the kinds of evaluative variables that shape them. The dividing line between the two is overt faith-dependence on God. That is to say, naturally free decisions neither affirm nor deny the historical self-revelation of God. Instead they simply prescind abstractly from God's saving action. They are naively (not maliciously) content to respond to legitimate spatio-temporal values but with no concern as to whether or not they incarnate the reality of God. Sin, on the other hand, is the abdication of gracious freedom through conscious opposition to the ultimate source of liberation and in despairing submission to the powers of darkness.

How, then, does natural freedom grow and develop? If natural, human freedom culminates in the conquest of ego-consciousness, an insight into the processes of human liberation must rest on a sound understanding of the stages of growth through which the normal human ego passes. We have paused to clarify several basic notions. Thus fortified, let us begin to climb in earnest.

Developmental Psychology

One who has thrown much light on the earliest phases in the development of the normal ego is Jean Piaget.[8] The emergent model of human experience proposed in Chapter III was formulated independently of Piaget. But Piaget's experimental work not only confirms the approach to experience proposed in Chapter III; it allows us to describe the genesis of ego-awareness in greater detail than heretofore.

An emergent anthropology concurs with Piaget in his suggestion that the laws governing ego-growth ought to be seen as a developmental extension and complexification of more fundamental biological patterns of behavior.

There are, as Piaget suggests, functional constants in the development of human experience. Biological constants are among the most basic. They include the developing organism with all of its functioning sub-units, its sustaining environment, and the modification of behavior that interaction with that environment effects.

An organismic, developmental theory of human experience discovers the same constants in the growth of human consciousness. It interprets intelligent human activity as the cumulative coordination of behavioral patterns in evaluative response to environmental impulses. More complex behavioral structures evolve from those that are more primitive.

An analysis of biological processes reveals two fundamental operational constants: organization and adaptation. Biological organization is the formation of self-sustaining organic structures. Adaptation seeks to relate already existing structures back to their impinging environment in ways that sustain and if possible enhance the organism's own vital processes.

Adaptation assumes two distinguishable forms: assimilation and accommodation. Biological assimilation adapts the environment to the structure of the organism. Food, for example, is ingested, broken down, and used to repair deteriorating neural, muscular, and skeletal structures. Biological accommodation is growth; it modifies the organism itself in order to relate it in new ways to its sustaining environment.

The same behavioral patterns appear in the development of human consciousness. Evaluative habits are first formed, then integrated into increasingly complex patterns of response. An assimilatory evaluation relates the environment to the mind's existing repertoire of interpretative structures. An accommodative response readapts the mind to reality by creating novel ways of responding evaluatively to the forces that shape experience.[9]

Piaget explains the genetic development of the human ego as the cumulative schematization of cognitive behavior. The term "schema" is, then, central to his theory. It designates a structure of cognition that grounds a class of similar evaluative responses. Schemata therefore lend regularity to human behavior and endow experience with its developing teleologies. Schemata are more or less complex. A schema, for example, grounds the infant's instinctive sucking and instinctive manual prehensions. A much more complex schema grounds the fantasies of the five-year-old or the mathematical inferences of the adolescent. There are schemata of assimilation and schemata of accommodation. The former bend the environment to the organism; the latter bend the organism to the environment.

In other words, the term "schema" in Piaget's system corresponds to the term "law" defined in Chapter III, with one important reservation. Piaget's "schema" designates a specific class of laws, namely those grounding the development of human ego-awareness. But if schemata are a special class of vectoral feeling, one may draw on Piaget's extensive descriptive and experimental work to outline the progressive legal schematization of different kinds of conscious human feelings.[10]

Piaget divides the early development of ego-consciousness into three periods. The first is the sensory-motor period. It ends when the child is approximately two years of age. The second period spans the years two to eleven. It is marked by the preparation and organization of concrete interpretative processes. The third period, from eleven to fifteen years, sees the emergence of abstract, propositional feelings.

Sensory-motor Development

The sensory-motor period effects the legal schematization of dative feelings. During it the child begins to explore the realm of literal meaning. This period develops in six stages.[11]

Stage 1 (0–1 month): In the first stage, the child gives no sign of intelligent behavior. It sucks, moves its tongue, swallows, cries, and engages in gross body movements. The sucking response is the first to undergo behavioral modification. It quickly acquires strength and control. In addition, the infant gives signs of sensing an evaluative difference between nourishing and nonnourishing suckables. Though the wailing of one infant may provoke another to cry, there is as yet no unambiguous evidence of imitative behavior. The child manifests only passive reaction to visual stimuli and seems to expect things to reappear at the point of disappearance. There is no sense of causality, although the child responds emotionally to its biological needs and rhythms.

Stage 2 (1–4 months): The infant's reflex responses begin to be transformed into controlled and repeatable behavioral patterns. Reflex sucking gives way to repeatable tongue movements and to thumb and finger sucking. Passive visual responses give way to looking at stationary objects and then to following their movements. An increasing number of objects become the center of such visual interest. But there is as yet no clear perception of the object as a thing in its own right. Vocalization patterns develop. Crying becomes more predictable. The infant begins to notice its own noises and to coordinate seeing and hearing, hearing and vocalization, vision and prehension, sucking and hand movements. Familiar sounds are recognized. Reflex closing of the palm under stimulation gives way to specialized grasping. Seen objects are grasped. Grasped objects are looked at. The infant repeats adult imitations of sounds it already knows how to make but will not yet attempt to imitate new sounds.

Stage 3 (4–8 months): The infant begins to endow the controlled, repeatable responses already mastered with new complexity. The child makes initial and usually futile attempts to keep interesting experiences going, often through primitive imitations. After a rattle stops shaking, for example, the child may begin to make shaking movements with its hands and legs.

Stage 4 (8–12 months): Novel signs of goal-oriented activity begin to emerge. The child now seeks to get at a favorite toy or other desired objects, provided, however, that the object is already visible behind whatever obstacle separates it from the child. Instruments are used to attain perceived goals. The schemata developed at stage two begin to acquire flexibility and coordination. Instead of merely passive response to visual signals, visually presented events begin to be anticipated before they occur. Merely rising to leave the room, for example, may occasion a flood of infantile tears that at an earlier stage of growth would have occurred only after the parent's disappearance. Objects that at stage three were employed as instrumentalities begin to be interesting for their own sake. Novel sounds and movements begin to be imitated. The child will now search for an object hidden before its eyes but is still inclined to look for it only at the point where it disappeared. That the vanished object might be elsewhere seems to be still incomprehensible. The infant now treats objects as three-dimensional and begins to be able to grasp concrete relationships among datively presented objects. It begins to comprehend constant size and shape despite shifts in visual perspective and to see things in depth relationships. There is a nascent sense of causality: the child, for example, now pushes aside an obstruction to a desired object and will try to make adults do for it what it cannot do for itself.

Stage 5 (12–18 months): The child begins to manifest a new capacity for creative improvisation. A chance action is reproduced again and again until it is integrated into the child's repertoire of activities. Imitation becomes more controlled and precise. There is a new ability to correct mistakes if a desired end is not immediately achieved. The child now remembers hidden objects and begins to search for them where last seen. But there is still no sense of the possibility of the unseen displacement of an object. The child begins to develop a conscious sense of the position of its whole body in space rather than just of its arms and legs. It studies changes in apparent shape and size, puts things into containers and removes them. The child begins a systematic exploration of its immediate environment. There is a nascent sense of systems of causes independent of the child. There is, for example, fascination in placing a ball on an incline and watching it roll. Persons are now recognized as causal centers of activity. And there is a recognition that other forces also affect the child's own body. The child will, for example, now release its grip on its playpen in order to drop to a sitting position on the floor.

Stage 6 (18 months on): The child can now not only discover new behavioral patterns accidentally; it can also create them spontaneously. When, for example, something it is pushing hits an obstruction, it can figure out how to remove the obstacle without experimentation. There is, in other words, a novel capacity to represent events symbolically through images. Complex behavioral patterns of others can now be imitated with ease. The child begins to enter into the fantasy world of allegorical meaning and make-believe. The displacement of unseen objects is understood and mastered. The child can keep running tab on its own body movements through space and react appropriately to unexpected environmental displacements. Concrete anticipatory analogues to inference begin to appear: a sound whose source is invisible will lead the child to search for its source. Past events can now be recalled as past. But there is as yet no clear grasp of the idea of causality.

Sensory-motor Thinking

Clearly, the legal schematization of experience during the period of sensory-motor development occurs largely through the recognitive structuring of dative feelings themselves. The neonate is, of course, already equipped at birth with very primitive affective responses. (S)he reacts spontaneously to pain with rage and fear, to pleasure with contentment and desire. As ego-consciousness grows, however, dative presentations acquire affective coloring through spontaneous association. But it is not until the final stage of sensory-motor development that the child begins to manifest signs of fantasy. In other words, during the sensory-motor period, the presented structures of dative consciousness seem to suffice for the development of concrete patterns of thought. The child can make concrete behavioral links between dative presentations and decisions, but it cannot relate creatively to events other than those that shape its immediate present. It can pursue immediate concrete goals but cannot criticize its own operational patterns. Its thinking is bound to the present moment.

The sensory-motor child learns gradually to discriminate between its bodily functions and its sustaining environment and then gradually to explore its immediate surroundings. At first, it grasps its world only in relationship to parts of its own body. Soon the body itself is grasped as a whole. By stage four, the child has developed a vague sense of the permanence of objects. By stage five, it has begun to search for hidden objects. By stage six, there is persistent search for an object that is not in the place anticipated. In other words, by age two, the child has developed the capacity to imagine independently changing things, to imagine a world.[12]

The Pre-operational Child

In contrast to the thought patterns of the sensory-motor child, pre-operational thought is formally and explicitly representational.[13] The child begins to relate to its environment through evaluative responses that create and evoke interpretative symbols. It can imagine relationships between events and enters into the archetypal world of fantasy and of allegorical meaning.

As we saw in Chapter III, dative feelings yield a more or less vague sense of the actual past as present, while physical purposes yield a more or less vague sense of transition beyond the present. The legal schematization of the realm of physical purpose, therefore, frees the child from its earlier entrapment in the present moment. Past and present are clearly differentiated, though the sense of the future remains vague.

The ego of the pre-operational child is still a delicate blossom. It is too small and fragile to be called "inflated." Nevertheless, it already manifests a profound tendency to "egocentrism." The term is Piaget's. It refers not only to the child's inability to see any other viewpoint than its own but also to its persistent refusal both to justify its own positions and to search for inconsistencies in its own thought patterns. Egocentric thinking focuses exclusively on a single striking quality of experience and refuses to attend to any other. It is blind to balancing and compensating factors. It is equally blind to its own blindness. Egocentrism tricks the child repeatedly into blunders as it grapples with its world. And it renders the socialization process painful.

Pre-operational thought is unable to transcend the realm of physical purpose. It remains imagistic and concrete. The absence of any integrating inferential abstraction leaves thought static and fragmented. The child's mind is ruled by events it lacks the capacity to control. Its "inferences" express the naive expectation that what worked before will work again. Thinking is a matter of repeated trial and error. It is spontaneous, imagistic, concrete, rather than controlled, abstract, and organized. There is as yet no ability to deal with abstract classifications of things based on a genuine abductive insight into an organizing rule.

Piaget calls the thought patterns of the pre-operational child "transductive." The term is an apt one and distinguishes the free and spontaneous associations of appreciative understanding from the conscious grasp of logical implication. Transductive thinking is syncretistic: images cluster without logical organization into all-encompassing wholes. Mere juxtaposition within experience is confounded with causal nexus. As a result transductive thinking has a facile "explanation" for everything. For the pre-operational child, the idea of chance is, then, inconceivable. At the same time, (s)he remains baffled even by concrete problems dealing with time, causality, space, measurement, number, quantity, movement, velocity. There is no clear distinction between play and reality. Transductive thought is relatively unsocialized, largely oblivious of the effect of communication on others, and thoroughly egocentric. It is self-contradictory, fluctuating, disorganized.

The chief structuring principle of transductive thought is not inference but memory. Piaget has correctly censured the attempt of philosophers and psychologists to portray memory as a faculty for reproducing perceived images subjectively. Memory emerges as the legal schematization of the physical purposes that transmute dative feelings. It makes environmental transactions possible. The very act of recall is motivated by the need to deal operationally with things. Those things we deal with on an occasional basis we find difficult to remember.

As the legal schematization of physical purpose proceeds, memory itself begins to assume subtler forms. Recognitive memory is rooted in dative feelings: I may, for example, come upon a familiar object and recognize it as the one I saw yesterday. Reconstructive memory is based on imitation: I may, for example, participate with zest in a game of follow-the-leader. In evocative memory, one image or feeling leads spontaneously to another. As its schematizations grow in complexity and therefore in flexibility, evocative memory becomes creative fantasy.[14]

As transductive thinking develops more complex patterns of recall and as egocentrism is partially eroded by the processes of socialization, the child's thought gradually begins to acquire self-regulating flexibility. It is not yet self-critical and still lacks the capacity to grasp underlying principles. But by the age of seven, the child's mind can deal with concrete problems in position and distance and in the relationship between concrete parts and concrete wholes.

But while the child can take apart and reassemble an object with facility, it cannot as yet add and subtract abstract classes of things. While it grasps spatio-temporal proximities, it is baffled by abstract, symmetrical relationships. While it has mastered concrete temporal sequencing, it does not yet grasp abstract, asymmetrical relationships. Because thought is still bound to the concrete, the properties of things must still be mastered one by one.

Propositional feelings in the strict sense do not emerge until around eleven years.[15] The child can now classify things abstractly without having to arrange them physically in clumps. Abductive classification is freed from concrete, spatio-temporal considerations. Between the ages of eleven and fifteen, the mind begins to develop deductive capacities as well. Different theoretical hypotheses can be entertained successively and their consequences examined and evaluated. Relationships need not be discovered in things. They can now be simply conceived.

The sensory-motor child lives almost wholly in the present moment created by dative feeling. The pre-operational child can relate present and past through memory but knows the future only as a vague fantasy or as the anticipation of a remembered experience. Abductive propositional feelings yield a vivid sense of the past become present; deductive propositions, of the present being transformed into a novel future. With the emergence of deductive inference, the adolescent discovers, therefore, a new and increasingly vivid sense of as yet unexperienced, theoretical possibilities.

At first adolescent dreams and plans for the future are unsullied by the need for rigorous inductive verification. They express a naive idealism and generate quixotic, intemperate schemes for reshaping nature, society, the world. In other words, the rapid legal schematization of the realm of abductive and deductive propositional feelings effected during adolescence combines with the narcissistic introspection that marks that period of growth in order to create a new kind of adult egocentrism. For while socialization mutes childish egocentrism, it never eliminates it altogether. In the course of a normal adolescence, egocentrism blossoms into ego-inflation.

Ethical Growth in Children
As ego-consciousness develops, so too does the child's sense of right and wrong. Piaget discovers four stages in the early development of moral judgment.[16] Though one may legitimately question the strictly "ethical" character of the kinds of judgments he examines, there can be no doubt that adult judgments of conscience are in fact conditioned by the kinds of childhood experiences Piaget describes.

The first stage is the individual, or motor, stage. It ends between ages two to five. It encompasses the period of sensory-motor development and extends into the early stages of pre-operational thinking. During this period, the child experiences regularity in its own biological rhythms and in other familiar patterns in its presented environment. But the legal schematization of experience during this first period of ethical growth betrays no conscious sense of rules as rules. Given a set of marbles, the child will, for example, suck them, roll and bounce them, fantasize them as eggs or rocks—nothing more.[17]

The second stage of ethical growth is the egocentric stage. It ends around age seven or eight. Sometime between the ages of two and five, the idea of a rule of behavior begins to dawn upon the childish mind. It is, to be sure, still a vague conception. The child senses that other children play according to rules and that parents expect the child's own behavior to conform to rules. The child begins to imitate both sets of rules, not because it understands them, but because at a deeper affective level it wants to feel like others, to win approval, and to avoid disapproval or punishment. As yet, there is not a clear sense that rules govern social intercourse. Even in group play that imitates the rule-governed games of older children, the egocentric child plays on its own without interest or regard for the rules other children in the group are following.

At this primitive stage of growth, the egocentric child perceives all rules as sacred, objective, immutable, handed down from on high. The child finds it unimaginable that new rules can be created by people, least of all by children. It is simply presupposes that things are now being done as they have always been done. Moreover, parental rules participate in the noumenal mystery and power of these great, mysterious personages.

Duty for the egocentric child is, then, heteronomous. It is something imposed upon behavior by another. For the egocentric child, conformity to rules is more important than the reasons that motivate them. Authority is experienced as external constraint. The reason for punishment is as vague and incomprehensible as the reason why rules must be obeyed in the first place. The best punishment is the severest, because it brings with it the surest conviction of guilt. Lacking a clear sense of causal relationship, the egocentric child tends to believe that all punishments are simply built into the existing scheme of things. They occur spontaneously and inevitably. In questions of personal decision, there is rigid dependence on parental guidance and authority.[18]

During the egocentric period, the authoritarian cast of the child's apperceptions reflects the primitive, syncretistic character of its own thought processes. The egocentric child endows everything it experiences with naive givenness. Rules fall under the same reifying tendency. While parental tolerance and open-mindedness cannot save the child from passing through a primitive authoritarian phase, an authoritarian upbringing can keep the child from advancing beyond heteronomy to cooperative and equitable behavior. The child will, then, be helped in its moral growth by parental care to explain the meaning and purpose of the rules it must obey and by the avoidance of harsh, vindictive punishment.

But the child's egocentric period of ethical growth is more than just an unfortunate inevitability. It marks an important moment in the process of socialization. The child must learn how to conform to rules before it can begin to assume conscious personal responsibility for their creation and transformation. Moreover, unless authoritarian upbringing freezes the child in an egocentric, heteronomous ethics, it will pass spontaneously, sometime around the age of seven, from an ethics of conformity to an ethics of cooperation.

Two important experiences mediate the transition. The discovery of fallibility and inequity in the parental code of expectations begins to undermine blind obedience to adult authority. More important, through socialization, the child discovers that children themselves create the rules of the games they play. This astonishing discovery creates a new sense of personal responsibility in children. To take it upon oneself to make a rule for others is to bind oneself in honor to obey it. To agree to obey the rules of others is to demand no less obedience from them.

During the period of cooperation, rules, then, lose their sacred, given character. But paradoxically, in the process personal obedience to rules is reinforced through dawning insight into their true social purpose. Peer pressures too reinforce obedient social conformity. Rules come to be seen, not as handed down from on high, but as the guarantees of organic social solidarity, especially with one's peers. Needless to say, there is no question in the cooperative child's mind of evaluating rules against an ultimate ground of morality.

Nevertheless, cooperative ethics marks an important advance in moral understanding. While the egocentric child operates according to a primitive notion of vindictive, punitive justice, the cooperative child has come to believe that justice is distributive. There is a new-found sense that punishments ought to fit the crime. It is, for example, accepted as just that one be deprived of something one has personally abused. Whereas the egocentric child wants punishments to be as strict as possible to convince the guilty of their wrongdoing, the cooperative child is concerned that only an eye be exchanged for an eye. Restitution is seen as a form of just punishment. Social ostracism or even censure may suffice for some misdeeds.

But when a child first begins to understand the meaning of cooperation and of shared responsibility, its sense of distributive justice is rigid and uniform. Egalitarian considerations outweight all others. What is demanded of one must be demanded of all, irrespective of persons and circumstances. As the socialization process proceeds, however, such leveling, democratic tendencies are softened somewhat by a more nuanced sense of equity.[19]

Around the age of eleven, the child enters a fourth and final phase of early moral development: the stage of codification. As its capacity for inference grows, the rules of social conduct become generalized, organized, institutionalized. Play follows rules universally accepted in the world of sport. Youth organizations are formed and endowed with constitutions. The codification and institutionalization of conduct prepares the way for assimilation to the rationally organized world of adult society.

Clearly, as the adolescent crisis approaches, a child's specific ethical agenda will vary considerably with personal upbringing. The child of authoritarian parents approaches young adulthood with precariously low ego strength and with a bellyful of repressed frustration, guilt, rage, and fear. Such a child's capacity for abstract insight is stunted. Thinking still follows spontaneously the concrete, stereotyped, syncretistic patterns of infantile egocentrism. Rage transforms social stereotypes into unabashed bigotry. Anything that threatens the young ego's precarious grip on its rampaging unconscious will tend to provoke aggressive, extrapunitive responses.

Criticism of sanctioned, codified values will be countered with vindictive retaliation. Having never learned the meaning of cooperative responsibility to a significant extent, the authoritarian adolescent will cling rigidly to its primitive, heteronomous morality. "Justice" will be vindictive and arbitrary.

The ego-assimilated child by contrast manifests greater emotional differentiation and greater capacity for abstract thought than his or her authoritarian peer. The ego-assimilated child is more inclined to shoulder personal blame than to lay it constantly at the doorstep of others. (S)he manifests sensitivity to a broader spectrum of human values and a greater freedom in seeking and creating new ones.[20]

The ego-assimilated adolescent will, however, be prone to naive idealism. (S)he will expect the adult world to be like the humane atmosphere of home. The shock of discovering otherwise can breed an unrealistic nostalgia for the halcyon days of childhood. If too intense, such nostalgia can inhibit authentic growth in hope by binding one emotionally to the futile search for a vanished past.

Affective Development in Children

Piaget's concerns are primarily epistemological. As a consequence, he has paid scant attention to emotional development in children. Archetypal analysis has, however, thrown considerable light on the basic emotional agenda of young boys as they move toward adulthood. The archetypes that dominate the development of male ego-consciousness from infancy to adolescence are the primordial circle; the Great Mother together with her consort, the World Father; the Hero, his birth, his adventures, and his conquest of the ring snake. Let us reflect briefly on some of the connotations of these images.

The circle (the sphere, the round) is a perennial archetypal symbol of eternity. One may trace a circle endlessly and still have only a circle. The primordial circle suggests the undifferentiated state of the cosmos at its point of origin. For, as Erich Neumann has observed, ". . . in its roundness there is no above and no below, no space." The primordial circle takes concrete shape in a number of common mythic images: the cosmogonic egg from which the universe is hatched, the eternal serpent swallowing its tail. As a symbol of undifferentiated sameness, the circle is an archetype of beginnings, both cosmic and psychic. Hence, the primordial circle evokes an appreciative sense of the aboriginal depths out of which personal consciousness and cosmic meaning emerge.[21]

The primordial circle is associated in transductive, syncretistic thought with the Great Mother, the feminine principle of life. She with her impregnating consort, the World Father, are in their union archetypal symbols of life everlasting. From their procreative activity all life proceeds. But the primordial circle is linked in myth to the feminine rather than to the masculine source of life. The womb of the Great Mother is the primordial circle whence all life proceeds. As a consequence, in the mythic imagination the snake devouring its tail is the Great Mother's common feral counterpart.[22]

The Hero is the child of the Great Mother. His birth and his adventures interpret the development of masculine ego-consciousness. As the child's world is expanded by syncretistic, pre-operational forms of thought, parental forces are felt vaguely as alternately benevolent or destructive, either as nourishing and sustaining the fragile ego in its first hesitant steps toward personal independence or as thwarting and inhibiting its growth. In moments of conflict, the Great Mother who gives birth to life can in the child's egocentric fantasies be transformed in a flash into the Terrible Mother who devours her own children.[23]

An example may be of help. The Great Mother is not only the encircling, primordial womb; she is the earth itself which, when inseminated, gives birth to food and life. Earth and orb fuse in the image of the cave. Descent into the cave thus becomes descent into the dark womb world ruled by the Mother Goddess.

The following is the terrifying dream of an eight-year-old boy whose mother had been repeatedly calling a minor disciplinary matter to his attention for several days. He dreamed that he and his friends went down into a dark cave to rescue some small boys who were stuck living in its walls. They managed to free several of them, until they came to one boy who could not be disengaged despite their best efforts. When they looked to see why he could not be freed, they found that he was being held tight in the wall by a giant female spider with huge teeth which had clamped in the unfortunate boy's back and kept him prisoner. At this point he woke in terror. His mother, who was anything but authoritarian, decided on hearing the dream to take up the disciplinary problem again at some later date.

The initial consolidation of stable ego strength is interpreted mythically in stories of the miraculous birth of the Hero. As soon as he emerges, the Hero enters into conflict with the parental powers. The mythic Hero often has four parents: the real parents who give him birth and their heavenly noumenal counterparts.

The Hero assumes many different forms in legend and myth. One of his common masks is that of the Trickster.[24] The childish ego senses that the forces governing the world of adult experience will overpower it if directly confronted. But the young ego can use cunning to outwit its antagonists. The child delights in posing riddles that baffle adults, in doing magic tricks that bewilder them, in using guile to get its own way. If the feral counterpart of the Great Mother is the ring snake, the feral counterpart of the Trickster is some small animal, like a rabbit or a fox, that is imagined to survive its predators through the use of cunning and cleverness. In the stories of Uncle Remus, two archetypal Tricksters, Br'er Rabbit and Br'er Fox, match wits to the perennial delight of children.

The growth processes by which the young ego reaches affective independence from parental control are archetypally interpreted in myths depicting the slaying of the Great Mother and her consort by the young Hero. Most parents will, no doubt, find such images distasteful and wholly repugnant to their preferred relationship with their children. But irrational conflict between rambunctious adolescents and their parents is as perennial as human experience. Moreover, from the child's or young adult's affective standpoint, matters are bound to be felt somewhat differently.

The mythic slaying of the world parents is an affective declaration of independence from their all-encompassing control. In mythic tales, the Great Mother may be slain in impersonal ways: in the killing of her high priests, in destroying her feral counterpart, the primordial dragon. In tragic myths, the Hero may succumb to the power of the Great Mother. And indeed many a male ego stands shackled at the threshold of emotional maturity. The fate of such men is reflected in the story of Sampson, who was blinded by feminine treachery and shorn of his strength-giving hair, or of Oedipus, destroyed and blinded by his incestuous fascination with his own mother.[25]

But the successful Hero emerges victorious from the dragon fight. He is Orestes, who not only slays his mother and her consort but with the help of Athena, goddess of Wisdom, triumphs finally over the Erinyes, the dark, feminine powers of the earth.

The World Father is the guardian of masculinity and the supervisor of education. In slaying him, the Hero comes of age sexually and emotionally. He destroys the threat that continued paternal control poses to adult independence, fame, achievement, social position. And he declares his intellectual independence from paternal patterns of thought.[26]

But the mythic Hero must not only destroy parental obstacles to emotional and intellectual autonomy. He must capture the prize that is his heart's desire and free the maiden who is his lady love. In the allegorical realm of appreciative understanding, such images must be understood archetypally, not literally. Erich Neumann puts the matter succinctly.

> The transformation which the male undergoes in the course of the dragon fight includes a change in his relation to the female, symbolically expressed in the liberation of the captive from the dragon's power. In other words, the feminine image extricates itself from the grip of the Terrible Mother, a process known in analytical psychology as the crystallization of the anima from the mother archetype.
>
> The union of the adolescent son with the Great Mother is followed by a phase of development in which an adult male combines with a feminine partner of his own age and kind, in the *hieros gamos*. Only now is he mature enough to reproduce himself. He is no longer the tool of a superordinate Earth Mother, but, like a father, he assumes the care and responsibility for his offspring, and, having established a permanent relationship with a woman, founds the family as the nucleus of all patriarchal culture, and beyond that the dynasty and the state. . . .
>
> So long as the man loves only the bounteous mother in woman, he remains infantile. And if he fears woman as the castrating womb, he can never combine with it and reproduce himself. What the hero kills is only the terrible side of the female, and this he does in order to set free the fruitful and joyous side with which she joins herself to him.[27]

The Hero's rescue of the maiden imprisoned by the dragon and his blissful union with her in a *hieros gamos* symbolizes the rational male ego's reappropriation of the affective side of his personality. The resulting affective wholeness is the prize, the treasure that beckons at the end of every heroic quest.[28]

In almost every culture, heroic imagery is profoundly sexist in character. The Hero is almost always male. Though heroic women like the Amazons or Wonder Woman appear from time to time upon the mythic stage, they tend to be the exception rather than the rule.

The myths that shape our culture school women to affective and intellectual passivity. It is always they who are being rescued from the dragon by some superior male power. In the *hieros gamos*, they are expected to find their fulfillment in buttressing and soothing the successful (and often inflated) rational male ego.

When authoritarian attitudes transform such cultural myths into bigoted stereotypes, the result is a network of familial, social, economic, and political structures whose combined effect is the systematic oppression and exploitation of women. Women are denied the opportunities to develop healthy egos and are censured and penalized for even trying. Theirs are the menial and boring tasks, the household chores that never end. They are denied access to education, to jobs, to most forms of human achievement other than the bearing and rearing of children.

The Human Conquest of Freedom

Freedom is the ability to act or not, to do one thing rather than another. Natural freedom is the fruit of personal evaluative development that prescinds naively from the historical self-revelation of God. It grows in response to other legitimate spatio-temporal values that foster human life and growth.

In an emergent universe, natural human freedom is not guaranteed by the possession of a fictive spiritual essence or by the formal object of a nonexistent intellectual faculty. It is the fruit of evaluative discrimination and of the subsequent interrelation of discriminated possibilities for decision. It is acquired with pain and sustained with difficulty.

Moreover, the forces that foster natural ego-development are identical with those that nourish freedom. Those forces are environmental, conceptual, perspectival, habitual, decisive.

a. *Environmental.* The shape of an environment is a function of the factual and legal variables present within it. The factual variables are presented datively; the legal variables, affectively and inferentially. As a consequence, environments shape the development of ego-consciousness in two ways: by their relative complexity and by their educational adequacy. Impoverished environments present a relatively small spectrum of dative values for further appreciation and understanding. The slum dweller is not free to evaluate one way or another the educational advantages available to the children of the wealthy. In New York, provided you have the money, you can on any given evening decide which of several concerts you wish to attend. The same options do not exist in Opelousas, Louisiana.

But environments, as Dewey saw quite clearly, must be organized in such a way as to foster evaluative growth. An environment whose complexity exceeds an individual's achieved capacity to respond creatively can stifle freedom through bafflement, discouragement, confusion, and the death of hope in repeated personal failure. Environments may even be organized in such a way as to stifle consciousness and freedom. Authoritarian environments do so through the systematic use of physical violence, intimidation, and institutionalized exploitation of the defenseless. They smother consciousness under a blanket of propaganda, double-talk, and other forms of obfuscation and deceit. They shackle the oppressed to their own self-hatred and rage. They are the seed bed of bigotry end of class warfare.

The healthy environment, by contrast, confronts the emerging self with an ordered set of interrelated problems that are endowed with increasing complexity and that stimulate novel insight, creative response, and growing conscious mastery of one's world.

b. *Conceptual*. One stands impotent before the environmental forces that shape experience until those forces are presented conceptually within experience for further evaluation and decision. To be presented, environmental variables must be conceptually discriminated.

Evaluative discrimination demands the elaboration of an adequate set of conceptual feelings for dealing affectively and inferentially with one's world. An individual who has known only rock and roll will, for example, probably be bored by the Beethoven Ninth. One whose only speculative diet has been comic books will not relish the *Divine Comedy*. The nonmathematician stands baffled before the nuances of relativity theory. In other words, freedom to deal creatively with one's world presupposes the capacity to elicit an evaluative response adequate to the environmental forces that shape experience.

c. *Perspectival*. But all conscious evaluations occur in a context. A context defines a specific evaluative perspective on the world. One's immediate context is defined by a specific question and by the answer one chooses to give it. Should marijuana be legalized? Is there a God? What is $3a^2$ multiplied by $4b^3$? Was Theodore Parker a Transcendentalist? How did the New Testament resurrection narratives come to be written? How can I express this passion in canvas and oil? What story will express this encounter with the Holy?

But specific questions arise in a larger heuristic context. A heuristic context is one that is common to a certain genus of question. Questions share a common heuristic context when they employ similar symbolic materials and can be resolved by similar operational procedures. Heuristic contexts define more or less broad areas of inquiry and expression: mathematics, physics, chemistry, biology, philosophy, theology, myth, presentational and significant art, etc.

Heuristic contexts develop in historical contexts. Historical contexts are defined by the more or less vague and ambiguous structures of meaning that shape a given epoch: its interests, biases, presuppositions, problems, insights, oversights.

A person's evaluative perspective on the world is, then, the interweaving of these evolving contexts and of the affective and inferential patterns of response they generate. A personal context focuses ego evaluations. It is both clarifying and blinding. It is clarifying to the extent that it sharpens differentiation. It is blinding to the extent that it excludes from evaluative consideration elements of experience that are irrelevant to a given context. Moreover, ego inertia tends to inhibit easy transition from one context to another. Such inability is yet another form of constraint.

d. *Habitual*. The ongoing acquisition of an immediate, heuristic, and historical perspective breeds generalized patterns of response. Such patterns constitute the legal schematization of the self. They ground habitual freedom. One of the most pernicious prejudices that infect American society is that true freedom is mere spontaneity. There can, of course, be no doubt that the healing of foolish inhibitions liberates affectivity. But its full liberation demands not only healing but schooling. The heart must be trained to respond to complex expressions of beauty. The mind must be trained to new ideas and to new methods of thinking. One must learn to be intelligently decisive. Moreover, until one has acquired adequate habits for dealing affectively, speculatively, and decisively with one's world, freedom of response, if it is present at all, is haphazard at best. Moreover, shared habits breed institutions. And institutions in turn either foster or stifle the growth of insight and of freedom.

e. *Decisive*. Habits are shaped by decision. As a consequence, one's ability to deal creatively with one's world is also a function of the intensity of the satisfactions achieved in the course of one's personal development. Satisfactions, as Whitehead saw, may be characterized as trivial or vague, as focused or broad.

A trivial satisfaction lacks coordination and reinforcement among the variables that function within it. Collecting garbage is an important service. But the satisfaction it yields the collectors is trivial in comparison with Michelangelo's satisfaction in carving the Pietá.

A vague satisfaction is one that suffers from faintness of contrast. In driving across west Texas, one is oppressively aware of the landscape. But as the journey wears on and on, one monotonous mile blurs into another. At the end of the drive, one is hard put to describe the terrain in any significant detail.

A focused satisfaction is tightly unified in its relational structure. But relational unity enjoys degrees of felt contrast. Unity may be achieved at the price of minimizing diversity. If so it degenerates into mere uniformity. Higher forms of unity, on the other hand, integrate the largest possible number of variables into a tight relational structure that combines complexity and focus. The difference between mere uniformity and the higher forms of unity is the difference between a scream and the Bach B-Minor Mass.

The breadth of a satisfaction is a function of the number of variables present within it. A two-week trip to Europe yields broader satisfaction than two weeks on the assembly line.

Achieved satisfactions shape the emerging self because they are the work of decision. The intensity of one's personal satisfactions is measured by the simultaneous unity and multiplicity one can integrate decisively within experience. Complex and integrated satisfactions enhance consciousness by intensifying the evaluative contrast present within experience. They also foster the ability to deal simultaneously with a broad spectrum of experienced variables. Both foster the growth of habitual freedom.

Ego and Freedom

That environmental, qualitative, perspectival, habitual, and decisive variables condition the waxing and waning of adult ego-consciousness should be clear. Stimulating environments intensify ego-awareness; boring ones stifle it. New feelings, new ideas, new questions, new techniques for dealing with reality—all enhance the developing ego. Their absence breeds tedium, atrophy, complacency. The peaks, plateaus, and depths of ego-growth are marked by satisfactions of greater or lesser intensity, vagueness, triviality, focus, and breadth.

The same variables shape ego-maturation through childhood and adolescence. Environmental and qualitative variables are crucial during sensory-motor development. The pre-operational child knows conceptual enrichment in the growth of fantasy. The operational child begins to explore the world of inferential evaluation. The legal schematization of each phase of experiential growth yields habits of decisive reaction, of recall, of inferential insight. The erosion of childish egotism opens up new evaluative perspectives, as does the adolescent's more or less systematic exploration of artistic, literary, scholarly, and scientific disciplines.

It should also be clear that the interweaving of environmental, qualitative, perspectival, habitual, and decisive variables in the growth of ego-consciousness gives incremental definition to the child's capacity to act or not to act, to do one thing rather than another. Freedom, then, when viewed in an emergent problematic, is a profoundly analogous concept. For the analogy of experience demands that no two individuals be free in exactly the same way. It demands too that one acknowledge the flickering character of one's own experience of freedom.

The scholar, for example, by shaping his body and his impinging environment to the exigencies of creative reflection, is free to engage in activities that the professional football player is not. The latter, by disciplining his body and environment to the exigencies of sport, is free to engage in athletic activity closed to the scholar. Both are free in different ways.

Moreover, each enjoys a different degree and kind of freedom in relationship to his peers. The quarterback is athletically free in a way that a tackle is not, and vice versa. The professional physicist enjoys intellectual forms of freedom that the philosopher does not, and vice versa. Yet neither intellectual nor football player is wholly bound to the kind of personal freedom he has professionally and painstakingly acquired. The thrust of the self toward the future leaves both open to cultivating new forms of personal liberation.

Natural Conversion

We have explored the growth processes that ought ideally to precede the experience of natural conversion. It is time to begin to explore the experience of conversion itself.

It should be clear from the preceding analysis that the thrust of natural and healthy ego-maturation is to conscious, personal autonomy in one's affective, speculative, and decisive responses. To assume conscious personal autonomy for oneself in any controllable area of personal growth is to experience conversion.

Normally, the term "conversion" is exclusively religious in connotation. Moreover, like the term "freedom" it has over the centuries acquired a number of narrow and misleading associations. The pietistic and the revivalistic traditions have tended to link conversion with "subjective" experiences of emotional upheaval. Denominationalism equates conversion with successful proselytization. In denominational religion one is converted from heresy and unbelief to objective creedal orthodoxy.

There is a half truth struggling to expression in both positions. Religious conversion does entail a change of heart, a healing of the memory, a readjustment of physical purpose. But its conscious affective impact may be more or less sudden, more or less violent, more or less intense. In no instance is it merely subjective. Similarly, authentic conversion does in fact bind one in love and compassion to others. It bears fruit, therefore, in incorporation into a community of faith. Nor are all creeds mutually compatible. To this extent the proselytizing preacher is correct in demanding ritual induction into a concrete religious community. But over the centuries denominational conflict has bred a rigidity of mind that is finally irreconcilable with integral conversion before God. For it objectifies creedal propositions in ways that are misleading.

Religious conversion may be correctly described as the assumption of personal responsibility for responding appropriately to the historical self-revelation of God. Religious conversion lives, then, at the level of decision. But it is motivated by attitudes and beliefs that have been touched by a sense of ultimacy. Because it is the decision to respond to the free and humanly transforming eruption of God into history, authentic religious conversion must be the work of grace. At the same time, to the extent that graced conversion involves the assumption of conscious responsibility for one's personal reactions, it has something in common with other growth experiences that can be wholly natural in origin. For I can in principle and in fact decide to assume responsibility for my personal affective, intellectual, and moral development in total abstraction from God, revelation, and grace. John Dewey is an outstanding and articulate example of such a posture.

Here, however, it is important to recognize that authentic natural conversion is not of itself sinful. It is not opposed to God. Through the processes of abstraction, it is simply religiously neutral. As a consequence, it is also incomplete. It needs to be pneumatically transformed.

The laws governing sound affective, speculative, and moral development are not the same. Psychology and psychotherapy are not logic. Ethics is different from all three. Hence, to cultivate conscious and responsible self-appropriation at one level is not necessarily to cultivate it at another. One may, then, in principle be affectively converted, but intellectually and morally unconverted, or intellectually converted but affectively and morally unconverted, or morally converted but intellectually and affectively unconverted. The ideal, of course, is to be integrally converted.

Affective Conversion
Karl Rogers has provided some useful insights into the normal progress of natural affective conversion. One may divide the conver-

sion process into eight possible stages.[29]

Stage one. At first one resists any discussion of personal feelings and attitudes. The physical purposes that shape personal experience are either ignored or disowned. Appreciative insight is dismissed as trivial. Close affective ties with others are felt as threatening. There is no felt need for affective healing, no desire for a shift in personal attitudes. Conscious rational processes are largely cut off from their deeper, subconscious motives.

Stage two. There is discourse about affectivity but resistance to discussing one's personal affective cramps and biases. There is an inchoate sense that present emotional attitudes are linked with the past. But discourse about feeling is still detached and "objective." For example, instead of saying "I am lonely and neglected," I will say "No one really appreciates what I do for them." There is only a vague differentiation of the feelings that motivate conscious behavior and a tendency to overgeneralize their impact upon experience. This tendency is expressed in phrases like: "I never do anything right" or "I am always putting my foot in my mouth." Contradictory attitudes are expressed but not named as such.

Stage three. One begins to talk more about oneself, but still in "objective" terms. Awareness of past affective attitudes is becoming more detailed, but it is still difficult to accept one's affectivity and to acknowledge present attitudes as one's own. There is, however, an inchoate ability to name past attitudes as merely affective. Contradictory attitudes begin to be recognized as such. There is an inchoate conscious acknowledgment that affectivity controls more of one's present behavior than one would like to admit.

Stage four. Affective discourse ceases to be bound to the past. Discourse about present affective states is, however, still couched in "objective" categories. Present negative attitudes begin to be begrudgingly and fearfully acknowledged. One begins to be aware of ego defenses against unwanted affections and to question one's former interpretations of one's own attitudinal stances. There is a growing desire to come to grips with conflicting physical purposes. There is conscious facility in naming different affective reactions and an initial concern to describe them with precision. Though close relationships are still threatening, one begins to risk exposing affective needs to others.

Stage five. Present affective responses are now freely expressed, although there is still some fear of confronting them fully or expressing them spontaneously in the present. There is a growing tendency to acknowledge personal responsibility for the way one feels and with such acknowledgment a growing desire to be affectively honest in dealing with others. There is less and less need to postpone facing present affective reactions. There is a growing sense of the conplexity of human affectivity. Personal attitudinal contradictions and incongruities are accepted with greater equanimity. Ego defenses against affective transparency begin to crumble.

Stage six. Affective responses begin to flow freely without inhibition or repression. They are accepted in all of their complexity. There is a constantly diminishing tendency to "objectify" one's attitudes. Feelings are expressed visibly and without fear in tears, sighs, bodily attitudes. There is a sense of liberation from former misleading beliefs about one's affectivity and about the place of physical purposes in human experience. Differentiation of diverse affective responses is now sharp and basic. Personal affective conflicts are no longer abstract problems to be solved but phases of growth to be lived through and resolved.

Stage seven. New affective responses are sensed and accepted immediately and their motives clearly acknowledged. There is affective freedom to face each new situation and deal with it in the present. Past traumas are less and less constricting. There is a healthy sense of one's fallibility in dealing with affective responses. There is a new-found sense of being able to choose new paths of growth and development.

Stage eight. This final stage crowns the process of initial conversion. It is marked by a conscious commitment to grow in understanding of one's affective attitudes and to cultivate balanced esthetic growth. Personal interest in artistic and literary explorations of the human heart is intensified. There is a growing attempt to rank esthetic satisfactions and to choose those that are genuinely liberating and ennobling. There is a concern with the impact of the environment on balanced affective development in oneself and in others.

Intellectual Conversion

Progress in natural intellectual conversion parallels affective maturation.

Stage one. Truth is affirmed naively and objectively. Subconscious affective or speculative motives for belief are either ignored or disowned. One is speculatively complacent, inclined to condescend to those of differing opinion.

Stage two. Theoretical objections to one's personal beliefs begin to be entertained. But they are handled polemically. One's concern is to refute alien positions rather than to understand and appreciate them for the potential insight they offer. One is inclined to admit past moments of ignorance and fallibility. But present beliefs are adhered to unswervingly. Argumentation is concerned with establishing objective truth or falsity. Moments of self-doubt produce feelings of speculative panic: one fears that any change in one's belief structure will demand the abandonment of all that one has formerly cherished.

Stage three. One begins to speak more freely about the reasons that motivate one's conscious creedal posture. There is a growing awareness that specific forces have shaped one's personal intellectual history. But one still resists assuming present responsibility for positions held personally to be true. There is an increasing tendency to appeal to authority to bolster familiar beliefs. But implicit in the appeal is a nascent admission of the possibility of present fallibility. There is, then, a dawning tendency to concede that not all of one's personal beliefs have adequate speculative grounding. But one still resists the suggestion that they are in fact revisable.

Stage four. The actual motives grounding specific personal beliefs begin to be subjected to critical scrutiny. Inadequacies in one's personal positions are conceded but still fearfully and begrudgingly. The positions of former adversaries are examined with greater sympathy. There is a growing awareness of one's need for present help in evaluating personal propositional stances. One begins to risk the admission of present doubts even about cherished beliefs.

Stage five. Doubts and hesitations about inadequately grounded beliefs are now freely expressed. Inadequacies or contradictions in one's own positions are immediately acknowledged. Prerational affective motives for personal speculative stances are candidly confessed. Appeal to authority is replaced by a growing willingness to trust one's personal guesses, hunches, hopes, in speculative matters. Reliance on personal speculative preferences begins to breed a new sense of intellectual freedom. The theoretical exploration of different points of view is no longer threatening. On the contrary, it is exciting, stimulating. There is a growing capacity to live with fallible, imperfectly grounded personal beliefs until one can bring them to more adequate conscious resolution. But in the absence of clear criteria for opting for one speculative position rather than another, taste begins to replace authority as the basis for speculative assent. Positions begin to be entertained because they are more appealing, interesting, stimulating, rather than because they are objectively true.

Stage six. There is a growing sense of the need to accept the speculative and practical consequences of one's personal beliefs. Beliefs are more easily revised now, especially in the face of clear internal contradiction or of new or overlooked evidence to the contrary. One begins to develop a sense of humor about one's own fallibility. One begins to differentiate which of one's beliefs would seem to have adequate speculative grounding, which are still held dogmatically or out of an appeal to authority or to esthetic preference. One senses the need to elaborate criteria for evaluating the truth, falsity, or degree of probability of specific propositions. The study of logic begins to take on fascination.

Stage seven. There is greater sureness concerning the predictable consequences of specific theoretical options. The possibility of creating a self-consistent personal system of belief becomes increasingly appealing. There is a growing desire to enter into creative dialogue with those of similar aspiration. Personal fallibility begins to be habitually assumed.

Stage eight. This stage crowns the initial conversion process. It is marked by the conscious and deliberate assumption of personal responsibility for one's fallible contribution to the human search for truth. There is a growing fascination with the processes that give normative shape to sound speculation. One is increasingly fascinated by the historical development of human beliefs and by the normative critique of different kinds of speculative presupposition. Thoretical frames of reference begin to be consciously and critically examined. One begins to establish critical norms for evaluating their relative interpretative adequacy.

Moral Conversion

Natural moral conversion may be schematized into a similar set of ideal stages. We shall return to the problem of ethical development in Chapter VII.

Stage one. One acquiesces spontaneously and unreflectively in the values incarnate in one's familiar environment. Other value systems and ways of living are either ignored or dismissed without thought. Challenges to the values that shape personal decisions and life-style are resisted as alien and threatening. There is no critical awareness of the historical forces that have shaped one's personal value system and socio-political relationships with others. There is no sense that the social ordering of one's life could or should be other than it already is.

Stage two. One begins to be aware that others espouse value systems contrary and even contradictory to one's own. But one's concern is to vindicate the superiority of personally familiar forms of social intercourse. That one's personal life-style may be in need of alteration is still not seriously considered. When ethical discourse occurs, it remains concerned with the objective truth or falsity of conflicting moral claims. There is an inchoate sense that one's habitual patterns of behavior are historically and culturally conditioned. But there is as yet no acknowledgment of significant bias or limitation in the conditioning process. Challenges to personal moral prejudices are met with strong affective resistance and elaborate argumentation.

Stage three. One begins to discuss the "objective" pros and cons relevant to specific ethical problems. There is a growing sense of specific historical influences that have conditioned one's personal life-style: sexual, familial, local, regional, national, religious. Speculative loopholes in one's personal value system are plugged by appeal to acknowledged moral authorities: parental, political, intellectual, religious. There is a tacit assumption that a thorough investigation of the reasons behind accepted sanctions for personal behavior would confound those of a different moral persuasion.

Stage four. The moral adequacy of personal ethical decisions begins to be consciously discussed. There is growing sympathy for the ethical dilemmas facing members of different social classes and groupings. There is a begrudging acknowledgment that the values shaping unfamiliar life-styles may pose a legitimate challenge to one's own. Appeal to authority begins to be eroded by a growing sense that responsible formation of one's conscience is the fruit of social dialogue. There is a nascent, begrudging admission that even cherished personal and traditional modes of conduct may be open to legitimate challenge.

Stage five. Doubts and hesitations about inadequacies in one's personal ethical positions are now freely acknowledged and their present motives begin to be scrutinized. The influence of physical purposes and of fallible propositional feelings upon personal decision is candidly acknowledged together with their historically conditioned character. In the absence of clear theoretical justification for one's personal ethical beliefs, there is a growing willingness to trust one's moral hunches. But there is as yet little attempt to criticize their presuppositions and consequences systematically. The attempt to understand alien value systems and life-styles begins to be more fascinating than threatening. As yet, however, one lacks evaluative criteria for judging among different ethical perspectives.

Stage six. There is a growing realization that personal moral options bring with them either destructive or life-giving consequences for oneself and for others. There is a growing sense of the need to be self-consistent in one's moral beliefs and personal decisions. Ethical positions begin to be modified when they are recognized as inconsistent, inadequate, or destructive. The different kinds of "oughts" that shape experience—affective, logical, moral—begin to be more sharply distinguished. There is a growing fascination with ethics.

Stage seven. There is growing clarity concerning the practical consequences of different ethical positions. Value systems incarnate in one's personal, social, economic, and political attitudes begin to be speculatively grasped. There is a growing conviction that the pattern of one's personal life as well as social, economic, and political structures should be better conformed to sound moral ideals. Acceptance of personal fallibility makes the revision of inadequate ethical postures easier.

Stage eight. This stage crowns the initial process of conversion. It is marked by the conscious decision to assume personal responsibility for one's judgments of conscience, fallible as they are, and for the ethical soundness of one's personal social, economic, and political decisions. The relative adequacy or inadequacy of different ethical frames of reference begins to be critically scrutinized, their historical antecedents examined, their inadequacies probed, although one's own approach to moral questions is still far from systematic. The causes of social oppression and injustice begin to be grasped. There is growing concern that one's own ethical categories and methods foster growth in personal moral responsibility as one attempts to contribute to the ethical reform of human society.

Christian Conversion

The experience of conversion is, needless to say, a profoundly personal one. It is shaped by the analogy of experience. The preceding account of natural conversion is, then, a frankly idealized portrait. Its purpose is to endow an unfamiliar term, "natural conversion," with a measure of concreteness by detailing the kinds of typical variables that can be expected to shape such an experience. The process described is a natural one because its evaluative form is untouched by religious faith.

American naturalism denies any reality to an encounter with the divine. It insists that what is felt in religious experience is not the reality of God but the reality of spatio-temporal forces imaginatively conceived in naive, mythic categories. And it presupposes that with the development of ego-consciousness, religious language must yield place to the language of science and of ethical philosophy.

The most articulate American exponents of such a position are, of course, George Santayana and John Dewey. For Santayana religion is an irrational ideal completely devoid of literal truth. He writes in *The Life of Reason:*

> The idea that religion contains literal, not a symbolic representation of truth and life is simply an impossible idea. Whoever entertains it has not come within the region of profitable philosophizing on the subject. His science is not wide enough to cover all existence. He has not discovered that there can be no moral allegiance except to the ideal.[30]

Dewey's atheistic naturalism was more morally strenous. He reduced the notion of "God" to the "active relation" between the ideal and the actual. Both men articulated experiences that claim to be untouched by a real, personal encounter with the Holy. For Santayana religion retained a certain anthropological and esthetic interest. Dewey reduced "the religious" to an aspect of natural morality.[31]

At the heart of a naturalistic estimate of religion is the presupposition that God is either by definition unexperienceable or that the experience of God is in no sense public. To establish its position, naturalistic polemic against religion seizes on the misleading language of subjectivism and of divine transcendence that mars dualistic forms of religion and then fallaciously supposes that such language is adequate to describe every instance of human religious experience. The position taken here is, by contrast, thoroughly convergent with that proposed in John E. Smith's *Experience and God.*[32] It also insists, however, that no human experience, whether religious or secular, is ever purely subjective. And it argues with Bernard Lonergan that within incarnational religion the public debate of issues is as applicable in theology as in any other speculative discipline.

More to the point, however, those who have known an authentic encounter with the Holy realize both that it cannot be explained away as subjective illusion and that it changes the felt quality of experience.

For Christian conversion is nothing else than the conscious pneumatic transformation of the processes of natural conversion. It transmutes the latter experience by submitting it through explicit faith and constant prayer to the transformative action of the Breath. It is disclosed experientially in the fiducial transvaluation of those values that shape natural conversion.

Christian Transvaluation of Affective Conversion

To transvalue a value system is: (1) to reverse the presuppositions on which it is grounded; (2) in so doing to create a new interpretative frame of reference; and (3) to reintegrate the categories of the transvalued frame of reference into the novel, interpretative context. This integration transmutes their meaning. A transmuted category will, then, retain elements of denotative and connotative significance derived from its former, transvalued frame of reference. But by integration into a novel, transvaluing interpretative context, the transmuted category acquires a wholly new capacity to illumine experience.

The pneumatic transvaluation of natural human values is effected by regrounding them in faith in the God who stands self-revealed in Jesus and the Holy Breath. Because it creates a new kind of consciousness, it brings new freedom. It is, then, a new exodus.

Hopefully the preceding methodological abstractions will acquire greater clarity as we reflect in more detail on the pneumatic transformation of each stage of the conversion process. Let us begin with affective conversion.

Affective conversion is structured by appreciative forms of understanding. Appreciative consciousness, it will be recalled, engages a broad spectrum of concrete evaluative responses: negative as well as sympathetic affectivity, archetypal images, remembered images, artistic and literary insights. The progressive differentiation of the evaluative form of appreciative thinking endows it with greater flexibility and freedom. Artistic creativity is freer than mere acts of recall; recall, freer and more spontaneous than archetypal thinking; archetypal thinking, freer than negative and sympathetic feelings.

Here, three points should be noted. First, archetypal categories endow appreciative understanding with universal significance. They give structure to the common fund of meaning present in imaginative modes of thought. Second, the relative lack of freedom attending archetypal thinking endows it with enormous power. As an archetype emerges within consciousness, it grips the heart. Third, the archetypes that ordinarily shape human appreciative insight are profoundly sexist in character. Erich Neumann has eloquently described the socio-political impact of uncritical acquiescence in traditional archetypal patterns of thought.

Neumann suggests that as human consciousness evolved, society was transformed from a matriarchal, woman-dominated culture to a patriarchal, male-dominated one. That civilization did in fact evolve in the way he suggests is questionable. It is far from clear that all primitive cultures were in fact matriarchal. But Neumann's reflections do cast considerable light on the mythic roots of contemporary sexism. For the standard archetype of the ego in male-dominated cultures is masculine. In patriarchal myths, it is always men who are imagining, reasoning, doing, creating. As a consequence, the patriarchal imagination associates rational insight with being male, appreciative insight with being female. Myths, however, do not traffic in literal truth but in the connotative integration of appreciative understanding. As a consequence, it is folly to characterize any form of human understanding as literally "masculine" or "feminine." But when myths shape experience unconsciously, that truth is often ignored.

Neumann also points out that the high premium placed upon abstract, analytic thought in male-dominated cultures bears bitter fruit in rationalism and technocracy. Together they breed a life-style that is increasingly schizophrenic. For the more ego-consciousness is focused upon rational modes of reflection, the more reason is dissociated from the subconscious motives that give shape to human hope. In advanced cultures, repressed negative feelings are, then, apt to surface in strange ways.[33]

When, for example, the heroic, archetypal imagery that interprets the growth of male ego-consciousness is co-opted by an inflated, technocratic masculine ego, it can be quickly transformed into a bigoted, sexist stereotype. Women are systematically excluded from experiences and opportunities that foster the growth of ego-awareness: education, job opportunities, and the exercise of religious, artistic, literary, intellectual, social, economic, and political leadership. When masculine obtuseness is augmented by overt authoritarianism, the result is not only the social segregation of women but their persecution and public degradation. Women are not merely sentimentalized out of competition with males, they are exploited, raped, and otherwise transformed into chattel and sex objects.

Christ the Hero
Authentic Christian conversion effects the transvaluation of the Hero myths that give affective shape to patriarchal culture. It does so by employing them to interpret the significance of the life and mission of Jesus of Nazareth, the Son of God. Let us reflect on what this means and on how it occurs.

That Jesus is described in the New Testament in heroic, archetypal imagery cannot be denied. He is miraculously born of the Virgin Mary. He leaves His humdrum life at Nazareth to hear the preaching of the Baptist. At the Jordan He comes to a conscious sense of divine mission in the power of the Holy Breath sent Him from the Father-Creator. He is subsequently drawn into conflict with Satan, the father of lies and serpent-tempter of the World Parents. His initial victory over the prince of darkness in the desert is, however, only a prelude to a lifelong conflict with the demonic forces that oppress human life. At the height of that conflict He is betrayed by Judas, the malignant shadow presence whom He encounters at the threshold of the underworld and whom He persists in calling "friend" even in the moment of betrayal. He is crucified and apparently defeated. But His descent into the shadow realm of death is in fact the supreme ordeal every authentic Hero must face. His triumphant return from the underworld in risen glory is His public vindication by the Father-Creator and the prelude to His sacred marriage with the Church, who is the virgin bride He has rescued from the ancient dragon. His gift to His bride is the bread of life and the cup of salvation, which foreshadow the messianic wine, the saving elixir of life He will bestow when He returns again to judge the living and the dead.

Many of the heroic images applied to Jesus by New Testament writers are not, of course, peculiar to Christianity. They are transcultural and lend imaginative shape to other religious traditions as well, as a perusal of Joseph Campbell's *Hero with a Thousand Faces* will show. But in New Testament theology, heroic imagery is sharpened and endowed with transmuted theological meaning by being associated syncretistically both with Old Testament imagery and with the life and teachings of Jesus Himself. The image that unifies the theological use of heroic categories in the New Testament is that of Jesus as the new David, the messianic King of Kings.

Although heroic figures like Sampson or Judas Maccabeus emerged from time to time in Jewish history, David towers over them all as the hero of Israel. Chosen and anointed by Yahweh, his fidelity to his call from God transforms a lowly shepherd boy into the regal pastor of Israel. Victorious in battle, he brings the ark of the covenant to Jerusalem and transforms it into the "City of David." The historical David was himself of heroic stature. But the promise of divine blessing to the house of David gave imaginative shape to Jewish, post-exilic messianism. In the process the image of the "new David" was born. When God's Anointed came to rescue His people, he would like David be a heroic defender of the ark of the covenant, would triumph over the enemies of Israel, and establish a golden age of peace.[34]

Luke's infancy gospel clusters messianic, Davidic images and focuses them on the person of Jesus and on His career. Jesus, even during His lifetime, seems to have been called more than once "son of David." Nor did He reject the title. His triumphal entry into Jerusalem, the City of David, made unmistakable messianic claims.

And His proclamation as Davidic king in the post-resurrectional Church was in part motivated by His own unremitting proclamation of the "reign of God." Moreover, it is Jesus' conception of the scope of the kingdom that provides the interpretative context that transmutes the allegorical significance of traditional heroic imagery.[35]

When used outside of a New Testament frame of reference, heroic imagery interprets the natural development of the masculine ego. When masculine ego-consciousness follows its natural dynamic, it thrusts toward rational, self-reliant conquest of its own destiny. It sets and controls the conditions for its own growth. And it seeks to found human society upon the insights of natural reason alone.

As we shall see in more detail in Chapter VII, Jesus in His life and preaching incarnated values that stand in flat contradiction to all of these masculine ego-ideals. In His preaching, He demanded, not the egocentric conquest of one's personal destiny, but the repudiation of egotistical self-reliance as the primordial human sin. He demanded, not the cultivation of autonomous, rational control of one's future, but unconditioned trust in God and unconditioned submission to the divine will, even when submission leads to Calvary. He demanded that human society be founded, not upon mere human insight, but upon the worship of the one, true God in the service of atoning and forgiving love. To proclaim Jesus as the divine Hero is, then, to repudiate the affective biases that the heroic myths shaping patriarchal cultures inculcate.

This transvaluation of patriarchal myths demanded by authentic Christian conversion has important socio-political consequences. For if consent to Jesus as the divine Hero demands the repudiation of those values on which patriarchal cultures rest, it also demands as its inevitable consequence the transformation of sexist, patriarchal institutions. The Pauline churches glimpsed that truth in their baptismal rituals, which proclaimed that Jesus had abolished all distinction not only between "Jew and Greek, slave and free" but also between "male and female." As Wayne A. Meeks has shown, this ritual phrase, thrice repeated in Paul's letters, seems to have expressed a nascent realization on the part of the first gentile Christians that Jesus had in fact overturned the sexist values of "this world." The gospel of John hints at the same truth when it ascribes the first public proclamation of Jesus' messianic mission, not to Peter and the apostles, as the synoptic gospels had, but to women: to the Samaritan woman, to Martha, to Mary of Magdala.[36]

But whatever the initial impulse in Christian circles to abandon patriarchal biases and institutions, it was soon stifled by cultural inertia. Sexist tendencies in the Hebrew tradition and in Greco-Roman society set the pattern for ecclesiastical organization and polity. These institutional patterns have gone largely unchallenged for almost two thousand years. But what the Church has in fact become provides no automatic measure of what it ought to be. For Church institutions have justification only to the extent that they incarnate integral conversion before God. If, however, as Scripture tells us, the coming of Christ has indeed abolished the distinction between male and female, then sexist discrimination in the Christian community is in fact an abuse and an injustice. And it has been for two thousand years.

Christ and Osiris

One can sense more keenly the revolutionary implications of New Testament use of heroic imagery to interpret Jesus' life, teaching, and resurrection by contrasting the heroic figure of the glorified Christ with the mythic figure of Osiris. The Osiris myth is a myth of transformation. Though of ancient origin, it was still enormously influential at the dawn of the Christian era.

Osiris was the national god of Egypt. In the myth recounting his career, he is drowned in the Nile and then castrated and dismembered by his evil brother Set. Set is a desert god, a symbol of the destructive, desiccating powers that stood as a constant threat to Egyptian life and civilization. The castration of Osiris points to his origin in primitive matriarchal fertility cults. It recalls rites in which the phallus of the young king who was sacrificed annually to the Great Mother was mummified as a symbol of impregnating male potency and preserved until the death of his successor the following year.[37]

But Osiris is more than a primitive fertility god. For through the intervention of his sister-wife Isis, he returns from death imbued with a new, incorruptible, spiritual fertility. Osiris the incorruptible was worshipped because he was the Self-perfected. He proclaims in *The Book of the Dead:* "I have knit myself together; I have made myself whole and complete; I have renewed my youth; I am Osiris, the Lord of Eternity."[38]

Osiris is, then, a mythic image of the male principle self-transformed and immortalized.[39]

The victory of Osiris is also the victory of his son Horus. Horus is the avender of his father; and when the latter returns to the region of celestial light, it is Horus who is endowed with his father's supreme temporal dominion. Horus's enthronement as reigning son of Osiris found ritual expression in Egyptian religion in the coronation and veneration of the Pharoah. Horus is a heroic figure, an archetypal symbol of the male ego. The transformed Osiris, a masculine archetype of the Self. The exaltation of Horus in the power of Osiris is a mythic rendering of the masculine ego triumphant. Neumann is once again illuminating:

> The Pharoah, too, in imitation of Osiris, is at his death changed into a spirit dwelling in heaven; he undergoes an "Osirification" which consists in the union of his soul parts, and the first condition of this is the preservation of the mummy and its magical resuscitation. The whole purpose of the ritual *Book of the Dead* is to make the earthly body immortal by uniting the parts and preventing it from being dismembered. . . . Thus all the essential elements of the hero myth are to be found in the myth of Horus and Osiris. There is only one qualification, and that has to do with the patriarchal conquest of the Terrible Mother. The myth contains traces of the terrible Isis, but the fact that Horus beheads her and commits incest with her in the Memphis festivities is clear proof that she has been overcome. In general, however, her negative role is taken over by Set, and Isis becomes the "good mother."
>
> In this way, the hero myth develops into the myth of self-transformation, the myth of man's divine sonship which is latent in him from the beginning, but can only be realized through the heroic union of the ego (Horus) with the self (Osiris). This union had its first exponent in the mythical Horus, and then in the Egyptian kings who succeeded him. These were followed by the individual Egyptians—though in their case identification with the king was a matter of primitive magic only—and finally, in the course of further spiritual development, the principle that every man had an immortal soul became the inalienable property of every individual.[40]

There is a superficial similarity between the mythic figure of Osiris and that of the risen Christ. Both present themselves as religious symbols of the passage through death to life. But there any real similarity ends. For while Osiris was a purely imaginative figure, Jesus was a concrete, historical man. While the return of Osiris from death was a mythic symbol of psychic integration, the resurrection of Jesus was an experienced reality. While the myth of Osiris lent pseudo-religious sanction to an oppressive, patriarchal political power structure, the risen Christ reveals that same power structure to be Satanic in inspiration. While the Osiris-Horus myth describes the enthronement and apotheosis of the male ego, Jesus, the suffering servant of the Lord, the new, pneumatic Adam, the Son of Man (*Ben Adam*) demands the renunciation of patriarchal (and matriarchal) ego-inflation and inaugurates the age of the Holy Breath.

Our Mother in Heaven

It was Jesus' unique mediatorial relationship to the Breath that transformed Him in Christian aspiration into the new Adam, the head of a new race of men and women pneumatically consecrated to God. The old Adam by his sin inaugurated the patriarchal oppression of women; the new Adam reverses the sinful disobedience of the old and brings liberation from sexist oppression by the saving power of the Breath. For not only does the Breath reconcile Jew and Greek, slave and free, male and female in atoning, forgiving love, but the Breath also inspires the handmaidens as well as the male servants of the Lord to do great deeds in the divine name. Moreover, it is possible to argue that the Breath stands self-disclosed to the Christian imagination as a feminine principle.

It took the Christian community several centuries to vindicate unambiguously the personal character of the Holy Breath.[41] In Hebrew piety, the Breath of Yahweh was an impersonal force. In this respect, Lukan pneumatology would seem to betray certain affinities to Old Testament patterns of thought. But the Pauline and Johannine traditions both spoke of the Breath in terms that are more clearly personal in connotation.[42]

By the time the personality of the Breath was clearly enshrined in the Christian creed, however, the iconography of the Holy Breath had already been fixed. Its inspiration was the New Testament. But New Testament images of the Breath, derived as they were from the Hebrew Scriptures, were either feral or impersonal. The divine Breath was imagined as fire, as wind, as a dove. The connotative inadequacy of such images to express the reality of the Breath as a person is suggested in an anecdote about a Japanese missionary. In the story a catechizing priest is confronted by a perplexed Japanese catechumen who is trying to understand the doctrine of the Trinity. The latter insists: "God the Father and God the Son I understand. But who is the Honorable Dove?"

It is not difficult to grasp why an impersonal, Old Testament iconography of the Breath has sufficed in Christian piety for centuries. By the time the personality of the Breath had been vindicated theologically, Her experienced role in the economy of salvation had been theologically obscured. Paul the apostle, for example, described the Breath on more than one occasion as being the "mind of God and of Christ." The Holy Breath functions as the interpretative link between Father and Son, between Jesus and His Church. Such phrases took on concrete, experiential meaning in a community that was consciously responding to the gifts of the Breath. With the waning of popular charismatic piety, the religious experiences that gave significance to this Pauline phrase faded, until in the Logos Christology of the Fathers, Jesus Himself, not the Breath, came to be associated with the divine intellect, the divine mind. At the same time, orthodox vindication of the divinity and personality of the Breath had led to creedal insistence on the Breath's adorability.

These insights were important theological advances. But an eternal Breath who is the object of adoration is experienced differently from a Breath who is an immanent charismatic divine principle of teaching and of light. And indeed with the passage of the centuries, theological discourse tended more and more to objectify the Breath and then to locate Father, Son, and Holy Breath in a Platonic eternity far removed from human space and time. By the fourth century a theology of the Breath and of gift had given way in the West to an anti-Pelagian theology of "grace." The language of the "divine Breath" and of "gift" informed popular Christian piety less and less, until finally, during the Middle Ages, the cult of the Virgin replaced the cult of the Breath in importance and popularity.

One may then argue that the Christian community has rested largely content with feral and impersonal icons of the Breath because as charismatic fervor waned and as speculation about the Spirit became increasingly abstract, the person of the Breath lost any strong affective hold upon the Christian heart. By the early nineteenth century, the Breath could in fact be aptly described as the forgotten God. During the nineteenth century, however, Catholic theology began to rediscover the Holy Breath. The earliest work proceeded at a fairly esoteric, scholarly level. It attempted to become pastoral in the papal encyclicals *Divinum illud munus* and *Mystici corporis*. But only with Vatican II was the charismatic activity of the Holy Breath officially restored to its full importance in Catholic teaching. Moreover, in the wake of Vatican II, there has been a significant renewal of all the Pauline gifts in the popular piety of the churches.

One may argue, then, that the time is also ripe for a renewed iconography of the Holy Breath, one that is integrally and explicitly

Christian. The only doctrinally adequate contemporary Christian image of the Divine Breath is, however, a personal one. Now there are different ways of defining "person" abstractly. But there are only two ways to imagine a person concretely, either as male or female. The foundational issue is, then, clear: in a renewed, Christian, personal iconography of the Breath, how ought the Paraclete to be imagined, as a man or as a woman?

There is no question here of the literal application of sexual categories to the Christian deity. Appreciative understanding deals in connotative, not in logical, truth. Christians have for centuries imagined the Father as an old man with a white beard riding on a cloud. No one was upset by the image as long as no one mistook it for literal, logical truth. An image interprets experience with connotative truth if it has the capacity to draw spontaneously to itself a cluster of other images that lend appreciative insight into the reality that is in need of affective understanding.

Here it is important to remember how archetypes organize affective understanding. They do not seek to define the essence of the reality they present. Instead they function as the interpretative center of an image cluster that orients more or less vague aspirations toward a reality that is otherwise grasped appreciatively through a miscellany of disparate, unrelated images. One may argue that the archetype of the feminine as a positive transformative force can perform just such an interpretative function for many of the images traditionally associated in Christian piety with the person of the Holy Breath.

In the gospel of John, for example, the Breath is imagined as proceeding in an inchoate way from the new Adam as He hangs upon the life-giving tree of the cross. The Breath who raises Jesus from the dead is, then, the force, the living water that transforms the tree of death into the tree of life.

Images such as these are traditionally linked to the archetype of the feminine. The menstrual flow links the feminine with the ocean tides and with their mysterious depths. As the image of water gathers religious significance to itself, it is transformed into the water of life that quenches the longings of the heart and bestows immortality. Similarly, Mother Earth is the source of life-giving plants. In many mythologies, the image of the feminine is, therefore, traditionally associated with the religious image of the tree of life.[43]

In traditional Christian piety, the Breath is also the source of divine enlightenment and wisdom. The Breath is the soul of the Church, the animating principle in its charismatic and its sacramental, eucharistic worship. The Breath effects rebirth, immortality. The

Breath inspires the Scriptures, the prophets, the Apocalypse. These images too are connoted by the archetype of the feminine.[44]

The womb is linked syncretistically to caves and to cave-like places. Among such places are churches. The medieval imagination knew as much when it identified its great cathedrals with the Virgin herself. The cathedral of Chartres is not dedicated to Our Lady; it is, as Henry Adams has shown, Notre Dame herself.[45] Similarly, imbibing divine wisdom is frequently likened even in Christian piety to drinking milk from the breast. The breast is thus transformed imaginatively into a sacred cup of truth, a chalice, the holy grail, the cup of the eucharist. As Earth Mother, the feminine principle is traditionally imagined as imparting both life and inspiration through the kinds of food she produces. In Christian belief, the supreme life-giving food is the bread of life, which derives its vital force from the action of the Breath. As transformative, the archetype of the feminine is traditionally imagined as the source of rebirth into immortality and as the divine principle of ecstasy, inspiration, vision, and heavenly wisdom.[46]

Finally, as we have already noted, the feminine is a personal archetype. Clearly, then, it has the capacity to integrate syncretistically a number of images that are linked in the Christian tradition with the reality and saving action of the Breath. Needless to say, the preceding suggestions need to be argued in greater theological detail. Our purpose here is merely to sketch how such an argument might proceed and to suggest some of its consequences for a theology of human emergence.

Before proceeding, however, there is need to recall one important law of psychic development. One cannot argue oneself into the interpretative use of an archetype. Archetypal thinking is not rational, controlled, deliberate. It is spontaneous, syncretistic, and engages deep, subconscious motives. The emergence of an archetype into consciousness is closer to an event than to a deliberate choice, although it can galvanize choice. All theological argument about archetypal thinking can accomplish is to vindicate in principle the connotative relevance of this or that archetype to some aspect of Christian faith and practice. The archetype's concrete aptness for interpreting the reality in question can be felt only as the heart becomes attuned to its power and richness. No one then will be able to imagine the Breath as feminine who is not appreciatively sensitive to the beauty and mystery of woman and open to the abolition of sexism from human society.

Sexual Politics and the Dark Night of Sense

The preceding reflections, if sound, cast an important foundational light on the meaning of the dark night of sense. Ordinarily, as we have seen, the term refers to the preliminary healing of repressed anger, fear, and guilt through self-discipline and the action of the Breath. But the realm of physical purpose encompasses archetypal thinking as well. The archetypal images that shape human attitudes are, however, profoundly sexist in character. If, then, the dark night of sense demands the healing of disordered affectivity in such a way that authentic Christian hope can be born, then it must include the healing of sexist attitudes as well.

That healing is effected by cordial consent in faith to the transvaluation of patriarchal, mythic values effected by the mission of Jesus and of the Breath. Cordial consent to the Breath demands, as we have seen, a capacity to respond affectively to the beauty of the feminine. It demands the healing of patriarchal egotism and the heartfelt acknowledgment of the feminine as a potential incarnation of divine life. It also demands the creation of a social order in which it is possible for women to develop graced egos and to use them on an equal basis with men for the betterment of the world and of society.

For belief in the Holy Breath (as opposed to abstract propositional belief that there is a Holy Breath) demands practical openness to the call of the Breath in prayer. The Breath's call is Her gifts, or charisms. An integrally converted Church is, then, a fully charismatic Church, one in which each person, male or female, stands responsibly open to the promptings of the divine Breath. It is the gift-giving Breath, then, not the sexist prejudices and institutional structures of patriarchal cultures, who must give concrete shape to the Christian community. To exclude any person in the community a priori from the possibility of receiving any charism of the Breath is to set arbitrary limits to the Breath's saving action. In an integrally converted Church, women should have public access to any form of service for which they are competent and to which they are moved by the Holy Breath. Clearly, then, the hearts of Christians will not be completely transformed in the power of the Breath until Christian hope finds courage to end the patriarchal captivity of the Church.

If so, however, then in addition to masculine and feminine symbols of graced wholeness, the Christian community is also in need of masculine and feminine symbols of the graced transformation of ego-consciousness. The historical Jesus functions in a Christian conversion experience as an interpretative symbol of the graced transformation of the masculine ego. So do the male saints. The great feminine saints ought then to perform a similar function for Christian women.

Too often, however, the heroism of women saints has had to flourish in the narrow social confines dictated by a male-dominated culture, although St. Joan of Arc stands as a stubborn Gallic reminder that Christian women need not confine their service solely to activities that are socially acceptable to the patriarchy. The same lesson can be learned from a contemporary prophet like Dorothy Day.

An integrally converted Church would, then, not only allow women full scope to exercise their charismatic gifts in obedience to the Breath's call, but it would stand prophetically opposed to all bigoted, patriarchal social structures. It would denounce those who oppress women, who deny them educational access to ego-skills, and who refuse them the right to exercise such skills charismatically for the loving service of others.

These reflections also enjoy more abstract, speculative implications. Liberation theologians have been calling for the elaboration of a spirituality of socio-political involvement. They have correctly censured substance theology for "privitizing" theological understanding of human freedom. Substance thought, however, privatizes not only the notion of "freedom" but those of "reason" and "affectivity" as well. For it transforms every evaluative experience into a "subjective" process that must transpire within a reality that exists in itself but not in anything else.

An emergent foundational theory of the human negates the notion of substance and insists on a social, relational understanding not only of freedom and of thought, but of affectivity as well. For the healing of the heart demanded by the dark night of sense will be accomplished only partially and with difficulty as long as human experience is shaped by socio-political structures that oppress and thwart balanced emotional development. The patriarchal oppression of women creates environments that breed unconscious sexist prejudices and shallow rationalizations of sexist bigotry.

The dark night of sense will not be completed, therefore, until it sets the Christian community and each person in it in prophetic opposition to *machismo* and to the oppression that is its fruit. Nor is a spirituality of liberation complete that confines its attention to political and economic questions while ignoring the defense of women's rights.

By the same token, however, a feminism that refuses to submit to the healing power of the Breath can be expected to embody all of the aberrations of unhealed human egotism. For it is selfish egotism and repressed sadistic tendencies that render patriarchal cultures oppressive.

The pneumatic healing of sexism in the Church and in human society demands, then, not the establishment of an all-powerful matriarchy to replace an oppressive patriarchy. Nor does it demand the withdrawal of women from a masculine world in narcissistic self-congratulation and lesbian sterility. It does demand a thoroughly androgynous social order in which each person's gifts, both natural and pneumatic, are valued, nurtured, and integrated into the fabric of human and religious society.

We have scarcely begun to imagine what such a society would be like. The power of the patriarchy is political and economic. Its prejudices are woven into the fabric of our emotions and institutions. Like every oppressive structure, it moves quickly to its own defense. Its capacity to rationalize the status quo is enormous. Its intransigence is all too symptomatic of repressed fear and animosity.

The Catholic community has only begun to face its unconscious sexist biases. The recent statement of the Sacred Congregation for the Doctrine of the Faith provides some indication of the present attitude of Roman officialdom toward women. But despite its presumably good intentions, the document is far from being a final statement about either the status of women in the Church or their admission to ordained ministry. It is, moreover, a statement of a congregation, not of the Pope.

In point of fact, the document gives evidence of being a somewhat hasty response to the recent Detroit conferences. Both endorsed the ordination of women in the Catholic Church. The recent decision of the Episcopal Church to admit women to orders may also have motivated the Congregation's action.

The document, however, fails to take into adequate account a number of important facts. And as a consequence it leaves a number of important questions unanswered. It offers three theological reasons why women should not be ordained: (1) that it is contrary to the intention of Jesus that women should be priests, (2) that their ordination is contrary to the "constant tradition" of the Church, (3) that the minister of the eucharist must bear a "natural resemblance" to Jesus. All three arguments are open to serious theological question.[47]

To establish Jesus' "intentions" in this matter, the Sacred Congregation points to the fact that when Jesus chose the Twelve, He chose only men. Hence, the Congregation argues, Jesus intended that only men should enjoy priestly office in the Church. That Jesus acted as the Sacred Congregation suggests is true. That His action manifested the personal intention they suggest is an affirmation that is unsupported by evidence either in the sayings of Jesus or in any other New Testament document.

The argument implicitly presupposes that the Twelve were the only apostles in the first Christian community. The New Testament makes it clear, however, that such was not the case. The first apostolic college also included persons who, like Paul, had seen the risen Christ and testified to that fact in the community.[48] Since we know that there were women who saw the risen Christ, it is not beyond the realm of historical possibility that women functioned in the first apostolic college.

There is another anomaly in the first argument proposed by the Sacred Congregation. It presupposes that in choosing the Twelve, Jesus intended to appoint them priests. If such was in fact the case, it is odd that the Christian community seems to have been oblivious of the fact for two centuries. The notion that the ordained leaders of the Christian community are "priests of the new covenant" analogous to the levitical priesthood emerges in the third century after the establishment of the monarchical episcopate and after the consolidation of ritual functions in the hands of ordained leaders.[49]

To argue against the ordination of women from the "constant tradition" of the Church is also less than conclusive. The traditions surrounding ordained ministry are complex. But one fact emerges clearly from their examination. Ordained Christian ministry is an evolving institution and was so from the beginning. The appointment of the first deacons was the first important institutional transformation of ordained ministry. It was undertaken to meet clear pastoral needs in the community. The episcopacy was created for similar motives.[50] Moreover, while Jesus called the Twelve, the episcopacy seems to have been largely the creation of missionary apostles like Paul.

Not only have the structures of ordained ministry evolved, so too has our understanding of its meaning. Vatican II has made it clear that the basis of ordained ministry is charismatic and that the Advocate distributes Her charisms as She wills. The Catholic community has only begun to assimilate the implications of these teachings.[51]

To argue that Jesus bequeathed to the Church a clear blueprint for the shape and scope of ordained ministry in the twentieth century is, then, simply not supported by the evidence. It is, however, true that the struggle for women's rights has only been with us for about a century and a half. Also true is the fact that it took the Church several centuries to realize clearly that there were serious moral problems with the institution of slavery. The industrial revolution too was a *fait accompli* before the Church began to critique its destructive presuppositions.

An impartial examination of the traditions of the Church suggests that the Church very early acquiesced uncritically in the patriarchal biases of Greco-Roman society just as it was initially content to tolerate the institution of slavery. Far from being of clear divine institution, the patriarchalization of ordained ministry gives every evidence of having been human, all too human.

The third argument proposed by the Sacred Congregation would seem to involve a startling departure from traditional sacramental theology. One of the permanent doctrinal acquisitions that resulted from the Donatist controversy was the notion that the conferral of grace in a sacrament is in no way contingent upon the moral uprightness of its minister, provided the latter is authorized to administer the sacrament and intends in the process to "do as the Church does."[52]

In suggesting that a sacramental minister must also bear a "natural resemblance" to Jesus, the Sacred Congregation seems to be proposing a new and paradoxical thesis. For if this novel doctrine is true, it would seem to follow that, while God can confer sacramental grace through the instrumentality of a morally unworthy minister, God's hands are tied unless the minister has male sexual organs. The mere affirmation of such a thesis is not its justification. And the evidence we now possess would seem to indicate that the only person in the history of the Church to suggest such a notion is the author of the recent declaration.

The simple truth of the matter is that to function as a sacramental minister one needs only the authorization of the Church. And to represent Christ in the administration of any sacrament, any authorized minister need only "intend to do as the Church does." The character, shape, or size of the minister's sexual organs is simply irrelevant.

Far from settling the debate over the ordination of women, the recent decree has only added fuel to the fire. To deny women ordination is a serious matter and should be supported by serious reasons. If the arguments against the ordination of women are no better than those suggested by the Sacred Congregation, then must not the Catholic community face an inevitable conclusion? For if we continue to refuse ordination to women who are competent to engage in official ministry and who have been inspired in faith with the desire so to serve the Church, then are we not in fact repressing the action of the Holy Breath? Unless the Sacred Congregation can offer more convincing reasons for its present stand than the ones it has suggested, it may find that its declaration has had a very different effect from the one it seems to have intended and that the document will be remembered theologically with the Biblical Commission's defense of the Mosaic authorship of the Pentateuch.[53]

Notes

1. Ex. 3:7–10; Ez. 16:4–14; Dt. 4:37, 6:5, 7:8, 10:12–15.

2. Ex. 11:5, 12:12–13, 27, 23:15, 18, 34.

3. Jn. 1:29–36, 18:28, 19:14, 36, 31:42; Mk. 14:22–24; Ac. 20:7; 1 Co. 10:1–6; 1 P. 1:18ff.; Rv. 21:1–22.

4. Jn. 6:1ff.; 8:37–39.

5. Ga. 5:3–26.

6. Ga. 5:1–13; cf. 4:26–31; 1 Co. 7:22; 2 Co. 3:17; Col. 1:13ff.; He. 2:14ff.; 1 Jn. 3:14; Jn. 5:24; Rm. 6:15, 7:1–6, 8:2.

7. The approach to human freedom suggested in these pages differs somewhat from both a Whiteheadean and a substance account of human liberty. Whitehead postulates that every occasion of experience is internally (or self-) determined and externally free. His understanding of freedom is linked to his belief that experience is finally atomic in structure and that each occasion of experience is the entire universe seen from a specific viewpoint. An emergent account of experience rejects both of the latter beliefs and so is forced to ground freedom in a different set of speculative premises.

Similarly, substance philosophy equates the growth of freedom with liberation from the limitations of matter. It therefore locates human freedom in the spiritual faculty of the will. It restricts freedom of choice to intellectual, spiritual beings and discovers the ultimate guarantee of freedom in the possession of a spiritual essence. An emergent anthropology by contrast eschews the philosophical categories "spirit" and "matter." And it repudiates faculty psychology. While it acknowledges degrees of freedom, it grounds the possession of liberty in processes of evaluative discrimination that are natural until transformed by grace. Such natural liberty would seem in some measure to attend every instance of spatio-temporal experience. Moreover, as we shall see, an emergent anthropology discovers the uniqueness of human freedom, not in some fictive spiritual essence, but in the fact that it can and ought to be the fruit of conversion.

Cf. Whitehead, *Adventures of Ideas*, pp. 19–20, 31–32, 38–42, 54–56, 75ff., 200; *Process and Reality*, p. 33; *Summa Theologiae*, I, QQ. lxxx-lxxxiii; I–II, QQ. x-xviii.

8. An excellent introduction to Piaget's psychology is: John H. Flavell, *The Developmental Psychology of Jean Piaget* (New York: Van Nostrand, 1963). An inciteful supplementary study is Hans G. Furth, *Piaget and Knowledge: Theoretical Foundations* (Englewood Cliffs: Prentice-Hall, 1969).

9. Flavell, *op. cit.*, pp. 41–52.

10. *Ibid.*, pp. 52–84.

11. For a more detailed summary of the material that follows, see: Flavell, *op. cit.*, pp. 84–164.

12. Furth, *op. cit.*, pp. 43–51.

13. *Ibid.*, pp. 164–201. Santayana was sensitive to the child's world of fantasy but interpreted the imaginative construction of a world inaccurately, I believe, as the projection of subjective feelings onto an objective, external environment rather than as the vague disclosure of environmental vectors in which the laws that shape one's sustaining environment and the laws that shape one's emerging personality are vaguely and therefore imperfectly distinguished; cf. George Santayana, *The Life of Reason: Reason in Common Sense* (New York: Scribner's, 1922), pp. 35–95.

14. Furth, *op. cit.*, pp. 158ff.

15. Flavell, *op. cit.*, pp. 202–236.

16. For a helpful introduction to Piaget's ethical thinking, see: Ronald Duska and Mariellen Whelan, *Moral Development: A Guide to Piaget and Kohlberg* (New York: Paulist, 1975).

17. Jean Piaget, *The Moral Judgment of the Child*, trans. Marjorie Gabain (New York: Free Press, 1965), pp. 51–53.

18. *Ibid.*, pp. 57–61, 111–194.

19. *Ibid.*, pp. 199–323.

20. *Ibid.*, pp. 279–323.

21. Neumann, *Origins and History of Consciousness*, pp. 5–16.

22. *Ibid.*, pp. 16–38.

23. *Ibid.*, pp. 39–169; *The Great Mother*, pp. 3–208.

24. Jung et al., *Man and His Symbols*, pp. 108–109.

25. Neumann, *Origins and History of Consciousness*, pp. 52–169.

26. *Ibid.*, pp. 170–191.

27. *Ibid.*, pp. 199.

28. *Ibid.*, pp. 194–219.

29. Carl R. Rogers, *On Becoming a Person* (Boston: Houghton Mifflin, 1961), pp. 125–259. Roger's developmental stages in affective self-appropriation were elaborated under the influence of process thought. When read in the light of the work of Jean Piaget and Lawrence Kohlberg, they suggest the possibility of similar growth processes at a speculative and moral level. What emerges is a more detailed (if idealized) descriptive analysis of Kohlberg's stage 4.5.

30. George Santayana, *The Life of Reason: Reason in Religion* (New York: Collier, 1962), p. 72.

31. John Dewey, *A Common Faith* (New Haven: Yale, 1934), pp. 42–53.

32. John E. Smith, *Experience and God* (New York: Oxford, 1968).

33. Neumann, *Origins and History of Consciousness*, pp. 311–444.

34. 2S. 5:2, 6:1–19, 7:24–27; Ps. 132; Is. 55:3.

35. Mt. 1:1; Lk. 1:67–71, 2:21, 41–50.

36. Wayne A. Meeks, "The Image of the Androgyne: Some Uses of a Symbol in Earliest Christianity," *History of Religions*, XIII (February, 1974), pp. 165–208.

37. Neumann, *Origins and History of Consciousness*, pp. 220–228.

38. *Ibid.*, p. 228.

39. *Ibid.*, p. 239.

40. *Ibid.*, pp. 239, 252.

41. George Montague, *The Holy Spirit* (New York: Paulist, 1976); Edmund J. Fortman, *The Triune God* (Philadelphia: Westminster, 1972).

42. G. W. H. Lampe, "The Holy Spirit in the Writings of St. Luke," in *Studies in the Gospels*, ed. D. E. Nineham (Oxford: Blackwell, 1955), pp. 159–200.

43. Jn. 7:38–39, 18:1–9, 19:25–30, 20:19–29; Neumann, *The Great Mother*, pp. 39–83, 240–267; Cf. Eliade, *Patterns in Comparative Religion*, pp. 154–330.

44. Neumann, *The Great Mother*, pp. 72–73, 281–336.

45. Henry Adams, *Mont S. Michel and Chartres* (New York: Doubleday, 1933).

46. Neumann, *The Great Mother*, pp. 39–54, 120–146.

47. Sacra Congregatio pro Doctrina Fidei, *Declaratio circa Quaestionem Admissionis Mulierum ad Sacerdotium Ministeriale*, pp. 6–21.

48. 1 Co. 15:3–8; Raymond Brown, *Priest and Bishop* (New York: Paulist, 1970); James A. Mohler, S.J., *The Origin and Evolution of the Priesthood* (New York: Alba, 1970), pp. 1–31.

49. Mohler, *op. cit.*, pp. 51–107.

50. Brown, *op. cit.*, pp. 47–86.

51. *Lumen gentium*, 4, 12.

52. DS 1262, 1315, 1611, 1617, 3126, 3318, 3874.

53. DS 3394–3397. Cf. Eugene Bianchi and Rosemary Reuther, *From Machismo to Mutuality* (New York: Paulist, 1976); Rosemary Reuther, *New Woman, New Earth* (New York: Seabury, 1975); Joseph Blenkensopp, *Sexuality and the Christian Tradition* (Dayton: Pflaum, 1969); Paul Jewett, *Man as Male and Female* (Grand Rapids: Eerdmans, 1975); see also *Theological Studies* (December, 1975), an issue devoted entirely to the problem of the status of women in the Church.

VI. Through a Glass Darkly

In the last chapter we began to reflect on the Christian exodus experience. That reflection will continue to preoccupy us in the present chapter and in the two that follow.

At the end of the analysis of the last chapter we found ourselves standing once again above the trailhead that marked the beginning of our ascent. We began our climb by attempting to understand the meaning of the Christian search for salvific integration. In our initial reflections on the meaning of the Christian exodus, we have begun to glimpse the truth that the salvific integration of experience is not only its pneumatic transformation but also its liberation in the power of the Holy Breath. Liberation, pneumatic transformation, coming to wholeness in God—these are simply three facets of one and the same process.

But if Christian conversion is the pneumatic transformation of the natural processes of conscious self-appropriation, it must effect the transformation not only of the heart but of the mind as well. Speculative development is mediated by the growth of propositional feelings. And propositional feelings shape experience most significantly during adolescence and young adulthood. For it is during this period of life that one ought ideally to construct and to consolidate a rational, adult ego. How then ought one to go about the task of ego-building responsibly and in faith? As we shall see, we will be unable to answer that question without addressing ourselves to another question as well. It is the third question we raised at the close of Chapter III, namely, "What is the locus of present experiential access to God?" Clearly, the trail ahead promises to be fraught with a number of complex windings. Before embarking on the next stage of our climb, let us then take care to check out the terrain.

Once again our initial ascent is through the Christian images that cast appreciative understanding on the problem we now face. But this time, our progress through the terrain of the imagination promises to be more arduous than before. This fact should come as no surprise, however; the higher the elevation, the steeper the landscape.

The image that presides over Christian aspiration for the pneumatic transformation of propositional feelings is, I would suggest, the image of Jesus as the New Adam, the firstborn of a pneumatic race of brothers and sisters charismatically anointed in His image. We shall, then, begin our reflections by examining the Adamic myth and the unique shape it gives to Christian hope.

But before beginning our serious climbing we will pause once again for a granola break. For if the image of the risen Christ as the bestower of the charism-giving Breath is the image that presides over the gracing of speculative conversion, a foundational insight into the human dynamics that shape this phase of the conversion process must rest on an understanding of how each of the charisms contributes to the progressive transformation of human experience. This is a problem treated in *Charism and Sacrament*. We will then recapitulate briefly the main points of that argument as immediate preparation for the next leg of our climb. Then we will begin our ascent.

Intellectual, or speculative, conversion bears fruit in the construction of an adult ego. The person who has seen most deeply into the psychodynamics of that process is Carl Jung. Our first set of switchbacks will, then, consist of a brief exposition of the salient features of Jung's descriptive analysis of personality types. On the basis of this analysis we will conclude that the charismatic transformation of experience is in fact the gracing of adult ego-consciousness.

Our final set of switchbacks promises to be the most taxing of all. In the course of it, we will draw upon our newly won insights into the psychodynamics of charismatic development to argue that the only adequate locus of initial, experiential access to God is a Christian charismatic community of faith in which all of the charisms of the Advocate are operative.

At this point in the climb, the terrain will begin to level out again. And we will use it as an opportunity to reflect briefly on two practical problems related to our discussion: the problem of discerning one's charism of service and the problems facing Christian educators.

The trail beckons. It begins with an examination of the Adamic myth. Let us begin to climb.

The Adamic Myth

Paul Ricoeur has argued correctly that the Adamic myth recorded in Genesis simultaneously corrects and transmutes religious values that are present in other mythic traditions. "The pre-eminence of the Adamic myth," he writes, "does not imply that the other myths are purely and simply abolished; rather, life, or new life is given them by the privileged myth."[1]

Ricoeur contrasts the Adamic myth with other mythic accounts of the origin of evil. He distinguishes three other such accounts:

theogonic myths, tragic myths, and Gnostic myths. We have already reflected on some of the foundational implications of Gnostic mythology. Let us now turn our attention to theogonic and tragic myths.

Theogonic myths tell the story of the genesis of the divine principle. In theogonic myths, the god of life functions as the principle of cosmic order. That order must, however, be achieved and sustained from year to year, and with it the life and sway of the benign deity. In such a mythic system, chaos is felt affectively as either anterior to or equiprimordial with the benevolent god. In Ricoeur's words, in a theogonic system one is led to affirm ". . . that evil is as old as the oldest being; that evil is the past of being; that it is that which was overcome by the establishment of the world; that God is the future of being." [2]

In theogonic myths, violence plays an important part. Creation is felt as the violent overthrow of the forces of confusion and destruction. Since, moreover, theogonic deities tend to be national gods as well, the victory of the creator God is believed to be reenacted in each victory of the king over the nation's adversaries. [3]

This interweaving of national and religious hopes was projected ritually into the cultic reenactment of the drama of creation. As in the cult of Osiris, the cultic function of the king was heroic. For in theogonic religion, the national creator god had to be born anew each spring and thus reaffirm control over the divine powers of chaos and destruction. [4]

As Ricoeur suggests, such myths reflect specific kinds of human attitudes. He observes:

> I see the ultimate outcome of this type of myth in a theology of war founded on the identification of the Enemy with the powers that the god has vanquished and continues to vanquish in the drama of creation. Through the mediation of the king, the drama of creation becomes significant for the whole history of mankind, and particularly for all of that aspect of human life which is characterized by combat. In other words, the mythological type of the drama of creation is marked by the *King-Enemy* relation which becomes the political relation *par excellence*. . . . According to that theology, the Enemy is a Wicked One, war is his punishment, and there are wicked ones because first there is evil and then order. In the final analysis, evil is not an accident that upsets a previous order; it belongs constitutionally to the foundation of order. [5]

Tragic myths, on the other hand, present a different kind of appreciative understanding of human salvation. The tragic vision is, perhaps, best exemplified in Greek mythology. Tragic myths are haunted by a sense of "fate." Both gods and humans are caught up in an inexorable cosmic determinism that forces them into conflict and suffering. The Greek deities are ego-inflated; they are subject to hybris and blind self-infatuation. As often as not their conduct is ruthless and vindictive. The divine and the human confront one another as shadow presences locked in a love-hate relationship in which both stand in need of repentance and transformation. Because tragic myths project into the godhead the foibles and follies of human ego-consciousness, they present a vision of divinity that is both terrifying and unthinkable.[6]

Greek religious aspiration provided two different solutions to the tragic dilemma—one artistic, the other philosophical. On the one hand, the ritual dramatization of the divine and human tragedy provided a purgative release from the emotional tension generated by human confrontation with a fallible and vindictive divine principle; on the other hand, Greek philosophy groped for a speculative alternative to affective, mythic religion.

The inadequacy of both efforts is symbolized in the tragic death of Socrates. For the esthetic purification of affectivity through religious drama offers finally no escape from the tragic vision it dramatizes. As Plato saw all too clearly, in the world created by Greek tragedy one must continue to conceive of the gods as either the vindictive cause of evil or as callously indifferent to the misery of the human condition. At the same time, the abstractions of Greek philosophy propounded an Apollonian religion unable finally to touch the human heart.[7]

The Adamic myth, Ricoeur suggests, avoids the limitations inherent in both a theogonic and a tragic vision of God. At the same time, it fulfills what is valid in both traditions. It locates the origin of evil in "an ancestor of the human race as it is now whose condition is homogeneous with ours." Moreover, even though Adam is the protagonist of the myth, the tragic fate of humanity is the work, not of Adam alone, but of the first couple. As Ricoeur has seen, every male is seduced in Eve; every woman sins in Adam.[8]

The Adamic myth insists that goodness is both divine and primordial. And it affirms a radical separation between the origin of good and the origin of evil: evil is the work of a creation whose creator is abiding and indestructible goodness. In the eschatological vision articulated by the Adamic myth, it is out of the question that any power of evil could even hope to vanquish the divine principle.

Moreover, the Adamic myth offers an appreciative insight into the religious significance of history itself. It presents evil as historical in origin and as destined to be overcome by the Lord of History.[9]

As Ricoeur points out, however, elements of tragic and theogonic mythology are selectively preserved and transformed in the Adamic myth. Adam and Eve are together tragic figures seduced not by God but by the serpent, who enters the myth as a vague, chthonic symbol of those environmental, personal, and social forces that set humans in blind and foolish opposition to one another and to a good and just God. The serpent, therefore, also personifies the cosmic forces of evil over which the mercy of God will eventually triumph. But the image of the serpent relegates those forces to a creaturely status. Does Christian faith and foundational theology have any light to throw upon these Hebrew images?[10]

The New Adam

Christian faith proclaims Jesus to be the author of the Adamic reversal, the one who sets into motion pneumatic forces that are God's answer to the very problem of evil to which the Adamic myth sought to give conscious appreciative access. As a consequence, New Testament catechesis, especially in its Pauline formulations, repeatedly interprets the historical figure of Jesus in categories that reverse the characteristics traditionally used to describe the mythic figure of the first Adam. While the first Adam was sprung from the earth, the new Adam descends from heaven. While the first Adam was the author of human ambiguity and sin, the second reveals the scope of God's saving plan and the extent of divine love and forgiveness. While the old Adam was the first human hypocrite, the new Adam frees us from pharisaical self-deception. The list of contrasts could be expanded.

In *Charism and Sacrament* I have attempted to discuss some of the more obvious ways in which the figure of the new Adam combines symbolically with other images to lend evaluative structure to Christian baptismal consent. Our concern here is not, however, with sacramental theology but with the relevance of Adamic imagery to the pneumatic transformation of natural, intellectual conversion. A leading Christian image that yields an appreciative insight into that process is that of the new Adam viewed as pneumatic progenitor. As pneumatic progenitor, Jesus brings into existence a race of men and women who are in process of being transformed in His image by the charismatic activity of the Mother Advocate.[11]

Where Adam had failed utterly, then, Jesus had succeeded. He had vanquished the ancient serpent. Unlike the first Adam who had proudly arrogated divinity to himself, the new Adam had emptied himself in love, trusting in the Father to exalt Him and establish Him as Lord of all creation. From the old Adam came disobedience, condemnation, death; from the new comes obedience, justification, life, and mutual service in a charismatic community of faith.[12]

Implicit, then, in the proclamation of Jesus as the new Adam is a persistent summons to repentance, to faith, and to charismatic openness to the Holy Breath. For as the mythic figure of the old Adam illumines the universal state of humankind in its sinfulness, so the glorious figure of the new Adam reveals the divine destiny to which all are summoned: total transformation in God through the sanctifying, gift-giving power of the Advocate.[13]

Granola Break

The gift of tongues is not ordinarily the gift of speaking a foreign language; it is a gift of prayer that expresses a vague, felt response to an impulse of the Breath of Jesus. When seen as an experience, glossolalia is, therefore, a conscious dative presentation of the presence of the Breath to the glossolalist and through shared glossolalic prayer to the believing community. Moreover, through the inclusion of Acts in the canon of Christian Scriptures, glossolalia has come to serve as a vivid reminder of the first arrival of the Breath on Pentecost day. The active presence of the gift in the believing community recalls, therefore, that salvific event lying at its origin. Moreover, tongues is an event, not a teaching or an act of mere ritual recall. It recreates in the present an important symbolic aspect of the first Pentecost.[14]

The interpretation of a tongue is not its literal translation but the reduction of a message in tongues to intelligible discourse. Moreover, the interpreted tongue functions, as Paul tells us, in the shared prayer of a community in the same way as prophecy. The prophetic word is, however, a confrontational word. It demands a readjustment of attitude. It therefore integrates a physical purpose with an abductive propositional feeling whose formulation is a conscious human response to an impulse of the Breath. Since the development of more complex physical purposes is mediated by imagist thinking, prophetic discourse manifests an affinity for poetic, mythic language. Prophecy and the interpretation of tongues effects, then, the charismatic transformation of conscious physical purposes.[15]

The gifts of teaching of which Paul speaks effect the proclamation and explanation of the message of salvation. Prophetic discourse is oracular and abductive. Teaching involves abductive thinking, but it extends conceptual activity into the realms of deductive and inductive inference. Kerygmatic proclamation is a form of teaching. Since faith healing always occurs in the context of the proclamation of God's word, the gift of healing is nothing else than a ministry of kerygmatic teaching that is blessed by visible signs of healing. Teaching and healing, therefore, both effect the charismatic transformation of propositional feelings.[16]

The gift of discernment mediates communal consensus concerning which alleged pneumatic and charismatic activities in the community truly proceed from the Breath of Jesus. From a logical standpoint, the exercise of a gift of discernment is an inductive inference. But the conclusion reached through discernment also engages appreciative forms of insight. Discernment yields a judgment concerning the truth or falsity, authenticity or inauthenticity, adequacy or inadequacy of specific charismatic impulses in the believing community. It does so in the light both of sound teaching and of a felt sense in prayer of the kinds of forces that are shaping the religious experiences of individuals and of groups. Discernment, then, effects the simultaneous charismatic transformation of primitive physical purposes and of inductive propositional feelings.

The action gifts, like gifts of official leadership, administration, almsgiving, etc., transmute the realm of decision. Marriage and celibacy mediate the charismatic transformation of human sexuality. Apostolate looks to the good of the entire community. It evokes and coordinates the other charisms.[17]

This correspondence of the Pauline gifts to every phase in the natural growth of human experience has both sacramental and anthropological significance. In *Charism and Sacrament*, I have attempted to show that it makes concrete sense out of the sacrament of confirmation. In confirmation, the covenanted Christian makes a lifelong commitment to stand in openness to whatever gifts of service Jesus' Breath may impart. Its anthropological significance begins to appear when we reflect that the ego in the course of its adult development becomes increasingly, though not exclusively, focused on specific phases of human evaluative response. Such focusing yields a personal sense of vocation, or call.[18]

The Adult Ego

One of the persons who has seen most deeply into the dynamics of adult ego development is Carl Jung. In his therapeutic work, Jung began to be sensitive to two very general but distinguishable attitudes in his patients.

Those possessed of the first tended to live in a world apart, largely abstracted from their environments, preoccupied with their own evaluative responses. He called the first group "introverts." The second group displayed an opposite dynamic. They were habitually absorbed with the environmental forces that shape experience and tended to be insensitive to their own personal evaluative processes. This second group Jung called "extraverts."[19]

No one, of course, is ever pure introvert or pure extravert. And Jung correctly protested against the facile labeling of individuals. He dismissed such exercises in pop psychology as "a childish parlor game, every bit as futile as the division of mankind into brachycephalics and dolichocephalics."[20] He insisted that extensive probing of personality is necessary before its true fundamental orientation can begin to appear. That such orientations exist, however, he had no doubt; and he began to grope for ways to distinguish these two attitudes.

Dwelling habitually in an evaluative world of his or her own creation, the introvert tends to feel more or less at sea when confronted with the concrete and the practical. The inability to deal effectively with environmental forces leaves introverts susceptible to compulsive sentiments of inferiority. Needless to say, such feelings only reinforce the introvert's habitual tendency to withdraw into the self. The introvert finds confrontation with the practical and the concrete a threatening experience. Aping the behavior of extraverts is felt as a sham and a mockery. The need to exercise some sort of conscious control over one's world persists, however. But the problem is solved by orienting fantasy and speculation toward power goals. What the introvert cannot accomplish through action, (s)he seeks to accomplish through personal feeling and thought, often to no avail. While the extravert explodes with enthusiasm, the excited introvert becomes all the more silent and withdrawn.

The extravert manifests the opposite personality traits. (S)he empathizes spontaneously with things and in peak experiences knows a kind of mystical participation with environmental forces.

The extravert remains, however, ill at ease in the world of ideas and of affectivity. If an extravert apes the skills of an accomplished introvert, the result is usually superficial or clownish. Speculative self-understanding and the confrontation with one's own personal attitudes threatens extraverts. While the introvert needs to dream a manageable, idiosyncratic world in order to avoid dealing directly with environmental problems and forces, the extravert is doomed to act in unconscious subjection to a host of unacknowledged and unconscious personal motives.

As a consequence, the extravert tends to be troubled by compulsive melancholia and hypochondriacal brooding. Fantasy and insight are valued primarily for their content rather than cultivated for the power they yield. Contemptuous of the abstracted dreamer, the extravert longs to change and revitalize the world through deeds. Hence, while enthusiasm deepens the introvert's self-absorption, it galvanizes the extravert and leads to ever deeper immersion in the world of hard fact.[21]

Jung believed that the distinction between introvert and extravert rested on some sort of biological basis, although he rejected out of hand the attempt to ground personality traits in physiological causes alone.[22] Moreover, as he pondered the personality theories of Sigmund Freud and of Alfred Adler, he found each of them myopically biased either to an introverted or to an extraverted account of the psyche. In his *Psychological Types*, he observed:

> How fantasy is assessed by psychology, so long as this remains merely science, is illustrated by the well-known views of Freud and Adler. The Freudian interpretation reduces fantasy to causal, elementary, instinctive processes. Adler's conception reduces it to the elementary, final aims of the ego. Freud's is a psychology of instinct, Adler's an ego-psychology. . . . The basic formula with Freud is therefore sexuality, which expresses the strongest relation between subject and object; with Adler it is the power of the subject, which secures him most effectively against the object and guarantees him an impregnable isolation that abolishes all relationships. Freud's view is essentially extraverted, Adler's introverted. The extraverted theory holds good for the extraverted type, the introverted theory for the introverted type.[23]

Jung's own personality theory is the attempt to create a more comprehensive hypothesis that can account for the valid insights of both Freud and Adler.[24]

Long before Jung formulated his own personality theory, William James had been insisting that temperament and affectivity give shape in unacknowledged and unconscious ways to allegedly objective scientific and philosophical speculations. In *The Varieties of Religious Experience*, James had distinguished three affective types: the healthy-minded, the sick soul, and the twice-born convert. We have already reflected on the foundational implications of these distinctions.

The Varieties was, however, a relatively early effort on James's part. His second attempt to grapple with the problem of personality types was *Pragmatism*, the philosophical study to which *Varieties* was a propaedeutic. In this later work, he tried to sharpen his earlier insights by delineating two kinds of thinkers whose habitual approach to the world rests upon specific emotional biases. With typical linguistic concreteness, he called the two types "tough-minded" and "tender-minded."[25] He described them in the following terms:

Tender-minded	*Tough-minded*
Rationalistic (going by "principles")	Empiricist (going by "facts")
Intellectualistic	Sensationalistic
Idealistic	Materialistic
Optimistic	Pessimistic
Religious	Irreligious
Free-willist	Fatalistic
Monistic	Pluralistic
Dogmatical	Sceptical

Jung found James's suggestions both stimulating and in need of qualification. And in his *Psychological Types* he devoted considerable space to commenting on James's hypothesis.[26] Moreover, Jung's critique of James is, on the whole, sound. But he was by profession a psychiatrist. And he had, I believe, only an imperfect grasp of the import of American pragmatism. Certainly, both Peirce and Dewey would have dissociated their own philosophies from Jung's description of pragmatism as a movement "which restricts the value of 'truth' to its practical efficacy and usefulness, regardless of whether or not it may be contested from some other standpoint."[27]

The overriding concern of the best expressions of American pragmatism is not practical utility but inferential precision. Peirce's thought inspired the movement, and he was a man who saw and saw quite correctly that hypotheses remain fuzzy until their theoretical and practical consequences are explicated and tested. He realized that an unclarified hypothesis is potentially misleading just as an untestable hypothesis lacks speculative significance, since there is no way to tell whether or not it is true. Such principles sound platitudinous until one begins to examine the methods that subtend a great deal of human speculation. The trivial character of much American and European theology lies in its failure to observe these basic principles.

Jung, in his criticisms of James's character typology, is on more solid speculative grounds. He finds Jamesean categories "too broad" and too exclusively concerned with thinking qualities to provide an adequate personality theory. He observes:

> It would not be difficult to show that such and such a quality is equally characteristic of the opposite Jamesean type, or even of several of them. There are, for instance, empiricists who are dogmatic, religious, idealistic, intellectualistic, rationalistic, etc. just as there are ideologists who are materialistic, pessimistic, deterministic, irreligious, and so on.[28]

Jung's own typology evolved as his clinical experience broadened and as his thought matured. At first he was inclined to regard introverts as thinkers and extraverts as doers. But with time he rejected the idea as too pat. There are, he realized, extraverted thinkers whose minds probe the realm of the concrete. He also discovered individuals who were preoccupied with dative values but for deeply personal, idiosyncratic reasons. He therefore sensed the need to introduce a new explanatory variable into his own hypothesis.

He accordingly differentiated the habitual "attitude" that shapes a personality from its acquired evaluative "functions." An attitude is more generalized than a function; a function lends specificity to an attitude. Attitudes are either "introverted" or "extraverted" in the sense described above. There are four personality functions: "sensation," "feeling," "intuition," and "thought."

Personality Attitudes

In his more detailed descriptive rendering of personality attitudes Jung distinguishes carefully between the conscious and subconscious motivations of both introvert and extravert. At a conscious level, the extravert orients personal activity in accordance with environmental data. If, for example, there is a weather change, the extravert will be sure to bring warm clothes. The absent-minded introvert might well freeze. The extravert's conscious attitudes tend to conform to what is socially acceptable. Extraverted beliefs rest upon solid factual evidence. Personal decisions must be above all hard-headed and realistic. Extraverted life-styles and personal moral conduct coincide with the prevailing laws and customs. Tasks are performed efficiently and satisfy the common social expectations, sometimes at the expense of personal health.

The Achilles heel of the extraverted types is their capacity to become lost in a world of mere "objects." The medieval contemplatives sensed that this tendency is the death of an introverted, Christian, Neo-Platonic mysticism and never tired of warning against *effusio ad exteriora*, or pouring oneself out on externals. There is a wisdom in their warning. Obtuseness concerning personal motives leaves the extravert the easy victim of unconscious and sometimes destructive forms of psychic compensation.[29] As Jung observes:

> The egoism which characterizes the extravert's unconscious attitude goes far beyond mere childish selfishness; it verges on the ruthless and the brutal. . . . The catastrophe can, however, also be subjective and take the form of a nervous breakdown. This invariably happens when the influence of the unconscious finally paralyzes all conscious action. The demands of the unconscious then force themselves imperiously on consciousness and bring about a disastrous split which shows itself in one of two ways: either the subject no longer knows what he really wants and nothing interests him, or he wants too much at once and has too many interests, but in impossible things. The suppression of infantile and primitive demands for cultural reasons easily leads to a neurosis or to the abuse of narcotics such as alcohol, morphine, cocaine, etc. In more extreme cases the split ends in suicide.[30]

The introvert dwells in a different realm of ego-consciousness and is as a consequence faced with a different set of personality problems. The introvert is, of course, aware of environmental influences and challenges but lacks the conceptual and perspectival equipment to deal with those forces effectively. For the introvert, personal interest and preference rather than environmental demands are the decisive determinants of personality development. As a consequence, the introvert values things, not for their own sake, but for their idiosyncratic appeal, for the way they are felt or thought of personally. The introvert is strongly prone to read meanings into things that are derived, not from the things themselves, but from past experiences and habits of thought or affection only indirectly connected with the reality at hand.

Moreover, as in the case of the extravert, the structure of introverted ego-consciousness is shaped by deep-seated subconscious tendencies. For the introverted ego focuses with extreme selectivity only upon certain aspects of personal evaluative response. As subconscious dynamisms entrap the introverted ego in an evaluative world of its own making, the personality becomes increasingly self-preoccupied, egocentric, ineffectually autocratic and autoerotic.

The neuroses of the introvert leave the personality at the mercy of environmental forces that elude understanding and conscious control. Typically, introverted geniuses die in poverty.[31] Jung's own words are enlightening:

> As a result of the ego's unadapted relation to the object—for a desire to dominate it is not adaptation—a compensatory relation arises in the unconscious which makes itself felt as an absolute and irrepressible tie to the object. The more the ego struggles to preserve its independence, freedom from obligation, and superiority, the more it becomes enslaved to the objective data. The individual's freedom of mind is fettered by the ignominy of his financial dependence, his freedom of action trembles in the face of public opinion, his moral superiority collapses in a morass of inferior relationships, and his desire to dominate ends in a pitiful craving to be loved. It is now the unconscious that takes care of the relation to the object, and it does so in a way that is calculated to bring the illusion of power and the fantasy of superiority to utter ruin. The object assumes terrifying proportions in spite of the conscious attempt to degrade it. In consequence, the ego's efforts to detach itself from the object and get it under control become all the more violent. In the end it surrounds itself with a regular system of defenses (aptly described by Adler) for the purpose of preserving at least the illusion of superiority. The introvert's alienation from the object is now complete; he wears himself out with defense measures on the one hand, while on the other he makes fruitless attempts to impose his will on the object and assert himself. These efforts are constantly being frustrated by the overwhelming impressions received from the object. It continually imposes itself on him against his will, it arouses in him the most disagreeable and intractable affects and persecutes him at every step. A tremendous inner struggle is needed all the time in order to "keep going." The typical form his neurosis takes is psychasthenia, a malady characterized on the one hand by extreme sensitivity and on the other by great proneness to exhaustion and chronic fatigue.[32]

Personality Functions

Introversion and extraversion give shape to the leading principle of adult personality development. That is to say, they define a dominant, generalized way of relating both consciously and unconsciously to the forces that shape personal experience. Personality functions, on the other hand, focus these generalized attitudes upon one or other phase of human feeling. Both are legal schematizations of the self, but functions are more specialized.

The function of sensation focuses conscious ego-development upon incarnate, factual value, both dative and decisive, for every decision enters into the dative phase of the next stage in the growth of feeling.[33] Jung notes:

> Objects are valued in so far as they excite sensations, and, so far as lies within the power of sensation, they are fully accepted into consciousness whether they are compatible with rational judgments or not. The sole criterion of their value is the intensity of the sensation produced by their objective qualities. Accordingly, all objective processes which excite any sensations at all make their appearance in consciousness.[34]

The function of feeling focuses conscious ego-development upon vague, pre-archetypal forms of physical purpose.[35] As we saw in Chapter III, as the affective continuum grows in evaluative differentiation, the realm of physical purpose bifurcates into two distinguishable realms of feeling. On the one hand, there are vague sympathetic or negative affections that are linked more or less directly to experiences of pleasure and of pain. And on the other hand, there are more highly differentiated archetypal and imaginative feelings. The first, pre-archetypal phase in the growth of experience corresponds to what Jung calls "feeling"; the archetypal, imaginative phase, to what he calls "intuition."[36] The function of "thought" corresponds to the realm of abstract, propositional inference.[37] In Jungian theory, then, a personality function endows a specific phase in the development of experience with normative evaluative importance. In other words, as the adult personality matures, there is a cumulative tendency to squeeze the whole of experience into the procrustean bed of a severely limited range of human values. Both attitudes and functions belong to the realm of law, for both are vectoral feelings that ground certain kinds of evaluative response.

Personality Types

In Jungian theory, there are, then, six primary variables that give structure to the adult ego: the attitudes of introversion and extraversion and the four functions of sensation, feeling, intuition, and thought. When combined in concrete individuals, they give rise to eight general personality types. For each personality function lends specificity either to an introverted or to an extraverted attitude. Moreover, the antagonism among functions initially precludes the conscious mastery of more than one. The eight types are the introverted sensation type, the extraverted sensation type, the introverted feeling type, the extraverted feeling type, the introverted intuitive type, the extraverted intuitive type, the introverted thinking type, the extraverted thinking type. Each personality type enjoys certain strengths and certain weaknesses as attitude and function blend to create conscious expertise and unconscious neurotic tendencies.

The extraverted sensation type is a hard-headed realist. (S)he values things above all and is most concerned to preserve and develop the values that shape the surrounding environment. Often such persons manifest a high esthetic sensitivity as well. The extraverted sensation type is especially alien to the rarified atmosphere of academia and must return very quickly to things in order to breathe again. There is a robustness in the love of such persons for the physical that keeps human life solidly anchored in the concrete.[38]

The introverted sensation type is attuned to the personal values that accrue to objects; but, being self-preoccupied, such a person often finds difficulty in articulating such feelings. Moreover, the object's associations are of much more importance than the object itself. While, for example, an extraverted sensation type would be concerned that a sea-shell collection be complete and each shell a perfect specimen, the introverted sensation type will treasure shells for their purely personal esthetic appeal or because they have been retrieved from places that are rich in individual memories. Moreover, the memory will be treasured more than the shell.[39]

The extraverted feeling type has an uncanny sense for the correct handling of social situations. Such a person knows instinctively how to do things *comme il faut:* what is or is not socially suitable, what would or would not please, what would unite, what would threaten and divide.[40]

The introverted feeling type by contrast knows both the heights and the depths of personal affective response. But introversion renders such persons silent, inaccessible, enigmatic. They are slow to reveal their motives, although one senses in them a harmonious range and depth of sensitivity. They are prone to contemplation and to mystical, or quasi-mystical, experiences.[41]

The extraverted intuitive type is the practical world reformer. Far from valuing things for their own sake, this personality is suffocated by external stability. (S)he must always be abustle after new reality values: new techniques, new experiences, new inventions, new forms of personal and community endeavor. Such people long to create a novel and concrete future. They are the entrepreneurs, the developers, the political and economic leaders, the social reformers. They have the capacity to inspire hope in others and to mobilize groups to achieve some common purpose.[42]

The introverted intuitive type is by contrast poet, artist, seer, prophet. Such individuals are persons whose creative but profoundly idiosyncratic vision sets them apart from others. At the same time it deprives them of the practical, managerial, or administrative skills demanded for effective social leadership.[43]

The extraverted thinking type is not a social or political leader, but the abstracted intellectual with an attitudinal bias to things. Such a person will tend to value "objectivity" as the ultimate criterion of truth, not only as a matter of personal preference but as a rule to which all others ought to conform. (S)he will tend to place high value on personal fidelity to "objective" responsibilities and will demand the same of others. The extraverted thinker delights in the speculative elucidation of the forces that shape our sustaining environment.[44]

The propositional abstractions of the introverted thinker lead in a very different direction. Like the extraverted thinker such persons place greatest value upon abstract considerations, but their thoughts seek to probe the private corners of their own minds. Immanuel Kant and Friedrich Nietzsche are typical intellectual introverts, as are C. S. Peirce and George Santayana. Peirce died in poverty while groping for an elusive metaphysical synthesis. Santayana's final intellectual efforts were attempts to transform his life and thought into a beautiful esthetic illusion. If the vision of the introverted intellectual is sound, however, (s)he can articulate deep insights into the morphology of experience that transcend in some significant measure personal idiosyncrasies. Nevertheless, the thoughts of the introverted thinker are often formulated in such uniquely personal terms that they remain inaccessible to others and need to be recast by some faithful Boswell in order to be understood.[45]

The Tower of Babel

As we saw in Chapter IV, the morphology of Christian hope that begins to take shape under the healing influence of the dark night of sense demands of the integrally converted Christian that (s)he live in openness to every realm of meaning and of value. With William Lynch we differentiated four such realms: the literal, the allegorical, the anagogical, and the tropological. We noted that these four realms of meaning correspond to the four stages in the growth of human experience described in Chapter III.

If, however, Jungian personality theory is sound, then each adult ego has something important to contribute to the conscious exploration of meaning. For as the adult ego grows in attitudinal and functional focus, it acquires new conscious appreciation and understanding of a relatively narrow spectrum of differentiated human values, which correspond in turn to the four realms of meaning. Sensation and feeling types are attuned to literal meaning; intuitive types, to allegorical meaning; thinking types, to anagogical meaning; extraverted thinking types, to tropological meaning.

Moreover, the natural ego tends spontaneously to regard those values it regards as "really important" as finally normative in any decision-making process. Decision in turn shapes the emerging self. The self is a complex of habitual reactive tendencies. As a consequence, in the natural course of ego development, some measure of entrapment in a self-created world of value is psychically inevitable.

The more focused the ego in individuals and in society, the sharper the sense of conscious isolation is apt to be. Moreover, the shadow presence lurking behind every conscious ego infects social intercourse with fear, suspicion, and hostility. Neurotic and psychotic tendencies render the conscious ego rigid, aggressively protective of the meager conceptual results it has been able to scratch from the soil of the unconscious.

The extraverted sensation type can degenerate into a crude pleasure seeker or a shallow esthete. The environment comes to be ruthlessly exploited then, not treasured or enhanced. As the personality is increasingly devoured by things, repressed neurotic impulses begin to surface: suspicion, jealousy, irrational fears and compulsions. Morality becomes punctilious, pharisaical. Religion degenerates into superstition. As hostility toward rational functions grows, the power of judgment decays.[46]

Neurotic tendencies in the introverted sensation type prevent the individual from keeping valued objects in realistic evaluative perspective. Repressive controls over alienating feelings begin to develop, notably, the dampening of enthusiasmms and of extravagance as a way of keeping the all-important influence of objects in proper focus. Repression breeds emotional passivity and submission to the dominance of others. Resentment of domination gives rise to stubbornness and vengefulness. Thought becomes banal, unimaginative. The surrounding world becomes increasingly fantastic and unreal. Irrational fear of vague, sordid, dangerous influences grows. Hysterical tendencies are obscured under symptoms of exhaustion.[47]

Within ego-consciousness, feeling and thought are mutually antagonistic. The extraverted feeling type tends, therefore, to dismiss out of hand abstract, theoretical insights that stand in conflict with a personal sense of propriety. As this tendency ossifies under neurotic influences, the personality is increasingly entrapped in the feelings of the moment. As the personality fragments, expressions of feeling become extravagant. This extravagance is in fact an over-compensated attempt to establish a felt rapport with one's environment. But its very eccentricity makes it self-defeating. Hostility to self-critical reflection leaves one susceptible to prejudice and bigotry. The ego is increasingly vulnerable to waves of unconscious feeling that strip formerly valued objects of personal significance. Cynical depreciatory ideas become increasingly obsessive and in the latter stages of personality disintegration give way to hysteria.[48]

The introverted feeling type is spontaneously inclined to personal reserve. The desire to break out of this reserve breeds the attempt to force others to conform to one's deepest personal feelings. As such tendencies become neurotic they produce vain, despotic, tyrannical behavior: the Don Juan, the *femme fatale*. There is a growing obsession with what others might think. Imagined plots spring from the ground like mushrooms. The disintegrating ego is plagued by rumors and devises counter-intrigues that lead to mindless clandestine rivalries. The exhaustion born of endless conflicts ends in neurasthenia.[49]

The extraverted intuitive type lives in the dream of a world transformed. As a consequence, (s)he can exhaust personal psychic reserves chasing down blind alleys. As in the case of the extraverted sensation type, the repression of thought and feeling gives way to personal hollowness. The primitive character of subconscious thought processes breeds a host of sexual suspicions, fears of financial disaster, forebodings of illness or other forms of misfortune. The individual establishes destructive social ties and more and more exempts conduct from rational control. Repressed thought patterns begin to shape behavior. Conduct is increasingly dominated by childish, hair-splitting ratiocinations and by the welter of sensations spontaneously aroused by environmental stimuli. There is a growing tendency to run roughshod over persons and things. And this insensitivity eventually gives way to hypochondriacal ideas and phobias and to obsession with absurd bodily sensations.[50]

The introverted intuitive type dwells in an idiosyncratic world of personal fantasy that leaves the ego socially isolated. There is a growing sense that one's dreams make no practical difference either to oneself or to others. Futile symbolic gestures substitute for practicality. The concrete configuration of things recedes before unconscious and intemperate affective impulses. Compulsive ties to persons or objects are established and hypochrondriacal symptoms emerge.[51]

The extraverted thinking type is spontaneously prone to insensitive dogmatism. As neurosis warps the mind, there is a growing insistence that everything conform to one's personal beliefs. Social dealings become dry, detached, impersonal. As one's social relationships deteriorate, even the most vital personal, financial, and moral concerns are sacrificed to vindicate one's increasingly eccentric ideals. All criticism is dismissed as ill will and prejudice. Insinuation replaces argument. The mind becomes petty, mistrustful, crochety, conservative, rigidly dogmatic. The irrational basis of one's theoretical positions becomes obvious to everyone but oneself. Religion is transformed into the compulsive worship of abstractions of the absolute. At the same time, the personality is gripped by paroxisms of doubt. There is growing fascination with intuitive persons of the opposite sex. Predictions become increasingly dependent on unacknowledged irrational motives. Transductive thinking is palmed off as logical argument. There is a growing ruthlessness in dealing with one's adversaries.[52]

The introverted thinking type has a different personal agenda. The inability to relate thought to fact leaves one increasingly absorbed in a world of impractical abstractions. The world of mere possibility becomes one's whole world, even as it acquires an increasingly fantastic character. Reality recedes behind a fog of abstractions. Thought lapses into pseudo-mystical vagueness. It becomes effete, esoteric, increasingly dominated by a welter of magical, irrational, contradictory influences. Speculation reverts to primitive, syncretistic patterns of evaluation. Futile attempts to reestablish contact with the concrete world end in cerebral exhaustion.[53]

Clearly, if left to its own spontaneous, wholly natural dynamic, the focusing of adult ego-consciousness gives rise inevitably to social fragmentation and misunderstanding. For the natural ego can achieve adult rational focus only at the price of repressing other legitimate needs and functions.

Moreover, as Jung suggests, specific evaluative functions give evidence of being mutually antagonistic. Thought and feeling stand in such a relationship; so do sensation and intuition. That is to say, the propositional schematization of feeling tends to inhibit thought, and vice versa. The propositional schematization of intuition tends to inhibit sensation, and vice versa.

Repressed attitudes and functions give structure to the unconscious. Repressed extroverted tendencies enter into the shadow of the introvert; repressed introversion, into the shadow of the extravert. Repressed feelings shape the shadow of the thinking type; repressed thinking, the shadow of the feeling type. Repressed intuitions enter the shadow of the sensation type; repressed sensation, the shadow of the intuitive type.

As obtuseness to whole realms of value waxes, so does suspicion and fear of those who dwell habitually in such realms. For terror of the shadow motivates the projection of repressed feelings upon those whose personalities reflect back to the conscious ego its own unwanted shadow self. Indeed, Jung suggests, and not without plausibility, that the fragmentation of the Christian community has over the centuries been motivated in more than one instance by the mutual fear and antagonism that divides introverts and extraverts.

Such social fragmentation becomes personal sin when it is pursued in conscious defiance of the divine command that all people become one in mutual forgiveness and love. The biblical symbol of such sin is, of course, the tower of Babel.[54] Interestingly enough, the rational construction of the tower is motivated by terror of being overwhelmed by the sea. The sea is, of course, a perennial symbol of the mysterious depths of the unconscious. The punishment exacted of such human pride is the scattering of the nations in a babble of mutually unintelligible tongues. Babel, then, symbolizes the unravelling of the social fabric that is the result of unhealed, sinful ego-inflation.

The Christian remedy for Babel is Pentecost, which in Lukan theology effects a new glossolalic confounding of the tongues of all the nations.[55] Its effect is to undo the sin of Babel by uniting all the people of the earth in heartfelt praise of the living God. Pentecost, however, also inaugurates the visible charismatic transformation of the Church.

Charism and Ego

When asked in Acts 2 about the practical import of Pentecost, Peter's reply is bald and direct: "Repent and believe the good news."[56] Christian repentance transpires in an ecclesial matrix of mutual acceptance in atoning love. Acceptance by others in the name of God nourishes the hope that the faith of the accepting community is true. Belief that that hope is justified yields freedom to confront the shadow and to seek reconciliation with oneself and with those one has offended. For the Christian, then, trust in the present saving power of the Breath as Her action comes to experiential visibility in a faith community of atoning love is the indispensable precondition to the healing of ego-consciousness.

Egos are not, however, sinful of themselves. The healthy growth of ego-consciousness is the progress of history and of culture. The abandonment of egotistical self-reliance is not, then, the repudiation of ego-development but its submission to charismatic transformation in the power of the Holy Breath. That submission demands that one's personal future be placed unquestioningly in the hands of God. And it demands as well that the law of the Holy Breath replace the law of natural reason as the ultimate basis of human social development.

Jung himself seems to have sensed that certain personality types manifest a natural affinity for specific charismatic gifts. He characterized the Hebrew prophets, for example, as introverted intuitive types. And he suggested that introverted feeling types are spontaneously inclined to personal mysticism. Jung himself pursued the matter no further. But with a little reflection, it is easy to see how other analogies are possible.[57]

Thinking types, whether introverted or extraverted, are naturally susceptible to the charism of teaching, although one may hypothesize that the extraverted teacher would be more temperamentally inclined to a ministry of kerygmatic proclamation, or in Paul's phrase, to "teaching with widsom." The ongoing catechesis of the community in all of its diverse forms, or "teaching instruction," would appeal to introvert and extravert alike, although the former might be more temperamentally inclined to pursue such teaching along scholarly lines.

Feeling types, whether introverted or extraverted, would seem to be naturally susceptible to the gift of discernment. Jung characterizes the function of feeling as "rational" and opposes it together with thought to the irrational functions of sensation and intuition. At the same time he correctly distinguishes judgments based primarily on feeling from those based primarily on abstract, theoretical considerations.

Discernment in its logical structure is, as we have seen, an inductive inference. It is dependent upon sound teaching for the abstract criteria it employs. The judgment of discernment is not, however, based on inferential considerations alone or even primarily.

It is a conclusion felt concretely in prayer and in a graced empathetic response to persons, to situations, and to the movements of the Breath in one's own heart.

Extraverted discerners would be more inclined temperamentally to a public ministry of discernment. Introverted discerners will be more inclined to explore contemplatively the recesses of their own hearts. Their gift is personal knowledge of the whole gamut of religious affections. But their shyness inclines them to share their wisdom with the community indirectly in books like *The Interior Castle, The Ascent of Mount Carmel,* or *A Treatise Concerning Religious Affections*.

The extraverted intuitive type is temperamentally susceptible to charisms of community leadership: to apostolate, to pastoral leadership, and to different facets of community organization. The fact that intuition is an irrational function suggests that normally community leadership should not be entrusted to academicians and intellectuals but to individuals with a flair for practical organization. Above all leaders should have the capacity to mobilize the gifts and endowments of others for concerted action.

Extraverted sensation types are attuned to concrete reality. Their hardheaded sense of the practical limits imposed by fact serves as a healthy counterbalance to the more mercurial leadership of the intuitive extravert. Since the ordained leadership of the Christian community is collegial and shared rather than individual and monarchical, the college of ordained apostolic leaders would do well to have a healthy supply of extraverted sensation types. Such persons are also naturally suited to tasks that concern the proper ordering of community affairs: to official administrative functions, to the supervision and distribution of goods to the poor, to assisting in practical ways in community projects.

In *Charism and Sacrament*,[58] I have suggested that the gift of tongues is a kind of dative feeling. In the introvert, the function of sensation is, however, focused upon dative presentations, not for the sake of their literal value but out of a felt fascination with their personal significance. One may, then, argue that the introverted sensation type would be temperamentally susceptible to the gift of tongues.

Here, however, a certain caution is in order. Approximately 85 percent of those involved in the Catholic charismatic renewal claim to have received the gift of tongues. Can there be so many introverted sensation types in charismatic prayer groups?

Protestant Pentecostal styles of prayer certainly manifest a bias to introversion. But another more plausible explanation is possible. The functions of sensation, feeling, intuition, and thought are never the exclusive property of any one personality type.[59] Rather, a personality function endows a specific realm of human evaluative response with an enhanced, conscious sense of importance. Other functions, however, contribute more or less consciously to the evaluative morphology of every human personality. Every adult personality will, then, enjoy in some measure the sensitivity of the introverted sensation type, although one would anticipate that such conscious sensitivity would be most atrophied in the extraverted intuitive type.

Moreover, the action of the Holy Breath cannot be completely circumscribed by human personality. All of the charisms are capable of both ordinary and extraordinary manifestations. The ordinary manifestation of a charism consists in the pneumatic transformation of natural ego-functions. The less basis there is for the action of the Breath in a given individual's personality, the more extraordinary the charism in question.

Clearly, then, while Jungian personality theory and a theology of charism would suggest that introverted sensation types are likely to be especially susceptible to the gift of tongues, there is no warranty for affirming that such personalities have an exclusive corner on the glossolalic market.

It is, then, theologically plausible to regard the charisms of the Holy Breath as the gracing of adult ego-consciousness. How then does an adult ego come to be charismatically transformed? As the response of Peter on Pentecost suggests, its pneumatic transformation proceeds in two phases: first repentance, then the submission of the developing ego to the obedience of faith through habitual openness to the Breath in shared and personal prayer. In the normal process of Christian development, these two phases of growth succeed one another with a certain regularity. And so the ascent of the mystic spiral begins.

In this alternating process of transformation, repentance effects the liberation of the ego from the first of the dark powers. Its fruit is the gradual healing of neuroses and personality crochets. Charismatic submission to the Breath transforms the way in which ego functions are performed. Here perhaps a personal example might be of help. My predominant attitude is introverted; my functional bias, thought. That I should pursue an academic career was wholly predictable. I have been a fairly successful teacher in both primary and secondary educational institutions. It was not until I became involved in the charismatic renewal, however, that I began to pray for the gift of teaching on a regular basis. I found that over the span of a semester of such prayer, my entire approach to the academic process had subtly, almost unconsciously, changed. I began to pray about what I would teach and for those whom I was instructing. I became more attuned to my own faith needs and to those of my students. The classroom ceased to be a place where I could flaunt my Ph.D. It was instead an opportunity to proclaim Christ and to summon myself and others to deeper repentance and faith through critical philosophical and theological insight. My students sensed my own change in attitude and seemed to respond more consciously to what I did in faith. In a word, the charismatic healing of my academic ego changed, not the things I did, but the quality of the faith with which I did them. In *Charism and Sacrament* I have attempted to describe how the natural human experience of marriage can come to be charismatically transformed. So too can every other legitimate, natural aspiration of the human ego.

Kilian McDonnell has on more than one occasion protested against "Pentecostalizing" the charisms.[60] To Pentecostalize the gifts is to approach them with a fundamentalistic belief in the "literal truth" of Scripture, to reduce the Pauline lists of charisms to exhaustive catalogues instead of reading them as indications of typical charismatic services performed in the first gentile Christian communities. If, however, the preceding analysis is sound, then there are as many charisms as there are different kinds of adult personality.

To be more specific, prophecy is only one way in which an introverted intuitive type can experience the charismatic transformation of ego-consciousness. Such an individual could also develop into a Christian artist or poet. But when art and poetry are charismatically anointed they breathe of a divine inspiration that touches the heart and invites it to hope and faith in God. The same is true of other personality types as well. The charisms of the Breath are then as diverse as adult egos and cannot be reduced facilely to fixed catalogues. The faith-filled scientist, the Christian politician, the prayerful community organizer—all such people can be charismatically anointed in their work.

Intellectual Conversion

Intellectual conversion is not, then, the conversion of an intellectual. It is the conscious assumption of personal responsibility for the propositional schematization of experience. That schematization lends structure to every adult ego-function, whether introverted or extraverted, although it is of course more pronounced in thinking types. The kind of intellectual conversion demanded of each individual will, then, differ as the evaluative form of the adult personality if functionally and attitudinally focused upon different aspects of human experience.

By the same token, other forms of conversion will tend to assume spontaneous importance for different kinds of personalities. Moral conversion will probably come more easily to extraverts; intellectual and especially affective conversion will probably be more difficult. Introverts will be apt to face the opposite problem. Attuned to the need for affective sensitivity or intellectual honesty, they may well find difficulty in assuming full responsibility for the practical consequences of personal decisions. Similarly, as ego functions develop, the need to deal with different aspects of the shadow will vary at different stages of growth. Clearly, then, the specific character of an intellectual conversion will differ according to personality type and degree of personal maturity.

The Problem of Faith
The preceding reflections cast light on two interrelated theological problems: the problem of faith and the problem of Christian education.

The problem of faith should be distinguished from the commitment of faith. The commitment of faith is here defined as the decision to live in constant faith-dependence on the Holy Breath of Jesus. The problem of faith is defined here as understanding the correct motives for such dependence. If, then, Christian faith results from the pneumatic gracing of the propositional feelings that shape the developing adult ego, the problem of faith is reducible to the problem of adequate inferential access to God. It asks the question: On what terms is such access possible?

We stand before the final set of switchbacks in this leg of our climb. For to respond to the problem of faith is to answer the question: "What is the locus of initial, experiential access to God?" Let us, then, adjust our packs and begin to ascend. But first, let us pause for another granola break.

In order to understand the meaning of a phrase like "adequate inferential access to God," we must first clarify the meaning of the term "adequacy." As we shall see in Chapter VIII, mystical experience offers us some grounds for affirming that the evaluative form of the Divine Experience differs from that of human ego-consciousness. As a consequence, it eludes comprehensive propositional insight. But if the Divine Experience eludes exhaustive propositional explanation, then no inferential insight into the reality of God can ever fully grasp the Divine Experience itself. The adequacy of an inferential approach to God is not, then, measured by its ability to explain away the mystery of God. The adequacy of any inferential approach to God is its adequacy to the dynamics of healthy personal development in faith. The problem of faith may, then, be reformulated more precisely in the following terms: Does my iterential approach to religious experience allow me to achieve true propositional insights into the historical self-revelation of God that can be transcended as soon as any contextual inadequacy surrounding them has been discovered?

If the reflections of the present chapter have been so far sound, adequate inferential access to God can be achieved only in an integrally converted charismatic community of faith.[61] Let us begin to reflect on what this might imply. Our initial approach to the problem of faith will be dialectical. Since, moreover, an American theology should reflect the problems and insights of the American speculative tradition, we will approach the problem of faith by attempting to derive from the work of major American thinkers a set of principles that clarify its meaning and hopefully point the way to its proper resolution.

"Realism" vs. "Mysticism"

The problem of adequate propositional access to God is only one facet of a larger epistemological problem, namely, the problem of adequate propositional access to experience in general. In the late nineteenth and early twentieth centuries both questions exercised the fertile minds of three major American thinkers: Josiah Royce, William James, and Charles Sanders Peirce. The three men had very different speculative interests. Royce's were ethical and metaphysical; James's were affective and psychological; Peirce's were logical and metaphysical.

Royce delivered his Gifford lectures in 1903, eighteen years before the publication of Jung's *Psychological Types*. But Royce had already sensed in a vague, inchoate way that inflated, extraverted preoccupation with "objectivity" on the one hand, and inflated, introverted preoccupation with "subjectivity" on the other had in the course of human thought produced myopic and inadequate philosophical accounts of what finally is real.

In its extremest forms, extraverted thinking gives rise to what Royce called philosophical "Realism." Like every philosophical term, "realism" is subject to a host of possible definitions. Paradoxically, in Royce's mind, the term was almost synonymous with "nominalism." Roycean "Realism" is an over-focused preoccupation with the factual, the "objective" aspects of experience to the exclusion of personal evaluative response.[62] In such a "Realistic" philosophy, the real is an object that "is *to be seen*, or *at hand*, or can be *found*, or is *marked*, or is *plain*, or *stands out*, or is *there*, or, as the Germans also say, is *vorhanden*; while the unreal has *no standing*, or is *not at hand*, or is *not to be found*, or is *not there*."[63]

A myopic search for pure objectivity leads the Roycean Realist to affirm that the objects of human knowledge are completely unaffected by the relation of cognition, since they are of themselves "totally indifferent to being known or not known." Royce himself believed that such an extraverted account of "the real" rendered knowledge finally impossible, for it sundered the meaning of things from the meaning predicated of them by human minds.[64]

To the objective metaphysics of the Realist, Royce's dialectical mind opposed the subjective metaphysics of the mystic. The Roycean "mystic" like the Roycean "realist" is something of a speculative stereotype, for as we shall see, there is more to mysticism than Royce's philosophical definition allows. In *The World and the Individual*, the revised version of his Gifford lectures, he observed:

> The genuine essence of Realism consists, as we saw, in defining any being as real precisely in so far as in essence it is wholly independent of ideas that, while other than itself, refer to it. We insisted, at the last time, that this thesis implies an absolute dualism within the world of real being, since an idea also is an existent fact, and is as *independently* real as is the supposed independent object. . . . For the mystic, according to the genuinely historical definition of what constitutes speculative Mysticism, to be real means to be in such wise Immediate that, in the presence of this immediacy, all thought and all ideas, absolutely satisfied, are quenched, so that the finite search ceases, and the Other is no longer another, but is absolutely found. . . . If a realist, viewing your progress from without, observes hereupon that you are simply ignoring the manifold realities of the finite world, you reply that those so-called realities, just because they are many, and because they pretend to be independent beings, are illusory, and that in forsaking such a world, you simply spare yourself errors. . . . For your very discovery of *that which is*, would involve the forgetting of

your finite personality as an illusion, an error, an evil dream.[65]

Thus the Roycean Mystic dismisses the world of facts as mere illusion, as *maya*. The real lies only within.

The reader may pursue Royce's examination of the inadequacies of both Realism and Mysticism by reading *The World and the Individual*. The psychological truth that lends present interest to his analysis is the spontaneous tendency of the inflated thinking ego to shape reality to the procrustean bed of its personal attitudinal bias. These reflections suggest, then, an initial insight into the terms under which adequate propositional access to experience is possible: (1) *Adequate propositional access to experience will be possible only in a speculative frame of reference that transcends the limitations inherent in both introverted and extraverted theories of the real.*

Royce himself suggested, correctly I believe, that to transcend the limitations of an extraverted "Realism" or of an introverted "Mysticism" one must do justice to the partial truth that is in each position. He therefore insisted that an adequate propositional approach to the real must acknowledge not only the realm of "external meaning" so dear to the extravert but also the realm of "internal meaning" cherished by the introvert. Moreover, these two realms of meaning must be seen as unintelligible in isolation from one another. To be knowable, he argued, reality must be conceived in relational terms; and relational reality must be conceived in such a way as to include the relationship of knowledge.[66]

Royce and James

When read in the light of Jungian personality theory, the lifelong philosophical debate between James and Royce is also relevant to the present discussion and instructive as well. The personalities of the two men had a clear functional bias. Royce was a thinker, at home in the world of abstractions. James had genuine intellectual interests, but he was most at home in the realm of feeling.

In Jungian personality theory feeling and thought are antagonistic functions. One must be repressed if the other is to develop. As a consequence, the thinker and the feeler tend to confront one another as shadow presences. Royce and James were good friends. But there is in fact evidence that their affection for one another was haunted by the shadow. Their friendship was an endless debate.

James seems to have been somewhat intimidated by Royce's capacity to reel off one abstract metaphysical treatise after another, while he himself seemed unable to advance metaphysically beyond his defense of the speculative legitimacy of grounding certain kinds of personal philosophical beliefs in "passional" motives. Royce's Apollonian metaphysics, by contrast, denied in principle even the possibility of unconscious psychological motives. In *The World and the Individual*, Royce insisted, incredibly enough: "The Unconscious we reject, because our Fourth Conception of Being forbids all recognition of unconscious realities."[67] With time, however, the two men came to a certain appreciation of the other's viewpoint. In *The Sources of Religious Insight*, Royce acknowledged his indebtedness to James's *Varieties*. In *Pluralistic Universe*, James avowed his speculative debt to Royce.[68]

The case of James and Royce is, then, instructive, for it suggests another basic principle that must subtend adequate propositional access to experience: (2) *An adequate inferential approach to experience must seek to create an interpretative frame of reference that transcends the functional biases that shape personal ego-consciousness.* By ambitioning with Whitehead a normative account of experience that is both applicable and adequate to experience in general, a foundational theology of human emergence attempts to do precisely that.

Royce and Peirce

The philosophical interchange between Peirce and Royce holds other relevant insights into the realm of propositional feeling. On reading *The World and the Individual*, Peirce recognized it as Royce's "great work." He was no doubt also pleased that Royce's book had shown a certain sensitivity to the series of metaphysical articles Peirce had published in *The Monist*. But Peirce also discovered serious lacunae in Royce's vision and wrote him urging him to undertake a serious study of logic. Anyone familiar with the thought of the two men will have no difficulty in guessing at least one of Peirce's motives.[69]

In *The World and the Individual*, Royce had suggested that Kantian critical philosophy was an important attempt to bridge the gap between a Realistic and a Mystical conception of reality. But he had found the Kantian solution inadequate, largely for its failure to provide cognitive access to the concrete and the particular as such.[70] Peirce would, no doubt, have agreed; but the logician in him would have also sensed Royce's failure to take account of what Peirce felt was a more fundamental Kantian failure, namely, Kant's uncritical acquiescence in the belief that deduction is in fact the only form of inference. Peirce's own logical studies had convinced him quite early that there are in fact three distinct and irreducible forms of inference: abduction, deduction, and induction.[71]

This insight, Peirce saw, had far-reaching consequences. First of all, it invalidates Kantian transcendental method. For it reduces Kant's "transcendental deduction" of the conditions for the possibility of human knowledge to the status of one abductive hypothesis among many. But if Kant's transcendental deduction yields only a hypothesis, not a conclusion, it is actually a hypothesis posing as a conclusion, an abduction masquerading as an induction even as it calls itself a deduction.

Kant's own transcendental thinking led him to conclude that the categories of the logic of his day constituted the necessary and universal conditions for the possibility of human knowing. Joseph Maréchal a century later would use the same method to argue that thirteenth-century Thomistic psychology and metaphysics constitute the necessary and universal conditions for the possibility of human knowing. Who is correct? Left to its own resources, Kantian transcendental method offers no methodological criterion for choosing between these mutually exclusive suggestions. For in confronting abduction with induction, transcendental deduction equivalently arrests argument at the level of abductive inference.[72]

Peirce's critique of Kant led him to several important conclusions concerning the limitations of propositional inference. Abduction and induction link reference to the concrete and to the actual. But the fallibility that attends both forms of inference entails that human inferential processes can never transcend the level of personal belief. In the world of propositional feeling there are, then, only initial fallible beliefs, deductively clarified but still fallible beliefs, and verified (but potentially reversible) inductive beliefs. In other words, Peirce saw quite clearly that the logical structure of the inferential process demands that: (3) *Adequate propositional access to experience must rest on a sound insight into the laws of inference and therefore on the conscious personal profession of a contrite logical fallibilism.*[73] As a consequence, the human claim to irreversible metaphysical insights, i.e., to insights that are necessarily and universally true and adequate to experience, is a philosophical fiction concocted by the extraverted and probably neurotic thinking ego.

At the same time, Peirce was careful to distinguish logical fallibilism from epistemological skepticism. Sound logic demands that no belief be doubted without a legitimate speculative reason. There are three such reasons: first, the existence of facts that contradict one's beliefs or are inexplicable in terms of them; second, logical contradiction or inconsistency within one's present belief system; third, the elaboration of a more adequate frame of reference than that in which one is accustomed to think.

Peirce also realized that genuine belief is impossible without commitment to the best human understanding of reality available under the circumstances. To believe anything is to be willing to accept the consequences of one's personal propositional affirmations, including their revision if they prove inapplicable or inadequate to experience.[74] In other words: (4) *Adequate propositional access to experience demands that a contrite logical fallibilism be counterbalanced by the recognition that the commitment to stand by the consequences of personal beliefs is constitutive of thought itself and that no propositional belief should be doubted without a sound logical reason.*

Peirce also suggested, with considerable plausibility, that there are at least four possible techniques for fixing one's personal belief: tenacity, authority, taste, and shared systematic inquiry. Tenacity refuses to acknowledge the existence of legitimate, unanswered questions that cast doubt on personal beliefs. It is the last-ditch effort of a threatened ego to maintain its going sense of identity.[75]

The fixation of belief through authority appeals to the wider experience and superior judgment of another whom I accept as more competent than myself, in order to resolve a given problem. The authority may be an individual, a community, or a tradition that one is willing to trust.[76]

The fixation of belief through taste appeals to esthetic preference as the basis for personal affirmation. It differs from tenacity in that it acknowledges the legitimacy of problems and questions the tenacious mind denies. But it resembles tenacity in that it rests belief in the last analysis on uncriticized feelings. The method of taste also labors under a certain insensitivity to the wider experience and more competent judgment of those who might legitimately challenge one's inflated personal biases.

At the same time, the appeal to taste has the advantage of trusting one's (hopefully educated) instincts. And such trust is, as Peirce also saw, one of the basic principles of sound abductive inference. Unfortunately, however, the method of taste, like Kantian transcendental deduction, terminates inquiry at the level of abduction and runs the serious risk of canonizing personal prejudice arbitrarily as the truth.[77]

The method of fixing one's belief that is, however, truest to the dynamics of propositional experience is not taste; nor is it tenacity or authority. It is, as Peirce realized, the method of shared systematic inquiry.[78]

Shared inquiry avoids the dogmatism that characterizes the method of tenacity and allows instead for legitimate questions and problems to be faced and resolved as best one may. Like the method of authority, it calls upon the evaluative responses of other persons as a check to one's potential myopia and prejudice. But unlike the method of authority, shared systematic inquiry challenges each individual engaged in a reflective process to publish the fruits of personal reflection for critical evaluation by others. Like the method of taste, it trusts educated, instinctive hunches and guesses as the key to sound abductions. But unlike the method of taste, shared systematic inquiry extends the inferential process beyond abduction to deductive clarification and inductive verification. We may, then, conclude that: (5) *Adequate propositional access to experience is mediated by personal commitment to shared systematic inquiry.*

Peirce willed his papers to Royce as the one person most competent to complete the metaphysical synthesis that had eluded Peirce himself during his declining years. During a personal convalescence, Royce found relief from his heavy academic schedule to read and ponder the Peirce papers at leisure. As he did so, he sensed as Peirce had the convergence of their philosophical stances. And he began to glimpse the potential religious significance of Peirce's vision of an ideal community of shared inquiry.

Moreover, Royce was sensitive to the fact that the search for truth in community intensifies rational ego-consciousness. The reason is not far to seek. In an emergent problematic, ego-consciousness is a function of evaluative differentiation and evaluative synthesis. That is to say, it is a function of the degree of contrast in the evaluative form of an experience between what is and what is not; between what is and what is not yet but could be. It is also a function of the interpretative interrelation of evaluatively discriminated factors within an experience.

By engaging the dative feelings of as many individuals as possible, shared inquiry increases the number of factual variables available to conscious evaluation. The differentiation of factual variables through dialogue thus intensifies evaluative contrast between what is and is not, since one fact is not another. Similarly, by blending into a unified dialogic process the affective and inferential evaluations of as many individuals as possible, shared inquiry maximizes the number of conceptual variables present in experience. Since physical purposes and the later stages of inferential evaluation disclose the possible vectoral thrust of experience into the future, shared inquiry enhances the contrast between what is and what is not yet but could be. Finally, shared inquiry seeks consensus. When successful, therefore, it yields the best synthetic, interpretative integration of experience available to a given community under the circumstances.

As his own philosophy reached maturity, Royce became increasingly fascinated with a complex philosophical problem: What conditions, he asked himself, must be fulfilled before a community of dedicated truth-seekers can achieve consciousness of itself as a community? As he pondered the question he discovered ten such conditions.[79]

The first condition for achieving community consciousness is the sharing of past experiences. In a smaller community, like a family or friendship, much of the past is shared directly, through immediate personal interaction. But even in small groups, experiences must be regularly recalled if community consciousness is to thrive. In larger social bodies, a common past must be recovered systematically through historical research and disseminated through teaching. The members must discover in history some common originating event from which the community derives its origin as a community.

The second condition for the emergence and development of community consciousness is, then, implied in the first. It is that the members of the community have the same basic understanding of the meaning of the originating event. Such consensus is best achieved through shared systematic inquiry, but its emergence is not infallible. When interpretative agreement concerning the meaning of the originating event disintegrates, community awareness is correspondingly diminished, and with it any shared sense of present communal identity. One need only recall the theological debates of the Reformation to understand what this second condition implies.

Third, since interpretative access to the originating event is mediated by intervening historical events, a conscious community must also seek to reach consensus through shared systematic inquiry concerning the significance of those historical processes that link it to its origins.

Fourth, because consensus as to the concrete character of the historical origins of an emerging human community shapes its present sense of identity, it also grounds the possibility of an affective and inferential projection of a common future. Common hopes and plans for the future further intensify community consciousness. Insight into what a community ought to become engages not only historical but normative patterns of thought. It therefore implies the eighth condition for community consciousness indicated below.

Fifth, the achievement of full consciousness as a community demands the practical realization of the shared future to which the community aspires. Shared activity must reduce shared plans and hopes to shared satisfactions that mediate growth in shared freedom.

Sixth, the intensity of the concrete satisfaction available to a given community through shared activity will in part be a function of its ability to treasure and preserve an enriching and broad diversity of gifts and talents among its members. The suppression of individual differences will breed a depressing uniformity. But diversity alone trivializes satisfaction. The unique contribution of each member to the shared satisfactions of the community as a whole must be coordinated in such a way as to render each contribution mutually reinforcing. Diminished satisfaction, as we have seen, yields diminished consciousness and diminished freedom. Enhanced satisfaction enhances consciousness and freedom.

Seventh, the practical, communal sharing of personal gifts demands the presence in a community of a variety of different kinds of leaders with competence to direct and mediate different kinds of group activities.

Eighth, the efficacious sharing of personal gifts must be accomplished freely. Oppression diminishes consciousness.

Ninth, since, as we have seen, freedom is the fruit of conversion, a community will achieve shared awareness to the extent that each of its members is integrally converted and actively committed in free consent to the realization of a common hope and a common ideal.

There is, then, also need for a tenth and final condition for the possibility of communal growth in consciousness: each member of the community must be committed to every other member in atoning love. For only a love that can absorb the suffering, the blunders, and the oppression born of natural myopia and of sinful egotism can sustain a community in the minimal unity necessary to survive the personal and communal crises that mark the development of shared ego consciousness. Moreover, as we shall see in Chapter VIII, love can become a form of knowing that transcends ego awareness.

We may then conclude that: (6) *Adequate propositional access to experience is possible only in a community that fulfills the conditions for the possibility of shared consciousness.*

The Psychodynamics of Community Consciousness

To the end of his life Royce remained insensitive to the cognitive demands of the subconscious. The human implications of his analysis of the growth of community consciousness become clearer, therefore, when they are read in the light of Jungian personality theory. Jungian psychology expanded Freudian theory in several ways. Most obviously, it extended the Freudian unconscious to include archetypal patterns of thought. But Jung also modified Freud's theory of repression. In a Jungian account of the psyche, the shadow symbolizes all the repressed negative feelings Freud discovered in the unconscious. But as Jung studied the dynamics of personality development, he became convinced that not only negative emotions but many good and natural processes must be suppressed for the adult ego to achieve personal individuation. He discovered antagonisms between specific ego functions—between thought and feeling, between sensation and intuition.

As we have seen, however, when an ego attitude or function is suppressed, it atrophies and becomes increasingly neurotic. When this happens, thinkers and feelers, sensation types and intuitive types, introverts and extraverts confront one another as shadow presences. So do those whose activity reflects back to the conscious ego its own repressed anger, fear, and guilt. Neurotic terror of the shadow causes it to be projected compulsively onto others. As a consequence, those who confront one another as shadow presences within community are subconsciously divided by mutual hostility and fear. The result is an inevitable breakdown of communications with a concomitant lowering of shared awareness.

These psychological insights lend further speculative warranty to Royce's suggestion that any human community is morally certain of being betrayed by its members. In *The Problem of Christianity*, he observed:

> Contrasts, rivalries, difficult efforts to imitate some fascinating fellow-being, contests with my foes, emulation, social ambition, the desire to attract attention, the desire to find my place in my social order, my interest in what my fellows say and do, and especially in what they say and do with reference to me,—such are the more elemental social motives and the social situations which at first make me highly conscious of my own doings.
>
> Upon the chaos of these social contrasts my whole later training in the knowledge of the good and the evil of my own conduct is founded. My conscience grows out of this chaos,—grows as my reason grows, through the effort to get

harmony into this chaos. However reasonable I become, however high the grade of conscientious ideals to which, through the struggle to win harmony, I finally attain, all of my own conscientious life is psychologically built upon the lowly foundations thus furnished by the troubled social life, that together with my fellows, I must lead.[80]

Moreover, there can, as Royce saw, be no doubt that conscious motives also fragment community life and consciousness.

Since the adult ego can focus consciously on only a limited range of experiential variables, it is clear that adequate propositional access to experience is unavailable to the isolated adult ego. We may then draw the following conclusions on the basis of the preceding reflections: (7) *Adequate propositional access to experience in general demands the presence in any community of every kind of personality type. It demands too that each member of the community live in sustained openness to the legitimate ego attitudes and functions of every other.* (8) *The conflict of conscious ideals and ambitions combines with the influence of the shadow upon subconscious evaluative processes to make such sustained openness morally impossible for the natural human ego.* (9) *To the extent that mutual openness is sustained among the members of a truth-seeking community, it is mediated by a repentant confrontation with one's shadow and by the ongoing healing of conflicts and misunderstandings among those who confront one another as shadow presences.*

Knowing God: James and Peirce

It is time to turn our attention to the problem of adequate propositional access to God. In an experiential problematic: (10) *Propositional access to God is the inferential schematization of a personal encounter with the Holy.*[81] *Since such an encounter is an instance of human experience, the normative principles governing adequate propositional access to experience in general also govern adequate propositional access to God.*

The two American thinkers who have seen most deeply into the problem of propositional access to God are, I believe, James and Peirce. Both were friends of Chauncey Wright, whose agnostic positivism posed a severe speculative challenge to their personal religious beliefs.[82] Their response to Wright reflected the differences in their respective personalities. James attempted to vindicate his right to believe in God on irrational, affective grounds. In his "Will to Believe" he argued that when a belief is of vital and momentous importance and when one's stand for or against it is a forced one, in the absence of contradictory evidence, one may fix one's belief on purely passional motives.[83] He observed:

> Our passional nature not only lawfully may, but must, decide an option between propositions, whenever it is a genuine option that cannot by its nature be decided on intellectual grounds; for to say, under such circumstances, "Do not decide, but leave the question open," is itself a passional decision,—just like deciding yes or no,—and is attended with the same risk of losing the truth.[84]

In more recent times, Michael Polanyi has advanced and nuanced James's germinal insights.[85] He has argued, quite correctly, that rational inquiry cannot be sustained or ever properly conducted in an affective vacuum. Polanyi has pointed out, again quite correctly, that all human cognition is irreducibly personal in character. He has seen that the personal contribution of the theoretician to the speculative enterprise demands a repudiation of naive claims to scientific objectivity. And he has suggested that the true criterion of such "objectivity" is in fact "intellectual satisfaction." To give "intellectual satisfaction" a theory must be formulated in abstract terms that render it independent of the experience of individuals or groups. And it must be deserving of universal acceptance by rational creatures. But the formulation of such abstract theories remains a profoundly personal (though not a purely "subjective") process.

Polanyi has seen that human passion is indeed an indispensable tacit component in every scientific and speculative endeavor.[86] Not only does passionate involvement with a problem motivate the theoretician to endure the labor and the sacrifices serious thinking demands, but the "heuristic passions" actually lead and nourish creative insight. Affectivity breeds hunches, guesses, and the intuitive breakthroughs that advance human science. Moreover, such passionate interests are public and shared, not merely individual and private. Finally, Polanyi is as insistent as Peirce and Royce upon the need for a convivial social context that advances rational inquiry, one in which shared convictions can be critically nourished by adequate social contact and fostered by liberating economic and political structures.

Peirce too was convinced that creative insight emerges from the free play of the prerational mind. But he was more keenly aware than James that abductive thinking, or the passionate formulation of an initial abduction, is only the first phase in the logical fixation of belief. As Peirce pondered the logic of abduction, he realized that, unlike deduction or induction, a good abduction cannot be logically pro- grammed in advance. There are no rules for coming up with a novel, creative solution to an unsolved problem.

As his insight into abductive logic matured, he became con- vinced that its proper task was not the formulation of a set of rules that govern creative hypothetical insight but the elaboration of a set of criteria for evaluating the potential speculative worth of proposed solutions to unsolved questions. He suggested that a good initial hypothesis will be marked by caution, by breadth, by testability, and by instinctive simplicity.[87]

An hypothesis violates the canon of caution when its testing exceeds the available resources of energy, time, and money. For even if such a hypothesis were true, how would anyone know? A hypothesis that is both cautious and testable will be broken into its smallest logical components for separate verification or falsification. Partial verification is better than none; partial falsification may lead to a better formulation. An abduction will have breadth if its verification or falsification has implications in other areas of human inquiry.

Finally, a sound explanatory hypothesis should be marked by instinctive simplicity. That is to say, all other things being equal, the more spontaneous an educated guess, the more likely it is to be expressive of the instinctive thrust of the mind toward understanding. Like many a scientist before him, Peirce was fascinated with the ability of great geniuses to select from out of a potentially infinite set of explanatory possibilities the one theory that eventually proves to be the correct one. This capacity convinced him that too much meddling in the instinctive workings of genius is speculatively coun- terproductive.

These reflections yield an important insight into the problem of adequate propositional access both to experience and to God: (11) *Adequate abductive propositional access to experience and to God is mediated by the free play of affectivity and by conscious sensitivity to the intimations of heuristic passion.*

Peirce, like James, was a religious man. Wright's skeptical bad- gering had forced Peirce to abandon his early Transcendental religi- ous creed. His first solution to this crisis of faith was to keep religious belief and scientific speculation carefully segregated. He now felt that in order to develop properly, the scientific mind needs freedom from the a priori, dogmatic restraints so easily imposed by conservative religious feelings and traditions. At the same time, he was convinced that instinctive human religious sentiments need to be protected from the inroads of scientific skepticism and fallible, theoretical abstractions. For he also remained convinced that religion lies closer to the primordial sources of human life than do the abstractions of scientific theoreticians.

But in the twilight of his career, Peirce began to glimpse the possibility of effecting the wedding of religion and science. Moreover, what mediated this advance in his thought was his growing conviction concerning the instinctive basis of sound abductive inference.[88]

From the first, Peirce had been ill at ease with the individualism and the irrationalism in James's "will to believe" in God. And in his "Neglected Argument for the Reality of God" he set about correcting what he felt were the logical oversights in James's "pragmatic" religion. In his own approach to God, Peirce conceded to James that initial cognitive access to the divine is imbued with an element of the irrational. A sound approach to God, he suggested, ought to begin with the free play of the mind before the mystery and complexity of the universe. His term for mind-play was "musement."[89]

As Hugo Rahner has shown, such "musement" has over the centuries been a source of perennial human and speculative fascination. Rahner's *Man at Play* is a eulogistic study of the virtue of "eutropelia," of the balance of character that frees humans to engage in play.[90] The authentic play of the mind, he suggests, leaves it "in a kind of Mozartian suspension between laughter and tears, between merriment and patience, a state of the soul in which the early Fathers of the Church wrote some of their loveliest pages, speaking of this our earthly life as a 'divine children's game.' "[91] Mind-play is indeed the key to conceptual openness to experience in all of its diversity. It demands the abandonment of close rational control of cognitive processes, a kind of active, Hiedeggerian listening to the world and to one's heart. It presupposes affective balance and wholeness, and it finds expression in a liberating sense of peace and joy. Mind-play demands, in other words, initial freedom from domination by the first of the dark powers.

Peirce was convinced that when the playing mind, as opposed to the controlled rational ego, confronts the wonder and mystery of life, it knows a self-transcendence that suggests instinctively the possibility of a God, a real source of ultimate meaning and of purpose lying at the basis of the cosmos. Even more, the playing mind is just as instinctively drawn by the beauty of its own vision to an initial belief in God. Abraham Maslow's investigation of the peak experiences of healthy adult egos tends to confirm Peirce's suggestion.[92]

So too does Jungian personality theory. In reflecting on the endless philosophical debate over the alleged speculative superiority of an extraverted cosmological proof for God's existence as opposed to an introverted ontological or ethical argument, Jung observes:

> *Esse in intellectu* lacks tangible reality, *esse in re* lacks mind. Idea and thing come together, however, in the human psyche, which holds the balance between them. . . . Living reality is the product neither of the actual, objective behaviour of things nor of the formulated idea exclusively, but rather of the combination of both in the living psychological process, through *esse in anima*. . . . The psyche creates reality every day. The only expression I can use for this activity is *fantasy*. Fantasy is just as much feeling as thinking; as much intuition as sensation. There is no psychic function that, through fantasy, is not inextricably bound up with the other psychic functions.[93]

Jung's suggestion takes on added foundational significance if one is willing to concede the situational character of human affectivity and to abandon the scholastic suggestion that the "spiritual faculties" of intellect and will give us our most basic form of cognitive access to God. In an emergent universe initial cognitive access to experience and to God is mediated by appreciative forms of understanding. Moreover, Jung's sensitivity to the power of archetypal thinking made him more sensitive than Peirce to the fact that openness to appreciative insight creates the possibility of being consciously grasped by God.

Peirce, however, has a sharper sense than Jung of the logic that ought to shape human religious affirmations. He saw quite clearly that initial religious propositions, like every abductive propositional feeling, need deductive clarification and inductive verification. Religious beliefs need to be coordinated with other beliefs. They need to be measured against relevant factual data and judged by the way they lead human experience. False, inadequate, or destructive religious beliefs should be abandoned; true, adequate, life-giving beliefs should be nurtured, clarified, and when possible developed and enhanced. The laboratory of religious thought is, then, history itself. For in the course of the evolution of historical consciousness, the grounds and the consequences of specific religious propositions come to be tested for their applicability and adequacy to human religious experience.[94]

Peirce's "Neglected Argument" yields, then, yet another insight into the problem of adequate propositional access to God: (12) *Adequate propositional access to. God demands the willingness to subject abductive religious propositions to deductive clarification and to historical verification through shared systematic inquiry into the ultimate meaning and purpose of human religious experience.*

The Problem of Faith

The preceding reflections cast foundational light on the complexity of reaching and sustaining adult faith consciousness. For authentic religious faith is the attempt to formulate an adequate propositional response to the historical self-revelation of God. But if in Jesus the very Word of God has indeed become flesh, then every adequate inferential approach to God must take that religious fact into account and must be willing to accept its consequences. Hence, (13) *Adequate propositional access to God is possible only in faith, i.e., in conscious response to the divine act of self-revelation incarnate in Jesus and illumined by the action of the Holy Breath.*

Jesus, however, as we shall see in the following chapter, demanded of His followers a trust in God that was unconditioned. In the post-resurrectional era, unconditioned trust in God is mediated by unconditioned submission to every authentic impulse of the Holy Breath. As we have seen, however, the pneumatic transformation of human propositional feelings is the charismatic transformation of adult ego-consciousness. Hence, we may also conclude: (14) *Adequate propositional access to God is mediated only by active, prayerful participation in the shared activity of that universal, charismatic community that is the living Church.*

We have already criticized substance theory for having privatized human affectivity by portraying it as a "subjective" rather than a situational response. The same criticism needs to be leveled against a substance view of reason and of faith. Reason is not primarily or in the first instance the subjective thinking capacity of an individualized substance. It is most fundamentally a social, dialogic process that hones personal habits of thought to greater and greater precision. Faith is the same process pneumatically transformed. It is the propositional shaping of adult ego-consciousness through the active sharing of all the charismatic inspirations of the Divine Breath.

The Psychodynamics of Charismatic Communities

If, however, the preceding reflections are sound, one can anticipate that the psychodynamics of normal adult ego-development will condition human interaction within a charismatic faith community.

As we have seen, the Pauline gifts can be correlated with different adult personality types, a fact that suggests the natural susceptibility of certain types of persons for receiving certain charisms.

But experience testifies that the charismatic transformation of adult ego-consciousness does not eliminate totally the lurking power of the shadow self. One may anticipate, then, that in Christian charismatic communities, charismatic introverts will continue to threaten charismatic extraverts. Charismatic activists will tend to fear and suspect charismatics of more pietistic bent, and vice versa. Antagonistic ego functions will also tend to breed division and misunderstanding. Intuitive prophets will terrify more pedestrian kinds of administrators, and vice versa. Thinking teachers will live in obtuseness to the realm of feeling that fascinates discerners. Discerners will live in suspicion of teachers who attempt to academicize the discernment process. Extraverted teachers will live in mortal terror of "subjectivistic" forms of affective piety. Intuitive administrators will be frustrated by the alleged myopia of fact-oriented officials, while the latter will tend to live in hostile suspicion of the harebrained schemes of prophets and visionaries. At least, all of this will be so to the extent that the members of a charismatic community resist facing the shadows that haunt them or refuse to submit subconscious impulses to the healing light of God.

These suggestions only underscore, however, the wisdom of Pauline teaching concerning the Mystical Body of Christ. It is the ego-inflated charismatic who resists the correction of other gifts. Aberration in a charismatic community is never, however, the effect of the charism itself. Charisms heal, they do not distort. Division and misunderstanding in a charismatic community are always symptomatic of a failure to submit to the conscious leading of the Breath. At the same time, as Paul also insisted, the test of authentic charismatic piety is growth in mutual forgiveness and love.

We have completed our final set of switchbacks, the most strenuous portion of this part of our climb. But if the preceding reflections have been sound, they raise two important practical and pastoral questions: How concretely do I go about discerning my personal charism of service? And how ought Christian educators to go about the task of fostering the growth of charismatically anointed, adult, Christian egos? Before closing this chapter let us ramble briefly through these two problems.

Discerning One's Service Gift

Among Christian saints and mystics, the one who understood

most clearly the complexities of discerning one's personal charism of service was, perhaps, Ignatius Loyola. Indeed, the first two weeks of his Spiritual Exercises are a very practical program for discerning the exercitant's personal charism of service within the Christian faith community.

In the course of Chapter IV we had occasion, in discussing the dark night of sense, to reflect on the first phase of the Ignatian program. It included: the desire for liberation from oppression by dark powers, heartfelt conviction of the mercy of God historically revealed in Jesus and in His Breath; frank and detailed confrontation with the sinful aspects of one's own shadow; a repentance that results in the practical reform of one's life; progressive liberation through faith-healing from the first of the dark powers; a growing affective sensitivity to the divine beauty incarnate in Jesus that nourishes Christian hope.

The second phase of the Ignatian program for discerning one's personal charism of service also proceeds in an orderly fashion. It should not begin until hope has intensified to the point that it gives rise to a personal desire for greater generosity in the service of our Savior and Lord. Once such generosity does emerge, it ought to motivate a new and more positive kind of self-examination, namely, a prayerful assessment of one's natural ego-strengths and weaknesses, of one's present vocational involvement, and of the other alternatives to service to which one might devote one's life.[95]

But reasonable clarity concerning potential vocational options does not of itself provide sufficient grounds for discerning a charism of service. Hence, Loyola also demanded that the maturing Christian first pass three important tests in prayer with the discerning help of a sound religious guide.

The first test engages the propositional feelings that shape religious experience. More specifically, the maturing Christian must face realistically the fact that the following of Jesus the servant Messiah leads every disciple to a personal Calvary. It demands the willingness to be poor with Christ poor, to be despised with Christ despised. It demands freedom of heart to share even needed spatio-temporal supports to one's own life with others. It demands the willingness to trust one's future to God rather than to rely on the rich and powerful of this world. When the maturing Christian can consent from the heart to such a program of life, (s)he is ready to pass on to the next test.[96]

The second Ignatian test of generosity looks to decision rather than to the understanding. One must do more than understand what it means to serve others in the image of a crucified Lord. One must also be willing to follow whatever call to service God may give, directly, immediately, without hesitation or substitute.[97]

The third Ignatian test of authentic Christian generosity is affective. Loyola anticipated that the maturing Christian who had passed the second of his tests would probably begin to find certain forms of Christian service more spontaneously appealing, others more instinctively repugnant.[98] One individual might, for example, prefer personally to serve God in the business world but sense the possibility of a deeper call to work directly with the poor. Another might be biased to academic research but sense the possibility of a deeper prophetic call that will entail distasteful confrontations. The list of possibilities could be expanded indefinitely.

Ignatius was convinced, and correctly so, that I will not be affectively free to hear God's own call to service until instinctive repugnance to every realistically possible call has been healed in faith. He suggested as a test of whether such healing had indeed occurred the freedom of heart to pray the following prayer in perfect peace: "Dear Lord, I desire with all my heart to be completely free to respond to every prompting of your Breath. If then it be to Your greater glory and praise, choose me for that form of service for which I feel the greatest instinctive repugnance."[99]

Such a prayer is not the charismatic anointing of the Breath. It is a preliminary test of affective freedom to respond to such an anointing when it occurs. For Ignatius saw that until I am affectively free enough to imagine the worst that might realistically happen to me in serving God and to accept it in advance, I lack the personal freedom of heart to discern and respond to the charismatic promptings of divine grace.

When the charismatic anointing of the Breath finally occurs, it brings with it a clear sense of divine election.[100] For one can choose in faith only that form of service for which one has been chosen by God. This is the pun lurking behind Ignatius's use of the term "election."

My charismatic call may come suddenly, in a single moment of unmistakable, graced clarity. Or it may be the fruit of a "lingering out sweet skill." When no clear charismatic prompting occurs in prayer, Ignatius allows the exercitant to make a tentative, personal choice of vocation during a moment of tranquillity. But he demands that that choice be subsequently confirmed, either suddenly or gradually, by the illumination of the Breath in prayer.[101]

To discern a personal charism of service demands greater subtlety of mind and heart than the discernment of initial repentance. For the person seeking to respond to a charismatic call is not choosing between belief and unbelief, or between good and evil, but between possible forms of ecclesial service, all of which are good. The temptations such a person experiences are not, then, temptations to what is sinful, but temptations to complacency and lack of generosity. Moreover, anyone who has wrestled with such a choice before God knows how easy it is for the natural ego to rationalize its unacknowledged anxieties about the future. As a consequence the principles that govern the discernment of a personal charism of service need to be more complex than those that judge the authenticity of an initial conversion experience.

Those who seek the Breath habitually in prayer know that Her touch always brings consolation, contentment in God, and deep spiritual joy. She dispels sadness, discouragement, and all the dark forces that bind and oppress the human heart. The habitually prayerful person gradually learns to recognize these divine consolations even in the midst of physical and psychic suffering.[102]

As one learns to unmask personal self-deception and demonic illusion through prayer and discernment, one begins to understand their deeper subconscious motives. As one sinks more deeply into prayer, one senses that one's life is being gradually, gently, almost imperceptibly shaped to God's own ends, as water drops fill a dry sponge one by one. As sensitivity to the gentler action of the Breath grows, so too does sensitivity to the violence, confusion, and turmoil that unholy impulses breed.[103]

Prayer begins to be marked by unmistakable interventions of divine grace. These graced peaks are marked by greater passivity before God and by a disproportion between the illumination received and its immediate human antecedents. A discerning approach to such a strange and unmistakable impulse of grace will, however, be careful to distinguish the moment of illumination from subsequent, self-initiated reflections upon it. For while the Breath never deceives Her children, Her children are capable of enormous self-deception in their attempt to interpret the movements of grace. The pattern of self-deception is ordinarily clear enough. It begins with holy and pious reflections that are compatible with the original passive grace. But as one's evaluative response develops, disturbing and disrupting thoughts begin to surface, until by the end of the process, one has lost any clear sense of the grace originally given.[104]

Christian Education

In the last chapter we noted the fairly widespread failure of South American liberation theologians to address the moral problems raised by sexist bigotry. Liberation theology has, however, made a solid contribution to critical reflection on the purpose of Christian education. It should, moreover, be clear to the reflective reader that the preceding analysis of the human foundations of Christian faith implies a number of educational corrolaries. The theology of education provides, then, the possibility of serious dialogue between liberation theology and foundational theory.

Liberation theology has insisted quite correctly that Christian education should be "conscientizing," a term to which we will return in Chapter VII. Moreover, in their critique of education, liberation theologians are heavily indebted to the work of Paolo Freire.[105] In his *Pedagogy of the Oppressed*, Freire contrasts what he calls a "banking theory" of education with a truly revolutionary pedagogy.[106]

In a "banking" pedagogy, the teacher talks and the student listens. Students are expected to memorize and regurgitate the teacher's ideas whether or not they find them meaningful or helpful. "Banking" pedagogy lays great emphasis on memorization. It instills passivity in the student, minimizes creativity, and discourages critical thought. It is manipulative and in the last analysis itself a form of human oppression.[107]

The true goal of education, Freire insists, is by contrast "conscientization": the liberation of the adult conscience to deal intelligently and responsibly with social and political questions of serious moral import. A liberating pedagogy, Freire suggests, will be one that engages both teacher and student in a shared learning experience. Those who seek to educate the oppressed should stand with them, not over them. A liberating pedagogy will be sensitive to the situation of the oppressed and will attempt to heighten their personal awareness of the environmental forces that deprive them of both basic human rights and the means to effect a just social order.[108]

The goal of a liberating pedagogy should be concrete and practical: the humanization of society. A liberating pedagogy should, then, unmask the oppressive designs of the dominant social elites. Those designs are the conquest, the manipulation, and the cultural invasion of the oppressed. The conquest of the oppressed is accomplished by dividing them, by reducing them to passivity, and by controlling social, economic, and political power with a view to preserving the status quo. Manipulative propaganda persuades the oppressed to eschew any activity not sanctioned by the bourgeois ethic of the ruling elite. Cultural invasion instills in the oppressed a sense of human inferiority through sloganistic propaganda that seduces them into internalizing the heteronomous authority structures that shackle them.[109]

The social mission of the oppressed is to effect not only their own liberation but that of their oppressors as well. For the oppressing elite are possessed by the tools of power to which they cling. A liberating pedagogy will, then, instill in the oppressed a love for the world and for all humanity, a belief in human ability to create a just and humane social order.[110]

It is impossible for the student of Dewey's educational philosophy to read Freire without a slight feeling of *déja vu*. Freire takes the class struggle more seriously than Dewey. His pedagogy is more overtly Marxist than Dewey's. But in other respects Freire's educational theory and Dewey's are remarkably convergent.

Both envisage the goal of education as preparation for responsible social action. Both espouse a progressive (and somewhat utopian) social ideal in which the common dedication of all to the enhancement of human life corrects social injustice and eliminates economic and political oppression. Both insist on the importance of pedagogical sensitivity to the situation of the learner. Both insist on the dynamic interplay of theory and practice within the learning process. Both condemn indoctrination as an educational ideal and censure rote memorization as pedagogically inadequate. Both place high value on student initiative and creativity. Both envisage the teacher as a participant in the learning process.[111]

Dewey has already had a profound impact upon American education. Hence, the convergence of his and of Freire's pedagogies probably helps explain why the principles underlying Freire's pedagogy sound somewhat less than revolutionary in the ears of American educationists. But while the United States enjoys one of the freest forms of government in the history of human civilization and while affluence and social mobility render revolution unpopular here, our country still knows oppressed minorities. And despite moments of moral responsibility it has done its share to contribute to the economic exploitation of developing nations. As a consequence, Freire's pedagogy of liberation has much to teach American society and the American Church.

It also has something to teach John Dewey. For Dewey, education is training for responsible participation in a free, progressive, democratic society. As a consequence, the ethical ideals inculcated by Deweyan pedagogy would not seem to transcend the fifth level of ethical consciousness described by Lawrence Kohlberg.[112]

We will have occasion to reflect on Kohlberg's ethical theories in greater detail in the chapter that follows. Here it suffices to note that he is a developmental psychologist of the same ilk as Jean Piaget. His chief interest is in the cognitive morphology of human ethical growth.

In his investigation of human growth, he has discovered six, possibly seven, stages in moral maturation. The fifth stage corresponds to the official, public morality enshrined in the American constitution. An individual at the fifth stage recognizes the need to act on ethical principle but is committed to government by consensus and to fidelity to existing laws until they have been modified by due process.

According to Kohlberg, the sixth stage of moral growth effects a personal deepening of one's ethical horizon. In the sixth stage of development, the human conscience recognizes the need for fidelity to personal moral principle, irrespective of what individuals and governments may think or do. If Kohlberg is correct, Freire, in establishing personal conversion as the ultimate goal of his pedagogy, holds out to the learner a more adequate ethical ideal than does Dewey.

Dewey, however, also has a few things to teach Freire. By grounding his pedagogical theory in a systematic, critical investigation of the dynamics of esthetic, intellectual, and moral development, he avoids some of the limitations inherent in Freire's espousal of "praxis" as a speculative method. As a speculative method, praxis has clear advantages. It recognizes that thought and action stagnate in mutual isolation. And it demands that speculation be relevant to specific social and political problems.

But practical relevance can be too narrowly conceived. And thought that is too closely bound to concrete situations will in the long run be irrelevant to the experience of most people. The proponents of praxis have, then, much to learn from the critical commonsensism of C. S. Peirce. The founder of American pragmatism was anything but insensitive to the speculative importance of practical consequences. He never tired of insisting, however, that the most practical insights are the most abstract and universal, provided one takes the time to explicate their implications for human life and decision.[113] Freire's pedagogy is most relevant to those who are politically oppressed. Dewey's is relevant to those who are human. Moreover, his abstract, philosophical orientation allows him to address a wider spectrum of educational problems than Freire.

Freire, like Dewey, is a humanist; his educational ideals are humanistic ideals. But if the preceding analysis has been sound, Christian personal and moral development must transcend mere naturalistic humanism. The purpose of education from hearth to graduate school is the nurture of an adult ego. The Christian, however, can grow to a full awareness of what it means to be an adult person only in response to the charismatic anointing of the Holy

Breath. For a charism is an enabling divine call to grow in sanctity, in service. Allegedly "Christian" education that is not explicitly and overtly charismatic is to that extent profoundly inadequate and inauthentic. It will tend to breed at best only natural self-reliance, at worst sinful ego-inflation.

American Catholic education has been in a state of crisis since its inception. But in an earlier age the threats to its future were largely extrinsic—immigrant poverty on the one hand and nativist and anti-Catholic bigotry on the other. As long as immigration gave decisive shape to the American Catholic community, the goals of Catholic education were also clear: the preservation of lay orthodoxy in a heretical Protestant environment, the Americanization of the immigrant poor, and their elevation from the lower to the middle class.

By the mid-twentieth century, therefore, Catholic education in the United States was headed for a serious internal crisis even had Vatican II never happened. For the educational institutions established at great sacrifice by the immigrant Church had accomplished all too well everything they had set out to do. The end of immigration, the election of John F. Kennedy, the numerical expansion and thorough bourgeoisification of the Catholic community had set for Catholic schools and colleges a new pedagogical agenda that they were all too slow to recognize. The dawning of Catholic ecumenism in the wake of Vatican II only widened the gulf in Catholic educational circles between pedagogical needs and original institutional goals. As a consequence, since the sixties, Catholic education in this country has been in a serious state of drift. Aimlessness had bred a growing "liberal" tendency to ape the religiously bland procedures of secular centers of learning. As a result the quality of religious instruction has in many places declined alarmingly.

If, however, the preceding analysis has been sound, American Catholic education can rediscover a sound sense of purpose if it espouses the following principles:

(1) The goal of Christian education from cradle to graduate school is the evocation and charismatic transformation of an adult ego.

(2) One becomes an adult through conversion. Hence, the purpose of Christian education is to lead young people to integral conversion before God.

(3) Since conversion ought to crown the passage through adolescence into the world of adult responsibility, sound Christian education must respect the laws of human experiential growth.

(4) Since human experience emerges from a spatio-temporal

environment, the first concern of the Christian educator must be the creation of a learning environment that leads young people to integral conversion before God.

(5) Since a "banking" pedagogy fosters infantilism rather than sound ego-development, a sound educational environment will employ instead a pedagogy that is integrally conscientizing and genuinely liberating.

(6) A truly liberating pedagogy will: (a) respect the valid insights of developmental psychology; (b) engage teacher and student in a shared growth experience; (c) foster needed ego skills; (d) advance the student by stages to deal creatively and responsibly with forces that shape adult society; (e) be overtly and explicitly charismatic.

(7) A learning environment will be charismatic: (a) if those who direct the educational enterprise are themselves integrally converted, personally open to the Breath of Jesus, sharing their gifts and charisms in a community of prayer, concerned that the entire educational enterprise proceed in docility to the leading of the Breath and (b) if students are inspired by the conversion and faith witness of their instructors to similar charismatic openness to God.

(8) Since Christian conversion mediates the pneumatic transformation of affective conversion, and since experiential access to God is initially affective and only subsequently propositional, Christian education will take as its most fundamental task the nurture of Christian hope.

(9) The nurture of Christian hope demands the healing of the human heart through repentance, the repudiation of sexist attitudes and values, the cultivation and charismatic transformation of appreciative consciousness, openness to every authentic prophetic impulse.

(10) Since propositional feelings are born of physical purposes and since Christian faith is born of Christian hope, authentic Christian education will respect the laws of adequate propositional access to experience and to God.

(11) Since Christian faith grows through the charismatic transformation of intellectual conversion and since intellectual conversion is the assumption of personal responsibility for the cultivation of an adult ego, authentic Christian education will lead young people to a sound insight into the strengths and weaknesses of their own ego and to a sound discernment of their personal charism of service.

(12) Since integral Christian conversion demands the pneumatic transformation of moral conversion, not only will authentic Christian education be conscientizing, in Freire's sense of that term, but it will

also teach the young to evaluate every moral situation according to the mind of Jesus.

(13) A conscientizing Christian pedagogy will deprivatize every aspect of human experience. Hence, it will lead students to the realization that integral conversion is impossible without commitment to social reform. It will, therefore, lead them to acknowledge by their lives that: (a) authentic, graced affective conversion sets the Christian in opposition to sexist values and institutional structures; (b) authentic, graced intellectual conversion dedicates the Christian to the ongoing reform and charismatic transformation of educational institutions; (c) authentic, graced moral conversion dedicates the Christian to active opposition to oppressive economic and political structures and to the re-creation of a just and loving human society in the power of the Breath of Jesus.

We have so far reflected on the pneumatic transformation of natural affective and intellectual conversion. It is time, then, to consider the pneumatic transformation of natural moral conversion. To do so we must begin to explore the morphology of Christian love.

Notes

1. Ricoeur, *Symbolism of Evil*, p. 309.
2. *Ibid.*, p. 178.
3. *Ibid.*, pp. 181–183.
4. *Ibid.*, pp. 191–198.
5. *Ibid.*, pp. 197–198.
6. *Ibid.*, pp. 211–224.
7. *Ibid.*, pp. 225–231.
8. *Ibid.*, pp. 232–235.
9. *Ibid.*, pp. 235–278.
10. *Ibid.*, pp. 306–346.
11. Gelpi, *Charism and Sacrament*, pp. 121–131.
12. *Ibid.*, pp. 123–125.
13. *Ibid.*, pp. 63–110.
14. Kilian McDonnell, *Charismatic Renewal and the Churches* (New York: Seabury, 1976); Morton T. Kelsey, *Tongue Speaking: An Experiment in Spiritual Experience* (New York: Doubleday, 1968); William Samarin, *Tongues of Men and Angels* (New York: Macmillan, 1970).
15. George Montague, *The Spirit and His Gifts* (New York: Paulist, 1974); Gerhard von Rad, *Old Testament Theology*, trans. D. M. G. Stalker (Edinburgh: Oliver and Boyd, 1970).
16. Avery Dulles, *The Survival of Dogma* (New York: Doubleday, 1973); Donald L. Gelpi, S.J., "The Ministry of Healing" in *Pentecostal Piety* (New York: Paulist, 1972), pp. 3–58; Louis Monden, *Signs and Wonders* (New York: Desclee, 1966); Francis McNutt, O.P., *Healing* (South Bend: Ave Maria, 1974).
17. Michael Buckley, S.J., "The Structure of the Rules for Discernment

of Spirits," *The Way*, Supplement #20, vol. 2, (1973) pp. 19–37; Jonathan Edwards, *A Treatise Concerning Religious Affections*, edited by John E. Smith (New Haven: Yale, 1959); Gelpi, *Charism and Sacrament*, pp. 92–93.

18. Gelpi, *Charism and Sacrament*, pp. 142–153.

19. Whitmont, *Symbolic Quest*, pp. 128ff.

20. G.G. Jung, *Psychological Types*, trans. H.G. Baynes (Princeton: Bollingen, 1974), p. xiv.

21. *Ibid.*, pp. 48, 62, 102, 130–131, 138, 168–169, 171, 182–183, 293, 326–327.

22. *Ibid.*, pp. 273–288.

23. *Ibid.*, pp. 61, 63.

24. *Ibid.*,

25. William James, *Pragmatism* (New York: Meridian, 1960), p. 22.

26. Jung, *Psychological Types*, pp. 300-319.

27. *Ibid.*, pp. 319–320.

28. *Ibid.*,

29. *Ibid.*, pp. 330–341.

30. *Ibid.*, p. 339.

31. *Ibid.*, pp. 373–380.

32. *Ibid.*, p. 379.

33. *Ibid.*, pp. 362–363, 393–395.

34. *Ibid.*, p. 362.

35. *Ibid.*, pp. 354–356, 387–388.

36. *Ibid.*, pp. 366–368, 398–401.

37. *Ibid.*, pp. 342–346, 380–383.

38. *Ibid.*, pp. 363–366.

39. *Ibid.*, pp. 395–398.

40. *Ibid.*, pp. 356–359.

41. *Ibid.*, pp. 388–391.

42. *Ibid.*, pp. 368–370.

43. *Ibid.*, pp. 401–403.

44. *Ibid.*, pp. 346–354.

45. *Ibid.*, pp. 383–387.

46. *Ibid.*, pp. 364–366.

47. *Ibid.*, pp. 396–398.

48. *Ibid.*, pp. 357–359.

49. *Ibid.*, pp. 390–391.

50. *Ibid.*, pp. 369–370.

51. *Ibid.*, pp. 402–405.

52. *Ibid.*, pp. 348–354.

53. *Ibid.*, pp. 385–387.

54. Gn. 11:1–9.

55. Ac. 2:1–21; Montague. *The Holy Spirit*, pp. 271–288.

56. Ac. 2: 37–39.

57. Jung, *Psychological Types*, pp. 390, 400.

58. Gelpi. *Charism and Sacrament*, pp. 70-78.

59. Jung, *Psychological Types*, pp. 405-407.

60 Kilian McDonnell and Arnold Bittlinger, *The Baptism in the Holy Spirit as an Ecumenical Problem* (Notre Dame: Charismatic Renewal Services, 1972); "The Holy Spirit and Christian Initiation," in *The Holy Spirit and Power* (New York: Doubleday, 1975), pp. 57–85.

61. Gelpi, *Charism and Sacrament*, pp. 97–110.

62. Josiah Royce, *The World and the Individual* (2 vols.; New York: Dover, 1959), I, pp. 62–77.

63. *Ibid.*, I, pp. 52–53.

64. *Ibid.*, I, p. 76.

65. *Ibid.*, I, pp. 142, 144–145.

66. *Ibid.*, I, pp. 265–345.

67. *Ibid.*, II, p. 241.

68. Josiah Royce, *The Sources of Religious Insight* (New York: Scribner's, 1940), pp. 27–28; William James, *Pluralistic Universe*, pp. 114–115, 173, 182ff., 207, 212, 265.

69. Royce mentions the incident in *The Problem of Christianity* (2 vols.; Chicago: Regnery, 1968), II, pp. 114–117.

70. Royce, *The World and the Individual*, I, pp. 185–222.

71. Murphey suggests that Peirce's critique of Kant is in need of nuancing on this point but concedes the originality of Peirce's final position; cf. Murphey, *The Development of Peirce's Philosophy*, pp. 55–63.

72. Rahner's suggestion that there is a special relation between the Logos and human nature would, for example, fall under this stricture, unless I mistake his meaning; cf. Karl Rahner, "On the Theology of the Incarnation," *Theological Investigations*, IV, pp. 105–120; Donāld L. Gelpi, *Life and Light: A Guide to the Theology of Karl Rahner* (New York: Sheed and Ward, 1966), pp. 3–14.

73. Peirce, *Collected Papers*, 1. 14.

74. *Ibid.*, 5. 358–376, 388–410.

75. *Ibid.*, 5. 377–378.

76. *Ibid.*, 5. 379–381.

77. *Ibid.*, 5. 383.

78. *Ibid.*, 5. 385–387.

79. Royce, *The Problem of Christianity*, see especially vol. II; Francis Oppenheim, S.J., "A Roycean Road to Community," *Proceedings of the Jesuit Philosophical Association* (April, 1969), pp. 20–61; Gelpi, *Charism and Sacrament*, pp. 101–103.

80. Royce, *The Problem of Christianity*, I, pp. 136–137.

81. Rudolf Otto, *The Idea of the Holy*, trans. John W. Harvey (New York: Oxford, 1950); Mircea Eliade, *The Sacred and the Profane*, trans. Willard Trask (New York: Harvest, 1959); Abraham Maslow, *Religions, Values, and Peak Experiences* (New York: Viking, 1970).

82. Edward Madden, *Chauncey Wright and the Foundations of Pragmatism* (Seattle: University of Washington, 1963).

83. William James, *The Will to Believe and Other Essays in Popular Philosophy* (New York: Dover, 1956), pp. 2–4.

84. *Ibid.*, p. 11.

85. Michael Polanyi, *Personal Knowledge: Towards a Post-Critical Philosophy* (New York: Harper and Row, 1958), pp. 4ff.

86. *Ibid.*, pp. 133.

87. Reilly, *Charles Peirce's Theory of Scientific Method*, pp. 23–55.

88. Peirce, *Collected Papers*, 1. 616–677. 6. 428–450.

89. *Ibid.*, 6. 452–467.

90. Hugo Rahner, *Man at Play* (New York: Herder and Herder, 1967).

91. *Ibid.*, p. 28.

92. Peirce, *Collected Papers*, 6. 466–467; Maslow, *Religions, Values, and Peak Experiences*, pp. 59–68.

93. Jung, *Psychological Types*, pp. 51-52, 63.

94. Peirce, *Collected Papers*, 6. 468–493.

95. Puhl, *The Spiritual Exercises*, #97; Peters, *op. cit.*, pp. 71–78.

96. Puhl, *op. cit.*, #136–148; Peters, *op. cit.*, pp. 91–99.

97. Puhl, *op. cit.*, #149–156; Peters, *op. cit.*, pp. 100–105.

98. Puhl, *op. cit.*, #157; Peters, *op. cit.*, pp. 122–124.

99. Puhl, *op. cit.*, #165–167.

100. *Ibid.*, #169–174; Peters, *op. cit.*, pp. 120–129.

101 Puhl, *op. cit.*, #175–188.

102. *Ibid.*, #329–334.

103. *Ibid.*, #333.

104. *Ibid.*, #336.

105. Paolo Freire, *Pedagogy of the Oppressed* (New York: Seabury, 1973), p.

106. *Ibid.*, pp. 27–51.

107. *Ibid.*, pp. 57–64.

108. *Ibid.*, pp. 68–84.

109. *Ibid.*, pp. 88–177.

110. *Ibid.*, pp. 40–42.

111. John Dewey, *Democracy and Education* (New York: Macmillan, 1961).

112. Lawrence Kohlberg, "The Claim to Moral Adequacy of a Highest Stage of Moral Judgement," *Journal of Philosophy*, LXX (October, 1973), pp. 630-346.

113. Peirce, *Collected Papers*, 5. 438-462.

VII. God or Mammon

We are approaching the end of our climb. We have our hiking legs and are finding it easier to keep up a rhythmic pace. Our lungs have adjusted to the new altitude. The trail is familiar now, almost like home. Each turn yields a new angle on our path of ascent, while towering above us bright peaks beckon.

In the course of our ascent we have had occasion from time to time to address the fourth question raised at the close of Chapter III, namely: "What are the practical consequences of consent to Jesus as the revelation of God and source of the Holy Breath?" We have examined some of those consequences in reflecting on the theological basis for sexual politics and on the foundational principles of contemporary educational reform. But the time has come to face this same question squarely and systematically. For though we have reflected on the pneumatic transformation of affective and intellectual conversion, we have not reflected on the pneumatic transformation of human ethical development. Once we have done so, we will be in a position to begin our final ascent.

The terrain that lies ahead divides clearly into five different rock strata. It begins, as our method demands, with a reflection on the salient images that have shaped Christian aspiration for the pneumatic transformation of natural moral conversion. That hope is shaped by the image of Jesus as the New Moses.

Implicit in the New Testament proclamation of Jesus as the New Moses is the claim that He was in fact an ethical teacher. It is a claim that a number of contemporary theologians are, however, unwilling to make. To justify such a claim we will have first to establish the plausibility of approaching Jesus as an ethical teacher. To do so we will attempt to isolate an ethical strain in His teaching. We will then apply dialectical method to the results of contemporary exegesis to formulate a hypothesis about the basic moral demands of new covenant religion. By this time, we will have reached a third stratum of foundational issues.

As we shall see, the writers of the New Testament inculcated an ethics of faith that stands in clear contrast to the natural law ethics taught by Stoic morality. But any contemporary foundational attempt

259

to reflect on the pneumatic transformation of human ethical development must be aware of the historical impact of Christian Stoicism upon the evolution of Christian moral theology. As we pass through this third stratification of problems, we will examine some of the speculative motives that mediated the theological assimilation of a natural law ethic. The realization that we need to elaborate a new foundational model for the Christian conscience will introduce us to a new stratum of reflection.

As we pass through this fourth stratum, we will begin our search for a developmental model for the Christian conscience. At this point in our climb we will examine the work of Lawrence Kohlberg and Jean Piaget, and we will subject their work to foundational critique.

We will then be in a position to ascend through the last rock stratum in this portion of our climb. During our passage through this section of the trail we will attempt to elaborate an emergent model for the Christian conscience that illumines the growth processes shaping the pneumatic transformation of natural moral conversion.

Having paused to get our bearings, let us begin our ascent through the first of these five strata. To do so we must reflect on the image of Jesus as the New Moses.

The New Moses

The figure of Moses is multifaceted. The first Moses was both a child of oppression and the liberator of an oppressed people. He was the mediator of the Sinai covenant. He was a prophetic voice who denounced the sinfulness of Israel and taught fidelity to the divine law. An intimate of Yahweh, he was intercessor for a sinful people before God. In his face, the glory of God was revealed at Sinai.[1]

The first Christians found these same traits abundantly fulfilled in Jesus. For only the incarnate Son of God knows the Father truly and intimately. A poor man, Jesus proclaimed liberation to the oppressed; as Messiah He announced an endless season of Jubilee. Moses sealed the Sinai covenant through animal sacrifice; Jesus sealed the new covenant with His own blood. By His death He atoned for sin and pleads for us now at the right hand of God. His risen glory surpasses that of Moses and is reflected in the faces of all who stand covenanted to God through Him.[2]

In His own ethical teachings Jesus acknowledged both the authority and the divine origin of the Torah. He lived in personal submission to the Law. He preached that fidelity to its ethical precepts is the gateway to eternal life.[3]

But Jesus also repudiated unequivocally every form of legalistic formalism. He demanded a piety that went beyond the hair-splitting debates of the rabbis. He was careless about ritual purifications and denounced the rigid enforcement of religious ceremonials that were of human rather than of divine origin. He rejected pious rationalizations that subverted the true intent of the Law, and He proclaimed that intent to be growth in love, mercy, justice, compassion.[4]

Moreover, Jesus did not hesitate to make ethical demands of His disciples that went beyond those of the Mosaic code. And He imposed these obligations with personal authority. He demanded a purity of heart that went deeper than mere external conduct. He abrogated Mosaic divorce practices, forbade the use of oaths, demanded the love of one's enemies, and proscribed violent retaliation to injustice.[5]

In the course of His ministry, Jesus also found Himself increasingly drawn into conflict with Pharisaism. He openly criticized its self-righteousness. He rebuked its propensity to substitute concern with legal niceties for concern with the needs and miseries of living persons. He denounced substituting meticulous attention to ritual purity for authentic repentance and faith in God. Again and again He challenged Pharisaism prophetically as a seed bed of complacency and as a source of serious scandal. As the battle lines hardened, His words seem to have assumed a harsher, more uncompromising character.[6]

The gospels testify clearly, therefore, to an ambivalence in Jesus' attitude to the post-exilic piety of His people. While He submitted personally to the Law, He rejected what He judged to be mere human legal traditions that subverted its true intent. Moreover, while Jesus acknowledged the divine origin and binding force of the Law, correctly interpreted, the focus of His own ethical teaching was not conformity to legal prescriptions but a repentance and conversion to God that was the prelude to lifelong discipleship lived in expectant faith of the coming reign of God.

The repentance Jesus required of His disciples demanded, first of all, an acknowledgment of personal sinfulness and of one's personal need for forgiveness. It was this demand that set Him on a collision course with Pharisaism. It was the publicans and the harlots who responded to His preaching and that of the Baptist, not the self-righteous Pharisee.[7]

The repentance Jesus demanded of His followers bore positive fruit in personal faith and personal discipleship. That faith was more than mere intellectual assent. It was a bond of life linking the disciple to the Father. It came to practical expression in a willingness to accept the free, divine gift of salvation Jesus Himself proclaimed. Hence, in His preaching Jesus identified faith in God with faith in Jesus' own message, mission, and person. He insisted that the true disciple must be assimilated to the Master, must follow Him in His own unswerving obedience to the Father's commands, even when obedience leads to Calvary.[8]

Granted the ambiguity present in Jesus' own attitude to the legal piety of His time, it is no wonder that divergent theological theories concerning the place and importance of the Mosaic code emerged in the apostolic community.

In Pauline preaching, Jesus' Breath and doctrine provides the necessary and sufficient basis for Christian moral practice. Paul portrays moral conflict as the struggle against the "flesh." The "person of flesh" is sinful. But in Pauline usage, "flesh" is not simply synonymous with "sin." Nor does it designate the "material" aspects of the human person alone. The "person of flesh" signifies the total person viewed under the aspect of natural human weakness and limitation. "Flesh" is then the state of humanity before it is grasped by the transforming power of Jesus' Breath. The "person of flesh" stands under the condemnation of the Law, for (s)he lacks the pneumatic life-force that alone frees one to live up to the Law's demands.[9]

Pauline moral preaching thus explicated a theme that is only implicit in the preaching of Jesus Himself, namely, the possession of a personal conscience. In Paul's teaching, the chief function of the conscience is to testify to one's personal guilt or innocence before God. The testimony of the conscience is, moreover, fallible, for even the witness of a clear conscience must await the day of the Lord for its final vindication or condemnation.[10]

More important still, Paul insisted on the presence of a conscience in all persons. In the pagan, the conscience is as soteriologically impotent as the Law. For the pagan whose heart is closed to the Breath of the Lord stands, like the unconverted Hebrew, condemned before God for personal inability to live in fidelity to those precepts conscience knows to be morally binding.[11]

These Pauline insights were destined to have profound impact on the development of Christian ethical theory. But Rudolf Schnackenburg is, I believe, correct to insist that Pauline teaching about the human conscience can in no sense be interpreted as an endorsement of Stoic or Neo-Platonic natural law theory. "St. Paul's 'by nature,' " he writes in commenting on Rm. 2:14,

cannot simply be equated with the moral *lex naturalis*, nor can this reference be seen as straightforward adoption of Stoic teaching. The Stoic was so certain that the *lex naturalis* was a part of human nature that he maintained that everyone who recognized it could also live by it. That was definitely not St. Paul's opinion. He uses the expression φύσει in an unphilosophical, popular sense, as meaning perhaps "by what you are, of yourselves."[12]

Like those of the apostle of the gentiles, the letter of James is at pains to insist that faith in Jesus must bear fruit in good works. But it is some measure of the contrast between its ethical optic and that of Paul that James never once mentions the Breath of Jesus as a force within Christian morality. The letter does, however, refer to the Christian covenant as "the law of liberty." Despite its high moral tone, however, the letter of James offers the reader at best a scattered miscellany of moral admonitions. The letter seems, indeed, to have been more concerned to correct popular distortions of Pauline doctrine.[13]

The gospel of Matthew offers yet another approach to the question of Christian morality. The gospel portrays Jesus as another Moses whose teaching fulfills the substance of the old Law by rendering its moral imperatives more radical. In Matthew's gospel, the binding force of the Law is never questioned. And it is taken for granted that consent in faith to Jesus includes acceptance of the authentic moral demands of the Mosaic code. But for the author of Matthew, Jesus demands more, not less, than does the Mosaic law.[14]

The Problem of New Testament Ethics

Thomas Jefferson, like many an eighteenth-century *philosophe*, believed that a demythologized New Testament was in fact a delicious morsel of ethics. Contemporary theologians are, however, on the whole disinclined to look on Jesus as another Socrates. Some question whether there is even a consistent ethical doctrine in Jesus' teachings and suggest that the Christian Scriptures proclaim a revealed reality rather than a revealed morality. Those who claim to discover an ethical doctrine in the New Testament are often hard put to reduce its moral message to a systematic code of conduct.

Our own reflections on Jesus' moral message will proceed in five steps. First, we will attempt to establish the plausibility of approaching Jesus as an ethical teacher. Second, we will attempt to isolate an ethical strain in His doctrine. Third, we will attempt to derive from the New Testament an initial foundational hypothesis concerning the basic moral demands of new covenant religion. Fourth, we will examine the sayings of Jesus to see whether our hypothesis can interpret the ethical strain in His doctrine. Fifth, we will examine several other New Testament authors to see if the same moral doctrine is reflected in their ethical teaching. Having sketched in broad outline the value system inculcated by new covenant religion, we will then turn our attention to a host of related foundational questions.

The Politics of Jesus

In his book *The Politics of Jesus*, John H. Yoder has argued that not only was there an ethical doctrine at the heart of Jesus' preaching but that it posed a genuine social threat to the religious and economic power structure of His day. For Yoder, Jesus' death was a direct consequence of the revolutionary character of His preaching.

Yoder argues with considerable plausibility that Jesus' proclamation of the reign of God derived much of its ethical inspiration from the Jewish year of Jubilee. The Jubilee year was a fallow year in which the land was allowed to rest and renew itself. But it was also a time of moral renewal and of social transformation. During the year of Jubilee, all debts were cancelled, all slaves were freed, all family property was restored.[15]

Yoder discovers similar themes in the preaching of Jesus. In the Lord's prayer, he observes, Jesus calls for a cancellation of all debts. In His preaching He summons the rich to distribute their possessions to the poor and the dispossessed. And in Luke's gospel especially, He is portrayed as divinely anointed to proclaim a season of Jubilee.[16]

Jesus' baptism by John also gives clear evidence, as Yoder, C. K. Barrett, and others have noted, that He was moving in the same religious circles as the Baptist. The religious vision of the Baptist was colored by the Jewish apocalyptic of his day. And in his preaching, the Baptist demanded vigorous moral reform. He called for economic and social justice. He summoned his listeners to share freely their material blessings, to active concern for the poor; and he demanded moral uprightness of powerful political leaders. Moreover, in the synoptic gospels, the imprisonment and assassination of the Baptist is presented as an understandable foreshadowing of Jesus' own death.[17]

The gospels also tell us that Jesus' words touched especially the poor and the dispossessed. Through table fellowship with sinners, He reached out to social outcasts. As a result of His Galilean ministry, He developed a popular following in the northern provinces. His symbolic choice of twelve assistants could not have gone unnoticed by Jewish authorities: this Galilean carpenter was presuming to construct a new Israel out of fishermen, tax collectors, and whores.

Moreover, the gospels suggest that it was only after Jesus had consolidated a following in Galilee and won from the apostles an acknowledgment of His messianic mission that He entered into serious confrontation with the Jerusalem authorities.[18]

His triumphant entry into Jerusalem was an act of effrontery that made unmistakable messianic claims; [19] His assault on the money changers in the temple, a defiant challenge to the religious power structure and a summons to repentance. To the Jerusalem authorities Jesus must have appeared, and rightly so, as the head of a swelling popular movement that posed a real threat not only to their religious authority but also to the limited political autonomy they enjoyed under Roman rule.

Yoder is, then, quite correct to insist that Jesus' proclamation of the reign of God involved more than the cult of religious interiority or an other-worldly faith in an immanent apocalyptic termination of human history. The reign of God envisaged an economic redistribution of material goods, the abolition of social barriers, the reform and renewal of existing religious institutions, and the repentant submission of Jewish authorities to the teachings of a Galilean carpenter.[20]

But Yoder is, I believe, also correct in portraying Jesus as rejecting the violent revolutionary tactics of Jewish Zealots and as opting instead for nonviolent opposition to religious hypocrisy and to economic and social oppression. If so, it is also entirely plausible that Jesus Himself realized, perhaps from the beginning, that at the end of the nonviolent path He had chosen lay His own violent death at the hands of the intransigent power structure He opposed.[21]

The Teaching of Jesus

Even though rabbis in Jesus' day did not ordinarily engage in a ministry of healing and forgiveness as Jesus did, and even though Jesus' own teachings were enunciated with an authority that transcended ordinary rabbinic discussions, John T. Palikowski is, I believe, correct in characterizing the bulk of Jesus' ministry as "rabbinic."[22] The Letter to the Hebrews, of course, portrays Jesus' death and resurrection as a priestly sacrifice that terminated the animal sacrifices of the old covenant.[23] But Hebrews is a belated Christian theologization of the meaning of Jesus' life and ministry. In the course of His career, however, Jesus eschewed cultic leadership. If we are to believe the fourth gospel, He did not even baptize His own disciples.[24] But He was popularly known as "Rabbi." Indeed, He seems never to have exercised anything like a cultic role until the Last Supper. There, in a gesture that was more prophetic than purely cultic. He assimilated His immanent death to a covenant sacrifice.[25]

Of all the gospels, Mark is least concerned to preserve the sayings of Jesus. Markan theology reflects early Christian hope that the second coming would be soon. Moreover, like the fourth gospel, the first attempts to portray Jesus' public self-disclosure as a gradual process of revelation. But instead of depicting that process as the mounting conflict of the forces of light and darkness, Mark resorts to a series of cumulative proclamations. Jesus is named Messiah and Son of God, then suffering servant, and finally glorious Son of Man. His progressive self-disclosure is the revelation of His "messianic secret."[26]

Markan theology colors the arrangement of the few sayings of Jesus the gospel preserves as continuous discourses. The evangelist inserts a few parables at the beginning of Jesus' ministry, for the parables are the most enigmatic of Jesus' sayings. As a consequence they suggest the obscurity of Jesus' initial self-disclosure. They contrast, moreover, with the more extended apocalyptic discourse recorded at the end of the gospel. The other gospels also testify to the presence of both a parabolic and an apocalyptic strain in Jesus' preaching.[27]

Joachim Jeremias has, moreover, discovered several doctrinal themes running consistently through the parables of Jesus. The parables announce the immanent accomplishment of some decisive salvific act. They give assurance of God's abiding forgiveness for sinners. They insist that despite its humble beginnings, the reign of God proclaimed by Jesus will be established upon earth. They promise that God is faithful and that the Father will hear the prayers of the poor and of all who turn to Him in faith. They warn that time is running out and that there is no postponing a decision concerning Jesus and His message. They speak of immanent catastrophe for those who ignore the good news. They warn that for some it may already be too late to turn and be saved. They challenge religious complacency, popular ethical and religious prejudices, and hypocritical self-infatuation. They demand mutual reconciliation, faithful discipleship, and humble acceptance of the good news.[28]

As one would expect, the apocalyptic strain in Jesus' preaching has more overt political overtones. Jesus identified powerfully with the glorious image of the Son of Man described in the Book of Daniel. The image was both messianic and political: it is to the Son of Man that domination of the nations of the world is divinely awarded. Jesus also prophesied, perhaps more than once, the end of temple cult and the destruction of the Holy City. The prophecy was an issue at His trial. He warned of the tribulations of the end time. He urged readiness for the divine judgment soon to be visited upon a faithless generation.[29]

Besides a parabolic and an apocalyptic strain, Jesus' teaching possessed a third, argumentative strain as well. The evangelists assure us that Jesus engaged other rabbis in regular public debate and that His wit and wisdom was frequently tested by probing and sometimes malicious questions. The gospels indicate some of the debated issues: Which commandment in the Law is the greatest? Is it proper to heal on the sabbath? What is the relationship of Jesus' teaching to the Law and the prophets? Is divorce legitimate? By what authority does Jesus proclaim the forgiveness of sins? Do the dead rise? Should Jews pay Roman taxes?[30]

A fourth strain in the teachings of Jesus finds expression in His solemn warnings, promises, and direct statements of personal self-revelation. He declares that He alone has the power to reveal the Father. He promises that He will sanction the actions of His true disciples, that He will build His community upon the rock of Peter, that some of His contemporaries will see the glory of the Son of Man, that He will establish the Twelve as judges in the New Israel. He claims authority to forgive sins. He attempts to convince His apostles that as Messiah He must enter into the atonement of the suffering servant of Yahweh.[31]

There may be other distinguishable strains in Jesus' sayings as they are recorded in the New Testament. The preceding rapid survey is, however, sufficient for our present purpose, namely, to isolate within Jesus' teachings a fifth doctrinal strain. For in proclaiming the reign of God, Jesus was at frequent pains to describe the style of living proper to the true children of God, i.e., to those who live in committed expectation of His coming reign. As we shall soon see, it is in these practical instructions for life that the substance of Jesus' ethical teaching is expressed. From them new covenant religion derives its distinctive moral character. Let us, then, begin to examine this fifth strain in Jesus' teachings to see if we can discover within them some kind of coherent pattern.

The Christian Covenant

Moses mediated the Sinai covenant. Implicit, then, in Christian proclamation of Jesus as the new Moses was the conviction that through Jesus' ministry, death, and glorification and through the action of the Holy Breath, the new covenant once promised by Jeremiah had in fact been sealed in the hearts of the members of the

New Israel. Jesus Himself had, of course, provided the immediate historical basis for Christian covenant piety by proclaiming in prophetic word and gesture at the Last Supper that His impending death would in fact be a covenant sacrifice. That gesture not only founded eucharistic devotion; it endowed Christian baptism with its salvific meaning, namely, ritual participation in the covenant death and resurrection of the Lord.

One of the defining ethical traits of covenant religion is, however, that it makes one's ethical stance toward one's covenant sisters and brothers the test of the authenticity of one's commitment to God. In the earliest forms of Mosaic religion, membership in the covenant tended to be conceived in narrowly racial terms. In post-exilic Judaism, however, a more catholic strain of piety emerged that extended the divine promise to the nations as well. Christian religion expanded this nascent universalism by opening its doors to uncircumcised gentiles.

One would, then, expect early Christian baptismal catechesis to have included some organized instruction concerning the ethical demands of faith in the God who stood revealed in the new covenant. The existence or content of such a catechesis is, however, far from self-evident. The explicit baptismal catechesis articulated in the letters of Paul focuses, for example, primarily on the archetypal and religious symbols that give ritual baptism its mysterious meaning. Paul portrays baptism as a Christian exodus, as incorporation into the body of Christ, as mystical death to sin and rebirth to risen life in the transforming power of the Holy Breath. Paul argues that baptism is pneumatic circumcision of the heart and therefore the necessary and sufficient condition for admission into the New Israel. There can, of course, be no serious doubt that in addition to these doctrinal considerations, Pauline baptismal catechesis included some kind of ethical instruction. But as Joseph Fitzmyer and others have observed, it is difficult for the exegete to reduce Paul's moral exhortations to anything like an ethical system.[32]

The letters of Paul are not, however, our only New Testament source for reconstructing the baptismal catechesis practiced in the early Church. Both the synoptic tradition and the gospel of John offer rich insights into the meaning of Christian initiation. Moreover, as we shall see, it is the synoptic tradition that provides the clearest key to the ethical demands of new covenant religion.

The synoptic accounts of Jesus' own baptism and temptation give clear evidence of being colored by early Christian baptismal instruction. Moreover, as we shall see, the different theological treatment given these two events by the three synoptic evangelists provides some of our best insights into how one strain of early Christian baptismal teaching evolved.

Markan Baptismal Catechesis

Mark's account of Jesus' baptism and temptations introduces all of the catechetical themes Matthew and Luke will seek to embellish.

(1) *Christian and Johannine Baptism.* Mark is the first gospel and the only one to record Jesus' baptism as an event. Matthew mentions Jesus' intention to be baptized and introduces a brief dialogue between Jesus and the Baptist in which the latter protests the impropriety of what he is about to do. Both Matthew and Luke refer obliquely to the baptism as an accomplished fact. The fourth gospel omits any reference whatsoever to Jesus' baptism at the hands of John and reduces the Baptist's salvific role to that of witness to Jesus' ministry and message.[33]

All this theological pussyfooting suggests the following: (a) Early Christian baptismal catechesis sought to vindicate the superiority of Christian baptism by contrasting it with Johannine baptism. But (b) the fact that Jesus had undergone Johannine baptism seemed to belie the superiority of Christian baptism and was a source of doctrinal embarrassment in the apostolic church. Hence, (c) Christian teachers were led to soft-pedal the fact of the baptism. But (d) since the baptism was a fact, the theological problem could not be so easily dismissed. Indeed, its repeated handling suggests that it may have been one of the standard objections raised by those who opposed Christian baptism.

Among those opponents may well have been disciples of the Baptist himself. The New Testament records instances of conflict between Jesus' disciples and those of John during Jesus' lifetime.[34] And the conflict probably continued after Jesus' death. The presence of such a controversy would, moreover, help explain why Mark's gospel makes the superiority of Jesus' mission and baptism the exclusive concern of the Baptist's witness to Jesus.[35] The other evangelists embellish the Baptist's teaching for both historical and theological reasons. But they also have the Baptist reiterate Mark's insistence that Jesus and Jesus alone baptizes with the Holy Breath.[36] In all four gospels, therefore, the witness of the Baptist endows Jesus' baptism with symbolic significance for the Christian catechumen. For Jesus' pneumatic anointing on the occasion of His baptism inaugurates His historical revelation as the true Breath-baptizer.

(2) *Jesus, The New Israel.* Mark's gospel also describes Jesus'

messianic commissioning at the time of His baptism. In Mark's account that commissioning occurs in an apocalyptic vision to which Jesus alone is privy. In Matthew, however, the voice from heaven proclaiming Jesus Messiah speaks, not to Jesus alone, but to the reader and through the reader to the world. Luke separates Jesus' messianic vision and pneumatic anointing from His baptism. In Luke, this momentous event occurs after John has finished baptizing and while Jesus is alone at prayer. There are two reasons for these textual variations in Luke. First, Luke desires to make it quite clear that Jesus' messianic commissioning is in no sense the effect of John's baptism. Second, because Luke wishes to parallel Jesus' messianic anointing by the Breath with Her descent on the apostles at Pentecost, he depicts both Jesus at the Jordan and the apostles in the upper room as divinely commissioned while at prayer.

In all three synoptics, however, Jesus' messianic anointing is linked theologically to Christian baptism, not only by the Baptist's witness but by the images that structure Jesus' messianic vision. Indeed, the witness and those images are intended to illumine one another mutually. Let us reflect on the theological connotations of the images in question.

All three synoptic writers include the same four elements in Jesus' vision: (1) the rending of the heavens as a sign of the inauguration of the last age of salvation; (2) Jesus' anointing by the Breath; (3) the descent of the Breath under the sign of a dove; and (4) the divine voice from heaven proclaiming Jesus to be Messiah in the image of the suffering servant.

The Divine Breath over the waters suggests the first creation. The dove over the waters suggests Noah's dove. Hence, the descent of the Breath upon Jesus is presented to Christian faith and hope as a salvific re-creation of the world that recalls its re-creation after the apostasy of Babel and the flood of retribution. Moreover, as we shall see in Mark and especially in Luke, the motif of the new creation forms an important symbolic link between Jesus' baptism and His desert temptations. For in both gospels Jesus confronts Satan in the desert not merely as the beginning of a New Israel but also as the new Adam, as humanity pneumatically transformed.

But the dove has a third symbolic meaning. It was a common rabbinic image for depicting Israel as the pet of God and as the object of Yahweh's special delight. The Breath, then, descends upon Jesus in all three synoptics under the sign of the dove because She comes to begin His revelation as the beloved Son of God and as the beginning of a new, pneumatic Israel.

Finally, the Breath descends in order to sanction the witness of the Baptist that Jesus alone is divinely empowered to baptize with the Holy Breath of Yahweh. And lest there be any doubt on that score, the voice from heaven confirms the testimony of the Baptist by designating Jesus, not John, as Messiah, i.e., as the one divinely anointed with the plentitude of the Holy Breath.[37]

It should by now be clear that the description of Jesus' baptism in all three synoptics endows that event with symbolic meaning that is intended to illumine the meaning of every Christian baptism. Not only does Jesus' messianic commissioning designate Him as the only authentic Breath-baptizer but the descent of the Divine Breath in messianic plentitude inaugurates His revelation as the personal beginning of the New Israel and as humanity pneumatically re-created.

But (and this is important) as the personal embodiment of a new, pneumatic Israel and of a humanity transformed in the power of the Divine Breath, Jesus in His baptism and messianic commissioning confronts every catechumen and every baptized believer not only as savior but as model. To enter through baptism into Jesus' dying and rising is to inaugurate a lifetime of discipleship and faithful following in the footsteps of the Lord. Accordingly, Mark's account of Jesus' baptism depicts the Messiah as the suffering servant of the Lord. His intent is clear: Whoever is baptized in the Breath of Jesus must seek to be assimilated to a messianic leader who was also the *ebed Yahweh*. This fundamental demand of Christian baptismal catechesis is, moreover, reinforced by portraying Jesus' desert temptations as the immediate outcome of His baptismal anointing.

(3) *Jesus Tempted.* That Jesus is indeed intended to be the model for all the baptized is both explained and reaffirmed by the story of His temptations. In Mark it is the Holy Breath that "drives" Him into the desert to be tempted. Jesus' testing is, then, the first and most immediate consequence of His baptismal anointing. That His testing lasts forty days is a textual reminder that Jesus submits to this ordeal not simply in His own person, but as the beginning of the New Israel. Mark's intent is, then, clear: let every member of the Israel of Christ remember that Breath-baptism is baptism into a lifetime of testing in the image of a crucified savior.

Mark depicts Jesus as surrounded in the desert by wild beasts. The image would seem to be deliberately ambiguous, at once sinister and salvific. The beasts suggest the animals named by the first Adam, hence, Jesus in His desert victory over Satan stands as the symbol of human kind re-created. For His victory reverses the defeat of the first Adam at the hands of the Adversary. But desert animals were not uncommon biblical symbols for dark, demonic forces. They also suggest, therefore, the bestial, devilish powers against which Jesus must contend with the angelic aid sent Him by the Father.[38]

(4) *The Figure of Satan.* In *Charism and Sacrament* I have attempted to reflect on the symbolic significance of Satan in Christian baptismal catechesis.[39] There is no need to repeat that analysis again. Here it suffices to note that in His temptations Jesus confronts the Adversary precisely as the beginning of the New Israel and therefore in the name of all His faithful disciples. Satan enters the narrative, therefore, as a symbol of the same principalities and powers against which the true disciples of the Lord must contend. If, moreover, as some exegetes suggest, Mark wrote for a community under harassment and persecution, the symbolic meaning of Satan's harassment of the Lord would not have been lost on them.[40]

Matthean Baptismal Catechesis

But if Mark's account of Jesus' baptism and temptations provides some important insights into early Christian baptismal instruction, its theological reformulation in Matthew's gospel offers an insight into how synoptic baptismal catechesis evolved. We have already noted some of the ways in which Matthew's account of Jesus' baptism and temptation differs from Mark's. Matthew has embellished the Baptist's teaching, refers only obliquely to the event of the baptism, inserts the Baptist's protest and Jesus' reply, and portrays the voice from heaven as addressing the world, not just Jesus alone.[41]

There is another significant difference in Matthew's account of the Baptist's witness. Unlike Mark, Matthew is concerned to contrast the descent of the Breath upon Jesus under the sign of the dove with Her descent upon the baptized disciple under the sign of fire.[42] The contrast of images suggests that while the Breath descends upon Jesus as Messiah, as Breath-baptizer, and as personal beginning of both the New Israel and a new creation, She descends on the believer in purification and in judgment. Matthew, then, insists more clearly than Mark that while Jesus' baptism illumines the meaning of Christian baptism, the baptized Christian can in no way claim to stand in the same relation as Jesus to the Father and to the Breath. It is a theological qualification of Markan catechesis that Luke will also endorse.

Nevertheless, Matthew preserves intact most of the imagery in Mark's account of Jesus' baptism and temptation.[43] This overall endorsement of the substance of Markan teaching is important. For it provides the context for understanding Matthew's chief departure from Markan theology, namely, his expansion of Mark's cryptic reference to Satan into an extended and highly dramatic dialogue between the tempter and the Messiah.[44] In other words, with Mark, Matthew locates the uniqueness of Christian baptism in the fact that it is baptism in the Breath of Jesus. With Mark, he sees Jesus revealed in His own Baptism as the beginning of the New Israel and therefore as both Breath-baptizer and model for all believers. With Mark, he sees Jesus' temptation in the desert as a foreshadowing of the confrontation between every believer and Satan. Hence, Matthew's catechetical expansion of the temptation narrative should be read as an instruction concerning the kinds of temptations the true disciple of Jesus can be expected to face as (s)he enters into conflict with the principalities and powers of this world.

But the dialogue between Satan and Jesus in Matthew betrays other theological concerns as well. More than any other gospel, Matthew reflects the world of rabbinic thought. Matthew is concerned to preserve and codify the sayings of Jesus in a way that Mark is not. Moreover, in his infancy gospel, Matthew is at pains to present Jesus unambiguously as a new Abraham and a new Moses. Matthew's theology also qualifies somewhat the vibrant eschatological hope voiced by Mark. In Matthew, concern with an immanent parousia has begun to be replaced by a sense of the importance of history, especially with the past. Yes, Jesus is coming, Matthew assures us; but it is nevertheless important to situate Him within sacred Jewish history, to see Him as the fulfillment of an earlier and more primitive revelation. Luke will, of course, expand this nascent historical concern to include the early growth of the apostolic church. For Luke, the meaning of Jesus is illumined not only by the past out of which He emerged but even more by the consequences of His death and glorification.

The descriptive details of Matthew's temptation narrative lack factual plausibility. Jesus is whisked from the desert to the pinnacle of the temple without explanation.[45] This lack of verisimilitude could be the result of literary naiveté. But Matthew's gospel is not literarily naive. In eschewing factual plausibility, Matthew is, I believe, attempting to signal to the reader that his expansion of Mark's temptation narrative is more doctrinal than historical in intent. That is to say, it is a doctrinal explication of the kinds of temptations the baptized Christian can expect to face in confronting Satan and his minions.

One might be inclined to object at this point that such an interpretation of the temptations is unwarranted because they are addressed to Jesus as Messiah and Son of God, and that since Jesus alone is

Messiah, the temptations have no significance for the disciple of the Lord. Such an objection overlooks, however, three important elements in Matthew's text.

First, in Matthew as in Mark, precisely because Jesus is the messianic Breath-baptizer, He is tempted not simply in His own person but as the embodiment of the New Israel. As the New Israel personified, He confronts its members not only as founder but as model.

Second, precisely because the temptations are messianic, Jesus' response to them reveals the meaning and scope of the reign of God that Jesus is about to begin proclaiming in Mt. 4:17. Jesus' responses to the tempter should, then, be read as an important key to the meaning of the teachings of Jesus that Matthew, with scribal care, has culled and thematically grouped in the course of his gospel.

Third, in replying to the tempter, Jesus never speaks in His own words. Instead, He always cites the Torah.[46] When read in the light both of Matthew's endorsement of the broad lines of Markan baptismal catechesis and of his own special concern to present Jesus as the new Moses, the purpose of those citations becomes clear. They provide the Christian catechumen with a handy mnemonic key to those precise aspects of the Old Law Jesus has come to fulfill.

Lukan Baptismal Catechesis

Luke reworks Matthew's account of Jesus' temptations. But his innovations, as we shall see, are largely an attempt to radicalize Matthew's basic doctrine. While Matthew reflects the world of rabbinic debate, Luke is intensely preoccupied with the gentile mission of the Church and its impact on faith and religious practice. Sensitivity to the universal scope of salvation motivates Luke to balance Matthew's catechetical portrait of the new Moses with an image that is biblical but less exclusively Jewish. Luke's temptation narrative therefore explicates and reaffirms unambiguously the Adamic imagery only hinted at cryptically in Mark's account. Luke does so by inserting a genealogy of Jesus (reminiscent of the genealogy that opens Matthew's gospel) between the account of Jesus' baptism and that of His temptation. Luke traces Jesus' lineage, not to Abraham, but to Adam, the father of the race.[47]

Similar concerns seem to have motivated Luke's reordering of the three temptations. By locating the last temptation on the temple pinnacle,[48] Luke parallels the dramatic movement of Jesus' encounter with Satan with the dramatic movement of his entire gospel. Both climax in Jerusalem. Jerusalem was, of course, the city of

David; and Luke's infancy narrative is filled with Davidic imagery. In Acts, moreover, Jesus' victory in Jerusalem will inaugurate the proclamation of the new covenant to the entire gentile world. By placing Jesus' temptation on the temple pinnacle last, Luke transforms it into a foreshadowing of Satan's final assault upon the Messiah in the Holy City. As a consequence, Luke is also concerned to depict Jesus' initial victory over Satan as decisive. The vanquished Satan withdraws in defeat until his final assault.[49] In this detail Luke's handling of the temptations contrasts with that of Mark, who sees the desert temptations as the inauguration of a lifelong struggle between Jesus and the minions of Satan.

Luke also introduces two other modifications into Matthew's temptation narrative: he abbreviates Jesus' first reply to Satan, and he has Satan insist on his dominion over the kingdoms and principalities of this world.[50] Neither modification affects the substance of Matthew's doctrine. Luke's tempted Messiah continues to function within the narrative as a new Moses.

Luke's abbreviation of Jesus' first reply to Satan possesses, however, interesting theological connotations. In Matthew, Jesus rejects the temptation to turn stones into bread with the words: "Man shall not live by bread alone but by every word that proceeds from the mouth of God." Luke abbreviates Jesus' response to: "Man shall not live by bread alone." Later in the gospel, Luke will also abbreviate the first of the Beatitudes. "Blessed are the poor in spirit" will become "Blessed are the poor."[51]

As we shall soon see, the first temptation is not a temptation to gluttony but to egotistical self-reliance before God. To such sinful self-reliance, Jesus opposes trust in God rather than in oneself or one's possessions. Moreover, as we shall also see, in both Matthew and Luke, Jesus will teach that the practical test of one's trust in God is one's willingness to share the spatio-temporal supports of life, one's "bread," with the needy and the dispossessed.

The gospel of Luke was written at a time when the eschatological expectations of many in the Christian community were beginning to undergo serious qualification. It had become clear that the parousia would not be as soon as many believers had at first anticipated. Since the free sharing of worldly possessions was originally linked to Christian faith that the present age would rapidly pass away, the waning of that hope may well have put a crimp in the freedom with which many Christians reached out to the poor and dispossessed. Such may or may not have been the case. What is clear is that Lukan theology is uncompromising in its insistence on practical concern for the poor, the helpless, the downtrodden. If, then, Luke modifies Matthew's understanding of the basic tenets of the new covenant, it is in the direction of rendering them more radical. Make no mistake about it, Luke warns, the true disciple of a servant Messiah cannot live by bread alone.

The preceding reflections are dialectical, not exegetical. But they have allowed us to formulate an initial foundational hypothesis concerning the most basic moral tenets of new covenant religion. They are (1) that the believer live, not by bread alone, but by every word that comes from the mouth of God; (2) that the believer never put God to the test; (3) that the believer worship and serve, not the prince of this world, but God alone. Let us focus these three moral imperatives upon the ethical strain in Jesus' teaching as they are preserved in Matthew and in Luke to see if the same three themes are reflected there. If they are, we have been able to advance from exegesis through dialectic to an initial foundational insight into some of the most basic moral precepts of the Christian covenant.

Temptation and Commitment: The First Christian Precept

In both Matthew and Luke, Jesus' response to His messianic anointing is twofold: (1) He descends into the desert as the messianic embodiment of the New Israel in order to repeat the original desert experience of God's people. But while the first Israel had repeatedly failed its desert tests, Jesus will emerge from the desert victorious. (2) In the desert Jesus undertakes a fast.[52] His descent into the desert and fasting are, moreover, symbolically connected. For the Jew, unlike the pagan Stoic, fasted, not in order to exert rational control over lower animal appetites, but as an expression of a personal desire to live in dependence upon the "mannah" provided by the Lord. The same sort of day-to-day trust in God was, as we have seen, an important theme in Jesus' parables and is crystallized in the fourth petition of the Our Father.

Satan's first temptation is not, then, a temptation to gluttony but a temptation to abandon the fast with all that it symbolizes. It is, in a word, a temptation to egotistical self-reliance before God. That this is the intent of the temptation is clear from Jesus' reply: "Man shall not live by bread alone but by every word that comes from the mouth of God."[53]

The first precept of the Christian covenant is, then, clear: Christian baptism demands the renunciation of egotistical self-reliance for a life of faith-dependence on the Lord. Moreover, the test of authentic faith involves the believer's attitude toward "bread" taken as a generalized symbol of the physical, spatio-temporal supports of human life. Do we find such a notion reflected in the ethical strain in Jesus' teaching?

Christian Sharing

In the gospels, Jesus is repeatedly portrayed as having taken an ambivalent stand toward the physical supports of life. On the one hand, He acknowledged legitimate human needs for food, drink, shelter. He urged the children of God to look to the Father in heaven to provide for all such wants. "Look at the birds of the air: they neither sow nor reap nor gather into barns and yet your heavenly Father feeds them. Are you not of more value than they?"[54]

At the same time, Jesus found the social uses of physical possessions tainted by human sinfulness. If falsely idolized, physical possessions become "mammon." When that happens, they are in need of redemptive transformation through proper use that is motivated by living faith. "Do not lay up for yourselves treasures on earth, where moth and rust consume and where thieves break in and steal. For where your treasure is, there will your heart be also."[55] He warned, then, against any tendency to turn money into a God: "No one can serve two masters; for either he will hate the one and love the other, or he will be devoted to the one and despise the other: You cannot serve God and mammon."[56] And He commended as salvific Zacchaeus' repentant determination to recompense generously all the injustices he had perpetrated during a lifetime of greed.[57]

More positively, Jesus summoned the true children of God to share their possessions with one another as an expression of their desire to live in expectation of the coming divine reign. This strain in Jesus' preaching may well have been a development of the ethical doctrine of the Baptist. Luke portrays the Baptist as having offered similar counsel. "And the multitudes asked him, 'What shall we do?' And he answered them, 'He who has two coats, let him share with him who has none; and he who has food, let him do likewise.' Tax collectors also came to be baptized, and said to him, 'Teacher, what shall we do?' And he said to them, 'Collect no more than is appointed you' Soldiers also asked him, 'And we, what shall we do?' And he said to them, 'Rob no one by violence or by false accusation, and be content with your wages.' "[58]

John began his ministry before Jesus; and Jesus certainly moved in the same religious circles as the Baptist. That Jesus would have proclaimed an ethical doctrine similar to John's should come as no surprise. Jesus, however, seems to have embellished the Baptist's doctrine on sharing by linking it to His own proclamation of the approach of God's reign. He also insisted explicitly on the gratuity and unrestricted scope of authentic faith-sharing. The true children of God must ignore the merits of those with whom they share. "You have heard that it was said, 'You shall love your neighbor and hate your enemy.' But I say to you, Love your enemies and pray for those who persecute you, so that you may be sons of your Father who is in heaven; for he makes his sun rise on the evil and on the good, and sends rain on the just and on the unjust. . . . You therefore must be perfect, as your heavenly Father is perfect."[59] Such sharing is more than a strategy for avoiding divine wrath. It is a profession of childlike trust in God as the ultimate source of life. Hence, it is also a sign of readiness to enter into the kingdom that is coming. "Come, O Blessed of my Father, inherit the kingdom prepared for you from the foundation of the world; for I was hungry and you gave me food, I was thirsty and you gave me drink, I was a stranger and you took me in, I was naked and you clothed me, I was sick and you visited me, I was in prison and you came to me."[60]

The sharing Jesus preached is also an act of atonement. It reconciles the disciple with fellow human beings in the active sharing of their goods and lives. Moreover, it is such mutual reconciliation that mediates the disciples' reconciliation to the Father and opens their hearts to the perfection of life He desires to give. "Forgive us our debts as we have forgiven our debtors."[61]

It is no surprise, then, that the faith-sharing provided the ecclesial context for the first celebrations of the Christian eucharist. The eucharist is the celebration of our reconciliation to God in Jesus through the power of His Holy Breath. For the apostle Paul, it was then unthinkable that anyone would participate in the Supper of the Lord while withholding any personal possessions spitefully from other members of the community. Moreover, the Pentecostal outpouring of the Holy Breath put Jesus' teaching concerning the sharing of God's gifts in a new light. For it revealed that the children of God have more to share than the spatio-temporal supports of life. In the last age of salvation over which the Breath presides, the true child of God is one who is concerned to share in community the charismatic gifts bestowed by the Mother Advocate.[62]

The faith-sharing Jesus demanded of the true child of God reaches across all social barriers. In Jesus' life and preaching both table fellowship with sinners and outcasts and the freedom to share one's blessings even with one's enemies stand as crucial tests of the authenticity of one's faith and trust in God. "If you love those who love you, what credit is that to you? For even sinners love those who love them. And if you do good to those who do good to you, what credit is that to you? For even sinners do the same. . . . But love your enemies, and do good, and lend, expecting nothing in return; and your reward will be great, and you will be sons of the Most High; for he is kind to the ungrateful and the selfish. Be merciful, even as your Father is merciful."[63] In its social consequences, faith-sharing seeks, then, the abolition of class distinction and with it the need for class conflict.

Christian faith-sharing must also be personal. It must include one's most intimate possessions. A hospitality that welcomes any person in the name of God is, therefore, an indispensable expression of an expectant Christian faith in the advent of the divine reign. "When you give a dinner or a banquet, do not invite your friends or your brothers or your kinsmen or rich neighbors, lest they also invite you in return, and you be repaid. But when you give a feast invite the poor, the maimed, the lame, the blind, and you will be blessed, because they cannot repay you. You will be repaid at the resurrection of the just."[64]

By the same token, dedication to the ideal of Christian sharing reorients the whole purpose of human labor. The Christian worker must abjure the selfish amassing of the fruits of personal toil. "Take heed and beware of all covetousness; for a man's life does not consist in the abundance of his possessions." One must labor then not only to avoid being an unnecessary burden upon others but also and especially so that one may have something to share with one's fellows in the name of God. The rich fool, Jesus warns, learned too late that the riches he might have shared with the needy during life would inevitably be distributed to others after he was dead and gone. "God said to him, 'Fool! This night your soul is required of you; and the things you have prepared, whose will they be?' So is he who lays up treasure for himself, and is not rich toward God."[65]

The Second Christian Precept

The Christian's commitment not to test God looks most immediately to personal attitudes rather than to personal possessions. To test God is to attempt to set the conditions under which one is willing to relate to Him. Not to test God is to allow God Himself to set the terms of one's covenant relationship. In other words, new covenant religion gives God a blank check. It demands that the believer's trust in the Father be as unconditioned as the love He has revealed to us in Jesus. "You know that the rulers of the Gentiles lord it over them, and their great men exercise authority over them. It shall not be so among you; but whoever would be great among you must be your servant, and whoever would be first among you must be your slave; even as the Son of man came not to be served but to serve, and to give his life as a ransom for many."[66]

But by the same token, if new covenant trust in God comes to social expression in one's willingness to share freely one's possessions, labor, and charismatic gifts with others, the refusal to test God, the determination to trust Him absolutely, must find practical expression in one's refusal to set any conditions on one's willingness to share with others in the name of Christ.

A practical love that is unrestricted in its scope excludes no one in principle from its concern. "Love your enemies, do good to those who hate you, bless those who curse you, pray for those who abuse you. To him who strikes you on the cheek, offer the other also; and from him who takes away your coat, do not withhold even your shirt. Give to every one who begs from you; and of him who takes away your goods do not ask them again. And as you wish that men would do to you, do so to them."[67] A love that is unrestricted in its conditions does not expect to be merited; it does not ask whether the one loved is worthy of one's commitment. "Those who are well have no need of a physician, but those who are sick. Go and learn what this means, 'I desire mercy, and not sacrifice.' For I came not to call the righteous, but sinners."[68] A love that is unrestricted in its consequences is sustained in the face of misunderstanding, rejection, and hatred. "When they came to the place called The Skull, there they crucified him, and the criminals, one on the right and one on the left. And Jesus said, 'Father, forgive them; for they know not what they do.' "[69]

Moreover, like the love of Jesus, the believer's love must be simultaneously forgiving and prophetic. While it refuses to pass judgment on any person, it nevertheless challenges others in the name of God to enter into a loving relation with God and with other people that reflects the quality of Jesus' own love.

The Third Precept

The converted Christian is also committed to worship and serve the Father rather than the prince of this world. This third covenant commitment required of the baptized is the sum and completion of the first two. It expresses the belief that the reign of God can never be established by mere legal means. Rather, the reign of God is established by the personal submission of every human heart to the moral exigencies of authentic new covenant worship.[70]

In the era of Pentecost, the first test of the authenticity of such worship is that it be Breath-inspired and Breath-led. But the practical test of the pneumatic inspiration of Christian worship is that it express forgiveness of others. "So if you are offering your gift at the altar, and there remember that your brother has something against you, leave your gift there before the altar and go; first be reconciled to your brother, and then come and offer your gift."[71] Personal repentance in the image of the lowly publican[72] and mutual reconciliation, these are the first and most basic touchstones of authentic Christian worship.

But mutual forgiveness and love are meaningless unless they find expression in deeds. Christian worship will, then, be inauthentic unless it occurs in a community that shares actively, freely, gratuitously, and unrestrictedly its goods and charismatic gifts with whoever is in need as the practical expression of mutual forgiveness in the image of Jesus. It must be a community whose members live in peace with one another and who are dedicated to the task of peace-making in the image of Him who said: "Put your sword back into its place; for all who take the sword will perish by the sword."[73] Authentic Christian worship is, then, incompatible with physical, social, and political acts of violence; with revenge, murder, rape, extortion, exploitation, war. Its political stance is pacifist and nonviolent.

At the same time, the true disciples of Jesus will take good care not to become the unwitting tools of political and economic manipulators. They will recognize the "foxes"[74] that infest the economic, political, and ecclesiastical power structure. And like Jesus and the Baptist they will summon these oppressors to repentance. The gospel becomes the tool of the oppressor when nonviolence is preached only to the powerless. It is the rich and the powerful, the oppressive ruling elites, who must abjure the calloused exploitation of the miserable and learn the works of peace. When Christians preach pacifism only to the poor they transform the Father of Jesus into the God of the oppressors and the Church into anti-Christ.

Pauline Ethics

It should be clear from the preceding reflections that the ethical strain in Jesus' teaching illumines and is illumined by the three precepts of new covenant worship proclaimed by Matthew's new Moses in His confrontation with Satan in the desert. But if these precepts are indeed a crystallization of the ethical demands of new covenant worship, one would expect to find them reflected in the moral catechesis of other New Testament writers as well.

Certainly, there can be no question that the first precept lies at the heart of Pauline doctrine. In Pauline ethics, as in Jesus' own, the most basic sin is not disobedience to the Law. It is sinful self-reliance before God. And its root is stinginess, cupidity, egotistical clinging to what is forbidden, finding security and salvation in a reality other than God. Moreover, for Paul as for Jesus, faith comes to expression in the free and gratuitous sharing of the blessings of God, both the spatio-temporal supports of life and the charisms of the Holy Breath. The free sharing of divine blessings is the practical sign of the bond of faith uniting Jewish and gentile Christians. It is a way of entering into Jesus' own covenant sacrifice.[75]

Sharing for Paul as for Jesus encompasses one's most intimate personal possessions: one's home and hearth. In Pauline catechesis, hospitality, especially to strangers and to the needy, is a fundamental Christian duty. But Paul also realized that fidelity to the ideal of Christian sharing takes one far beyond the demands of strict legal justice. One committed to share freely with others has, then, already abjured greed, theft, usury, swindle, extortion, economic exploitation, and any spirit of competition.

Jesus demanded that the mutual love and forgiveness of His disciples like the Father's own merciful love be simply there. Pauline ethics is concerned with explicating the practical consequences of such love. Not only, Paul warns, is it incompatible with murder and violence. It also excludes revenge, wrangling, feuding, quarrels, and bad temper. It demands the abjuration of slander, lying, deceit, dishonesty. It is incompatible with selfish egotism; with lust, sexual depravity, gross indecency. It demands a community unmarred by cliquishness, boastfulness, contentiousness, jealousy, and hypersensitivity. It demands patience, kindness, truthfulness, realistic opposition to what is wrong, readiness to excuse others and to forgive them.[76]

The third Christian precept is the worship of God in the service of atonement. Like Jesus, Paul insists that authentic worship be the expression of personal repentance and of mutual forgiveness and reconciliation before God. It must become incarnate in a prayer of joy, praise, and astonishment in the face of God's forgiving love made visible in Jesus and in childlike dependence on the promptings of the Holy Breath. Active mutual service in the image of the crucified demands tenderness toward all, sympathy, forgiveness. It abounds in a peace that nourishes faith and mutual commitment in love.[77]

James and John
The letter of James inculcates the same three precepts. It de-

mands a faith-dependence on God that stands firm under testing and temptation and proves itself by the free sharing of God's blessings with the needy. It insists that in a faith community of sharing there is no place for class distinctions, for rival cliques and factions, or for violence of any kind. The letter condemns the proud accumulation of wealth and the insensitive exploitation of the poor. And it insists that the test of authentic worship is mutual forgiveness and reconciliation before God.[78]

Johannine catechesis is more preoccupied with doctrinal than with ethical issues. Both the fourth gospel and the first letter of John seem to have been written to combat neo-Gnostic tendencies in the Christian community. Gnostic ethics, as we have seen, tended to veer between rigorism and antinomianism. It is then, no surprise to find the first letter of John repudiating any claim to salvific enlightenment that espouses an antinomian morality. The letter inculcates instead repentance, faith, mutual love, practical service, and the free sharing of God's blessings, especially with the needy.[79]

The fourth gospel inculcates the same moral catechesis as Matthew's temptation narrative, but treats its fundamental affirmations more cryptically and under a different theological rubric. In words that are clearly redolent of Matthew's first temptation, Jesus assures His disciples: "My food is to do the will of Him who sent me, and to accomplish His work." The gospel portrays the trial of Jesus as the supreme attempt of the powers of darkness to put God to the test. It holds up the "new commandment" as the test of authentic discipleship and demands that authentic worship be conducted in spirit and in fidelity to the truth of God made visible in Jesus.[80]

If the preceding reflections have been foundationally sound, we have warranty for the following conclusions:

(1) There is a coherent ethical vision proclaimed in the New Testament.

(2) That ethical vision was derived from the teachings of Jesus preserved in the first Christian community.

(3) It was summarized by Matthew in three precepts that both fulfill and transcend the ethical demands of the old covenant: (a) You shall live, not by bread alone, but by every word that proceeds from the mouth of God; (b) you shall not test God; (c) you shall serve God alone in the mutual worship of atoning love and in the image of the servant Messiah.

(4) Consent to the three basic precepts of the new covenant demands active commitment to the creation of a certain kind of faith community.

(5) In the Christian community, the free and gratuitous sharing of physical blessings and of charismatic graces is the practical test of faith. The unrestricted scope of such sharing is the practical test of the unconditioned character of one's faith. And personal repentance, mutual forgiveness, and mutual service in atoning love are the test of the authenticity of worship.

We have so far been primarily concerned with some of the historical facts and values that lend normative structure to the Christian conscience. It is time then to turn our attention to the legal tendencies, or vectoral feelings, that give dynamic shape to Christian moral development. Our argument will proceed in three stages. First, we will reflect on the speculative attempt of the Fathers and of medieval theologians to Stoicize the Christian conscience and on the speculative inadequacies of Christian Stoicism. Second, we will examine the efforts of contemporary developmental psychologists to articulate predictable stages of natural moral development. Third, we will subject a natural developmental model of the human conscience to critical theological examination. Fourth, we will attempt to articulate a working model of the Christian conscience that is consonant with both the teaching of Scripture and the results of developmental research into human moral conduct.

The Stoic Victory

Both Yoder and Schnackenburg have, I believe, correctly protested any facile assimilation of New Testament and Stoic ethics.[81] Yoder's analysis discovers several points of contrast between the two moral doctrines.

Stoic morality inculcated obedience to the natural law. It conceived that law as fixed and immutable. Though Stoicism inculcated civic responsibility, it appealed primarily to the individual conscience and to an aristocratic sense of noblesse oblige. Its chief moral sanction was the self-evident appropriateness of virtuous living; Stoic virtue is its own reward.

Yoder argues, quite correctly, that even New Testament exhortations having a superficial literary resemblance to Stoic moral maxims reveal on closer examination a very different kind of ethical vision. They inculcate, not fidelity to an immutable natural law, but fidelity to Christ and to the will of God revealed in Him. They find their justification, therefore, not in the metaphysical postulation of an eternal cosmic law, but in a decisive historical act of divine self-revelation. The Christian conscience is ecclesial and charismatic; Christian exhortations appeal, not to the isolated individual, but to the salvific call common to all believers. Far from being patrician and aristocratic, Christian moral exhortations appeal first to the lower strata in Greco-Roman society. When read in context that appeal has revolutionary implications. For it treats everyone as a responsible moral agent, even those who in pagan society were not even regarded as persons. Instead of inculcating aristocratic condescension, Christian moral maxims call for mutual service in forgiveness and in atoning love. Instead of looking to virtue to provide its own reward, Christian morality holds out the hope of eternal life with Christ in God.[82]

Moreover, Yoder also insists, again correctly, that while apostolic preaching attenuated in some respects the revolutionary political implication of Jesus' own socio-economic vision, early Christian catechesis was truest to the Lord's own teaching when it freed the believer's conscience to stand in pneumatically enlightened judgment on the moral adequacy before God of any human law or political system.[83]

But as patristic speculation appropriated the dualistic cosmology and anthropology of Neo-Platonic metaphysics, Christian ethics in its turn underwent a gradual Stoicization. Moreover, the two speculative processes were in fact mutually reinforcing. Neo-Platonic *logos* doctrine was profoundly influenced by Stoic belief in the existence of an immutable natural law. Neo-Platonism identified the eternal law of the cosmos with the divine Intelligence, or *Nous*. In Neo-Platonic cosmology, that Intelligence is the higher regulating principle (*logos*) that rules the lower, spatio-temporal universe. It is the archetypal pattern to which all natural processes and all authentic moral judgment must conform. The Greek Fathers assumed, though they never proved, that the eternal Intelligence of Neo-Platonic speculation was identical with the Logos of St. John. Both Augustine and Pseudo-Dionysus popularized the same assumption in the West.

It was this highly questionable theological presupposition that lent apparent speculative justification to the elaboration of a Christian natural law theory. For if, as Christian Platonism held, the incarnate Word (*Logos*) is in fact identical with the eternal, divine intelligence (*Nous*) that is the cosmic rule (*logos*) that gives normative structure to the natural cosmos, then ethical judgments reached through contemplation of the eternal *Logos* must include not merely the judgments of faith but the rational cultivation of natural virtue as well.

The cultural advantages of such a doctrine must be clear. It allowed Greco-Roman Christians to cultivate pagan virtues in the name of Christ. Unfortunately, however, the self-reliant cultivation of virtuous self-control inculcated by Stoicism stood in diametric opposition to the first precept of the Christian baptismal covenant. For that precept demands that trust in God, not rational self-reliance, be the ultimate motivation of every Christian moral decision. Eventually, of course, the attempt to Stoicize the Christian conscience bore fruit in the Pelagian heresy. But condemned heresies rarely vanish, and Pelagianism is no exception. As Stoic values continued to inform the Christian conscience, Jesus' enthusiastic, eschatological vision of a faith community of free and gratuitous sharing came, all too often, to be replaced by the dualistic cult of "virtuous apathy" toward the mutable things of this material world.

The discovery in the West of the texts of Aristotle in the twelfth and thirteenth centuries mediated an even tighter identification of Christian ethics and a philosophy of natural law. In his own day Aristotle had realized that in rejecting a Platonic theory of ideas, he had in fact also repudiated a Platonic moral philosophy. For Platonic moral ideals are a specific kind of eternal, archetypal form. Having denied the reality of all Platonic archetypes, Aristotle sensed the need to elaborate a new philosophical criterion for judging human moral behavior. He eventually replaced the Platonic cultivation of transcendent moral values with an ethics of the mean. Aristotelian virtue is not the attempt to imitate a subsistent, eternal archetype of virtuous action. It is the more pedestrian attempt to steer a middle course between two vicious extremes. Courage is, for example, the virtuous mean between cowardice and braggadocio.

Thomistic ethics sought to integrate an Aristotelian ethic of the mean with a modified theory of natural law. With the Christian Platonists, Aquinas continued to locate the ultimate norm of morality in the eternal *Logos*, or divine Intelligence. But with Aristotle, he denied the human conscience immediate cognitive access to the divine ideas. He held up as the intermediate norm of morality the immutable, natural, substantial, human essence that, he thought, underlies accidental change in the human person. An Aristotelian substantial essence is, he saw, as immutable as any Platonic idea. And it may be thought of as a kind of "law" as soon as one is willing to concede that it has been created by God in imitation of His own eternal idea of human nature. Since, moreover, Aquinas believed that the nature of the human substantial essence was revealed in the faculties that emanate mysteriously from it, faculty psychology, together with its operational dualism, became normative for "Christian" conduct. Actions contrary to the formal object of a faculty were taken as contrary to the "law of God."[84]

Aquinas also identified the "conscience" with the human, spiritual intellect judging the conformity or nonconformity of any given choice to divine law, whether natural or revealed. Moreover, Thomistic natural reason, whether theoretical or practical, proceeds deductively. Accordingly, Aquinas envisaged the development of the conscience as the deductive application to different moral situations of the immutable first principles of conduct, which, he postulated, are intuitively revealed to the human intellect through the action of a naturally infused "habit of first principles" called *synderesis*, after the Pauline term for conscience.[85]

Thomistic natural law theory also sought to enrich Christian Stoic morality with insights derived from Aristotelian ethics. It endorsed an Aristotelian theory of virtue and even went so far as to interpret faith, hope, and charity as "infused supernatural virtues" whose purpose is to enable the believer to grow in sanctifying grace. Moreover, it described supernatural charity as "informing" all the other virtues, including natural, moral virtues.[86]

Finally, Thomistic ethical theory also attempted a systematic account of natural rights and duties. It insisted correctly that the two notions are correlative and attempted to distinguish social, religious, personal, and proprietary rights and obligations.[87]

As Christian Aristotelianism replaced Christian Platonism in the fields of metaphysics and anthropology, Thomistic natural law theory came to exert enormous influence on Christian moral conduct. As a systematic ethical statement, it was hard to rival and impossible for Christian thinkers to ignore.

But Thomistic ethics labors under some fairly obvious speculative limitations. (1) It is grounded in an understanding of the human conscience that is heavily intellectualistic and voluntaristic. Hence, it describes ethical development in terms of an untenable operational dualism that subjects lower, material faculties to the higher, spiritual powers of intellect and will. (2) By reifying an abstract *essentia humana* it endows intellectual insight into human nature with a naive objectivity. (3) It fails to take adequate account of the place of feeling in the formation of conscience. (4) It rests on a privatized understanding of affectivity, of thought, and of freedom. (5) Its view of human nature is static and essentialistic. (6) It postulates without proving it the mind's ability to intuit the universal first principles of conduct, a postulate belied by contemporary logic, epistemology, and psychology. (7) By assuming the laws of nature to be immutable, it fosters a rigid, moral legalism. (8) It defines virtuous behavior, not as a creative reshaping of one's environment, but as unswerving conformity to the unchanging essence of things. Its ethical vision is, therefore, static and conservative rather than progressive and developmental.

In Search of the Christian Conscience

As the Thomistic revival has faltered under the combined impact of phenomenology, existentialism, and naturalism, Catholic ethical teaching has lapsed into speculative drift. At the basis of much of the contemporary confusion in Catholic morality is the lack of an adequate interpretative model for understanding the workings of the Christian conscience. The "first deductive principles" that once guided Thomistic ethics have lost the fictive self-evidence once attributed to them. Human judgments of conscience can no longer justify epistemologically naive claims to ethical "objectivity." The shift to an evolutionary cosmology has seemed to deprive the laws of nature themselves of any universal moral significance. For in a world in which cosmic laws are themselves in principle changeable, no legal structure of nature can lay claim to being ultimately or universally normative. Lack of theoretical and pastoral consensus concerning the norm of morality and growing skepticism both of canonical legalism and of traditional theories of natural law have left the Catholic conscience in a serious state of confusion. As liberal Catholic rationalists drift into various forms of antinomianism, Catholic conservatives fossilize in a fideistic authoritarianism. The resulting tensions are increasingly intolerable. Does an emergent theology of the human have anything to say to this complex and important problem?

The Kohlberg Alternative

An emergent anthropology espouses a developmental approach to human experience. As we have seen, its presuppositions are convergent with the developmental psychology of Jean Piaget. Piaget has been more concerned with epistemology than with ethics. But Lawrence Kohlberg has attempted to implement the methods of Piaget in a systematic investigation of the cognitive structure of human moral development.

Kohlberg's work is in part inspired by the naturalistic ethics of John Dewey.[88] Kohlberg was intrigued by Dewey's suggestions that there are three distinguishable levels of human ethical awareness: a premoral (or preconventional) level, a conventional level, and an autonomous level. Kohlberg's empirical researches confirm and nuance Dewey's suggestions, for they reveal within each of Dewey's levels two interrelated sub-stages of moral growth. Each stage is an organized way of thinking about moral problems. Each stage rests on specific principles that give it a distinctive evaluative orientation. Let us reflect on each stage in order.[89]

Stage One: Punishment and Obedience Orientation. Moral good or evil is measured in terms of the physical consequences of an act. The good is what is physically pleasant, enjoyable, satisfying. It is what either earns reward or escapes punishment. Evil is what brings physical punishment, physical pain, the depravation of physical satisfaction.

Stage Two: Instrumental, Relativist Orientation. At the second stage of moral growth, narcissistic self-preoccupation has begun to be attentuated, but only slightly. The good is still largely equated with whatever meets my needs, evil with what frustrates them. But at stage two, there is a tendency on occasion to take the needs of others into consideration. The criterion invoked in resolving equitably the conflict of personal interests with those of other people is one of "fair play." There is, however, still no awareness at all of the existence of generalized moral principles that ought to govern personal, ethical decisions. There is as yet no real appreciation of higher moral ideals like loyalty, justice, gratitude. Concern for others is concrete and crudely pragmatic; it is a question of "You scratch my back and I'll scratch yours."

Stage Three: Interpersonal Sharing Orientation. At the third stage of natural moral development the social awareness that began to emerge at stage two acquires enhanced sophistication and importance. The stage-three conscience appeals to social convention as the norm of moral judgment. It equates the good with what helps others, pleases others, and wins the approval of others. There is a concomitant willingness to take the intentions of others into account in judging the rightness or wrongness of their actions. Personal decisions begin to be justified by stereotyped appeals to the way "everybody" acts. There is also an enhanced appreciation of the importance of being "nice" to one another, although at stage three the personal cultivation of "nice" behavior is largely motivated by a desire for social approval.

Stage Four: Law and Order Orientation. The growing realization that not all people act nicely forces the developing natural conscience to search for a new basis for social responsibility. The natural conscience now acknowledges obligatory obedience to existing laws as a basic moral value. Moral good is now equated with the faithful and obedient performance of social duty irrespective of the personal sacrifices involved. There is a conscious need to defend the legitimate exercise of authority and to preserve the institutional guarantees of social order.

Stage Five: Social Contract Orientation. The stage-five conscience is still concerned with the preservation of law and order, but the conscience now realizes that laws are often as not inadequate. It realizes that the defense of law and order is bootless unless the processes by which laws come to be framed are also equitable. The conscience now concedes that the legal and institutional structures of human society are subject to critical review and to improvement provided the changes foster the common good and provided the revisions in question are agreed upon by the members of society themselves. There is also an initial recognition of the limitations of government. But when faced with problems not covered by existing laws, the stage-five conscience will insist on fidelity to binding agreements freely consented to by the involved parties rather than to universal principle or to logical self-consistency. In other words, the resolution of ethical problems is only inchoately rational and autonomous. There is, however, an enhanced sense both of individual personal rights before the law and of the relativity and diversity of personal value systems. There is also concern that proper procedures be established and followed to deal with this diversity effectively and equitably.

Stage Six: Universal Moral Principles. At the sixth level of moral development, the conscience acknowledges the inadequacy of both utilitarian and legalistic solutions to ethical problems. There is a new sense that in order to do one's duty, one may on occasion be obliged in conscience to stand in opposition to the existing legal or social consensus concerning correct conduct. And with this realization comes commitment to self-chosen ethical principles for dealing with important moral questions. In the formation of conscience, appeal to logical comprehensiveness, universal applicability, and internal consistency replace obedience to the law and the observance of due process as the ultimate court of ethical appeal. There is concern that the same ethical principles apply to all and that they be genuinely universal in scope. There is an enhanced sense of the ethical value and importance of each person.

Kohlberg's hypothesis recognizes that the pace of ethical maturation varies from individual to individual. Everyone, of course, begins at stage one. By age nine, however, most people have passed through stage two and have entered stage three, though some may make the same transition later. Entrance into stage four ordinarily occurs in middle or late adolescence. But Kohlberg's researches suggest that the odds are against the majority of Americans ever passing to stage five. If the transition occurs at all, it does so in the late teens and early twenties, or possibly even later. Kohlberg believes that relatively few people ever reach stage six. If they do, they are usually over thirty.

Kohlberg's theory is a working hypothesis. But it has been tested in such diverse cultural settings as the United States, Turkey, Mexico, Taiwan, Israel, Yucatan, Canada, and India. And its defenders claim that it applies across cultures.

Kohlberg's personal stance toward his own theory remains, however, critical and flexible. He has, for example, suggested the need to introduce a transitional stage between stages four and five. This intermediate stage is characterized by skepticism, egoism, and relativism. Skepticism results from the collapse of naive trust in the moral adequacy of existing legal solutions and social structures. Egoism emerges as personal taste replaces legalistic obedience as the criterion of ethical judgment. At stage four-and-a-half, therefore, there is a tendency to revert temporarily to a stage two morality. Relativism develops as the conscience recognizes that different moral tastes have the same claim to social recognition, if taste is indeed the only judge of right and wrong. Stage five fuses stage four and the intermediate stage that follows it into personal commitment to an argued, democratic search for the most reasonable solution to any given moral question possible under the circumstances. Clearly, then, Kohlberg's researches suggest that until the natural conscience passes to stage five, it fixes its ethical beliefs through a blend of taste and authority. The account of natural conversion in Chapter V is an attempt to give a more detailed descriptive rendering of the affective, speculative, and ethical variables that might ideally be expected to structure Kohlberg's stage four-and-a-half.

Kohlberg and Piaget

The independent researches of Kohlberg and Piaget overlap. Both have investigated the moral development of children. They both discover two stages in the conscious growth of childhood morality. But unfortunately they differ in their account of the values that lend conceptual structure to those stages.

Piaget's investigations assume that the child's earliest moral attitudes are revealed in its evaluative stance toward rules. He argues accordingly that parental relationships are of decisive importance at the first stage of moral development. The child's earliest consciously moral responses are therefore described as unreasoning submission to the heteronomous demands of adult authority.

Kohlberg, however, minimizes the importance of parental relationships at stage one. The stage-one child, he argues, is a hedonist rather than an authoritarian, although he also insists that infantile hedonism is devoid of any guile. Kohlberg finds that stage-one children confuse being punished with being a bad person. He concedes to Piaget that children show an egocentric deference to people with superior power and prestige. But he argues that their morality may be described as "heteronomous" only in the sense that stage-one children tend to judge the good and evil of an act by its pleasant or unpleasant consequences rather than by the intentions that motivate it.[90]

What, then, is the issue between Piaget and Kohlberg and what is its significance? For there is an issue and it is more than verbal. The fundamental question is this: Does a child at the equivalent of Kohlberg's stage derive its controlling sense of right and wrong from the demands of parental authority or does it equate "good" with the pleasant and "evil" with what is painful?

Both Kohlberg and Piaget agree that at the following stage a noticeable socialization of attitudes emerges. But their conflicting conceptions of the preceding stage lead them to conflicting descriptions of the stage of initial socialization. While Piaget interprets the stage of socialization as the initial democratization of an authoritarian, Kohlberg sees it as the initial socialization of a narcissist.

For Kohlberg, of course, the democratization of the conscience lies far down the path of evaluative growth, at stage five. But the "democratization" of attitudes Piaget describes falls short of Kohlberg's fifth stage. The social contract ethics of Kohlberg's fifth stage is an ethics of mature rational discourse. Piaget's "democratic" stage derives its cognitive structure from the transductive thinking of the pre-operational child. Similarly, Kohlberg locates the emergence of moral legalism at stage four rather than at stage one. But Kohlberg's socialized, conventional, law-and-order conscience has achieved a degree of conceptual sophistication unknown to Piaget's heteronomous conscience.

This examination of the more obvious issues dividing Kohlberg and Piaget is cautionary in intent. The fact that there is data supporting both theories suggests that both express a partial insight. Both may, then, need to be replaced by a more comprehensive account of the earliest stages of natural moral development. It is entirely plausible that at Kohlberg's stage one a child operates under a double standard of value in which infantile hedonism and infantile authoritarianism both function. That either exerts a more decisive influence over the child's sense of right and wrong has yet to be fully established. By the same token, it is plausible that the child's appropriation of parental rule-making activity at Kohlberg's stage two would facilitate a transition to the bargaining, market-place ethic that characterizes that stage.

The argument between Kohlberg and Piaget also suggests caution in labeling any given individual as an authoritarian. The strict authoritarian would seem to be someone who has yet to pass beyond Piaget's heteronomous stage. Kohlberg's law-and-order conscience is, however, several stages removed from Piaget's heteronomous conscience. Taken together the findings of both Kohlberg and Piaget suggest that much of society is made up, not of authoritarians in the narrow sense, but of legalists who are the easy dupe of authoritarian demagogues.

The resolution of the debate between Kohlberg and Piaget is a task for developmental psychology, not for foundational theology. Our own present concern is not primarily with the ethics of childhood, but with the morphology of the adult Christian conscience. Let us, then, begin to probe the implications of Kohlberg's hypothesis as a prelude to articulating an emergent theory of Christian morality.

Kohlberg's Rules for Natural Moral Growth

In addition to providing a descriptive account of different kinds of evaluative orientation that characterize the stages of natural moral development, Kohlberg's theory postulates a number of principles governing the transition from one stage to another.[91]

The first postulate affirms that the stages are not artificial or fictive but express invariant steps in the natural maturation of the conscience. At present it is, however, legitimate to ask whether the available data fully warrants this initial and fundamental postulate.

The second postulate is that at any stage of moral growth, one can achieve a conscious appreciation of the evaluative criteria habitually invoked by those in the next highest stage.

The third postulate is that the emerging conscience can comprehend the evaluative processes that characterize all the stages below its present level of development.

The fourth postulate is that in the course of personal ethical growth the conscience functions primarily at one stage of moral evaluation but on occasion invokes criteria from the stages contiguous to it. In other words, at any stage of growth the conscience may lapse into momentary immaturity. But it also knows moments of ethical self-transcendence. The former fact testifies to the force of habit; the latter prepares the transition to the next stage of ethical maturity.

The fifth postulate is that the transition from one stage to the next is mediated by insight into the inadequacy of one's present manner of reaching moral judgments. This insight usually results from confrontation with ethical dilemmas that are insoluble at the level of moral insight at which the conscience habitually functions. As a result the conscience is painfully torn between conflicting moral claims. The transition to a higher stage occurs when that conflict becomes intolerable.

The sixth postulate is that education that is sensitive to human developmental processes can facilitate transition to a higher stage of ethical judgment.

The seventh postulate is that transition to a higher stage is in no way automatic. The conscience may, then, become stuck at a particular level of moral maturation.

Objections to Kohlberg

Kohlberg's methods are similar to Piaget's: he employs interviews in which a subject is faced with a series of moral dilemmas describing an ethical situation that can be decided by a number of conventional, culturally sanctioned solutions. On the basis of the kind of solution habitually chosen by a given subject, trained scorers attempt to locate his or her level of ethical awareness within Kohlberg's scheme. When these results are combined with the use of extensive interviews, trained Kohlberg scorers can in fact achieve ninety percent agreement concerning any given subject's stage of moral consciousness.

Clearly Kohlberg's methods, like Piaget's, are suited to the exploration of ego-consciousness but fail to yield easy access to the subconscious bases of human ethical decision. If pressed, Kohlberg will acknowledge the influence of subconscious motives upon human decision. But he regards conscious evaluative processes as the most important single factor in human ethical development.[92]

It is, needless to say, difficult to weigh the importance of conscious moralization in the abstract. This much, however, is clear: conscious ethical argumentation can and often does mask a host of unacknowledged subconscious motives. Moreover, the influence of subconscious feelings on conscious moral decisions can cast light on the failure of more people to advance to autonomous morality. We will return to this problem in reflecting on the faith-healing of religious pharisaism.

Kohlberg has also been criticized for failing to demonstrate that a "higher" stage of moral evaluation is necessarily a "better" one. His reply to this objection takes us, I believe, to the heart of his theory.[93] Kohlberg suggests two criteria for judging the relative adequacy of ethical systems of thought: evaluative discrimination and evaluative integration.[94] In other words, an interpretative frame of reference enjoys greater adequacy if it allows me to think about things that are either ignored or only vaguely perceived in a different reference frame, and if it allows me to grasp relationships among discriminated elements in experience that were previously either ignored or only vaguely felt.

In the theories of both Kohlberg and Piaget, the higher stages of ethical growth do indeed reveal a cumulative sensitivity to new kinds of value and to new kinds of moral relationships. Piaget's democratized conscience recognizes the claims of parental authority but in addition invokes an enhanced sense of self-appreciation and an inchoate respect for others that are both absent at the preceding stage. Kohlberg's stage-two child has begun to recognize the legitimacy of other person's needs. Kohlberg's stage-three child engages in primitive, stereotyped ethical generalizations and discriminates between intentional and unintentional activity. The stage-four conscience appeals not only to social convention but to legal sanction; the stage-five conscience, to ethical dialogue and to the intelligent regulation of social structures that govern moral behavior. The stage-six conscience appeals to personal moral responsibility and to logical adequacy and self-consistency. The six stages do, then, mark distinguishable moments in the development of ethical ego-consciousness.

By the same token, as the conscience advances from stage to stage, its ethical conceptions are correspondingly enhanced. To illustrate this point, Kohlberg offers a schematic analysis of the shifting sense of "right" and "duty" as the conscience advances from one level of ethical awareness to another.[95]

The stage-one conscience equates having a right with the capacity to exert power and control over something or someone. There is as yet no sense of any limitation on the legitimate use of authority. Having a right is also confused with being right. "Duty" at stage one means standing under the claims of authority.

The stage-two conscience, however, distinguishes clearly between having a right and being right. It equates having a right with freedom to control one's own options. There is also a nascent sense of the limitation of rights: to violate the freedom of another or to injure another is felt as "wrong." The notion of "duty" is also expanded to include the relationship of means to ends: one "ought" to do those things that enable one to achieve those ends one has freely chosen.

There is also a recognition that not every command of authority need be the right thing to do.

At stage three the conscience recognizes that while specific personal decisions may entail specific obligations (think of making a promise), moral rights cannot be established by personal fiat alone. The stage-three conscience acknowledges that the claims of society ought to function in the definition of human rights. There is a new sense that one may earn the personal right to act in a certain way or to receive a reward by conformity to rules and to the social expectations of others. For example, a person who works harder or longer than another is felt to have earned the right to higher pay. The notion of "duty" is also expanded to include accepted social rules and socially sanctioned patterns of behavior. It is, for example, conceded that becoming a wife, a husband, a doctor, a teacher, brings with it specific social responsibilities, although there is only a vague, stereotyped understanding of the obligations involved.

At stage four, the notion of "right" has begun to acquire a measure of real generality. It now encompasses freedoms and expectations common to every member of society. There is also a new sense of a hierarchical order among rights. Common social rights are recognized as exercising a more basic moral claim than those consequent upon the performance of a specific social function. A starving person's right to food is, for example, seen as having ethical priority over a merchant's right to remuneration for foodstuffs. Duty is now seen to encompass social accountability. Social duties too begin to be hierarchically ordered. Those common to all members of society are seen to be more fundamental than those consequent upon the assumption of a social role.

At stage five, the conscience acknowledges that the most basic human rights (often called "natural rights") precede laws, conventions, and social expectations. And with this realization comes a recognition of the duty of society to protect the basic rights of each individual. At stage five, the conscience is also ordinarily concerned to restrict the right of society to limit the personal exercise of socially awarded freedom only to those instances when the exercise of such freedom stands in conflict with a like freedom in others. Duty is now identified with those things one has contracted to do in order to ensure the protection of one's own rights. But since obligations that are contingent upon social contracts freely entered shift as the terms of those contracts change, rational concern for the welfare of others is now differentiated from stable moral responsibilities.

At stage six rights are explicitly universalized. The moral claim of each person to just treatment is now felt to transcend social contracts or the mere protection of one's personal liberties. The same respect for justice is now expected of every person and is affirmed as binding upon all. Rights and duties are understood as reciprocal.

Kohlberg argues that the sixth stage of ethical awareness is higher than the preceding five because only at stage six can human rights and duties be conceived in a manner that is rationally self-consistent. To be fully rational, Kohlberg insists, moral judgments must be reversible, consistent, and universalizable. He is quite correct. Only reversible relationships can be applied with rational consistency and universal applicability. To affirm, for example, that $X + Y$ is the same as $Y + X$ is to assert a reversible relationship. Or to say that $X - Z = Y$ implies that $Y + Z = X$ is to assert a reversible logical relationship. Only when conceptual relationships are reversible can thought move rationally back and forth between premise and conclusion without distortion.[96]

This basic logical truth applies to moral judgments as well. Kohlberg observes:

> To say that rights and duties are correlative is to say that one can move from rights to duties and back without change or distortion. Universalizability and consistency are fully attained by the reversibility of prescriptions of actions. Reversibility of moral judgment is what is ultimately meant by the criterion of the fairness of a moral decision. Procedurally, fairness as impartiality means reversibility in the sense of a decision on which all interested parties could agree insofar as they can consider their own claims impartially, as the just decider would. If we have a reversible solution, we have one that could be reached as right starting from anyone's perspective in the situation, given each person's intent to put himself in the shoes of the other.
>
> Reversibility meets a second criterion of formalism: universalizability. As reversibility starts with the slogan, "Put yourself in the other guy's shoes and decide," universalizability starts with the slogan, "What if everyone did it; what if everyone used this principle of choice?" It is clear that universalizability is implied by reversibility. If something is fair or right to do from the conflicting points of view of all those involved in the situation, it is something we can

wish all men to do in all similar situations. Reversibility tells us more than universalizability, then, in resolving dilemmas, but it implies universalizability.[97]

Kohlberg's point is, then, clear. Only at stage six does ethical thinking become fully rational. Fully rational morality enjoys greater interpretative adequacy than morality that is less than fully rational. Hence, stage-six morality ought to be preferred to stages one through five.

Kohlberg also draws on the work of John Rawls to describe the processes by which the stage-six conscience reaches its moral generalizations. Faced with a moral dilemma, the stage-six conscience first imagines itself in the position of each person affected by the moral choice to be made, the chooser included. Second, the conscience asks: What would any just person do in such a situation? Third, the choice is made in the light of those reversible claims.[98]

In Kohlberg's scheme there is, then, a genetic link between stage-five and stage-six morality. At stage five the conscience is committed to the rational search for solutions to moral dilemmas but has yet to espouse ethical criteria that are themselves fully rational. Hence, stage six transmutes and fulfills the moral aspirations that implicitly motivate the conscience at stage five.

As in the case of rights and duties, one can, then, trace the idea of moral reciprocity through the six stages of moral development. At stage one, moral reciprocity is the *lex talionis*: an eye for an eye, a tooth for a tooth. At stage two it becomes contractual fairness: I will deal fairly with your needs if you deal fairly with mine. At stage three it becomes the Golden Rule; but at this early stage of moral growth the judgments of conscience lack logical reciprocity. Hence, the attempt to live the Golden Rule can prove perplexing. Kohlberg observes: ". . . in the Talmudic dilemma of a man with a water bottle encountering another man equally in danger of dying of thirst, a stage three interpretation of the Golden Rule logically leads to them passing the water bottle back and forth like Alphonse and Gaston." At stage four, moral reciprocity becomes uniform justice before the law. At stage five, it is respect for human rights that are prior to the law and fidelity to contractual agreements. At stage six it is the Golden Rule transformed into a principle of just dealing and interpreted with logical reversibility.[99]

In his more recent writings Kohlberg has alluded to a seventh stage in the growth of natural moral awareness. He characterizes it as a morality of sanctity or of supererogation. At stage seven, the conscience recognizes the existence of rights and duties that go beyond what could be expected of "any just person." Not only is it committed to doing the right, it is also ready, if need be, to suffer persecution for justice's sake.[100]

Kohlberg: A Foundational Evaluation

What, then, is the foundational significance, if any, of Kohlberg's work? In the pages that follow we will attempt to argue the following positions: (1) Taken together, the researches of Kohlberg and of Piaget provide a plausible account of the natural growth of moral freedom. (2) A developmental model of the human conscience based on their work casts light on the natural variables that structure different ethical systems. (3) New Testament ethics transcends every natural ethic by being an ethic of faith. (4) New Testament ethics challenges the inadequacies of natural moral systems and summons them to fulfillment in Christ. (5) When the Christian conscience appeals to natural reason alone in the resolution of moral dilemmas its judgments are necessarily morally inadequate. Finally, on the basis of these reflections we will attempt to propose a model for the Christian conscience that avoids the inadequacies of a Thomistic model.

(1) *Taken together, the researches of Kohlberg and of Piaget provide a plausible account of the natural growth of moral freedom.* The researches of developmental psychology have established beyond serious question that moral consciousness advances through stages as the natural ego grows in its capacity to differentiate and interrelate factors in experience relevant to choice. Further investigation into the processes of human growth will hopefully provide a more nuanced and detailed account of the character of each stage and may demand modification of existing hypotheses. But it seems unlikely that the existence of genetically linked levels of moral awareness will be disproven.

Kohlberg's studies are at present among the most extensive. But it is important to note the limited focus of his interest. His investigations are concerned only with naturally motivated choices. His work as a consequence casts no light on the growth of religious consciousness as such or on the impact of religious values upon human moral development.

Nevertheless, his account of the natural stages of moral growth is foundationally suggestive and thoroughly convergent with the account of human freedom suggested in Chapter V. Kohlberg acknowledges the role of environment and of decision in the growth of moral consciousness. He has provided a descriptive account of the conceptual and perspectival variables that condition the growth of the natural moral ego. His stages describe habitual schematizations of evaluative response. Since his theory takes into account all the variables that condition the growth of freedom—environmental, conceptual, perspectival, habitual, and decisive—we may conclude that, when appropriately qualified in the light of Piaget's and of subsequent researches, his theory offers a plausible, working description of the growth of natural, moral freedom.

(2) *A developmental model of the human conscience based on the work of Kohlberg and Piaget casts light on the different evaluative variables that structure diverse ethical systems.* During the late sixties Joseph Fletcher's *Situation Ethics* held considerable fascination for a large number of liberal American Catholics.[101] There can be no doubt that the going morality of many American Catholics in the decades immediately preceding Vatican II was a stage-four ethics of law and order. Fletcher's brand of situationism offered liberated American Catholics a rich vocabulary of invective against every form of moral "legalism." At the same time, Fletcher described the positive thrust of his thought in the following terms: "Situationism is a form of relativism as to both norms themselves and as to their use; for Christians it is a Christianly motivated form of ethical relativism." At stage four-and-a-half, the conscience, it will be recalled, is in a state of drift characterized by skepticism, egocentrism, and relativism. Once again Fletcher's words are revealing.

> The insistent demand to spell out the "content of love" masks an insistence on norms as prefabricated decisions. To "fill up" love with rules or laws is to slip back into a new form of legalism.
>
> An atheist could be a situationist, or an egoist, or a vitalist—anybody who, no matter what his formal imperative may be (love, self-interest, life, or whatever) cuts his coat to fit each situation.[102]

Fletcher cites the ethics of John Dewey as one of the inspirations for his own thought. The citation is misleading. Dewey's ethics, as we shall soon see, can be legitimately characterized as a stage-five morality. A stage-five morality is explicitly and overtly committed to rational discourse concerning moral problems. In his individualistic take-it-or-leave-it attitude to moral principles, Fletcher's situational relativism falls short of the solid commitment to reasoned, collective ethical solutions that characterizes Dewey's stage-five morality.

Fletcher's situationism is a legalistic ethic in transition to a social contract orientation, but it has not yet arrived.

This conclusion is not without its ironies. For it suggests that "liberal" Catholic morality in the late sixties had advanced to a stage of ethical awareness that under ideal circumstances ought to come in late adolescence. And indeed the liberated Catholic of the late sixties boasted on every possible occasion that (s)he had morally "come of age."

In their attempt to evaluate the theological significance of the theories of Kohlberg and Piaget, Roland Duska and Mariellen Whelan suggest that Vatican II can be interpreted as a serious attempt to move the Catholic community from a stage-four to a stage-five morality.[103] The suggestion does not do justice to the ethical teaching of the Council.

Certainly, the chief theological contribution of the American Church to the work of the Council was the Decree on Religious Freedom. One of its chief architects was John Courtney Murray. Murray had, it is true, devoted much of his energy and considerable intellectual genius to a theological defense of the "American proposition." But his moral doctrine has the traits of a stage-six morality. Murray's own refurbished natural law ethics, like the Declaration on Religious Freedom, summons the conscience to impartial justice. Both vindicate the right of the individual conscience to pass moral judgment on the ethical inadequacy of social contracts and political institutions. Both seek to ground moral judgments upon principles of conduct that are universally binding on all just persons.[104] Both recognize the full reciprocity of right and duty. Moreover, in addition to natural law theory, the ethics of the Council draws upon the ethics of faith proclaimed in the New Testament.

A truer assessment of the moral teaching of Vatican II would be that it summoned the Church as a whole to an ethics of faith and of justice. But it has left large segments of the Catholic community entrenched in moral legalism and has moved other parts of the community forward to an ethics of adolescence. Some few seem to have responded at the level of justice and of faith.

A better example than Vatican II of a stage-five morality is, I believe, the democratic liberalism of John Dewey.[105] Dewey's ethics is an ethics of progress. It acknowledges the need to subject the structure of society to constant critical review. Dewey was concerned with defending individual rights against the encroachments of tyranny and oppression. And he was convinced that the method of shared scientific inquiry provides the conscience with all it needs to effect the ongoing amelioration of the human condition. But Dewey's instrumentalism leaves moral ends thoroughly relativized. As Gerard Dalcourt has recently observed:

> In Dewey's view there is such intimate continuity and interdependence of ends and means that, contrary to the traditional theory, it is the means that determine our ends. Moreover, even though we do accept certain things as ends and values, any particular end-value is ultimate only in the tautological sense that it concludes one's appraisal of a particular case. Our ends then have of themselves no hierarchy of value. One will be preferred to another only to the extent to which it promises to resolve a conflict better. It follows for Dewey that the quest for really ultimate values is not only fruitless but actually harmful.[106]

What Dewey offers, then, is not a morality based on universal moral principles. The only principle binding on all is commitment to the method of science as the most effective instrument of intelligent social change yet developed by the human mind. That method engages one in a constant democratic dialogue. In *Liberalism and Social Action* Dewey observes:

> The problem under discussion is precisely *how* conflicting claims are to be settled in the interest of the widest possible contribution to the interests of all—or at least of the great majority. The method of democracy—inasmuch as it is that of organized intelligence—is to bring these conflicts out into the open where their special claims can be seen and appraised, where they can be discussed and judged in the light of more inclusive interests than are represented by either of them separately. There is, for example, a clash of interests between munition manufacturers and most of the rest of the population. The more the representative claims of the two are publicly and scientifically weighed, the more likely it is that the public interest will be disclosed and be made effective.[107]

Liberation theology is one of the most exciting theological movements to emerge from Latin America. It is the compassionate attempt of a relatively small group of sometimes embattled theologians to move the Latin Church to confront effectively the fact of class conflict and the plight of the poor and the oppressed.

Liberation theology aspires to a spirituality of active political involvement. It is a theology of socio-political commitment rather than a natural morality. But to the extent that it is shaped by considerations derived from natural reason, it exemplifies a stage-six morality in transition to stage seven. Not only do liberation theologians denounce social, economic, and political injustice; they also demand that those who seek justice share the lot of the oppressed and suffer with them in their struggle to end human exploitation and misery.[108]

(3) *New Testament ethics transcends every natural morality by being an ethics of faith.* It should be clear from the foundational analysis of new covenant ethics undertaken in the first part of this chapter that the Christian ethical vision differs from all the ethical perspectives described by Kohlberg in that it is an ethics of faith. It encompasses the highest values in Kohlberg's scheme. Like the defender of stage-seven morality, the Christian must be willing to suffer persecution for justice's sake. But by making faith the most fundamental test of moral authenticity, Christian ethics demands the transvaluation of all natural moral values.

First of all, new covenant ethics demands that the human instrument of moral judgment be divinely enlightened and pneumatically transformed. It demands, therefore, that moral insight be the fruit of repentant confrontation with the shadow and of dependence in faith upon the God revealed in Jesus and in the action of His Breath. Hence, the Christian must judge right and wrong, not only rationally, but prayerfully, with discernment, and in charismatic openness to the Breath. Hence, new covenant ethics demands that the procedures for reaching a judgment of conscience be faith-informed and transcend mere natural rational discourse.

Second, new covenant ethics demands that moral right and wrong be interpreted in terms that are consciously and overtly religious. Wrongdoing is transformed into sin, i.e., into wrong done before God; moral righteousness, into the obedience of faith.

Third, new covenant ethics provides a new basis for judging moral reciprocity. The golden rule ceases to mean: "Do what any just person would reasonably decide to do." It becomes instead: "Act toward others as you would want a merciful God to act toward you." In other words, the rational search for justice is replaced by the "new commandment": "Love one another as I have loved you."

Finally, new covenant ethics grounds the understanding of rights and duties, not in a reversible insight into the demands of natural justice, but in a reversible insight into the divine call to sanctity proclaimed by Jesus. That is to say, the adult Christian sees right and duty as completely correlative and in this sense rational. But in any situation, the Christian conscience measures both its duty and the corresponding rights of others, not by some abstract ideal of natural justice, but by the mind of Jesus, by His religio-ethical vision of an eschatological faith community dedicated to the ideals of open and gratuitous faith-sharing, and to the worship of God in the service of unrestricted atoning love.

(4) *New covenant ethics challenges the inadequacy of natural moral systems and summons them to fulfillment in Christ.* Christian ethics offers a word of encouragement and of challenge to the emerging natural conscience at each stage of its development. To the stage-one conscience, torn between infantile narcissism and authoritarian fear, it offers the assurance that the Father God and divine Mother Advocate are not eternal, threatening, heteronomous powers, but gentle, loving persons dwelling in the child's own heart and inviting it to love and trust others. Needless to say, the child of authoritarian parents will find that hard to believe.

To the stage-two conscience, it offers the vision of a covenanting God, but it reminds the conscience that the covenant of love revealed in Jesus is more than a marriage of convenience. Like the love of ideal Christian parents, divine love is always and simply there. At stage two as well, then, the Christian message will have credibility in the child's ears only if Christian parents relate to it in Christlike atoning love.

To the stage-three conscience Christian ethics brings the assurance that the Golden Rule does indeed fulfill the law and the prophets, but that it is preceded by another commandment: "You shall love the Lord your God with all your mind, all your heart, and all your strength." And it offers the concrete figures of Jesus and of the saints as models of Christian behavior to a conscience that is maturing but still only inchoately rational.

To the stage-four conscience, Christian ethics offers the assurance that Jesus has come, not to abolish the Law, but to fulfill it. It warns of the dangers of pharisaical self-righteousness, demands that the conscience submit finally, not to any legal code, but to the rule of the Mother Advocate. In the process, it insists that the Law is only a means to an end: "The sabbath was made for humans, not humans for the sabbath." New covenant ethics thus transforms the Law into a flexible instrument of order rather than seeing it as the ultimate ground of moral value. And it subordinates the demands of any law to judgment in the light of the ethical visions of Jesus.

To the stage-five conscience, Christian faith offers the assurance that the search for the moral good is indeed a shared human enterprise and that concern with due process and contractual fidelity are important. But it reminds the conscience that the only community capable of grasping the true meaning of responsible moral decision is not the natural, rationalistic, democratic community envisaged by the founding fathers of the American republic. It is instead the charismatic, faith-sharing community envisaged by Paul the apostle.

To the stage-six conscience, Christian ethics offers the assurance that those are blessed who hunger and thirst after justice, but that true justice consists in the submission of every heart to the reign of God proclaimed by Jesus. For God's justice is the restructuring of human society in faith, in gratuitous and unrestricted sharing, and in the worship of atoning love.

Finally, it invites the stage-seven conscience to enter actively into the death and resurrection of the Lord.

Similarly, new covenant ethics demands that philosophical and theological systems be judged in the light of the gospel of Jesus. It demands, for example, that the advocates of situation ethics recognize that the moral vision of the Christian adolescent of any age falls short of the moral demands imposed by Jesus. Of the Deweyan naturalist, it demands that the collective search for an improved social order submit to the charismatic guidance of the Mother Advocate and to the ethical vision of the Lord. Of the philosophical natural lawyer, it demands the recognition that the moral imperatives binding upon the Christian conscience cannot be derived from reflection on natural processes alone.

To the theologian of liberation, an insight into the foundations of Christian ethics offers a moral clarification and a summons to realism. In his *Theology of Liberation* Gustavo Gutierrez argues that the Christian must accept the class struggle as a fact.

> The class struggle is a fact and neutrality in this question is impossible. . . . The Gospel announces the love of God for all people and calls us to love as he loves. But to accept class struggle means to decide for some people and against others. To live both realities without juxtapositions is a great challenge for the Christian committed to the totality of the process of liberation. This is a challenge that leads him to deepen his faith and to mature in his love for others.[109]

There is a profound truth in what Gutierrez affirms. And there is an even deeper truth in his further insistence that dehumanizing poverty is an abomination in the sight of God and that its pious rationalization by apathetic Christians is rank hypocrisy.

But new covenant ethics also demands that the Christian social reformer be perfectly clear concerning the terms on which a disciple of Jesus can enter the political arena. The class struggle may be a fact. But the violent pitting of class against class is also Anti-Christ, as are those who maliciously or hypocritically create the oppressive conditions that make it inevitable. It is hard to confront Anti-Christ, politically without being corrupted by it. I believe, then, that, as Yoder suggests, an authentic spirituality of liberation is a summons to the moral heroism of a faith-filled, politically astute, committed pacifist.[110] Those who respond to that call should be clear in their own minds that they are setting foot on the same path that led Jesus to Calvary, and Gandhi and Martin Luther King to prison and to bloody assassination. Our God is a consuming fire. May He strengthen us all with courage to respond to His call.

The Emerging Christian Conscience

We are now in a position to sketch in broad outline a working model of the Christian conscience viewed as an emerging process. In the remaining sections of this chapter we will argue that: (a) An adequate interpretative model for understanding the workings of the Christian conscience should be true to the dynamic structure of human experience. (b) It should affirm the values inculcated by new covenant religion as ethically ultimate and absolute. (c) In its evaluative structure it should express a Christian sense of sin. (d) It should be sensitive to distinguishable stages in natural human development. (e) It should offer the hope of healing the pharisaical conscience and its analogues. (f) It should set Christians personally and collectively in active opposition to the powers of oppression. Let us reflect on each of the preceding propositions in turn.

(a) *An adequate interpretative model for understanding the workings of the Christian conscience should be true to the dynamic structure of human experience.* There is an important hint of the form such a model might take in C. S. Peirce's theory of the normative sciences. Peirce's division of the sciences was part of a much larger philosophical project, namely, his final, ultimately unsuccessful attempt to construct a systematic metaphysics based upon a survey of the available results of every field of human inquiry.

In reflecting on the field of philosophical speculation, he suggested that in addition to phenomenology and metaphysics, philosophy embraces three normative sciences: esthetics, ethics, and logic. In Peirce's division, esthetics is the science of what is finally and ultimately admirable. It studies the formation of correct habits of affective response. Ethics is the science of right and wrong. It attempts to articulate a theory of self-controlled and deliberate conduct. It derives from esthetics its understanding of what is supremely valuable and studies the formation of correct habits of choice. Logic is the science of self-controlled and deliberate thought. It studies how humans ought to think if they are to direct their actions intelligently and correctly to ends that are authentically sublime and ultimately valuable.[111]

The relevance of Peirce's proposal to the elaboration of an adequate foundational model for the Christian conscience becomes clearer when one reflects that implicit in his division of the normative sciences are two interrelated presuppositions. First, his division presupposes that in the natural development of human experience, it is possible to distinguish three different kinds of "ought": affective, moral, and speculative. Second, his theory presupposes that these three oughts are irreducible but nevertheless genetically interdependent. Let us reflect briefly on some of the foundational implications of these two proposals.

There can be no serious question that the laws of logic and the laws of morality are not identical. A clear head is no guarantee of a good character. Scientists have in the past become easy dupes for vicious and ruthless politicians. One can construct logically irrefragable arguments to support the most dastardly schemes. Similarly, ethically correct decisions can be reached for logically questionable motives, just as true strength of character exists in individuals whose minds are quite vague and logically muddled.

There can also be no serious question that human affectivity develops according to vectoral patterns that are neither logical nor ethical. Affectivity does follow developmental laws. The presence of similar archetypal structures of cognition among persons of different epochs and cultures does, for example, provide some evidence of predictable legal schematizations of human affectivity. Archetypal thinking is, however, not logical but transductive. And it is too vague and undifferentiated to be called formally and explicitly ethical. In fact it stands in need of both logical clarification and ethical evaluation.

If, however, archetypal thinking is prelogical and pre-ethical, more primitive affective experiences, whether sympathetic or negative, have even less claim to either moral or logical status.

Nevertheless predictable patterns do seem to emerge at the level of primitive affective response. As we have seen, the repression of negative affections leads to predictable stages of ego-disintegration. And Erik Erikson has suggested the presence of predictable stages of maturation at the level of pre-archetypal affective adjustment.

Erikson is a Neo-Freudian. His psychological preoccupations are, as a consequence, not with the archetypal phase of affective development but with more fundamental negative and sympathetic affections. In Freudian theory, the former drive toward death; the latter, toward life. Erikson suggests that the life-death struggle of primitive affections takes on a predictable character at different stages of human maturation.[112] The small child's first challenge is to acquire affective freedom to trust others. For without such trust the socialization of the personality cannot advance. The child riddled with fear and distrust becomes withdrawn and eventually autistic.

The socialization process raises, however, the specter of guilt. Toilet training opposes infantile desires for autonomy to an infantile sense of shame and guilt. As motor habits develop and as the child begins to discover its physical sexuality, the sense of guilt seeks to inhibit a burgeoning affective spontaneity. As a youngster moves toward adolescence, its growing sense of personal initiative tends to be further undermined by feelings of inadequacy and inferiority.

The affective conflicts of adolescence itself center around the search for an adult identity. The adolescent needs to develop the felt sense of a personal place in history, a clear sexual identity, and self-confidence in dealing with the challenges of adult existence. (S)he needs freedom to experiment with new social roles, must readjust personal attitudes to parental authority, and must develop a personal moral code. (S)he needs to pass through a period of apprenticeship to creative involvement in adult society. Failure to negotiate these multiple crises successfully leaves the personality confused and deprived of any clear sense of adult purpose and adult identity.

The young adult who has completed the adolescent rite of passage needs to learn the meaning of adult intimacy or suffer the pangs of loneliness and isolation. The mature adult runs the serious risk of falling victim to ego-inertia; hence, as the crisis of middle age approaches, affective conflicts center increasingly around the desire for continued growth and creativity, on the one hand, and the threat of stagnation and sterility on the other. In the twilight of life, a new set of problems emerges: the psyche now needs to preserve a sense of dignity and personal integrity despite temptations to despair in the face of physical and psychic deterioration and death.[113]

Erikson's eight stages of affective development pose, therefore, a cumulative series of interrelated affective alternatives: trust vs. mistrust, autonomy vs. guilt, initiative vs. guilt, industry vs. inferiority, identity vs. identity confusion, intimacy vs. isolation, generativity vs. stagnation, integrity vs. despair. A healthy resolution of affective conflict at one stage of growth prepares the psyche to cope with the problems and conflicts of the next stage.

These reflections on Erikson's stages might seem at first reading to be an irrelevant digression. But they are not. An adequate model for the Christian conscience must not only differentiate esthetic, logical, and ethical imperatives; it must also show their genetic interdependence.

Kohlberg has suggested, correctly I believe, that logical imperatives acquire ethical significance when they are seen to stand in relation to choice. Thus, a more adequate speculative frame of reference that allows for the evaluative differentiation of realities and relationships once only dimly and vaguely perceived and that as a consequence permits the resolution of otherwise unresolvable moral dilemmas is not only logically but ethically preferable to a less adequate frame of reference.

A similar argument might be made with regard to the growth of human affectivity. The resolution of an affective conflict that heightens appreciative consciousness, frees one to deal realistically and effectively with reality, and provides the basis for the next phase of affective maturation is clearly better than one that does not and ought to be preferred to the latter.

Here, however, a certain theoretical caution is in order. For if affective development and inferential insight take on ethical significance by relationship to decision, not every human decision is endowed with ethical meaning in the strict sense. Hence, the relationship to decision alone is not enough to render thought and affectivity morally significant. Let us reflect on why this is so.

The meaning of a decision is a function of the evaluative processes it terminates. But not every value is moral. Some values are, for example, ethically neutral. Of themselves, they are neither right nor wrong. Taking a walk, eating a hamburger, doing a crossword puzzle, and a host of other human activities yield specific satisfactions. They therefore incarnate certain kinds of value. But to the question are they morally right or wrong only one answer is possible, namely, it all depends. Depends on what? On the reason why they are performed and on the circumstances in which they are enjoyed. Most people would concede that under normal circumstances there is nothing wrong with eating a loaf of bread but that it would be wrong to do so when I am well fed and when the bread I devour is the only food available to someone who is starving.

In other words, values that are of themselves morally neutral acquire ethical significance when they are seen to stand in relationship to values that are morally significant. The same may be said of affective and speculative values. They acquire ethical meaning in the strict sense, not when they are seen to stand in relation to any human decision, but when they are seen to stand in relation to a human decision taken in the light of values that can legitimately be affirmed as moral values in the technical sense of that term. But when do values become fully moral?

Kohlberg has suggested correctly that any moral frame of reference that fails to achieve full and conscious rationality is ethically inadequate because logically inadequate. A fully rational morality is certainly better than one that is less than fully rational and should be preferred to the latter. But what makes a frame of reference ethical in the first place? Peirce is, I believe, moving in the right direction when he suggests that human evaluative processes acquire conscious ethical significance when they are judged in the light of a specific set of values that are affirmed as absolute and ultimate.

A value is affirmed as ethically ultimate when it is affirmed as the final goal of my personal striving. An ultimate value enters experience, therefore, as that goal, ideal, purpose beyond which I am willing to affirm no other. A value is affirmed as absolute when it is affirmed as worth striving toward under all circumstances.

The ethically neutral values that shape experience—whether affective, speculative, or practical—will, then, acquire moral significance to the extent that they are seen to stand in relationship to a set of ideals that I am willing to affirm absolutely and ultimately. By the same token, the values I affirm as ultimate and absolute will not enjoy ethical adequacy unless they can encompass and lend healthy dynamic orientation to the growth of affectivity and of thought and to the practical pursuit of legitimate pragmatic values.

(b) *An adequate interpretative model for understanding the working of the Christian conscience should affirm the values inculcated by new covenant religion as ethically ultimate and absolute.* In a recent controversial interview, James Empereur, S.J., has suggested that an option for a process problematic in philosophy and theology is an option for situation ethics.[114] The truth of the matter is that with the notable exception of Daniel Day Williams,[115] process theologians have failed in any significant way to address important ethical issues. Moreover, Williams's earliest moral speculations betray little influence of process, patterns of thought. Even his mature reflections on the ethical dimensions of a life lived in Christian love draw little inspiration from process categories.

There is, however, a theory of value implicit in a Whiteheadean cosmology. As theories go, however, it is scarcely reducible to the situation ethics of Joseph Fletcher. John Goheen's analysis of Whitehead's value theory is, I believe, an accurate portrait.[116] For Whitehead, events take on value as a consequence of their finite structure, for value emerges in the patterning of experience. The value of any event is, then, identical with its intrinsic reality, with the kind of experience it is, with its conceptual form. All purposive activity is, moreover, evaluative in character and evaluation endows experience with direction and purpose. The purposive patterning of experience bears fruit in a succession of finite satisfactions, and the quality of any satisfaction is a function of the simultaneous novelty and unity with which it is endowed.

In a Whiteheadean universe, good and evil both enter experience as positive forces: the good as positive and creative, evil as positive and destructive. For evil is felt most keenly in the mutual obstruction of creative processes and in the perpetual perishing of things. In such a universe, moral striving seeks to control the experiential process in such a way as to maximize the importance of any given satisfaction. Ethical control of experience is enhanced through realistic insight into the actual and potential structure of experience.[117] Whitehead's own words, though technical, are illuminating:

The point to be noticed is that the actual entity, in a state of process during which it is not fully definite, determines its own ultimate definiteness. This is the whole point of moral responsibility. Such responsibility is conditioned by the limits of the data, and by the categoreal conditions of concrescence. But autonomy is negligible unless the complexity is such that there is great energy in the production of conceptual feelings according to the category of reversion. This category has to be considered in connection with the category of aesthetic harmony. For the contrasts produced by reversion are contrasts required for the fulfillment of the aesthetic ideal. Unless there is complexity, ideal diversities lead to physical impossibilities, and thence to impoverishment. It requires a complex constitution to stage diversities as consistent contrasts.[118]

Here several points should be noted. First, Whitehead formulates the problem of moral responsibility in terms of each emergent subject's search for satisfaction through evaluative self-definition. Second, as each subject moves toward satisfaction it must take into account the limitations imposed by its immediate factual past. Third, satisfactions that yield the enhancement of experience are those that include "reversion." "Reversion" is a technical Whiteheadean term for the introduction of novel possibility into experience. The integration of novel possibility into an occasion of experience enhances its value by lending novel complexity to the conceptual pattern that shapes its satisfaction. Fourth, the ultimate ground of reversion is God in His primordial aspect. God, however, in His primordial aspect is the evaluation of the totality of possibility. As primordial, God sets the goal of the spatio-temporal process. Fifth, in Whiteheadean theory, the formation of conscience is portrayed in esthetic terms: as a totally engaging, creative, esthetic response to a divinely grounded vision of cosmic harmony and beauty that mediates the ongoing expansion and creative reharmonization of experience.

A Whiteheadean ethic seems, then, to be suggesting that in reaching responsible moral decision of any importance, not only ought one to come to a correct evaluation of the limiting factors that shape one's immediate past; one ought also, as far as possible, to seek to shape one's satisfactions creatively in such a way as to advance experience toward the goal of cosmic development set by God. As a consequence, a Whiteheadean conscience stands stretched between correct self-valuation and world loyalty. And loyalty to the world is measured in turn by loyalty to the ultimate goal of the universe decreed by God. Moreover, moral sensitivity is expanded beyond mere inferential processes and includes appreciative forms of understanding.

When these insights into a Whiteheadean ethic are read in the light of Peirce's theory of the normative sciences, they become foundationally suggestive. For Peirce, like Whitehead, sought to derive moral values esthetically. And both men locate religious consent in the heart's spontaneous response to a felt sense of divine beauty. Of the two, Whitehead links cordial consent to God more explicitly to consent to ideals that are ethically absolute and ultimate in the sense described above. But neither Peirce nor Whitehead provides an adequate account of what those ultimate values might be. In the closing pages of *Adventures of Ideas* Whitehead describes the aspiration of experience toward adventure, beauty, truth, and peace.[119] But his remarks are of little help in the practical resolution of specific moral dilemmas. For in a Whiteheadean universe, the goal of the cosmic process remains eternally shrouded in the transcendent mind of God. It is never really consciously available in any practical way for personal moral decision. And, needless to say, there is no developed ethical theory in the writings of Peirce.

For the believing Christian, however, matters stand somewhat differently. For the Christian conscience discovers the goal of the cosmic process concretely revealed in the apocalyptic preaching and religio-moral vision of Jesus. It also discovers moral absoluteness and moral ultimacy in the new covenant ethics He proclaimed. For the Christian conscience affirms the basic tenets of new covenant morality to be expressive of the very mind of God. And God enters Christian experience as a reality to be loved above all and in all situations and circumstances.

Moreover, as we have already seen in Chapter IV, cordial consent to the ethical demands of the new covenant mediated by the dark night of sense bears positive fruit in increasing sensitivity to the beauty of God made visible in Jesus. Appreciative insight into incarnate divine beauty is not, then, as both Brownson and Edwards knew, an expendable adjunct to Christian morality. On the contrary, it makes Christian moral striving possible. For it frees the heart to consent to those religio-moral ideals Jesus proclaimed. That consent creates the Christian conscience.

If these reflections are sound, another important conclusion follows, namely, that an adequate model for the Christian conscience must be true, not only to the dynamics of natural experiential development but also to the pneumatic transformation of those same experiential processes through lifelong conversion to Christ.

Conversion to Christ, however, endows experience with a dynamic structure that transcends the dynamics of natural human growth. For in a Christian consent to God, (1) religious conversion mediates between affective and moral conversion; (2) intellectual conversion seeks to inform affective, religious, and moral conversion; and (3) the ethics of faith demanded by converted consent to new covenant religion demands the transvaluation of the natural values that lend conceptual shape to affective, intellectual, and moral conversion. Let us explicate the meaning of each of these propositions.

Conversion, it will be remembered, is the decision to assume personal responsibility for one's own future development. Personal experience is, however, endowed with an affective, an inferential, and a decisive moment. Moreover, the gracing impulses of the

Mother Advocate function as a real force in one's total emergent environment. Integral conversion to God demands therefore a complex, fourfold decision: the decision to assume responsibility for one's personal affective development, for one's ethical development, for one's speculative development, and for the adequacy of one's responses to the impulses of the Divine Breath.

These decisions are dynamically interrelated by the same laws that link the different phases marking the growth of experience. Affective responses are the creative matrix of abductive inference. Affectivity and inference together shape the character of specific decisions. And decision not only defines my immediate personal past; it also shapes the character of the vectoral feelings that structure experience.

Religious consciousness is simultaneously affective and inferential. The great part of religion, as Edwards says, consists in gracious affections. For religious consciousness mediates a felt encounter with the Holy. But in covenant religion, religious conversion also yields enlightened commitment to certain values and realities as ultimately and absolutely important. For the Christian convert, therefore, the dynamic link between affectivity and moral decision is mediated by a religious conversion that supplies the conscience with those values that render it explicitly and formally ethical.

Speculative, or intellectual, conversion is, by contrast, the decision to assume responsibility for the propositional structuring of experience. But since affective, religious, and moral conversion are conscious processes, they are all conditioned by personal beliefs about them. Intellectual conversion, therefore seeks to inform and give guidance to the other forms of conversion.

But if natural affective, speculative, and decisive variables condition personal progress in religious conversion, the ethics of faith inculcated by new covenant religion demand the transvaluation of all natural value systems and the submission of all natural growth processes to the charismatic anointing of the Mother Advocate. We have already seen how a new covenant ethics of faith speaks a word of encouragement and of repentance to the natural conscience at each stage of its development. We have also seen how consent to God in faith demands the charismatic transformation of the inferential processes that structure adult ego-development. And we have seen how submission of the human heart to the healing action of the Holy Breath demands the transvaluation of mythic, patriarchal values.

To an infantile heart torn between trust and fear, Christian conversion offers the assurance of the unswerving love of the Father God and Mother Advocate and a summons to initial faith. To the childish heart, torn between the claims of ego-autonomy and ego-initiative on the one hand and guilt paralysis on the other, it offers assurance of abiding divine forgiveness in Jesus and a summons to healing and to hope. To the heart of the youngster torn between the need for creative involvement with the world and feelings of personal inadequacy, it offers both the assurance that each Christian is indeed called to creative charismatic service and a summons to begin to prepare the heart to hear that call. It reminds bewildered adolescents that the Mother Advocate has power to heal their chaos of personal feeling and to grace human sexuality by Her gifts of marriage and of celibacy. And it summons their troubled hearts to a patient, repentant discernment of their personal call to adult service in the Christian community. To the young adult torn between intimacy and isolation, new covenant ethics offers a constant summons to affective healing and to a practical atoning love. To the mature adult, it offers assurance that for the believer the successful negotiation of the middle-age crisis is a new exodus and the gateway to the fullness of Christian wisdom and of divine knowledge. To the aging adult, it offers the assurance of abiding personal dignity in the sight of God and sure knowledge that death is rebirth to wholeness and to eternal life.

A Christian conscience is, then, irreducibly charismatic in its structure. It measures rights and duties, not by some abstract rational norm, but by human growth needs measured in the light of the ethical imperatives inculcated in new covenant religion. The relation of gospel values to concrete human situations ought, then, to proceed under the prayerful guidance of the Mother Advocate.

(c) *In its evaluative structure, an adequate model of the Christian conscience ought to express a Christian sense of sin.* In Chapter III, we attempted to outline Paul Ricoeur's account of the growth of religious consciousness of evil. It will be recalled that he suggests that the religious awareness of evil progresses in predictable stages: from a sense of defilement and taboo to a sense of personal sin, from a sense of personal sin to the guilty sense of degrees of moral culpability, from a sense of guilt to the scrupulous attempt of the pharisaical conscience to free itself of all guilt before God, and from pharisaism to the Pauline insight that the scrupulous, self-reliant attempt to render oneself guiltless before God is itself sin.

Louis Monden has offered a simpler interpretation of the stages in the growth of sin-consciousness. Monden's first stage corresponds in large measure to Ricoeur's sense of defilement and to the religious morality of the infantile authoritarian. But while Ricoeur interprets the New Testament as inculcating an ethics of faith, Monden sees it as inculcating an ethics of love. Accordingly, Monden portrays the growth of religio-ethical awareness as the progressive interiorization of the law of love. Monden's conscience begins its progress with a heteronomous ethics of taboo. But at the second level of its development, it progresses to an ethics of autonomy and to the interiorization of the moral law. In its third and final stage of growth, it transcends moralism and legalism and learns to interiorize the Christian law of love.[120]

When Ricoeur and Monden are both read in the light of the new covenant ethic sketched at the beginning of this chapter, their insights can be recognized as convergent rather than contradictory. Once one grasps the meaning of the three basic precepts of new covenant religion, it becomes clear that a Christian ethics of faith is inseparable from a Christian ethics of atoning love. For the practical test of authentic faith in God in the image of Jesus is the open and gratuitous sharing of the spatio-temporal supports of life with those who are in need. By the same token, the free sharing of divine charisms and blessings, mutual forgiveness and mutual service in the worship of atonement must authenticate any act of worship that claims to be an expression of Christian faith. In other words, while Ricoeur's description of the Christian sense of sin focuses on the first precept of the Christian covenant, Monden's focuses on its practical consequences. But of the two theologians, Ricoeur has perhaps touched what is deepest in a Christian covenant commitment. For a religious love that is not grounded in a Pauline realization that the self-reliant attempt to live a moral life before God without faith is itself sin runs the constant risk of becoming arrogant, condescending, and Pelagian.[121]

(d) *An adequate interpretative model of the Christian conscience should be sensitive to distinguishable stages in natural human development.* (e) *It should offer the hope of healing the pharisaical conscience and its analogues.* When the theories of Ricoeur and of Monden are read in the light of the insights of developmental psychology into the growth of moral awareness, they all take on added foundational significance. For Ricoeur sin-consciousness emerges with the discovery of intentionality; for Monden, with the discovery of moral autonomy. Both hold that the second stage of sin-consciousness expands the horizon of moral awareness beyond a heteronomous, authoritarian ethics of taboo. Both recognize the need for the Christian conscience to transcend mere moralism and legalism.

Kohlberg's model is, of course, more empirically grounded and more detailed than the schemes of either Ricoeur or Monden. But there are points of convergence among the three. Kohlberg's model recognizes three levels of natural moral awareness of which his seven stages are subdivisions: a preconventional, a conventional, and an autonomous level. Transition from a preconventional to a conventional morality is mediated in part by the discovery of intentionality; transition to an autonomous ethic, by the transcendence of legalism. Moreover, Kohlberg's researches suggest that the failure to pass from a conventional to an autonomous morality is linked to terror of the growth processes that occur during late adolescence. The transition is terrifying enough—the collapse of one's conventional world of legal certitudes, the sense of moral isolation and of ethical drift, and, as the moral ego disintegrates, reversion to infantile patterns of ethical behavior.

It is possible to draw on Kohlberg's conclusions to complete and nuance the basic insights of both Ricoeur and Monden. More specifically, Kohlberg's work casts light upon the precise character of the pharisaical dilemma. For the pharisee is one who clings to a natural, law-and-order ethic in the face of a clear divine summons in Jesus to abandon a conventional legal ethics for an autonomous ethics of faith. At the root of pharisaical intransigence is terror of the shadow who lurks behind the pharisee's conscious facade of legalistic propriety.

But the transition from a conventional to an autonomous ethics is only one instance of natural moral development. As a consequence the sin of the Pharisee has its analogues at every other stage of natural moral growth. For to cling to any natural moral system rather than consent to the ethics of faith proclaimed by Jesus is to transform that natural ethic into sin. In other words, the human conscience is as capable of transforming any natural ethic into as much of a sinful idol as pharisaism, whether that ethic be a heteronomous ethics of taboo, or a narcissistic ethics of hedonism, or a market-place ethics of mutual pragmatic accommodation, or a social ethics of propriety, or a confused ethics of skeptical relativism, or a democratic ethics of progress, a rationalistic ethics of justice, or a naturalistic ethics of supererogation. All become sin when pursued in self-reliant defiance of Jesus' summons to repentance and to faith.

But if the practical meaning of sin shifts as the conscience advances from one stage of natural moral development to another, so too does the meaning of the Christian summons to repentance as human affectivity passes through successive stages of natural maturation. For to refuse to repent is to refuse to admit one's need for divine forgiveness. To refuse to acknowledge one's need for forgiveness is to refuse to acknowledge and to forgive one's shadow self. To refuse to love the shadow is to refuse to hope. Hope dwells in the heart. And repentance is the rending of the heart in faith before God. Hence, as human affectivity moves from one stage of conflict and of growth to the next, the meaning of religious repentance and of religious hope shifts correspondingly. To the infantile heart, whatever its physical age, repentance means learning to trust God and other persons. To the childish heart, it means learning to hope for the healing of guilt. To the youthful heart, it means trusting in God's power to lead one in a personal exodus from childhood to adult maturity. To the adolescent heart, it means facing a chaos of initially unintelligible feelings, submitting erotic love to charismatic transformation, and learning the meaning of adult, charismatic service. To the heart of the young adult, it means the healing of loneliness born of egotism and of selfishness. To the mature adult, it means the healing of anxieties that breed neurotic rigidity and personal sterility of life. To the aging heart it means the healing of disillusionment and despair in the hope of risen life.

(f) *An adequate interpretative model for the Christian conscience should set Christians personally and collectively in active opposition to the powers of oppression.* The gospel needs to be preached to the poor. But its word of repentance and of faith needs to be proclaimed in season and out to the rich and the powerful, to the ruthless and ambitious, to the slaves of money and of every false or inadequate value system, to the compromisers, to the sadistic authoritarians, to self-infatuated egotists, to the exploiters, to the war lords, to the demagogues, to the world of organized crime and of economic and political corruption.

For the good news proclaimed by Jesus is more than a program for personal salvation. It is that. But it makes personal salvation contingent upon personal commitment to the transformation of human society and to its submission in faith to the moral exigencies of the divine reign. The gospel of Jesus is a program for social transformation: for the sharing of economic resources, not according to human merit but according to human needs whether collective or individual, for the abolition of social barriers and of class distinctions, for the establishment of God's own justice upon the earth among individuals and peoples, and for the repentant submission of each human heart and institution to the ethical imperatives of new covenant religion and to the healing touch of the Mother Advocate.

The Christian community that fails to live up to the social challenge of the gospel should not delude itself. For in its failure it is transformed from a living sacramentalization of human experience into a living countersign to the gospel, into Anti-Christ. Instead of worshippers of the Father of Jesus such a community is in process of becoming the servant of Satan and of the principalities and powers of this world.

The Morphology of Christian Love

In Chapter V, we began to reflect on the morphology of Christian hope. In Chapter VI, on the morphology of Christian faith. In the present chapter, we have been concerned with the evaluative morphology of Christian love. We have suggested that Christian love derives its basic evaluative form from the three basic tenets of new covenant religion. We have concluded that so interpreted the consent of Christian love gives decisive ethical orientation to personal moral conduct. It demands the active pursuit of a religio-ethical ideal that has specific consequences for personal growth and for the transformation of human society. Far from breeding a legalism, as Fletcher fallaciously feared, the explication of the laws of Christian love stands as an enduring challenge not only to legalism but to every humanly concocted ethical system, including situation ethics.

The preceding analysis also transforms the ideal of experiential integration through mutual commitment in atoning love that we described at the close of Chapter III from a vague abstraction to a practical program of action. And it brings to a close the attempt to explain the meaning of the pneumatic transformation of natural conversion begun in Chapter IV. It has brought our reflections on the graced transformation of human growth from the cradle to the threshold of the middle-age crisis. One task still remains: to reflect upon the pneumatic transformation of the human experience of ego-disintegration, senescence, and death.

But before we do so, it will perhaps be helpful to note in passing that an emergent model for the Christian conscience avoids all of the speculative inadequacies we discovered earlier in the Thomistic conscience. It eschews intellectualism, voluntarism, essentialism, naive epistemological realism, and a privatized account of affectivity, thought, and freedom. It is not static but developmental; not dogmatic, but fallibilistic; not conformist, but the summons to be a divine instrument of the new creation. With the New Testament writers it grounds Christian moral obligation, not in some quasi-Stoic insight into the natural law, but in the preaching of Jesus and in the charismatic anointing of His Holy Breath. At the same time, it offers a theory of the natural evolution of the legal structure of experience that incorporates within itself a theory of the growth of moral freedom. Finally, it grounds a Christian sense of rights and duties, not in a rationalistic sense of justice, but in the summons of the Son of God to love all persons with the same forgiving, atoning love as He has loved us.

Notes

1. Ex. 1:8–22, 2:1–10, 3:1–15, 17:9–13, 18:79ff., 19:6ff., 32:11–14, 33:11, 17–23, 34:29–35; Nm. 14:13–20; Dt. 5:1–5, 18:15–18; Ho. 12:14.
2. He. 3:6; Jn. 1:17, 5:45ff.; 2 Co. 3:7–18.
3. Mt. 5:17ff., 8:4; Mk. 12:28–34, 19:16–22; Lk. 18:18–21.
4. Mt. 23:16–26, 9:10–13, 12:1–8, 15:1–20; 16:5–12; Mk. 2:15–3:6; Lk. 12:37–54.
5. Mt. 5:20–48, 19:1–12; Lk. 16:16ff.; Mk. 1:22, 2:21ff., 7:15–23.
6. Mt. 23:1–39; Lk. 11:37–54.
7. Lk. 13:1–5, 18:10–14; Jn. 8:7.
8. Mt. 10:24, 11:25–29; Lk. 10:23–26; Mk. 1:16–20, 3:13, 8:34–37.
9. Rm. 6:4, 7:1ff.; 1 Co. 6:11, 12:13ff.; Eph. 4:4ff.; Ga. 3:1–2.
10. Rm. 2:15, 9:1; 2 Co. 1:12.
11. Rm. 2:25-29.
12. Rudolf Schnackenburg, *The Moral Teaching of the New Testament*, trans. J. Holland Smith (New York: Herder and Herder, 1967), p. 291.
13. Jn. 1:25, 2:12.
14. Gunther Bornkamm, Gerhard Barth, and Henry Joachim, *Tradition and Interpretation in Matthew*, trans. Percy Scott (London: S.C.M. Press, 1963).
15. John H. Yoder, *The Politics of Jesus* (Grand Rapids: Eerdmans, 1972), pp. 34–39, 64–77.
16. *Ibid.*, pp. 26–34, 66; Lk. 4:19.
17. *Ibid.*, p. 29; C. K. Barrett, *The Holy Spirit and the Gospel Tradition*, pp. 25–42.
18. Yoder, *op. cit.*, pp. 26–27, 44–56.
19. *Ibid.*, pp. 48–46.
20. *Ibid.*, pp. 108–133.
21. *Ibid.*, pp. 80–102.
22. John T. Palikowski, "The Minister as Pharisee," *Commonweal*, XCV (January, 1972), pp. 369–373.
23. Hb. 10:1–18.
24. Jn. 4:2.
25. Joachim Jeremias, *The Eucharistic Words of Jesus*, trans. Norman Perrin (New York: Scribner's, 1966).
26. Mk. 2:9, 8:27–33, 9:2–8, 14:61–65.
27. Mk. 3:31–4:33, 13:1–37.
28. Joachim Jeremias, *The Parables of Jesus*, trans. S. H. Hooke (New York: Scribner's, 1972).
29. Mk. 13:1–37; Mt. 24:1–51.
30. Mt. 9:1–13, 12:1–8, 22–32, 15:1–20, 16:1–4, 19:1–9, 21:23–27, 15–46.

31. Mt. 6:2–4, 9:1–8, 10:37–42, 11:25–27, 12:28–30, 46–50, 16:17–20, 24–28, 18:18.

32. 1 Co. 10:1ff., 12:13; Ep. 2:11–12, 5:26; Col. 2:11ff.; cf. Joseph Fitzmyer, *Pauline Theology* (Englewood Cliffs: Prentice Hall, 1967).

33. Mk. 1:9–11; Mt. 3:13–16; Lk. 3:21; Jn. 1:19–34.

34. Mt. 9:14–17; Jn. 3:24–27.

35. Mk. 1:7–8; Mt. 3:11; Lk. 3:16; Jn. 1:32–34.

36. Mk. 1:9–11; Mt. 3:16–17; Lk 3:21–22.

37. Barrett, *loc. cit.*

38. Mk. 1:12–13.

39. Gelpi, *Charism and Sacrament*, pp. 117–121.

40. Mk. 1:13.

41. Mt. 3:13–15, 17.

42. Mt. 3:11.

43. Mt. 4:1–2.

44. Mt. 4:3–11.

45. Mt. 4:5.

46. Mt. 4:4, 6, 10.

47. Lk. 3:23–38.

48. Lk. 4:9.

49. Lk. 4:13.

50. Lk. 4:4, 6.

51. Lk. 6:20.

52. Mt. 4:1–2.

53. Mt. 4:4.

54. Mt. 6:25–34.

55. Mt. 6:19, 19:23–24.

56. Lk. 16:13.

57. Lk. 19:1–10.

58. Lk. 3:10–14.

59. Mt. 5:43–48.

60. Mt. 25:31–46.

61. Mt. 6:12.

62. 1 Co. 12:7–11.

63. Lk. 6:32.

64. Lk. 14:12–14.

65. Lk. 12:16–21.

66. Mt. 18:21–22.

67. Mt. 5:43–45.

68. Mt. 9:10–13.

69. Lk. 23:34.

70. Mt. 7:7–12.

71. Mt. 5:21–24.

72. Lk. 18:9–14.

73. Mt. 26:52–54.

74. Lk. 13:31–33.

75. Rm. 1:16–17, 8:1–39; 1 Co. 1:20–25, 11:17–14:40, 12:12–13: 27–31, 14:1; 2 Co. 8:1–9:15. Cf. Stanislaus Lyonnet and Leopold Sabourin, *Sin, Redemption, and Sacrifice* (Rome: Biblical Institute, 1970), pp. 50–51.

76. 1 Co. 5:9–13; Col. 6:9–11; Phil. 2:1–11.

77. 1 Co. 13:1–13; Ep. 3:16–19, 5:4, 19–20, 6:1–8; Col. 4:2–4; Phil. 2:1–11; Gal. 5:13–26; 1 Co. 10:31.

78. Jm. 1:1–27, 2:1–13, 3:7–12, 4:1–5:6.

79. 1 Jn. 1:5–11, 3:3–24.

80. Jn. 4:21–24, 35, 6:28–51, 13:1–20, 37–35, 18:12–19:16.

81. Schnackenburg, *loc. cit.*; Yoder, *op. cit.*, pp. 170ff.

82. Yoder, *op. cit.*, pp. 171–181.

83. *Ibid.*, p. 207.

84. *Summa Theologiae*, I–II, QQ. xciii–xciv.

85. *Ibid.*, I–II, Q. li, a. 1.

86. *Ibid.*, I–II, QQ, lv ff.

87. Cf. Austin Fagothy, S.J., *Right and Reason* (St. Louis: Moody, 1953), pp. 239ff.

88. Lawrence Kohlberg, "The Cognitive-Developmental Approach to Moral Education," *Phi Delta Kappan*, LVI (June, 1975), pp. 670–677; D. Sholl, "The Contribution of Lawrence Kohlberg to Religious and Moral Development," *Religious Education*, LXVI (1971), pp. 364–372.

89. For a discussion of Kohlberg's stages, see: Duska and Whelan, *op. cit.*, pp. 42–103; Edwin Fenton, "Moral Education: The Research Findings," *Social Education*, XL (April, 1976), pp. 188–193; Richard S. Peters, "Why Doesn't Lawrence Kohlberg Do His Homework?" *Phi Delta Kappan*, LVI (June, 1975), p. 678; Jack K. Fraenkel, "The Kohlberg Bandwagon: Some Reservations," *Social Education*, XL (April, 1976), pp. 216–222.

90. John H. Krahn, "A Comparison of Kohlberg's and Piaget's Type One Morality," *Religious Education*, LXVI (1971), pp. 373–376.

91. Fenton, *op. cit.*; Kohlberg, *op. cit.*

92. Kohlberg, *op. cit.*, p. 672.

93. Lawrence Kohlberg, "The Claim to Moral Adequacy of a Highest Stage of Moral Judgment," *The Journal of Philosophy*, LXX (October, 1973), pp. 630–646.

94. *Ibid.*, p. 636.

95. *Ibid.*, pp. 636–641.

96. *Ibid.*, pp. 641–642.

97. *Ibid.*,

98. *Ibid.*, p. 642.

99. *Ibid.*, pp. 642–643.

100. *Ibid.*, pp. 640–641.

101. Joseph Fletcher, *Situation Ethics* (Philadelphia: Westminster, 1966).

102. Joseph Fletcher, "Reflection and Reply" in *The Situations Ethics Debate*, ed. Harvey Cox (Philadelphia: Westminster, 1968), p. 252.

103. Duska and Whelan, *op. cit.*, pp. 80ff.

104. John Courtney Murray, *We Hold These Truths* (New York: Sheed and Ward, 1960); Thomas T. Love, *John Courtney Murray: Contemporary Church-State Theory* (Garden City: Doubleday, 1965).

105. John Dewey and James H. Tufts, *Ethics* (New York: Holt, Rinehart, and Winston, 1908); John Dewey, *Human Nature and Conduct* (New York: Modern Library, 1930); *Liberalism and Social Action* (New York: Capricorn, 1935); *Individualism Old and New* (New York: Capricorn, 1962); *A Common Faith* (New Haven: Yale, 1970).

106. George Dalcourt, "The Pragmatist and Situationist Approach to Ethics," *Thought*, LI (June, 1976), p. 137.

107. Dewey, *Liberalism and Social Action*, p. 79.

108. Gustavo Gutierrez, *A Theology of Liberation* (New York: Orbis, 1973); Dom Hélder Câmara, *Revolution Through Peace*, trans. Amparo McLean (New York: Harper and Row, 1971).

109. Gutierrez, *op. cit.*, p. 275.

110. Yoder, *op. cit.*, pp. 124–133.

111. For a lucid discussion of Peirce on the normative sciences, see: Vincent G. Potter, *Charles S. Peirce on Norms and Ideals* (Worchester: University of Massachusetts, 1967).

112. Erik H. Erikson, *Identity, Youth, and Crisis* (New York: Norton, 1968).

113. *Ibid.*, pp. 91ff.

114. James Empereur, S.J., "Process Theology," *National Catholic Reporter* (February, 1974), p. 45.

115. Daniel Day Williams, *God's Grace and Man's Hope* (New York: Harper, 1949); "Moral Obligation in Process Philosophy," *Journal of Philosophy*, LVI (1959), pp. 263–270; *Spirit and Forms of Love*, pp. 214–275.

116. John Goheen, "Whitehead's Theory of Value," in *The Philosophy of Alfred North Whitehead*, pp. 437–459.

117. Paul Arthur Schilpp, "Whitehead's Moral Philosophy," in *The Philosophy of Alfred North Whitehead*, pp. 563–618.

118. Whitehead, *Process and Reality*, pp. 297–298.

119. Whitehead, *Adventures of Ideas*, pp. 240–295.

120. Louis Monden, *Sin, Liberty, and Law*, trans. Joseph Donceel (New York: Sheed and Ward, 1965), pp. 4–17.

121. Ricoeur, *Symbolism of Evil*, pp. 118–157.

VIII. Death and Resurrection

We are about to begin the final leg of our climb. Our attempt to understand the human dynamics of Christian conversion has forced us to trace the path of human growth from the cradle to the middle-age crisis. The time has come to follow the way that leads from the middle-age crisis to death. For those without hope, that path is a descent into darkness. But for those whose hearts expand to the vision of Christ the way continues to mount.

Mountain peaks are places of austerity and of incredible beauty. Familiar vegetation is gone. Even the stunted growth that marks the tree line has been long since abandoned. But in these barren places, the heart knows silence and ecstasy.

Our topos tells us that this final ascent divides into four sets of switchbacks. The Christian experience of death and transformation in God is interpreted by the image of Jesus the crucified and risen Savior. As we ascend the first set of switchbacks, we will attempt to show how these images yield appreciative insight into the psychodynamics of the middle-age crisis. An examination of the writings of the Christian mystics will, however, also show that they envisage growth processes in the latter half of life that transcend anything described by contemporary psychology.

During the third stage of our climb we will attempt to probe the meaning of Christian mysticism. We will examine the contributions of William James and of Joseph Maréchal to this field. We will try to understand the shortcoming of their respective approaches. Then we will draw on the work of R. C. Zaehner to explore the varieties of mystical experience. We will then be in a position to make our final ascent.

As we mount our last set of switchbacks, we will reflect on the uniqueness of Christian mystical experience in order to come to a foundational insight into the meaning of salvation history. Then we will contrast the death of the mystic with the ordinary human experience of dying and of near death in order to provide anthropological underpinnings for a Christian theology of the "four last things."

The summit beckons. Let us begin our final ascent.

The Death and Resurrection of the Lord

Among the leading images that lend structure to Christian aspiration in the face of death are, of course, the images of Jesus the crucified Savior and risen Lord. As images they are inseparable. In Jesus crucified, the saving mercy of God stands already revealed; and at the same time the risen Lord bears in His glorified body the wounds of crucifixion. The fourth gospel makes the point plainly: being lifted up on the cross is the beginning of Jesus' exaltation in divine glory.

But while the images of the crucified Savior and risen Lord are complementary, each carries its own message. The cross endows Christian piety with stark realism. The Christian path to glory leads inexorably to Golgotha. On the other hand, the image of Jesus risen imbues Golgotha with its paradoxical meaning. In the light of Easter, Calvary is revealed, not as defeat, but as Jesus' victory over death. The glory of Easter transforms a rejected rabbi into the new Adam, the gibbet of the cross into the tree of life.[1] By the same token, then, Calvary is Easter in the making, the prelude to Jesus' vindication by the Father and His final transformation in the glorifying, revelatory power of the Holy Breath.[2]

The roots of this paradoxical faith and hope lie in Jesus' own preaching. That Jesus in contrast to the Sadducees believed in and proclaimed the resurrection of the dead seems to be beyond serious question. Moreover, the gospels all portray Him as predicting His own death and ultimate vindication by the Father.

Moreover, in foretelling His own violent demise, Jesus seems to have applied to Himself the image of the suffering servant of Yahweh. That He could have done so is historically plausible and would have been consistent with His teaching concerning bodily resurrection. For the suffering servant, by trusting to the divine fidelity even in death, finds vindication at the hands of God and triumphs finally over the grave.[3] As opposition to Him grew, the image of the *ebed Yahweh* might well have spoken to Jesus' heart with power concerning the quality of trust demanded of Him as Son.

Understandably enough, the meaning of Jesus' predictions of His passion remained vague and obscure in the disciples' minds until their encounter with the risen Christ. The New Testament describes two different kinds of encounter with the risen Lord. "Seeing the Lord" is a technical term that designates a personal apparition of Jesus risen and strangely transformed.[4] On the other hand, the experience of faith, of personal consent to Jesus as Savior and Lord in response to the proclamation of the gospel and in the transforming enlightenment of the Holy Breath is also described in terms that suggest an encounter with the risen Christ.[5] For to know Jesus in the enlightenment of faith is to enter into the same process of pneumatic transformation as He. In Jesus' case that process culminated in Easter. The believer, then, experiences Jesus' resurrection in its salvific consequences through the present action of the Breath in his or her own life and in the Christian community.

Consent in faith to the Lordship of Jesus engages the deepest eschatological aspirations of the Christian. It unifies Christian hope and therefore Christian belief as well. To proclaim Jesus as Lord is to proclaim His co-equality with the Father, His messianic sway over all the principalities and powers of this world, His gentle pneumatic presence in His Church and in its charismatic and eucharistic assemblies. It is to look forward to a cosmic exodus, to the salvific recreation of heaven and earth in the power of Christ, to the return of the Son of Man, to the vindication of His saints, to the descent of the heavenly Jerusalem, and to the holy marriage of the Lamb and His bride.[6] What light, if any, do such images throw upon an emergent theology of the human?

The Ego and the Self

Once again, Jungian theory offers some fruitful foundational leads. We have suggested that Jesus in His humanity enters Christian aspiration as a heroic symbol of the human ego charismatically transformed. The risen Christ, on the other hand, interprets Christian hope for total transformation in God. Such total transformation encompasses not only ego processes but the human self in the sense defined in Chapter III.

The emerging self is a vectoral feeling and must be distinguished from the archetype of the self described by Jung. The archetype of the self is a qualitative, conceptual feeling. It lends evaluative structure to conscious and unconscious ego processes. It is a symbol of integrating wholeness. In its positive aspect, it connotes the reconciliation of conflicting psychic forces. The mandala, the *hieros gamos*, the world navel, the axis of the universe, are all examples of the positive dimension of this controlling archetype. In its negative side, the self is demonic, diabolical, and in Christian iconography Satanic. The Hero and the Heroine are, as we have seen, archetypal symbols of the conscious ego. The integration or fragmentation of the emerging, legal reality of the self at a deeper level than conscious ego processes is, then, disclosed to appreciative understanding through the mediating archetype of the self. Once these distinctions have been made,

Jungian personality theory begins to assume some interesting foundational implications.

In the healthy personality, the conscious ego and the self exist in creative tension. The absorption of the conscious ego by the self is psychic disaster; it is the painful disintegration and destruction of conscious ego processes described in Chapter III. It reveals the dark, demonic side of the self. The absorption of the self into the ego, on the other hand, breeds ego inflation. It is the Hero or Heroine victimized by hybris and self-infatuation.

For as the rational ego acquires autonomy, independence, and personal individuation, conscious ego functions become detached from the rest of the personality. The conscious ego becomes increasingly self-assured and begins to assume autocratically the integrating, directive functions of the self. In this fatuous state of self-deception, the ego is more and more victimized by its own myopia and blindness. It grows increasingly deaf to the advice of others and to the promptings of the unconscious, until, as we have already seen, its hybris leads it to posit the "inflated act." That act is a deed of egotistical and foolish arrogance whose fruit is failure, rejection, disillusionment, and ego-disintegration.

The deflated ego feels wounded, fragmented, powerless. But in the normal processes of psychic growth, through humility, repentance, and acceptance by others, the ego reestablishes a dialogic relation with the self. From the self it begins to derive healing and new life. During this period of passive transformation, the convalescent ego begins to discover confidence. When fully reconstructed, it reassumes its former buoyancy, until its newly found confidence again becomes myopic and overweening and inflation generates another foolish decision freighted with destructive consequences. As we have seen in other contexts, this cycle of inflation, alienation, repentance, reconciliation, and reinflation is repeated again and again. Its final fruit is a fully developed adult ego.

But in addition to the shorter cycles of personality disintegration and reconstruction, there is a longer cycle as well. Somewhere around the age of forty, the normal, conscious adult ego, left to its natural resources, reaches the end of its rope. Some of the reasons were suggested in Chapter VI. To achieve specialized competence and abstract propositional focus, the developing conscious ego must repress many legitimate needs for personal growth. The maturing introvert is increasingly reduced to frustration and futility in dealing with an intransigent environment. The maturing extravert is increasingly harassed by repressed and rambunctious affections and thoughts. The thinking type is increasingly obtuse toward feeling; the feeling type, increasingly bewildered by abstractions. The sensation type is increasingly hostile to creative intuition; the intuitive type, increasingly terrified of practicalities. Jung puts the matter succinctly:

> The nearer we approach the middle of life, and the better we have succeeded in entrenching ourselves in our personal attitudes and social positions, the more it appears as if we had discovered the right course and the right ideals and principles of behaviour. For this reason we suppose them to be eternally valid, and make a virtue of unchangeably clinging to them. We overlook the essential fact that the social goal is attained only at the cost of a diminution of personality. Many—far too many—aspects of life which should also have been experienced lie in the lumber-room among dusty memories; but sometimes, too, they are glowing coals under grey ashes.[7]

The Crisis of Middle Age

The crisis of middle age is a period of mental depression and conscious disorientation. There is a new confrontation with the shadow. The life one has made for oneself now seems cabined, cribbed, confined, bound in to futility and boredom. The conscious ego feels disenchanted, alienated, trapped. The naive optimism of youth is no longer possible. Down the road lies, not the promise of sexual discovery and fulfillment, but the certainty of diminished potency and of inexorable physical debilitation and decay. The hopes and ambitions of youth have been replaced by adult routines. There is a gnawing sense that achievement lies in the past and that its best moments were somehow less than satisfying. The sense of the noumenous is lost. Life holds no more mysteries. It is flat and tasteless. The ego seeks with decreasing success to exert despotic control over its future. Repressed archetypes begin to be projected into persons and events. The response to environmental pressures and social demands begins to assume a bizarre, fantastic character. Guilt, frustration, and failure are rationalized, however, until finally they can no longer be denied.[8]

Not everyone negotiates the middle-age crisis successfully. Some remain miserably trapped in their own neuroticisms. For just as the neurotic youth cannot escape the traumas of childhood, so the neurotic adult remains imprisoned in the traumas and frustrations of youth. Instead of growing in wisdom, the aging, neurotic ego either clings consciously to the memory of fast-fading personal achievements or sits in embittered contemplation of the individual it never became.

The personality becomes rigid, persona possessed. The neurotic, middle-aged, conscious ego is increasingly dominated by the social functions it has created for itself. Personal identity becomes a matter of rigid conformity to social expectations. The temptation to be content with conscious satisfactions born of shallow social rewards is, moreover, strong because, as Jung also observes, the persona is always rewarded in cash. Plagued by a growing self-dissatisfaction and anxiety, the neurotic ego clings to visible signs of its worth rather than yield to the increasingly insistent claims of the unconscious for healing and for integration.

Clearly, for the aging, conscious ego, the path to psychic health lies in the opposite direction. Jung again says it succinctly: "From middle life onward, only he remains vitally alive who is ready to *die with life*."⁹ For the disintegration of the persona and the new confrontation with the shadow that typify the middle-age crisis can and should be the prelude to a period of enormously creative dialogue between the ego and the self.

Here, however, a methodological caution is in order. Jungian archetypes are denotatively vague and connotatively rich. As a consequence, they are capable of yielding appreciative insight into growth processes that are purely natural as well as those that are graced and touched by faith. Religious archetypes that are faith-derived can interpret growth processes that are purely natural. Naturally derived archetypes can interpret growth processes instinct with authentic religious faith.

With these reservations in mind, it is nevertheless interesting to note that the dismembered Hero is a standard archetype for the fragmented, alienated ego; crucifixion, a standard archetype of dismemberment. The image of the crucified Savior interprets, therefore, the ego disintegration that accompanies the middle-age crisis.

The Divine Father is an archetype of the Self: He is the divine source from which all things proceed and in whom all are to find unity and reconciliation. The human figure of Jesus enters appreciative understanding as the image of an ego wholly submissive to the Self: He is the divine Son who is obedient in every respect to the will of the Father. For the believer, then, His crucifixion is also a symbol of the kind of ego-death demanded by the obedience of faith.¹⁰

The risen and glorious Lord is, by contrast, a powerful Christian symbol of the ego creatively transformed in the vitalizing power of the divine Self, and therefore of the salvific wholeness that lies beyond ego-death in faith. In its risen state the humanity of Jesus radiates the transforming glory of His heavenly Father. Through the resurrection, the gibbet of the cross becomes the axis of the world, that point in time and space in which heaven and earth, the divine and the human, are wedded in love. Through Jesus' crucifixion and glorification, the malice of sin is taken up even into the Godhead and transformed into healing, salvation, and life.[11] Our Lady of Sorrows assumed into heavenly glory and wholly transformed in the power of the Mother Advocate could in a less adequate fashion perform a similar interpretative function for some Christian women. But we lack an adequate Christian iconography for the development of feminine ego-consciousness in faith.

Jung in discussing the Christian vision of Jesus risen as an archetype of the self engages in a prolonged and somewhat misguided polemic against the proposition that evil is merely the privation of good. The notion leads, he feels, to too optimistic a conception of evil and to too pessimistic a view of the human psyche. To say that evil is nothing, he argues, is to encourage the dangerous notion that it is negligible. In point of fact, the forces of evil are forces of enormous destructive power. At the same time, Jung fears, to portray the human soul as the exclusive source of evil is to tempt it to demonic and destructive inflation.[12]

Jung's polemic, whatever its psychological merits, is theologically misguided. For as Stanislaus Lyonnet and Leopold Sabourin have shown, New Testament theology does not reduce evil to the mere privation of good, even though one strain of biblical polemic against the folly of sin does move in that direction.[13] The patristic belief that evil is nothing more than the absence of good is strictly speaking Neo-Platonic in origin. Instead of being an attack on "Christianity" as he seems to presuppose, Jung's critique is of the Platonization of Christian faith at the hands of the Fathers. So pervasive is Neo-Platonic influence upon the writings of the Fathers, however, that Jung's overgeneralization is understandable. He was a psychiatrist and a genius, but not a professional exegete or theologian.

Similarly, Christian faith has never portrayed the human soul as the unique source of evil. Already in the Adamic myth, the serpent is present as a vague chthonic symbol of forces of evil beyond the individual person that seduce the heart and lead to sinful and destructive choices. In both Hebrew and Christian iconography, moreover, the serpent tempter fuses with the figure of Satan.[14]

When viewed from the standpoint of an emergent anthropology, every Jungian archetype, including the archetypes of the ego and of the self, are specific elements in the evaluative form of appreciative understanding. Appreciative knowing, it will be recalled, may be either conscious or unconscious. It defines the realm of physical purpose and constitutes one phase in the development of the human ego. One should, then, be careful not to reify such images uncritically, including the archetype of the self. The reason is not that such images are subjective but that they are vague. Their meaning is rich in connotation but logically obscure. To treat an archetypal category as if it were capable of logical verification is, then, methodologically perverse. This caution is in order, for Jung himself seems at times to ignore it. He and his disciples will on occasion speak of the archetype of the self as though it were the living reality of God and infer that since the archetype has a positive and negative side, God too must have a Jekyll-Hyde personality. As we shall see, another interpretation of the two faces of the self is possible.

Furthermore, it is important to keep reminding oneself that the archetypal images that structure appreciative insight into the Christian discovery of graced self-consciousness in God are finally inadequate to describe the event itself. For authentic Christian self-discovery in faith is the fruit of contemplative prayer. And mystical contemplation transcends every form of insight available to ego-consciousness, whether imagistic and archetypal or abstract and inferential. It is, then, to the Christian mystics that we must turn, if we are to reach an adequate foundational insight into the meaning of ego-death in faith and of the graced pneumatic transformation of human self-awareness.

Developmental Mysticism

Developmental psychology is a relatively recent arrival on the academic scene. As a consequence, it remains surrounded by the controversy that normally attends every scientific breakthrough. Such polemic is the normal result of both initial theoretical vagueness and of ego-inertia in the face of a new idea. But often it yields clarifying results.

Already in the sixteenth century, however, Teresa of Avila had enriched theology with what can, I believe, be legitimately described as a theory of developmental mysticism. Her mature description of the successive stages through which faith-consciousness passes is to be found in her *Interior Castle*. She undertook the book reluctantly, in obedience to her confessor at a time when age and ill health were plaguing her. It remains to this day a landmark in mystical theology.

Mystics, as we have seen, are especially attuned to appreciative forms of insight. Teresa's book is accordingly organized around a central unifying image. In the opening chapter she writes:

> While I was beseeching Our Lord today that He would speak through me, since I could find nothing to say and had no idea how to begin to carry out the obligation laid upon me by obedience, a thought occurred to me which I will now set down, in order to have some foundation on which to build. I began to think of the soul as if it were a castle made of a single diamond or of very clear crystal, in which there are many rooms, just as in Heaven there are many mansions. Now if we think carefully over this, sisters, the soul of the righteous man is nothing but a paradise, in which, as God tells us, He takes delight. For what do you think a room will be like which is the delight of a King so mighty, so wise, so pure and so full of all that is good? I can find nothing with which to compare the great beauty of a soul and its great capacity. In fact, however, acute our intellects may be, they will no more be able to attain to a comprehension of this than to an understanding of God; for, as he Himself says, He created us in His image and likeness. Now if this is so—and it is—there is no point in our fatiguing ourselves by attempting to comprehend the beauty of this castle; for though it is His creature, and there is therefore as much difference between it and God as between creature and Creator, the very fact that His Majesty says it is made in His image means that we can hardly form any conception of the soul's great dignity and beauty.[15]

One's own house or castle is a common image of the self. The mansions, or rooms, in Teresa's *Interior Castle*, are then nothing else than stages or levels in the growth of conscious self-awareness in God.

The door to the interior castle is prayer. Its first mansion, which is relatively cold and cheerless, is characterized by initial conversion to God. In it the God-seeker experiences repentant confrontation with the shadow. (S)he abandons habitual behavior that is seriously destructive in its consequences and makes preliminary, tottering steps in the path of prayer. (S)he begins to know the initial purification that characterizes the dark night of sense.[16] These are issues to which we addressed ourselves in Chapters IV and V.

In the second mansion, faith is a bit stronger but still in need of massive environmental buttresses even to stand firmly. The person who dwells here needs communal support in order to sustain a personal commitment to God in integrity. Instruction in Christian doctrine and in the basics of growth in prayer and in service are also strong imperatives. There is continued need for the eradication of sinful habits and for conscious personal growth both in self-discipline and in practical love. But what clearly differentiates the second mansion from the first is the conscious maturation of a sense of personal vocation or call.[17] To these issues we addressed ourselves in Chapter VI.

Teresa's third mansion is a period of religious consolidation. At the third level of faith-consciousness, the maturing religious ego acquires proficiency in ordering its many activities according to authentic Christian morality and according to the moral demands implicit in one's personal vocation. At the third level of faith-consciousness, signs of genuine sanctity begin to appear. Personal conduct begins to express the mind of Jesus. There is growing concern to use possessions justly and charitably, to share them freely with the needy as an expression of faith. Conduct and values contrary to the mind of Christ are instinctively recognized and rejected. Sin is genuinely abhorrent. Self-discipline has introduced an element of frugality, even of occasional austerity into daily routine. One's life is fairly rich in good works. In the last chapter we attempted to explore the values that ought increasingly to shape the faith-consciousness of those who dwell in the third mansion.

But as Teresa observes correctly, those who have entered the third level of faith-awareness still face a serious set of personal growth problems. They remain vexed with anxieties, many of them unconscious. Prayer is frequently arid. They know seasons of self-pity and discouragement. Under stress they blame God for misery produced by their own imperfections. When adversity is absent, those in the third mansion are apt to yield to complacency. The positive bent of their piety is rationalistic and fatuously self-assured. In describing their practice of penance, Teresa observes wryly: "You need never fear that they will kill themselves: they are eminently reasonable folk! Their love is not yet ardent enough to overwhelm their reason." Her wryness is an expression of concern. For the most serious problem facing those who dwell in the third mansion is the inability to pass beyond it to the higher levels of religious awareness.[18]

When Teresa's description of the third mansion is read in the light of Jungian personality theory, there can be little doubt that it corresponds to the ego-inflated piety of the young adult. For the personality problems that plague the maturing adult ego as it moves toward the middle-age crisis correspond almost point for point with those encountered in the third mansion: the growing alienation of the conscious ego from a larger sense of the self, affective aridity, the evaporation of a noumenal sense of mystery, the growth of largely unconscious neurotic anxieties, persona possession, rationalism, and the subjection of personal growth processes to the despotic control of the ego.[19]

The *Interior Castle* is not a scholarly study of mysticism in the manner of Evelyn Underhill. It is the personal testimony of one of the greatest mystics after an extraordinary career of personal growth in prayer and after considerable experience in helping others to grow. It should come as no surprise, then, that the mansions described by Teresa reflect discernible stages in her own religious odyssey. Teresa is critical of the good complacent people who dwell in the third mansion because she herself spent so much time there, time that she subsequently felt had been sterile and wasted, though her feelings may have been partially motivated by what Felix Marti-Ibañez has called the "mystic scruple." Still, it is true that after entering religion at the age of twenty, for eighteen years Teresa of Jesus knew only arid, affectively sterile prayer.[20]

Her own transition to the higher graces of contemplation commenced, therefore, only at the onset of middle age. It is then no surprise that her description of the fourth mansion corresponds in many of its details to Jung's account of healthy psychic growth after the successful resolution of the middle-age crisis.

In the fourth mansion conscious contact is reestablished with the deeper aspects of the self. The despotic control of the rational ego begins to break down. There is newfound passivity in prayer. The heart of the God-seeker becomes aware of a quiet center of recollected religious consciousness that is other than the busy ego, although the latter still bustles about like Martha with its images and abstractions. But ego-awareness has ceased to be the primary locus of one's conscious relationship with God. Teresa calls this new, passive form of prayer the "prayer of recollection." It sets the feet of the God-seeker on the path to infused contemplation. Teresa describes the experience:

> It is a form of recollection which also seems to me supernatural, for it does not involve remaining in the dark,

or closing the eyes, nor is it dependent upon anything exterior. A person involuntarily closes his eyes and desires solitude; and, without the display of any human skill there seems gradually to be built for him a temple in which he can make the prayer already described; the senses and all external things seem gradually to lose their hold on him, while the soul, on the other hand, regains its lost control.[21]

Recollection is the least of the contemplative graces, an initial schooling in passivity before God. It should not be confused with the grace of infused contemplation itself or even with the prayer of quiet. Teresa observes:

> One person told me of a certain book by the saintly Fray Peter of Alcántara (for a saint I believe he is), which would certainly have convinced me, for I know how much he knew about such things; but we read it together, and found that he says exactly what I say, although not in the same words; it is quite clear from what he says that love must already be awake. It is possible that I am mistaken, but I base my position on the following reasons.
>
> First, in such spiritual activity as this, the person who does most is he who thinks and desires to do least: what we have to do is to beg like poor and needy persons coming before a great and rich Emperor and then cast down our eyes in humble expectation. . . .
>
> The second reason is that all these interior activities are gentle and peaceful, and to do anything painful brings us harm rather than help. By "anything painful" I mean anything that we try to force ourselves to do; it would be painful, for example, to hold our breath. The soul must just leave itself in the hands of God, and do what He wills it to do, completely disregarding its own advantage and resigning itself as much as it possibly can to the will of God. The third reason is that the very effort which the soul makes in order to cease from thought will perhaps awaken thought and cause it to think a great deal. The fourth reason is that the most important and pleasing thing in God's eyes is our remembering His honour and glory and forgetting ourselves and our own profit and ease and pleasure.[22]

Those who dwell in the fourth mansion have begun to glimpse realms of consciousness that transcend ego-awareness. For as the God-seeker moves toward contemplative experiences there is both a therapeutic and a supernatural transformation of the personality.

At a therapeutic level, the anxieties that kept the conscious ego prisoner in the third mansion begin, as Jung suggests, to be healed. But for the contemplative, this deeper healing of memories is itself a passive grace, the fruit of openness to God in prayer.

Moreover, at the level of faith two new variables begin to structure human consciousness. First, there are planted the first seeds of a new kind of passive absorption in God that transcends the workings even of the graced charismatic ego. As recollection becomes the prayer of quiet and then ripens to infused contemplation, it yields a new kind of consciousness: one mediated neither by images nor by abstractions. Both John and Teresa, following the author of *The Cloud of Unknowing*,[23] describe it as the knowing that is loving. It is a passive grace that ripens, however, into the higher forms of mystical encounter.

But before we begin to reflect on such experiences, a few preliminary observations are in order. For if the preceding interpretation of the normal psychological underpinnings of the third and fourth mansions is sound, it casts light on the human growth processes that help ground the first two mansions as well.

In the first mansion, one experiences adult conversion to God. In the second, one responds charismatically to a divine vocational call. In the normal processes of human growth, initial conversion and vocational choice normally occur at some point during the adolescent crisis. Teresa's first mansion presupposes, therefore, an initial maturation of religious consciousness during childhood. Before we proceed to the more advanced stages of mystical growth, let us backtrack then for a moment and reflect on the human underpinnings that ground and precede the first two mansions.

The Religion of Childhood and of Youth

In his perceptive study of the stages of personal religious maturation, Gordon Allport correctly notes that the religion of childhood and of youth suffers from the same limitations as the infantile and youthful ego. In the course of socialization, the child absorbs religious ideas and attitudes from its milieu with the same spontaneity as natural ideas and values. It learns to perform religious gestures, partakes in ritual worship, recites rote prayers, but initially with little or no real understanding of their meaning. The child's spontaneous religious thoughts, like its other evaluative responses, are egocentric and transductive. They abound in free-floating fantasies and are concrete and anthropomorphic. Lack of any clear conception of causality leads the child to endow prayer with the same magical explanation as other events.

As the child matures, its religion becomes increasingly conventional. The religious beliefs and attitudes of parents are appropriated without question. The collapse of naive allegiance to the conventional world of childhood normally occurs during adolescence. When that collapse involves religious questioning, it produces the adolescent crisis of faith.[24]

Pierre Babin details some of the typical components of the adolescent faith crisis. The early adolescent still lives in a conventional world of family values and remains socially dependent for most personal attitudes. But as peer groups begin to provide an alternate social environment to the family, conventional patterns of religious behavior may be eroded and can eventually collapse, sometimes fairly permanently. The problem of evil, affective turmoil, rebellion against parental control, lack of a clear personal identity, pharisaical self-righteousness, moral conflicts, childhood neuroses—all these are typical components of the adolescent crisis of faith. As the confused adolescent gropes for a personal religious identity, conventional symbols of faith may, then, lose their former motivating power.[25]

Allport notes, however, that the temporary collapse of the religion of childhood should not be automatically interpreted as the abandonment of religion altogether. In young males, the greatest period of irreligiosity normally occurs in the early and middle twenties, when affective repudiation of parental values is most violent. But even the rebellious ordinarily acknowledge the continued influence of early religious training and continue to feel the need for some kind of personal religious orientation.[26]

Babin correctly observes that the resolution of the adolescent crisis of faith through conversion can be either decisive or implicit. A decisive conversion is characterized by the conscious discovery of a personal religious vision and by clear personal commitment to it as a meaningful ideal for living. In implicit conversion, one's religious attitudes gradually assume a discernible orientation but with little conscious reflection or decision. One drifts inauthentically into a personal religious stance whose motives are obscure even to oneself. Or the implicit convert may revert to the religion of childhood without ever subjecting conventional, childish beliefs to serious critical revision.[27]

Ideally, of course, conversion ought to be decisive. The adolescent ought to reach a conscious personalized religious commitment to God in Christ and in the power of the Holy Breath. The personal discovery of vocational identity ought also to share the same decisive character. But human history testifies that all too often it does not. Implicit conversion and implicit vocational decisions are the seed beds of adult religious inauthenticity. Vocational options normally occur in late adolescence or in the early stages of young adulthood.

We may, then, conclude that the first two mansions of Teresa's *Interior Castle* ought normally to correspond to adolescent religious development, the third mansion to the piety of young adulthood, and the fourth to the initial dialogue between the charismatic ego and the self that is the fruit of the successful negotiation of the crisis of middle age.

Visions, Voices, and Feelings

As the normal middle-aged ego relaxes its despotic control over personal consciousness, prayer may begin to be marked by a variety of parapsychological phenomena. The very term "parapsychology" suggests an important advance in contemporary understanding of the workings of the human psyche. The scientific study of the human person was first undertaken by individuals with highly developed thinking egos. As a consequence, in its earliest formulation psychology tended to be marked by a myopic rationalism and empiricism that automatically characterized unusual, prerational states of consciousness as pathological.

Today the academic climate has shifted somewhat. The contemporary study of altered states of consciousness has freed unusual forms of appreciative knowing from the automatic stigma of madness. Moreover, those who are attuned to charismatic forms of prayer know that the occurrence of such states in spontaneous affective, unscripted prayer is far from uncommon. The intensification of charismatic words and visions that mystics may know in the latter half of life would, then, seem in many instances to be psychologically linked to a new expansion of faith-consciousness into areas of religious feeling previously unavailable to the rationally controlled, ego-centered piety of the young adult.[28]

Of all the Christian mystics, John of the Cross has perhaps provided the most detailed descriptive analysis of the kinds of parapsychological phenomena that can emerge as the charismatic ego enters into dialogue with previously unconscious ego functions. John speaks of visions, revelations, locutions, feelings.

Graced visionary experiences may be either corporeal and sensible, intuitive and imaginative, or imageless and intellectual. Corporeal visions are psychologically akin to hallucinatory experiences. The vision is environmentally situated and seems to have a physical reality independent of the visionary. The visions of Bernadette at Lourdes exemplify such experiences. So too does the following experience related to me by a young Catholic woman almost a decade after its occurrence.

At the time the vision occurred, the lady in question was a young girl wrestling with the problem of vocation. In the course of a retreat of election, she decided she would marry rather than enter the convent. The election had been confirmed by the sister directing the retreat. But the young girl remained troubled by fears that she had chosen the less perfect thing.

The evening she returned from the retreat, she sat in bed reading before going to sleep. Her heart was still not at peace. She raised her eyes from her book and was astonished to see Jesus standing in the corner of her room. As she looked stupified, He smiled. Instantly the depression and confusion lifted, and she knew that her decision had been a sound one and according to God's will. Such experiences were never repeated.

At times, hallucinatory visions can engage the other senses as well. The visionary may experience smells whether sweet or foul. (S)he may seem to be physically touched, as Teresa of Avila did when transfixed by the seraph with the flaming dart.[29]

Imaginative visions are, by contrast, free of hallucinatory traits. The images that structure it are not environmentally located but are clearly felt to be an aspect of one's personal evaluative response to God in faith. Once, for example, a young male religious whose retreat I was directing received a clear locution on the first day of prayer. The word received was: "Wait upon me." It left both of us baffled. Subsequent to the locution, prayer became dry and routine. Then on the fourth day, he received a powerful grace followed by several hours of intense consolation.

He saw himself in his own imagination being drawn out of a black tarry substance, upwards into a light that was gradually stripping away his skin and hair. With the vision came the clear realization that the personal neglect of prayer was a source of serious disorder in his life and that he must reorder his commitments to make ample time for prayer. He also realized that this visionary grace unlocked the meaning of the locution that had occurred earlier in the retreat.[30]

Imageless intellectual visions yield the felt sense of personal presence. But the person is not presented under any visual or imaginative form. In shared charismatic prayer, there are moments in which the presence of the Breath is, for example, palpably felt, although She is neither seen nor imagined. A sister involved in the charismatic prayer community in New Orleans passed long periods in which she felt the presence of Jesus at her side, though there were no sensible or imaginative phenomena accompanying the experience. Teresa of Avila recounts a similar experience and notes that at times the invisible presence seemed to be clearly localized.[31]

In addition to visionary experience, John of the Cross describes experiences he calls "revelations." Revelations are often akin to locutionary experiences but seem to lack precise verbal formulation. They yield "an intellectual understanding or vision of truths about God, or a vision of present, past, or future events which bears resemblance to the spirit of prophecy."[32]

John insists that the first of these revelatory experiences, i.e., revelations of God himself, are of a privileged character and authority. They are accompanied by intense delight; but because they instantiate contemplative union with God they are largely indescribable. John's own words are helpful:

> This sublime knowledge can be received only by a person who has arrived at union with God, for it is itself that very union. It consists in a certain touch of the divinity produced in the soul, and thus it is God Himself who is experienced and tasted there. Although the touch of knowledge and delight that penetrates the substance of the soul is not manifest and clear, as in glory, it is so sublime and lofty that the devil is unable to meddle, nor produce anything similar (for there is no experience similar or comparable to it), nor infuse a savor and delight like it. This knowledge savors of the divine essence and of eternal life, and the devil cannot counterfeit anything so lofty. . . .
>
> These touches engender such sweetness and intimate delight in the soul that one of them would more than compensate for all the trials suffered in life, even though innumerable. Through these touches a person becomes so courageous and so resolved to suffer many things for Christ that he finds it a special suffering to observe that he does not suffer.[33]

But revelations concerning particular persons and events are of a very different character. John suggests that they instantiate either prophecy or discernment.[34] The suggestion needs qualification, for it reflects an unfortunate tendency in scholastic theology to assimilate prophecy somewhat narrowly to the prediction of future events. While the prophetic impulse can include such revelatory disclosures, it also encompasses locutionary and on occasion visionary experiences as well. What distinguishes prophecy from all the various experiences described by John is the impulse to proclaim the divinely received message to an individual or community and to do so in God's name. The revelatory graces described by John would also render any exercise of the gift of discernment rather extraordinary. Ordinary discernment is more pedestrian a process.

Verbalized revelations are termed locutions. As in the case of visions, some locutionary experiences are hallucinatory in character. One seems to hear the words spoken with one's very ears. In addition to such sensible auditions, however, John of the Cross distinguishes three other kinds of graced locution: successive, formal, and substantial.

Successive words occur in times of recollection. The mind is led by the Holy Breath from word to word, from insight to insight. John offers the following caution concerning successive locutions:

> Though in that communication or illumination itself there is actually no deception of the intellect, yet there can be and frequently is deception in the formal words and propositions the intellect deduces from it. That light is often so delicate and spiritual that the intellect does not succeed in being completely informed by it; and it is the intellect that of its own power, as we stated, forms the propositions. Consequently the statements are often false, or only apparent, or defective. Since the intellect afterwards joins its own lowly capacity and awkwardness to the thread of truth it had already begun to grasp, it easily happens that it changes the truth in accordance with this lowly capacity; and all as though another person were speaking it. . . .
>
> And I greatly fear what is happening in these times of ours: If any soul whatever after a bit of meditation has in its recollection one of these locutions, it will immediately baptize all as coming from God and with such a supposition say, "God told me," "God answered me." Yet this is not so, but, as we pointed out, these persons themselves are more often the origin of their locution.[35]

That John would have reservations about some of the exercises of prophecy in the charismatic renewal goes without saying.

Formal locutions occur without warning and whether or not one is recollected. They are more clearly from a different source than the self. John observes:

> Sometimes these words are very explicit and at other times not. They are like ideas spoken to the spirit, either as a reply to something or in another manner. At times only one word is spoken, and then again more than one; sometimes the locutions are successive, like the others, for they may endure while the soul is being taught, or while something is being discussed. All these words come without any intervention of the spirit, because they are received as though one person were speaking to another. . . .
>
> When these words are no more than formal they bear little effect. Ordinarily they are given merely for the purpose of teaching or shedding light upon some truth. Accordingly the efficacy of their effect need be no more than required for the attainment of their purpose. When God is the cause of the locution, this effect is always produced in the soul, for it renders the soul ready to accomplish the command and discerning in understanding it. Yet these locutions do not always remove repugnance and difficulty, rather they sometimes augment it.[36]

Substantial locutions are like formal in that they are passively received but, unlike formal locutions, substantial words change spontaneously the very character of one's relationship to God:

> For example, if our Lord should say formally to the soul: "Be good," it would immediately be substantially good; or if He should say: "Love Me," it would at once have and experience within itself the substance of the love of God; or if He should say to a soul in great fear: "Do not fear," it would without delay feel ample fortitude and tranquillity. . . .
>
> In this fashion He bestows substantial locutions upon certain souls. These locutions are important and valuable because of the life, virtue, and incomparable blessings they impart to the soul. A locution of this sort does more good for a person than a whole lifetime of deeds.[37]

Finally, Johannine mysticism distinguishes two forms of gracious feelings: "affections of the will" and "feelings in the substance of the soul." John's language is scholastic, but his intent is clear. His "affections of the will" are gracious aspirations that yield a more or less clear insight into the reality of God. "Feelings in the substance of the soul" are an intensification of the same grace. They come suddenly and lack a clear causal source. Their healing effect is loftier and more efficacious.[38]

Clearly John's mystical doctrine offers detailed descriptions of the charismatic transformation of every phase in the growth of ego consciousness: dative presentations, vague and primitive physical purposes, imagistic and propositional apperceptions—all are illumined by the touch of divine grace. But except for revelations of God and substantial locutions, he warns about the real possibility of error and deception in such experiences. When they occur in prayer they should be subjected to the discerning judgment of one competent to evaluate them and should be understood in the light of sound psychological, doctrinal, and moral principles. Their meaning and effects should be carefully weighed and should be judged by sound norms for discernment.

Needless to say, authentic visions, revelations, locutions, and gracious feelings are not the exclusive prerogative of the aging contemplative. But the intensification of such graces in the latter half of a lifetime dedicated to prayer should come as no surprise. For as the rational ego relinquishes despotic control over psychic processes, the life-long contemplative reestablishes contact not only with appreciative forms of knowing but with an affectivity that is increasingly docile to the healing impulses of the Holy Breath.

But the Christian mystics all insist that any religious experience that falls short of the grace of contemplation itself is relatively superficial and should not distract one from the major task confronting the God-seeker in the twilight and evening of earthly life, namely, growth in contemplative union with the Divine Reality.

John of the Cross insists on this point and never tires of repeating the same sound advice to the God-seeker who has already begun to advance in the grace of contemplative union: to cling to ego-centered ways of knowing God when one is being called by God to deepen in the knowing that is loving hinders the transforming activity of the Holy Breath.[39] Visions, revelations concerning particular events and persons, and successive and formal locutions should, he warns, be neither sought nor artificially induced. If they occur, one advancing in contemplative prayer should assume a passive stance toward them. For if they are from God, they will of themselves produce a good effect without any active response from the one so graced. If they are not from God, to attend to them in prayer will be at best distracting, at worst destructive.

But for one dwelling in the first four mansions, John's advice may be a bit premature. Even at the fourth level of religious awareness, one is still ignorant of contemplation in the strict sense. In the fourth mansion, the God-seeker has discovered only the gateway that leads to infused contemplation. Teresa, as we have seen, calls it recollection. Let us begin then to explore the fourth mansion in more descriptive detail.

Recollection and Quiet

In the fourth mansion, the God-seeker knows a season of healing and of peace. The aridity of the third mansion gives way to intense, healing periods of consolation. One begins to learn the meaning of praise. There are tears in prayer, healing tears, bittersweet in their assurance of divine love despite one's sinfulness. There is a newfound tranquillity of heart, a new lively quality to the grace of consolation. That grace is less mixed now with human passion: purer, more clearly divine in origin and purpose.

But the most important grace of the fourth mansion is the grace of recollection itself. In *The Way of Perfection* Teresa describes it in the following terms:

> If one prays in this way, the prayer may be only vocal, but the mind will be recollected much sooner; and this is a prayer which brings with it many blessings. It is called recollection because the soul collects together all the faculties and enters within itself to be with its God.[40]

In other words, recollection does not replace meditation or vocal prayer. The ego remains active. But within habitual forms of prayer, the God-seeker begins to discover a new conscious center for relating to the Lord. There is a felt sense that healing in prayer must henceforth be the work of God Himself. The God-seeker now begs that divine healing with growing confidence, certain that busy self-preoccupation in prayer will only be self-defeating, painful, and counterproductive. Sin has now become instinctively abhorrent. Meditation and vocal prayer continue; but the heart expands now as it turns to God with a newfound freedom. There is a felt sense of the greatness and reality of God. There is a new centeredness: a passive, wordless, imageless consent to God that anchors the heart despite the busy, sometimes frantic movement of fantasy and thought.

As this grace of passive openness to the Lord intensifies, it gradually calms the busy ego and eventually absorbs it into the prayer of quiet. In *The Way of Perfection* Teresa describes the chief traits of this new form of prayer:

> This is a supernatural state, and, however hard we try we cannot reach it for ourselves; for it is a state in which the soul enters into peace, or rather in which the Lord gives it peace through His presence, as He did to that just man Simeon. In this state all the faculties are stilled. The soul, in a way which has nothing to do with the outward senses, realizes that it is now very close to its God, and that if it were but a little closer, it would become one with Him through union. This is not because it sees Him either with its bodily or with its spiritual eyes. . . . It is, as it were, in a swoon, both inwardly and outwardly, so that the outward man (let me call it the "body," and then you will understand me better) does not wish to move, but rests, like one who has almost reached the end of his journey, so that it may the better start again upon its way, with redoubled strength for its task.
>
> The body experiences the greatest delight and the soul is conscious of a deep satisfaction. So glad is it merely to find itself near the fountain that, even before it has begun to drink, it has had its fill. There seems nothing left for it to desire. The faculties are stilled and have no wish to move, for any movement they may make appears to hinder the soul from loving God. They are not completely lost, however, since, two of them being free, they can realize in Whose Presence they are. It is the will that is in captivity now; and, if while in this state it is capable of experiencing any pain, the pain comes when it realizes that it will have to resume its liberty. The mind tries to occupy itself with only one thing, and the memory has no desire to busy itself with more: they both see that this is the one thing needful and that anything else will unsettle them. Persons in this state prefer the body to remain motionless, for otherwise their peace would be destroyed: for this reason they dare not stir. Speaking is a distress to them: they will spend a whole hour on a single repetition of the Paternoster.[41]

Here several points should be noted. In the prayer of quiet there is a significant quelling of ego functions. The business of fantasy and thought is now largely stilled. Their activity is replaced by an intensification of loving openness to God. There is a marked increase in passivity within prayer. There is even a quieting of physical processes that parallels the quieting of mind and heart. The inchoate quiet centering experienced during recollection is beginning to be consciously transformed into the knowing that is loving. The God-seeker stands poised at the boundary of contemplative union.

The prayer of quiet described by Teresa should be carefully distinguished from the doctrine of Quietism condemned in 1682. The history of Quietism is a curious affair. It drew its inspiration from the ascetical and mystical writings of Michael Molinos and from the religious experiences and reflections of Jeanne Marie Bouvières de la Mothe Guyon. Quietism was never an organized, popular movement comparable to Jansenism or revivalism, although it culminated in the empassioned confrontation of Francois de Salignac de la Mothe Fénelon and Jacques Benigne Bossuet. Fénelon's popularization and defense of Madame Guyon's spiritual doctrine eventually cost him his ecclesiastical career. But at no point was he the head of a broadly based movement of popular piety.[42]

Quietism was too precious a doctrine to have large popular appeal. But if taken seriously, Quietism was fraught with potentially misleading consequences. In condemning this teaching, the Holy Office took exception to the doctrine's tendency to speak disparagingly of meditation and to transform the mystic spiral into a one-way street. For when reduced to a classical position, Quietism assumes a smug, condescending attitude toward those who have yet to attain the graces of "higher contemplation." Classical Quietism also manifests iconoclastic tendencies; it disparages the use of images in prayer and seeks to exempt the true contemplative from ecclesiastical discipline.

All of these tendencies are diametrically opposed to Teresian mysticism. Submissive obedience to one's spiritual director and to ordained church leaders is a fundamental principle of her doctrine. She inculcates a self-knowledge and humility that precludes religious smugness in any form. And she recognizes that God can at any point withdraw the graces of contemplative prayer and leave the God-seeker in helpless confusion. She insists on the importance of liturgical and sacramental worship, on devotion to the sacred humanity of Jesus, and on the balanced use of vocal prayer, meditation, and religious images.

Nevertheless, both Teresa and John of the Cross recognize, together with all the great medieval mystics, that progress in contemplative prayer introduces the God-seeker into realms of religious experience that are not mediated by ego-consciousness. They both refer to this new species of God-awareness as the grace of "contemplation."

Contemplation, Rapture, Ecstasy

The experience of infused contemplation introduces the God-seeker into the fifth mansion. Teresa describes the experience in terms of an ego-death.

> This delectable death, a snatching of the soul from all activities which it can perform while it is in the body; a death full of delight, for, in order to come closer to God, the soul appears to have withdrawn so far from the body that I do not know if it has still life enough to be able to breathe.[43]

At the inception of infused contemplation ego functions are still further quelled. Teresa observes: ". . . the faculties are almost totally united with God but not so absorbed as not to function. . . . The faculties have only the ability to be occupied completely with God." There is an intensity of consolation unknown during the prayer of quiet. "This prayer," Teresa writes, "is a glorious foolishness, a heavenly madness where the true wisdom is learned; and it is for the soul a most delightful way of enjoying." The heart is now "bewildered and inebriated" with the love of God. It bursts with praises that are themselves divinely inspired. The heart seems stretched almost beyond its capacity. It knows at once the drunkenness of joy and the pain of purification. It is a time of complete abandonment to God, of passive transformation in the Holy Breath.[44] Teresa's own words are again helpful:

> Although this prayer seems entirely the same as the prayer of quiet I mentioned, it is different—partly because in the prayer of quiet the soul didn't desire to move or stir, rejoicing in that holy idleness of Mary; and in this prayer it can also be Martha in such a way that it is as though engaged in both the active and contemplative life together. It tends to works of charity and to business affairs that have to do with its state in life and to reading; although it isn't master of itself completely. And it understands clearly that the best part of the soul is somewhere else. It's as though we were speaking to someone at our side and from the other side another person was speaking to us; we wouldn't be fully attentive to

either the one or the other. This prayer is something that is
felt very clearly, and it gives deep satisfaction and happiness
when it is experienced. It is an excellent preparation so that
the soul may reach a profound quiet when it has time for
solitude, or leisure from business matters. It causes the soul
to go about like a person whose appetite is satisfied and who
has no need to eat but feels that he has taken enough so that
he wouldn't desire just any kind of food; yet he is not so filled
that he wouldn't eagerly eat some if it were tempting to the
appetite. The soul is therefore neither content with nor
desirous of the world's satisfactions, because it has in itself
what pleases it more: greater consolations from God—
desires to satisfy its desire to enjoy Him more and to be with
Him. Being with Him is what it wants.[45]

Here several points should be noted. First of all, as many com-
mentators on Christian mysticism have noted, the grace of contemplation is falsely characterized as a "subjective feeling." It is on the
contrary an experience of encounter in which the God-seeker is not
annihilated but responds actively to the Divine Lover. Second,
in contemplation love has finally matured to a way of knowing
God consciously. But it is a knowledge quite distinct from ego-
consciousness. It is in Paul's phrase the knowledge that is beyond all
knowledge. Third, as contemplative knowing intensifies it grows in
the power to interpenetrate conscious ego functions, whose superfi-
ciality is now vividly felt. The God-seeker now sees all too clearly
how easy it is for the poor ego to know without loving and to substitute its feeble capacities to distinguish and infer for union with God.
Fourth, as contemplative union with God deepens, it ceases to be
merely passive and becomes a reciprocal exchange between lovers.[46]
    Here, then, is the key to the apophatic rhetoric of John of the
Cross. The God-seeker must pursue the grace of contemplative union
relentlessly because it is finally the only knowledge of God that saves.
Inordinate attachment to knowledge of God that is based in ego-
consciousness, even in an ego that has been charismatically transformed, stands as a serious obstacle to total union with the Living
Breath. We shall return to this last point in reflecting on the dark
nights of faith, hope, and love. Here it is sufficient to observe that the
union with God experienced in the early stages of infused contemplation falls short of the grace of spiritual betrothal. Once again Teresa's
words are enlightening:

It seems to me that this union has not yet reached the point of spiritual betrothal, but is rather like what happens in our earthly life when two people are about to be betrothed. There is a discussion as to whether or no they are suited to each other and are both in love; and then they meet again so that they may learn to appreciate each other better. So it is here. The contract is already drawn up and the soul has been clearly given to understand the happiness of her lot and is determined to do all the will of her Spouse in every way in which she sees that she can give Him pleasure. His Majesty, Who will know quite well if this is the case, is pleased with the soul, so He grants her this mercy, desiring that she shall get to know Him better, and that, as we may say, they shall meet together, and He shall unite her with Himself. We can compare this kind of union to a short meeting of that nature because it is over in the very shortest time. All giving and taking have now come to an end and in a secret way the soul sees Who this Spouse is that she is to take.[47]

A further symptom of the preliminary character of the union now experienced with God is the appearance of ecstasy and rapture. Both Teresa and John view these as intermediate graces. Seen as a physical phenomenon, ecstasy is a state of trance, more or less deep, more or less prolonged. Body functions slow down. Breathing and blood circulation are depressed. The body becomes cold and rigid. Sometimes it is frozen suddenly in an awkward pose. Since the same physical symptoms can accompany extreme pathology, such experiences must be carefully scrutinized, instance by instance, before being authenticated.

When authentic, ecstatic states of consciousness yield total personal absorption in the reality of God. They are an impulse of divine love so powerful that in unifying and centering consciousness they leave ego processes to all outward appearances suspended and held in abeyance. The ego-death demanded by contemplative prayer is beginning to have clear physical side-effects. Teresa describes the experience:

While the soul is seeking God in this way, it feels with the most marvelous and gentlest delight that everything is almost fading away through a kind of swoon in which breathing and all bodily energies gradually fail. This experi-

ence comes about in such a way that one cannot even stir the
hands without a lot of effort. The eyes close without one's
wanting them to close; or if a person keeps them open, he
sees hardly anything—nor does he read or succeed in pro-
nouncing a letter, nor can he hardly even guess what the
letter is. He sees the letter; but since the intellect gives no
help, he doesn't know how to read it even though he may
desire to do so. . . . This prayer causes no harm, no matter
how long it lasts. At least it never caused me any, nor do I
recall the Lord ever having granted me this favor that I didn't
feel much better afterward no matter how ill I had been
before. But what illness can produce so wonderful a blessing? The external effects are so apparent that one cannot
doubt that a great event has taken place; these external
powers are taken away with such delight in order to leave
greater ones.[48]

In patholigical instances of trance, there is evidence of morbid
and compulsive preoccupation with a single idea. In the authentic
mystic, however, ecstasy yields a healing, a deepening, and a liberation of the personality. Teresa describes the effects of ecstatic prayer.
Love of one's neighbor is deepened and increased. There is a new
courage and generosity in serving God, new hope, new certainty of
the Divine Reality and victory. The mind is freed to discover new
meaning in things. The heart explores new realms of praise. At the
same time, there is a heightened sense of personal sinfulness and of
one's need for even deeper healing in God. The dissipation of ecstatic
consciousness leaves the God-seeker restless, dissatisfied, longing
for deeper transformation in the power of the Breath.

As ecstatic states grow in duration and frequency, they are
transformed into rapture. In rapture, ecstasy is abrupt, unpredictable, and increasingly prolonged. Teresa is again concrete and vivid:

The advantage rapture has over union is great. The
rapture produces much stronger effects and causes many
other phenomena. Union seems the same at the beginning,
in the middle, and at the end; and it takes place in the interior
of the soul. But since these other phenomena are of a higher
degree, they produce their effect both interiorly and ex-
teriorly. . . . In these raptures it seems that the soul is not
animating the body. Thus there is a very strong feeling that
the natural bodily heat is failing it. The body gradually grows

cold, although this happens with the greatest ease and delight. At this stage there is no remedy that can be used to resist. In the union, since we are upon our earth, there is a remedy; though it may take pain and effort one can almost always resist. But in these raptures most often there is no remedy; rather, without any forethought or any help there frequently comes a force so swift and powerful that one sees and feels this cloud or mighty eagle raise it up and carry it aloft on its wings.[49]

The God-seeker is now deeply wounded with love, longing for total union, increasingly appalled at personal weakness and sinfulness. John of the Cross describes the anguish that cessation of rapt union brings:

Where have You hidden,
Beloved, and left me moaning?
You fled like the stag
After wounding me;
I went out calling You, and You were gone.

Shepherds, you that go
Up through the sheepfolds to the hill,
If by chance you see
Him I love most,
Tell Him that I sicken, suffer, and die. . . .

How do you endure
O life, not living where you live?
And being brought near death
By the arrows you receive
From that which you conceive of your Beloved.

Why, since You wounded
This heart, don't You heal it?
And why, since You stole it from me,
Do you leave it so,
And fail to carry off what you have stolen?[50]

As mystical awareness intensifies, therefore, it sets the feet of the God-seeker on the ascending path of the seven-storey mountain of purgative suffering. It is the Calvary of the mystic.

The Dark Nights of Faith, Hope, and Love

Evelyn Underhill suggests that the dark nights of faith, hope, and love that are the normal concomitant of introduction into the higher states of mystical awareness find their psychological explanation in the fatigue and lassitude that is the normal psychic result of intense concentration. She observes: "When the higher centers have been submitted to the continuous strain of a developed illuminative life, with its accompanying periods of intense fervour, lucidity, deep contemplation—perhaps visionary and auditive phenomena—the swing back into the negative state occurs almost of necessity."[51] The mystics certainly attribute some of their suffering to natural weakness. But they also speak of a new confrontation with the shadow. Unhealed disorders of the heart, especially paralyzing anxieties, now stand glaringly revealed in the growing intensity of mystical light. The feeling of sinking back from ecstatic wholeness to a chaos of natural and sinful impulses rends the heart with bitter anguish. John of the Cross witnesses to the suffering of the night of the spirit in the moving terms of one who has known its full impact.

> Since this divine contemplation assails him somewhat forcibly in order to subdue and strengthen his soul he suffers so much in his weakness that he almost dies, particularly at times when the light is most powerful. Both the sense and the spirit, as though under an immense and dark load, undergo such agony and pain that the soul would consider death a relief. . . . The divine extreme is the purgative contemplation and the human extreme is the soul, the receiver of this contemplation. Since the divine extreme strikes in order to renew the soul and divinize it (by stripping it of the habitual affections and properties of the old man to which it is strongly united, attached, and conformed), it so disentangles and dissolves the spiritual substance—absorbing it in a profound darkness—that the soul at the sight of its miseries feels that it is melting away and being undone by a cruel spiritual death; it feels as if it were swallowed by a beast and being digested in the dark belly, and it suffers an anguish comparable to Jonas's when in the belly of the whale (Jon. 2:1–3). It is fitting that the soul be in this sepulcher of dark death in order that it attain the spiritual resurrection for which it hopes.[52]

Moreover, in addition to periods of lassitude following upon rapt and ecstatic states, John of the Cross seems to envisage longer periods of intense darkness and abandonment in which the God-seeker wrestles with personal demons. During such times, the only positive sign of the presence of God may be the mystic's inability to despair.

These periods of intense dryness and desolation have, however, a creative purpose: to wean the mystic from attachment to any reality that is not finally God. They free the heart from the remnant of any need to approach God via ego-consciousness, even via an ego-consciousness that is charismatically transformed. The weaning process involves two distinct moments. As the grace of contemplative union deepens, the mystic must learn total detachment from affective graces, visions, revelations, locutions. In periods of deflation, depression, and disorientation, one must cling in cliff-hanging faith to a God whose absence is keenly and painfully felt. It is the dark night of faith.

The dark night of hope effects a healing of the memory deeper and more efficacious than anything experienced earlier during the dark night of sense. In the night of sense, the healing of memories mediates, as we have seen, the healthy growth of ego-consciousness and its charismatic transformation in faith. But in the dark night of the spirit, the God-seeker is being asked to die to ego-consciousness itself. If then (s)he is to advance to the highest forms of mystical prayer, (s)he must not only be purified of any sinful residue from the dark night of sense but also of any anxiety that would lead the heart to cling for security to the past. Personal liberation from anxious attachment to any concrete good whatever that is not God is what John means by the dark night of love.[53]

Mystical Betrothal and Mystical Marriage

As memory, understanding, desire, are pneumatically transformed through the graces of contemplative union, the infused knowing that is loving intensifies and deepens. As it does so, it yields a new and mysterious kind of self-awareness born of transformation in the reciprocity of divine love. Christian mystics speak of two distinguishable stages of advanced contemplative union: mystical betrothal and mystical marriage.

John of the Cross was fond of assimilating the night of the senses to the twilight of mystical experience and the night of the spirit to its midnight. But he also insisted that midnight is only the prelude to a new dawn. Through the mystical midnight of faith, hope, and love the God-seeker is delivered from paralyzing and constricting anxieties that bar total union with God. As the passive, purifying healing progresses, the heart knows a season of increasing tranquillity, contemplative enlightenment, and peace. Anguished longing for an absent God and the complaints of apparently neglected love yield to longer periods of contemplative delight in divine union. There begins a gentle, loving interchange in prayer between God and the newly cleansed God-seeker. The latter, however, still knows times of divine withdrawal and its concomitant personal confusion and depression. But the mystic is now more sensibly aware that personal fears and imperfections are in the process of being passively healed through the fire of love. It is the time of mystical betrothal.[54]

Throughout the period of betrothal, contemplative union intensifies. Rapture and ecstasy are less traumatic, diminish in frequency. As the mystic sinks deeper and deeper into the mystery of divine love, betrothal gives place to the mystical marriage. John describes this culminating state of divine union in the following terms:

> This spiritual marriage is incomparably greater than the spiritual espousal, for it is a total transformation in the Beloved in which each surrenders the entire possession of self to the other with a certain consummation of the union of love. The soul thereby becomes divine, becomes God through participation, insofar as is possible in this life. And thus I think that this state never occurs without the soul's being confirmed in grace, for the faith of both is confirmed when God's faith in the soul is here confirmed. It is accordingly the highest state attainable in this life.[55]

It is a period of perfect love and perfect peace. Growth in virtue is experienced as God-given, God-wrought. It is a season of abiding, mutual surrender in love. In a theologically suggestive passage Teresa describes the process by which the God-seeker passes from betrothal to marriage:

> It is brought into this Mansion by means of an intellectual vision, in which by a representation of the truth in a particular way, the Most Holy Trinity reveals Itself, in all three Persons. First of all the spirit becomes enkindled and is illumined, as it were, by a cloud of the greatest brightness. It sees these three Persons, individually, and yet, by a wonderful kind of knowledge which is given to it, the soul realizes that most certainly and truly all these three Persons are one Substance and one Power and one knowledge and one God alone; so that what we hold by faith the soul may be said here

to grasp by sight, although nothing is seen by the eyes, either of the body or of the soul, for it is no imaginary vision. Here all three Persons communicate Themselves to the soul and speak to the soul and explain to it those words which the Gospel attributes to the Lord—namely, that He and the Father and the Holy Spirit will come to dwell with the soul which loves Him and keeps His commandments.[56]

In mystical marriage conscious union with God has ceased to be intermittent. Periods of desolation and abandonment all but cease, although suffering remains. But it too has become all love. Nor are ego functions totally suspended. The mystic may know seasons when the "faculties" are clearly functioning in purely natural ways. But despite all such experiences, the self knows at its deepest center a union with God in peace that is unbroken, undisturbed. Self-forgetfulness, joy in suffering, perfect detachment, a responsiveness to every touch of Divine Love—these are the fruits of mystical marriage. There is a growing longing for death as final and total transformation in God.

Mystical betrothal and mystical marriage are the sixth and seventh of Teresa's mansions. She speaks of no others. But before we attempt to reflect on the meaning of mystical death and rebirth, two preliminary reflections on this final state of mystical union are in order. First, an important practical test of the authenticity of divine union even in the seventh mansion is humility, knowledge of one's need and sinfulness without God, and active dedication to the service of others in deeds of love. In a very real sense, then, when the Christian mystic reaches the center of the interior castle, (s)he is transported back onto the streets in zealous dedication to the practical service of God in others. But service has become God's own action in the God-Seeker.

Second, as the God-seeker is lovingly transformed in the grace of contemplative union, (s)he grows in the capacity to view the world with God's own eyes. The Christian mystic broods over creation with the same compassionate, forgiving love as the God whose response to the problem of evil is to take its pain lovingly unto Himself. At no point, then, does Christian mysticism take one out of this world. Rather it binds the heart of the mystic to creation with the unshakeable fidelity of a God whose redemptive love for a sinful humanity is guaranteed by His inability to deny Himself.[57]

The Meaning of Christian Mysticism

Any attempt to understand the meaning of mysticism must begin with the human subject of mystical experience. Two pioneering investigations of the psychodynamics of mystical experience are William James's essay on mysticism in *The Varieties of Religious Experience* and Joseph Maréchal's *Studies in the Psychology of the Mystics*.

In the *Varieties*, James characterizes mystical experience as a passive, transient, noetic state whose specific character is ineffable.[58] When measured against the experience of the Christian mystics, his description needs nuancing at almost every point.

First of all, it is possible to exaggerate the ineffability of mystical experience. The Christian mystics all attest to the fact that the higher graces of mystical prayer are a direct confrontation with the divine mystery and defy direct description in categories derived from ego processes. But while the grace of contemplative union can never be adequately characterized in the images and abstractions of ego-awareness, it is not beyond all characterization whatever.

To say that in infused contemplation the love born of faith in God intensifies to the point where it becomes a form of knowledge in its own right is to articulate an important characteristic of Christian mystical experience and one that differentiates it from other forms of knowing. Moreover, as we have just seen, it is also possible to offer some account of the stages through which this new mystical awareness normally moves. One can speak too of the human preconditions that must be met if one is to begin the ascent of the mystic spiral. One can investigate the psychic underpinnings of mystical growth. And one can examine its personal and social consequences. In other words, while there is a dimension of mystical consciousness that eludes direct description, there is much that can and should be said about the development of mystical contemplation.

Second, the "transient" character of mystical experience to which James alludes also needs qualification. For while transiency characterizes the early stages of the growth of mystical consciousness, those rare individuals who penetrate into the seventh mansion speak of an abiding, habitual awareness of God.

Third, the "noetic" character of authentic Christian mysticism also needs precision and qualification. Neo-Platonic mysticism, being Greek and intellectual, spoke of mystical encounter in terms of *noesis*. And in its earliest formulations Christian mystical theology was profoundly influenced by the Neo-Platonism of the Fathers and by the Neo-Platonized mysticism of Pseudo-Dionysus. But over the centuries the experience of the Christian mystics themselves gradually reshaped Neo-Platonic language to fit the unique character of Christian God-consciousness. The contemplative flight of the soul to noetic union with the divine described in Neo-Platonic piety was gradually replaced in Christian mystical literature by the identification of contemplative knowledge with the knowing that is loving.

Finally, the passive character of mystical consciousness also needs qualification. For while the Christian mystics discover in the early stages of mystical experience a new kind of passivity before God, in describing contemplation, mystical betrothal, and mystical marriage they use the language of reciprocity rather than the language of mere passivity. The latter better characterizes recollection and quiet. Moreover, the Christian mystics insist that an authentic encounter with God bears fruit in active deeds of love.

James's conclusions concerning the meaning of mystical consciousness are also in need of qualification.[59] He correctly insists that the very existence of mystical states calls into question "the authority of the non-mystical or rationalistic consciousness." Mysticism does indeed provide evidence that ego-consciousness is not the ultimate or even the best way to know God. But mysticism does more than invite us to an irrational leap into the contemplative dark. For a careful reading of the Christian mystics reveals a subtle interplay within their religious experience between infused contemplation in the strict sense and charismatically transformed ego processes, an interplay that is, as we shall see, rich in foundational suggestion.

Moreover, there is also need to qualify James's proposal that the experiences of the mystics have absolute authority only for the person who undergoes them but can oblige no one else to consent uncritically to their reality and meaning. The great Christian mystics testify that certain experiences of God are self-validating. But their personal reaction to their own experiences is anything but uncritical. They are careful to probe and test the authenticity of their transports against the discerning opinions of others, to submit the doctrinal content of their experiences to the judgment of the Christian community acting in union with its leaders, and to employ the best available insight to the workings of the human psyche in order to evaluate the human variables that condition growth in God-consciousness.

The critical student of the mystics who approaches their writings in openness and humility can, moreover, find in their lives and in their works a summons to repentance and to faith that is touched with divine authority. When illumined by their personal testimony and by the action of the Mother Advocate, their example and witness can, then, function within the religious experience of another person either as an initial summons to faith or as a call from God to deepen in the faith one already professes.

If the insights of William James into the meaning of mysticism are in need of foundational qualification, so too is the mystical psychology of Joseph Maréchal.[60]

In attempting to explain the meaning of Christian mysticism Maréchal appeals, predictably enough, to his own theory of the natural dynamism of the intellect to know all being. That theory presupposes the interpretative adequacy of Thomistic faculty psychology and Thomistic formal object analysis. Since an emergent Christian anthropology rejects both with all their works and pomps, a foundational theology of the human will have to find a different explanatory hypothesis for interpreting the significance of Christian mysticism. An alternative approach, and one that is rich in foundational suggestion is that proposed by R. C. Zaehner.

The Varieties of Mystical Experience

Zaehner's *Mysticism, Sacred and Profane* is a vigorous protest against approaching mystical experience with bland, muddle-headed syncretism. He attempts to distinguish several varieties of mysticism: (1) psychosis masquerading as mystical encounter; (2) drug-induced mysticism; (3) nature mysticism; (4) a solipsistic mysticism of self-discipline; (5) and an authentic mysticism of encounter.[61]

Mystical psychosis is counterfeit mysticism. It is a manic state rooted in unacknowledged, unhealed affective disorder. As the psychotic ego disintegrates, it is increasingly victimized by its own illusions. Hallucinations, a compulsive sense of divine vocation, morbid fascination with bizarre religious rites and practices, are among the aberrations mystical madness breeds. These pseudo-religious phenomena are, moreover, accompanied by the pathological symptoms of personality dysfunction described in Chapter III.[62]

Psychotic mysticism can be embellished by a broad variety of fantasies that are purely natural in origin. Zaehner discovers four clusters of beliefs and images common in religious psychosis:

> (1) an intense communion with Nature in which subject and object seem identical. . . .
> (2) the abdication of the ego to another centre, the "self" of Jungian psychology;
> (3) a return to a state of innocence and the consequent sense that the subject of the experience has passed beyond good and evil. . . .
> (4) the complete certainty that the soul is immortal, and that death is therefore at least irrelevant and at most a ludicrous impossibility.[63]

As we shall see, these images and concepts can occur in other contexts and need not be symptomatic of religious psychosis. Zaehner is, however, correct in contrasting all of the aforementioned experiences with those described by Christian mystics. The closest analogue to authentic Christian mysticism is, perhaps, the second. But while Christian mystics invoke archetypes of the ego and of the self in their efforts to explain their experiences to others, they also insist that the self-discovery that transpires in infused contemplation transcends the kinds of psychic growth processes described by Jung. In the final analysis, infused contemplation, mystical betrothal, and mystical marriage instantiate forms of cognition unknown to Jungian personality theory. Nor can such experiences be reduced to the images the mystics use to describe them.

Drug mysticism is the artificial manipulation of ego processes through the use of hallucinogens. Appropriate drugs can indeed effect the relaxation of conscious, rational ego functions and stimulate a variety of conscious fantasies. Moreover, the use of drugs for allegedly religious purposes can be and often is, as Zaehner suggests, a coping device, a way of escaping from a world that is overwhelming and unmanageable. To the extent that its use is symptomatic of an inability to deal with one's environment in realistic ways, it is destructive and often is symptomatic of more or less pathological tendencies.

The normal effect of drugs is, moreover, to endow a perfectly trivial experience with an illusory sense of religious importance. Zaehner, for example, analyzes Julian Huxley's description of his mescalin experiences in *The Doors of Perception* and concludes that the drug led Huxley to mistake the vivid apperception of his flannel trousers draped over the back of his chair for an experience of the beatific vision.[64]

There is, of course, a legitimate clinical use of hallucinogens for therapeutic purposes. And there seem to be cases on record in which the use of drugs has helped a person of religious bent to traverse an emotional barrier to personal growth and development. Such positive experiences are, however, more the exception than the rule. And the indiscriminate use of drugs as a religious panacea has reduced more than one young brain to cottage cheese and plunged more than one life into a vortex of despair.

Nature mysticism is the peak experience of an inflated natural ego. In his study of the healthy personality,[65] Abraham Maslow found that the healthy ego knows with some regularity seasons of conscious self-transcendence. No one lives, of course, at an uninterrupted conscious "peak." And Maslow's mature theory envisages the alternation of peaks and plateaus in the growth of a healthy ego.

Peak experiences yield a sense of detachment from ordinary, day-to-day problems and concerns. There is a diminished sense of space and time. Peaks seem to be self-validating. They induce a feeling of passivity in the face of reality: a sense of mystery, of awe, of reverence, of humility, of surrender. They bring freedom from anxiety and inhibition. And they tend to produce permanently beneficial effects upon the personality.

Not every peak experience has a religious character. The sense of wonder and of mystery is not identical with the sense of God. Natural peaks are positive experiences. They seem to occur when a healthy ego is attuned to the sympathetic affections that form the matrix of its life and growth. Religious peaks, as we have seen, bespeak a healthy ego attuned to the beauty of the divine.[66]

Here four points should be observed. First, peak experiences are an event in the growth of ego-consciousness. When that event transpires in a context of living faith, it assumes a charismatic character. But even charismatic peaks fall short of the graces of infused contemplation described by the Christian mystics.

Second, natural peaks reflect the bias of individual egos. One may, for example, differentiate introverted and extraverted peaks. In the natural introverted peak, the ego seems to encompass the universe by its spontaneous personal thoughts and feelings. Emerson, for example, who was a notorious introvert, believed for a time that in moments of scientific and artistic creativity, the whole of cosmic reality was mysteriously encompassed within the subjectivity of the individual creative genius. In the natural, extraverted peak, by contrast, the ego seems to be emptied out into its sustaining environment. It and the world it loves fuse into an "objective" identity.

Third, natural peaks should be termed "visionary" rather than "mystical," if by mystical one means the graces of higher contemplation. For like the ego-self dialogue described by Jung, natural peaks are the fruit of normal psychic growth processes and, unlike infused contemplative prayer, fail to escape the confines and hazards of ego-awareness.

Fourth, natural, visionary peaks can instantiate ego-inflation. They can, therefore, be a source of cruel self-deception and, when religious, can provide hypocritically pious rationalizations for destructive, unacknowledged neurotic and psychotic tendencies. Such is especially the case in peaks that create the Gnostic illusion of essential innocence and of moral omnipotence. The visionary who is convinced that inflated personal dreams yield escape from ordinary moral restraint is a dangerous Raskolnikov.

It should be clear from the preceding analysis that the experiences of infused contemplation described by the Christian mystics are of an order different from psychosis, from the artificial manipulation of ego-consciousness through the use of drugs, or from the experiences of a peaking or inflated ego. True enough, the Christian mystics do describe charismatic experiences that accompany the grace of contemplation and that are ego-based: feelings, visions, locutions, revelations. But we must postpone any discussion of the relation between contemplative and charismatic forms of knowing until we have reached a preliminary insight into the uniqueness of Christian contemplation. To do so we must explore the yogic quest for freedom and immortality.

The Yogic Quest

There is a strain of oriental mysticism that seeks to liberate self-awareness from every natural, ego-based impulse. The instrument of liberation is yogic meditation and asceticism. Among the experiences described by yogins is, moreover, a wordless, imageless, aconceptual form of self-awareness that is the fruit of a disciplined assault upon all conscious and unconscious ego processes. Zaehner is correct to note that yogic self-discovery may or may not be overtly theistic in character. He describes the activity of the earliest yogins in the following terms:

> . . . though they had no clear idea of the nature of God, they knew that it was the business of the soul to isolate itself from *prakrti* or Nature which, with its three qualities of goodness, passion, and darkness, its attractions and repulsions, desires and hates, is plainly the same thing as Jung's collective unconscious. Their technique would seem to be explicitly designed with a view to shutting out the unconscious and all its works, including the "partial autonomous complex" which appears as the "God-archetype." By isolating consciousness from all contact with the unconscious they sought to realize their eternal essence, the "second self" which Proust discovered and which is so often dormant for such prolonged periods. The Muslims who had a very much clearer idea of God, did precisely the same. "What distinguishes the Sufis from all the others I have mentioned," says the tenth-century Sufi, Al-Sarraj, "is that they abandon what does not concern them and cut off every attachment which separates them from the object of their quest; and

they have no object of quest and desire except God Most High." "And they asked Junayd, 'What is Sufism?' and he replied, 'That you should be with God and free from attachment.' " The operative words are, of course, "with God"; for as Jung rightly points out, to empty the consciousness of all content is only to invite seven devils in from the unconscious. The possibility of God filling the vacuum can only be entertained if the soul has been wholly purged from sin; and this, in effect, is what Bhagavad-Gita and indeed all the major Hindu ascetical classics recommend. It is perfectly possible that the ecstasy experienced by the Yogin or Vedantin may in some cases be a genuine experience of union with God; for his intention is, in fact, the elimination of sin, or, in psychological parlance, the suppression of the whole contents of the unconscious. Thus the mere fact that he obtains a complete stillness of soul, irrespective of whether that stillness is the peace that passeth all understanding mentioned by St. Paul, shows that the "lower" soul of which the collective unconscious would appear to be the most substantial part, can in fact be suppressed, repressed, eliminated for good. Mystical religion proper, then, shows that the mystical state at which the religious man aims is the reverse of the natural mystical experience: it is the cutting off of one's ties with the world, the settling in quietness in one's own immortal soul, and finally the offering of that soul up to its Maker. The first stage is that to which the monist aspires: the second lies beyond and appears only to be attainable with the active help of God Who is felt to be other than the immortal soul.[67]

What Zaehner is suggesting is, then, that yogic meditation can lead one to two very different kinds of experience. The conscious transcendence of ego-functions can produce a theistic encounter with a Reality that transcends the yogi. But yogic contemplation can also yield merely an ego-transcending experience of self-isolation, nothing more. In such a solipsistic mysticism, there is a systematic emptying of the mind of specific ideas or images. There is a sense of liberation and of peace. There is apathetic detachment and separation from the things of space and time. There is a feeling of personal purification and wholeness. There may even be a healing of ego-based neurosis and anxiety. But there is no encounter with God. There is the discovery of a horizon of consciousness that transcends the particular, differentiated horizons that structure ego-consciousness. Moreover, the solipsistic yogi seems quite content with such an experience and knows no driving, spontaneous impulse to go beyond it.

We observe in passing that the very existence of solipsistic mysticism would seem to call into question the whole concept of the supernatural existential. As an expansion of the formal object of the intellect, the supernatural existential is the subjective component of Rahner's transcendental deduction a priori of the conditions for the possibility for divine self-revelation in the Word-made-flesh. It first postulates the natural thrust of the intellect to know the triune God. Then it expands the horizon of the intellect by an infused, non-salvific grace whose purpose is to save Neo-Thomism from crypto-Pelagianism.

The conclusions of any transcendental deduction a priori that is truly worth its salt are in principle necessary and universal. A single exception calls the theory and its method into question. If, then, the theory of the supernatural existential is a sound one, it should be impossible to transcend consciously the particular horizons of ego-cognition to an explicit awareness of the general cognitive horizon within which all ego processes transpire without discovering in that most general of all horizons a spontaneous impulse to know the God who is Being and to know Him in Christ.

Solipsistic mysticism would in fact seem to explicate the horizon of knowing within which both conscious and unconscious ego functions transpire. But to the embarrassment of transcendental method, it finds there neither Maréchal's dynamism of the intellect to know God nor Rahner's supernatural impulse to know Christ.

More directly to the point, however, Christian mysticism stands in dramatic contrast to a solipsistic mysticism of self-isolation by being a mysticism of loving encounter. The Holy Breath enters the experience of the Christian mystic as a power of love that burns away the disorder and sinfulness in the mystic's heart. She rearranges the mystic's personality, sometimes at the price of great pain. And She so transforms the person of the mystic that love becomes the mystic's way of knowing God and the world. In the early stages of this process of transformation the Christian mystic must learn passive docility to the Mother Advocate. But as the Christian contemplative advances to mystical betrothal and marriage, docility is transformed into a reciprocity of love, an intimate exchange between the Divine Lover and the beloved. Finally, in the culminating stages of infused contemplation, the Christian mystic bends over the broken world with something akin to Christ's own loving, compassionate desire to suffer with

creation in its wretchedness and sin and by the mysterious power of
loving endurance to encompass and overcome the mystery of iniquity
by following the strategy of the cross. Such experiences are simply
absent from a solipsistic mysticism of withdrawal.

Moreover, as Zaehner also observes, the latter gives no evidence
of being anything other than a natural state of consciousness achieved
through vigorous self-discipline. The Christian mystics, by contrast,
all insist that infused contemplation is something that God does to the
mystic. It is an experience that no natural asceticism can produce or
counterfeit.

But if Christian mysticism differs from a natural solipsistic mysticism by being a mysticism of loving encounter, it differs from
theistic forms of yogic meditation in other significant respects. Here
the work of Mircea Eliade is especially illuminating. In his perceptive
study of the varieties of yogic mysticism, Eliade articulates the four
"kinetic ideas" that lie at the heart of Indian spirituality:

> (1) The law of universal causality, which connects man
> with the cosmos and condemns him to transmigrate indefi-
> nitely. This is the law of *karma*.
> (2) The mysterious process that engenders and main-
> tains the cosmos and, in so doing, makes possible the "eter-
> nal return" of existences. This is *maya*, cosmic illusion,
> endured (even worse—accorded validity) by man as long as
> he is blinded by ignorance (*avidya*).
> (3) Absolute reality, "situated" somewhere beyond the
> cosmic illusion woven by *maya* and beyond human experi-
> ence as conditioned by *karma*; pure Being, the Absolute, by
> whatever name it may be called—the Self (*atman*),
> *brahman*, the unconditioned, the transcendent, the immor-
> tal, the indestructible, *nirvana*, etc.
> (4) The means of attaining to Being, the effectual tech-
> niques for gaining liberation. This corpus of means consti-
> tutes Yoga properly speaking.[68]

In other words, the religious hopes of yogic mysticism are profoundly shaped by the myth of the "eternal return." That myth lends
interpretative structure to yogic experience and endows it with a very
specific soteriology, one that contradicts Christian hope and faith in a
number of key respects.

In the myth of the eternal return, the cosmos is imagined along
vaguely Platonic lines. There is a spiritual, celestial archetype that
provides the eternal pattern for the material, terrestrial shape of

things, especially those shapes imbued with sacred significance.

The zone of the sacred is, moreover, the zone of Absolute Reality. Since the Absolute is imagined as eternally creative, religious contact with it is felt as a regression to cosmic origins, as a recreation of the world in the power of the Absolute, through the performance of paradigmatic ritual acts.[69]

In the myth of the eternal return, the ritual re-creation of the world is also the re-creation of time. It often marks the beginning of each new year. Implicit, therefore, in the myth is a specific view of history. It presents time as cyclic. Time turns back upon its own point of origin. It is the ring snake of the Great Mother, the eternal serpent swallowing his tail.[70]

Eliade contrasts the image of cyclic time inculcated by the myth of the eternal return with the imaginative view of history inculcated by the Judaeo-Christian tradition. Yahweh enters the pages of the Hebrew Scriptures as the Lord of history. His saving acts occur, not in mythic, but in real time. As Eliade observes:

> This God of the Jewish people is no longer an Oriental divinity, creator of archetypal gestures, but a personality who ceaselessly intervenes in history, who reveals his will through events (invasions, sieges, battles, and so on). Historical facts thus become "situations" of man in respect to God, and as such they acquire a religious value that nothing had previously been able to confer on them. It may, then, be said with truth that the Hebrews were the first to discover the meaning of history as the epiphany of God, and this conception, as we should expect, was taken up and amplified by Christianity.[71]

In Judaeo-Christian religion, therefore, time does not bend back upon itself. It moves forward to the goal set for it by the Lord of history. This shift in the mythic understanding of time, which would seem to be unique to Judaeo-Christian religious aspiration, provides, as we have in part already seen, a novel interpretative context in which mythic and archetypal images are theologically transvalued.

The victories of the Babylonian kings were, for example, as Ricoeur has correctly observed, interpreted by Babylonian myth as the restoration of the hegemony of the benign creator god over the powers of chaos and disorder. Military victory, therefore, restored a threatened cosmic order. It was a return to the scheme established at the beginning.

But for the devout Hebrew, the victories of God's people advanced history itself toward the final accomplishment of God's saving plan. For in Judaeo-Christian piety, the re-creation of the world, the restoration of lost innocence, lies not in some mythic past that must be eternally and nostalgically recaptured, but in the end time that is coming and that is even now in process of being realized.

Every religion, as Eliade suggests, has to deal with the "terror of history," with the fact that time moves inexorably toward death, leaving in its wake shattered hopes and empty, unrealized dreams. The terror of history is the perpetual perishing of things, it is the precariousness of human life, it is the mystery of futile suffering and oppression, it is the apparent victory of the forces of iniquity.[72]

Where time is viewed as a cyclic process, salvation lies either in nostalgia or in escape, either in the illusory attempt to recapture a vanished past or in a religious strategy of liberation from the terror of death and from the frustration and misery that haunt human existence. Babylonian religion opted for the first solution. Yogic piety, whether theistic or not, chose the latter path. Eliade puts the matter succinctly.

> According to the Indian conception, every man is born with a debt, but with freedom to contract new debts. His existence forms a long series of payments and borrowings, the account of which is not always obvious. A man not totally devoid of intelligence can serenely tolerate the sufferings, griefs, and blows that come to him, the injustices of which he is the object, because each of them solves a karmic equation that had remained unsolved in some previous existence. Naturally, Indian speculation very early sought and discovered means through which man can free himself from this endless chain of cause-effect-cause, and so on, determined by the law of karma. But such solutions do nothing to invalidate the meaning of suffering; on the contrary, they strengthen it. Like Yoga, Buddhism sets out from the principle that all existence is pain, and it offers the possibility of a concrete and final way of escape from this unbroken succession of sufferings to which, in the last analysis, every human life can be reduced. But Buddhism, like Yoga, and indeed like every other Indian method of winning liberation, never for a moment casts any doubt upon the "normality" of pain. As to Vedanta, for it suffering is "illusory" only insofar as the whole universe is illusory; neither the human experience of suffering nor the universe is a reality in the ontological sense of the word.[73]

But for the Christian, there is no salvation either in nostalgia or in the flight from history. Some nostalgia is, of course, only pleasant fantasy. But when nostalgia is absolutized to a religious creed, it betrays unhealed anxiety and fear. For when confronted with the terror of history, religious nostalgia clings in false security to a vanished past. It knows nothing of the dark night of hope. The Christian summons to repentance demands, however, that all such fears be acknowledged and submitted to transformation in the dark nights of sense and of spirit. For only then can human hope begin to expand to God's own future.

Equally unacceptable to Christian piety is the identification of salvation with escape from historical entanglement. For in the final analysis, such a soteriology divorces saving enlightenment from unconditioned commitment to this sinful world in the image of a crucified God. It is the Gnostic fallacy. Authentic Christian enlightenment is, by contrast, the knowing that is the love of atonement. It binds one to the world with the passion of the crucified Christ.

Moreover, a soteriology of escape presents the abolition of ego-consciousness as the key to liberation from the illusory circle of time. The suggestion, as we shall see, does not lack for insight. For there is an intimate connection between ego processes and the temporal structure of experience. But authentic Christian mysticism assumes a different stance toward both history and cognition. The Christian exodus to eternal life is a passage through history that is itself the experience of graced, pneumatic transformation in God.

Salvation and Time

In a suggestive essay on the meaning of salvation history, Karl Rahner has attempted to describe the complex relationship that obtains between sacred and profane history. Sacred and secular history are not, he insists, simply identical. Salvation history transpires within world history. It endows secular history with a meaning the latter does not of itself possess. Sacred history envisages the eventual abolition of secular history through an act of God that is as salvifically decisive as the resurrection of Jesus, but cosmic in its scope and in its effects. But for the Christian salvation history is a real process, and it is happening even now. It occurs whenever human lives are pneumatically transformed through openness to God in faith. The reality of salvation history can itself, then, be grasped adequately only in faith; for unless one is experiencing personal transformation in God, it will be difficult to recognize the same process in others or to enter deeply into its meaning.[74]

In an emergent Christian anthropology, history is itself the emergence and development of ego processes. For ego processes are, as we have seen, irreducibly spatio-temporal in their structure.

But if history is the development of ego processes, then salvation history is nothing else than its charismatic transformation. For until ego processes are subsumed into the transforming power of the Holy Breath, their evaluative form is either natural or sinful. Natural history is the growth of an ego whose evaluative form is untouched by God-consciousness. The history of sin is the dark side of salvation history. For sin-consciousness presupposes an awareness of God.

If the preceding reflections are sound, Jesus stands revealed as the Lord of history precisely in His mediation of the Pentecostal Gift-Giver. Jesus did not come to mediate the Holy Breath for the first time. She had been active in great charismatic leaders of the old dispensation: in Moses, in the prophets, in all the divinely anointed leaders of God's people. In Jesus, however, Her charismatic anointing is made universally available to all. It is, then, through the charismatic action of the breath of Jesus and through no other means that the whole of human history begins to be able to take on positive salvific significance. Oriental mysticism offers no such hope.

By the same token, the sending of the Advocate also creates the possibility of confrontation within history between the divine Breath and the dark forces of Anti-Christ. Anti-Christ is a counterfeit, charismatic impulse. Anti-Christ is the angel of darkness pretending to be the angel of light in order to lead astray even the chosen ones of God.

The activity of Anti-Christ is, then, Satanic. It tests the heart of each believer. Only those who are discerning enough to recognize and reject the forces of Anti-Christ are, then, truly moved by the Holy Breath of God.

Jesus in His second coming will, moreover, break the power of Anti-Christ for He will then also bring to an end the need for charismatic, propositionally mediated, sacramental access to God. The struggle between the Advocate and Anti-Christ is, then, the historical struggle between belief and unbelief, between authentic docility to the Advocate and destructive ego-inflated piety. That struggle engages the living Church in Jesus' own confrontation with Satan and with the principalities and powers of this world.

But while the children of God must stand in opposition to false mysticism, to pseudo-prophets, to inauthentic charismatics, and to demonic, diabolical, and oppressive forces in human society, they must themselves stand in lifelong openness to the charismatic and contemplative anointings of the Holy Breath. For it is through their response to Her authentic charismatic impulses that the saints of God are historically and sacramentally revealed.

In *Charism and Sacrament* I attempt to show that the charisms of the Breath are integral to the primordial sacramentality of the Church.[75] There is no need to repeat that argument here. Here it suffices to note that in mediating the divine Gift-Giver, Jesus reveals God's desire to sacramentalize every aspect of human ego-consciousness and thereby to render the whole of human history instinct with religious meaning it does not otherwise possess.

If, however, the preceding reflections are sound, the ego-death that marks the transition from charismatic to contemplative prayer is the dividing line between a God-consciousness that is historically, charismatically, and sacramentally mediated and a God-consciousness that is unitive, abiding, "atemporal." Here, however, if one is to avoid the Quietist fallacy, it is important to recognize the continuities that bind together contemplative prayer on the one hand and charismatic and sacramental prayer on the other.

Yogic mysticism offers the hope of liberation from a temporal process that is fraught with pain and illusion as well as ultimately purposeless and devoid of real significance. Even the rituals of tantric yoga and the mission of the compassionate bodhisattva have no other purpose.[76] Christian mysticism too offers the God-seeker the hope of eventually transcending the spatio-temporal functions of the ego even when they have been charismatically and sacramentally transformed in the power of the Holy Breath. But authentic Christian mysticism poses no false option between graced ego-awareness and mystical transcendence. Rather it preserves charismatic and sacramental piety on the one hand and infused contemplative consciousness on the other in graced, dynamic tension. Let us reflect on how this occurs.

Medieval theology distinguished quite correctly between two different kinds of charismatic anointing. The *dona Spiritus Sancti*, or seven gifts of the Holy Breath, were described as "sanctifying" and were opposed to the *gratiae gratis datae*, that is, to the Pauline charisms. The latter were described as being divinely given, not for personal sanctification, but for the upbuilding of the community.[77]

In *Charism and Sacrament* I have suggested that the gifts of sanctification can be legitimately interpreted as the pneumatic transformation of natural moral conversion.[78] These matters were discussed in Chapter VII. To grow in holiness is to put on the mind of Jesus. To put on His mind is to consent in the power of the Breath to the religio-ethical vision He proclaimed and to its lived consequences. To live in obedience to the new covenant is to serve others in faith. Authentic charismatic piety is, then, a school of love because it makes the measure of one's love for God the loving service of others in a community of atonement, forgiveness, and worship.

Authentic charismatic piety also demands in a preliminary way the death and penumatic transformation of the natural ego. Growth in charismatic piety is inaugurated by repentance and conversion. Repentance is a form of ego-death. It is confrontation with the pent-up demonic forces that infest and bind one's own heart. It demands reconciliation with those who reflect my own sinful, shadow self. But repentance is the prelude to conversion. And conversion bears fruit, as we have seen, in the pneumatic transformation of appreciative consciousness, in the charismatic gracing of the inferential ego, and in the conscious ordering of one's life in conformity to the demands of new covenant religion.

There is, moreover, a very real sense in which the ethics proclaimed by Jesus is an ethics of dying and rising. The most basic form of ego-consciousness is body-consciousness. But in new covenant ethics the most basic test of faith is the freedom to share the physical supports of bodily life with others, even when sharing means that one lacks necessities oneself. Christian sharing submits bodily cravings, then, to the obedience of faith. And faith can on occasion demand the sacrifice even of one's body in martyrdom.

As we have shown in *Charism and Sacrament*, the sacramental system ritualizes the commitment demanded by authentic charismatic piety. The sacraments too are a school of love and a school for the initial death and transformation of ego-consciousness. The dark night of sense is the natural fruit of authentic charismatic and sacramental piety. As the love born of fidelity to the sacraments and openness to the gifts intensifies, it is gradually transformed into the contemplative knowing that is loving.

The problems that plague the piety of the young adult—dryness in prayer, complacency, rationalism—betray an ego only partially submitted to the anointing of the Holy Breath. The young adult has, then, only begun to know the meaning of dying and rising with the Lord. The collapse of the natural ego defenses erected during the first part of life initiates the God-seeker into a new phase of death and transformation in God.

As we have seen, however, once the Christian mystic has left the third mansion, (s)he can anticipate an intensification, not a diminishment of charismatic forms of consciousness. Gracious affections, visionary and locutionary experiences, are likely to become more commonplace. This intensification continues even after infused contemplation has replaced charismatic prayer as the conscious center of the mystic's relationship with God.

In other words, as infused contemplative love intensifies, it draws a charismatically graced ego after it into a dizzying vortex of loving involvement with God. Even the higher graces of contemplative prayer enhance rather than totally abolish charismatic ego functions. The poetry of John of the Cross, his mystical doctrine—both were born of his contemplative experience. As divine love intensified, it freed his mind to articulate with precision the path of his ascent to divine union. It freed his eyes to see the world afresh. And it freed his heart to sing of his Beloved. The same contemplative grace freed Ignatius Loyola to find God in all things. And Teresa, hardheaded and practical as usual, insists that the highest graces of contemplative union nourish the faithful performance of deeds of service and of love.

A developmental mysticism insists, then, upon the continuity that links sacramental, charismatic, and contemplative prayer. Not every Christian mystic will harp upon such continuity, for articulated mystical experience, like every other human experience, is subject to the inadequacies of language and to the law of analogy. The language of the mystics often harbors unconscious and unexorcised dualisms. Nor is every mystical odyssey identical in its progress. For some mystics the transition to contemplative prayer seems to be especially painful and traumatic.

Such seems, for example, to have been the lot of John of the Cross. His mystical doctrine also has a specialized focus. He was particularly concerned to provide directors with a set of norms that would facilitate the transition to contemplation. He was moreover writing at a time when Spanish piety was marred by morbid preoccupation with specific charismatic manifestations of the Breath. John sensed in the morbidity the telltale presence of Anti-Christ. His apophatic approach to contemplation reflects not only these preoccupations but also his formal training in scholastic theology.

Teresa, on the other hand, had never been trained in abstract theology. She was incapable of poetry, though rich images fill her writings. She seems as a consequence to have experienced less need than John, the poet-theologian, to insist upon utter detachment from images and abstractions. She is less suspicious of charismatic phenomena than he. And her own transition to contemplative prayer seems to have been less traumatic.

It may well be, then, that the degree of natural development present in any given mystic's ego will increase the problems involved in the transition to contemplative prayer. For the mystic with a highly developed ego-consciousness has much more to lose in the ego-death that mediates contemplative self-discovery in God.

Be that as it may, a balanced Christian mysticism eschews the Quietist fallacy of forcing a false option between contemplation and ego processes. For it is when charismatic activity is nourished by the love born of contemplative prayer that the historical ego and its works are most powerfully suffused with sacramental meaning. In a world of *maya* ruled by the law of *karma* where history is cyclic and purposeless and where salvation is escape from spatio-temporal entanglement, such a vision of mystical contempation is unthinkable. For the authentic Christian mystic, no other vision is finally adequate.

There is another lesson to be learned from the mysticisms of Teresa and of John. Jungian personality theory suggests that the introverted feeling type has a natural susceptibility to mystical contemplation. And in point of fact Teresa gives evidence of having been an introverted feeling type. She loved the sequestered life of a contemplative nun from the beginning. She resonated most powerfully to the realm of feeling; but she was also open to the worlds of sense and of intuition. Typically, she was baffled by too many abstractions.

But John's personality, while introverted, gives evidence of having been oriented primarily to intuition. His conscious ego resonated most powerfully to images, to poetry. His apophatic asceticism was antipathetic to sensation. Teresa apparently used to twit him for his "stoic" seriousness. He was more open to the world of abstract speculation than Teresa. But he was not given to metaphysical system-building. *The Ascent of Mount Carmel* and *The Dark Night of the Soul* are his most systematic, scholastic works. Both lie uncompleted. His completed treatises are direct, linear commentaries on his own poems. He was attuned to the realm of feeling and a person of extraordinary discernment.

As we have already seen, Jung suggests that the introverted feeling type has a spontaneous affinity for contemplative experience. The mysticism of John suggests that Jung's observation is in need of qualification. Infused contemplation is a free gift of God. As a consequence, no single personality type may be said to have a corner on the contemplative market. Thomas Aquinas would, for example, seem to instantiate the thinking mystic. Ignatius Loyola may well have been an extraverted intuitive type. In his youth he was a romantic and a soldier. It took a cannon ball in his leg as well as a prolonged and painful convalescence to force him into introspection. He was no poet; but he was a visionary, an inspired leader, and an innovative administrator.

There is, then, some evidence in the lives of the mystics that every adult ego is capable in principle of advancing to infused contemplation and of being charismatically enhanced as contemplative graces intensify. Under such a hypothesis, the charismatic consequences of mystical union would differ somewhat from mystic to mystic and from personality to personality.

Christian Death

The experience of the Christian mystics does more than illumine the meaning of salvation history. It also casts light upon the meaning of Christian death and its aftermath.

In his suggestive essay on the theology of death Karl Rahner has attempted to probe the meaning of death as an event and as a consequence of sin. His insights are couched in scholastic and existential categories, and they deserve critical attention and evaluation.

When viewed as an event, death is, Rahner suggests, the separation of the soul from the body. He further suggests that when the soul leaves that portion of the spatio-temporal universe it informs, it ceases to be bound by the limitations of space and time. But being by its scholastic essence matter-oriented (it is *essentialiter* the form of a body), it does not lose its relation to the spatio-temporal universe. As a consequence, death modifies rather than terminates the soul's relation to the cosmos. In death that relationship expands automatically to universal proportions. In the event of death, the soul begins, therefore, to participate in some sense in God's own attitude toward creation.

Rahner suggests too that when viewed as an event, death is the passage from time to eternity. Hence, at the moment of death one's attitude toward God and toward the world becomes fixed and immutable. This fixation of personal commitment at the time of death constitutes one's personal judgment.

Rahner is correct to suggest that the event of death becomes a consequence of sin when it is shrouded with salvific ambiguity. When the event of death is graced, the believer ripens to it as a fulfillment. As we shall see, the experience of the Christian mystics makes concrete sense out of this hypothetical suggestion. But unlike the mystics one can die spurning God or in a state of soul still marred by doubt, fear, resentment, guilt, selfishness. Moreover, death as we experience it in others does not involve the transformation of the physical, spatio-temporal supports of personal life. The corpse disintegrates, returns to dust. It is the food of plants and worms. Even for the mystic, then, death retains an element of ambiguity. It is not the parousia.[79]

Rahner's argument is as usual a transcendental deduction a priori. That is to say, it is a hypothesis, not a conclusion. It needs to be measured against the data we now possess concerning the dying process. That data is of two sorts: interviews of dying and near-death patients and the approach to death described by the Christian mystics.

The Dying Process

Elisabeth Kübler-Ross has for many years now been engaged in an investigation of the process of dying. In her interviews of dying patients, she has uncovered what she believes to be a common developmental pattern in ego-consciousness as it confronts the fact that its physical supports to life are about to be destroyed. Even if it is not applicable in every instance, her scheme provides a useful insight into the typical coping devices the ego employs when it discovers that its vital basis in body-processes is about to be destroyed.

A common first reaction of a dying patient who learns that (s)he is suffering from terminal illness is to deny that the news is either possible or true. Subconsciously such patients know that denial is a subterfuge. Denial is then usually replaced very early by partial acceptance of the inevitable. But exceptionally stubborn or defensive patients can persist in denial to the bitter end. Moreover, initial acceptance often brings a profound sense of loneliness and isolation.[80]

Soon denial and loneliness are replaced by anger and bitterness. Rage that had long been repressed surges into consciousness as the dying ego begins to crumble.[81]

But if there is time, rage is frequently replaced by a new tactic. Many of the dying begin, like the hero of *The Seventh Seal*, to bargain with the grim reaper. When this fails, the typical patient moves to a fourth stage: depression and self-pity.[82]

Depression in the face of death is often linked to emergence of unhealed feelings of shame and guilt, to the sadness of parting and of loss, to the discouragement and frustration born of growing physical weakness.[83]

But for those who are allowed time to die, depression is replaced by a final season of relative peace. Happiness is too strong a word. But in the final stage of the dying process, the ego has ceased to struggle against death. Conflict diminishes. One acquiesces in the inevitable.[84]

Throughout the process, Kübler-Ross discovers in most patients an enduring thread of hope.

The people interviewed by Kübler-Ross and others like her have been ordinary, average people. The great Christian mystics are, however, anything but average. And their approach to death contrasts in notable respects with the portrait of the dying process suggested by Kübler-Ross.

As contemplative union deepens and intensifies within mystical marriage, the Christian mystic is increasingly consumed with a longing for total transformation in God. Conscious that the purifying action of the Holy Breath has freed the heart in its deepest center from disordered affectivity and from attachment to anything that is not God, death becomes a consummation devoutly to be wished. John of the Cross observes:

> It should be known that the death of persons who have reached this state [of mystical marriage] is far different in its cause and mode than the death of others, even though it is similar in natural circumstances. If the death of other people is caused by sickness or old age, the death of these persons is not so induced, in spite of being sick or old; their soul is not wrested from them unless by some impetus and encounter of love, far more sublime than previous ones, of greater power, and more valiant, since it tears through this veil and carries off the jewel, which is the soul.
>
> The death of such persons is very gentle and very sweet, sweeter and more gentle than was their whole spiritual life on earth. For they die with the most sublime impulses and delightful encounters of love, resembling the swan whose song is much sweeter at the moment of death.[85]

Even granting an element of hyperbole in the preceding passage, we should be able to discern in the death of the mystic at least two characteristics that distinguish it from the dying processes described in Kübler-Ross. First, the mystic is palpably conscious of living in and through the power of the Holy Breath. (S)he has discovered a conscious center different from ego-awareness. Contemplative union with God has been transformed into a habitual loving exchange between the self and God. And in the process, the Breath has come to be felt as a sustaining matrix of life. The mystic, then, knows that relinquishment of the body will in no way be the relinquishment of every source of life. The true, conscious source of the mystic's life is the living God. Nor will death hinder contemplative union. On the contrary, bodily involvement is felt as the only remaining obstacle to perfect union with God.

Second, the mystic has already passed through the dying process

Kübler-Ross describes and much worse. Mind, heart, commitment, have all been purified, healed, and liberated in the living flame of divine love. The fear, the rage, the shame, the attachments that make death difficult for most, have been cauterized and healed. The joy of divine union is so intense that the heart bursts with the desire for face-to-face vision. There is no reason, then, to deny death or to bargain with it. As a consequence, the mystic does more than acquiesce in death. (S)he longs for it as the final exodus, the ultimate liberation.

> O living flame of love
> That tenderly wounds my soul
> In its deepest center! Since
> Now You are not oppressive,
> Now Consummate! if it be Your will:
> Tear through the veil of this sweet encounter!

> O sweet cautery,
> O delightful wound!
> O gentle hand! O delicate Touch
> That tastes of eternal life
> And pays every debt!
> In killing You changed death to life.[86]

The experiences of the great mystics yield, then, some concrete insight into the way in which the salvific ambiguity that normally surrounds the dying process can be dispelled by the action of the Mother Advocate. The mystic ripens into death. Some ambiguity still remains, of course, even in the death of the mystic. But the mystic knows that (s)he is so far advanced in the dying process that (s)he will not face its final stages alone.

Life Beyond Life

But the death of the mystic is the exception rather than the rule. What lies beyond the grave for those who have not known mystical purification and conscious contemplative union with God in this life?

It has long been a known medical fact that patients pronounced clinically dead can sometimes be revived even after several minutes of apparent clinical death. Until relatively recently, however, there seemed to be no general interest in investigating the experiences of near-death patients while in that moribund state. In point of fact, many revive recounting experiences that display remarkable similarities.

Raymond A. Moody has written an interesting and provocative summary of the kinds of experiences reported by near-death patients. His work should soon be supplemented and confirmed by the findings of Kübler-Ross.

Those who return after near-death experiences insist that what they encountered at the threshold of death is of a different order from everyday human experience and therefore difficult to describe. Many recall hearing themselves pronounced dead by physicians or spectators. But far from being dismayed, their first feelings are ordinarily those of warmth, comfort, and peace. Some report a period of annoying auditory phenomena: buzzing, roaring, clicking. But the sounds may be pleasant as well: music or the tinkling of bells. At the same time there is often the sense of being drawn through a dark space, like a cave, tunnel, or well.

After passage through the dark, the subjects interviewed seemed to float out of their own bodies. They rise above their bodies, and they gaze down from above on their own death scene and on the activities of those attempting to revive them. At this point many are filled with understandable confusion. This aspect of their experience can be tested. And investigations show that after reviving, they can describe in detail events that transpired around their unconscious and apparently dead bodies.

The confusion that accompanies seeing one's own body usually passes, however, as the subject recognizes that (s)he is dying. (S)he seems to possess a new and different kind of "body," one that lacks solidity but that seems to have something like articulated limbs. Moody suggests that it resembles the spiritual body to which the apostle Paul alludes in his letters. The senses seem to be intact but freed from their ordinary physical limitations. Communication with those still inhabiting the body is, however, impossible; and the dying person often feels a momentary pang of loneliness. But this is soon dispelled by the realization that one is not alone. There is often a sense of the presence of a loved one who has come either to ease the passage to the next life or to bring the message that the time for dying has not yet arrived and that the moribund person must return to his or her own body.

Some near-death patients describe an encounter with a "being of light," a wonderful noumenal presence who is identified most frequently in categories derived from the subject's personal religious background. In some mysterious way the "being of light" establishes communication with the dying subject, often putting probing questions but never judgmentally or in condemnation. The subject is lovingly asked: "Are you prepared to die?" "What have you done with your life?" "Have you done enough?" "What have you to show me?" The dying subject experiences this gentle cross-examination as freeing and illuminating rather than as threatening. Important symbolic events pass rapidly in review and yield liberating self-understanding.

Some near-death patients recall finally being drawn toward some kind of border or limit. It is felt under the guise of different images: a lake, a fence, a door, or in some cases simply a line. The border is never passed, however, and the subject is at some point recalled to the body. (S)he returns often regretfully, reluctant to be separated from the "being of light." Some feel called back for a specific purpose, to accomplish some specific mission. The return is often through the same dark tunnel through which the subject emerged.

Those whose near-death was caused naturally or accidentally tend to find themselves broadened and deepened by the experience. Many know a healing of memories, a significant change of heart and attitude. The experience seems to remove all former fear of dying.[87]

Moody has extended his investigations to include near-death suicides. In their case he finds a very different kind of experience. He puts the matter succinctly:

> These experiences were uniformly characterized as being unpleasant. As one woman said, "If you leave here a tormented soul, you will be a tormented soul over there too." In short, they report that the conflicts they had attempted suicide to escape were still present after they died, but with added complications. In their disembodied state they were unable to do anything about their problems, and they also had to view the unfortunate consequences which had resulted from their acts. . . .
>
> Others who experienced this unpleasant "limbo" state have remarked that they had the feeling they would be there for a long time. This was their penalty for "breaking the rules" by trying to release themselves prematurely from what was, in effect, an "assignment"—to fulfill a certain purpose in life.[88]

Evaluating Near-Death Experiences

Not everyone who experiences near-death recalls the kinds of phenomena just described. Some revive and remember nothing at all. Moreover while patterns emerge in recalled experiences, they are not uniform.

Even if one is willing to grant the authenticity of such experiences, the evidence they furnish is relevant, not to death itself, but to near-death. For the subjects examined seem to have preserved some link to their physical bodies, at least to the extent of being able to resuscitate its vital processes after the ordinary medical signs of life had vanished.

Nevertheless, near-death experiences raise a number of interesting questions. Of special interest are: (1) the evidence they provide that the self is in fact capable of survival without the physical body; (2) the fact that the experiences described seem to have transpired in the realm of ego-consciousness; (3) the presence of psychopomps; (4) the character of the encounter with the "being of light"; (5) the contrast between near-death experiences and the experience of mystical prayer; (6) the contrast between natural and suicidal near-deaths.

Moody and Kübler-Ross both suggest that the experience of floating out of the body described by near-death patients lends support to religious and philosophical belief in personal survival after death. There is merit in their suggestion. And in the present context, it is perhaps worth noting that the experience would seem to be inexplicable in terms of a strict Whiteheadean authropology.

Whitehead was understandably cautious about discussing personal survival after death. On the one hand, his rationalism left him blind to the grounds for belief in personal survival supplied by mystical experience; on the other, his failure to supply the human individual with a principle of vital continuity distinct from the physical and conceptual feelings that shape experience left him hard put to explain how personal survival might be possible, except as a memory in the mind of God.

His normal strategy was to counsel trust in the enlightened self-interest of the Deity. For, he argued, divine satisfaction would be enriched if human, personal survival is possible. And Whitehead's God is concerned to achieve the greatest possible satisfaction from the world. God will then preserve whatever can be preserved out of each personal human nexus of actual occasions.[89]

But in contrast to Whitehead's scheme, an emergent anthropology affirms the existence of legal, vectoral feelings as the principle of unity and continuity within experience. And it concurs with both Moody and Kübler-Ross in suggesting that the extracorporeal experiences described by near-death patients provide evidence that supports belief that the emerging human self is not totally dependent on its own body for personal survival. In addition, however, an emergent Christian anthropology looks to mystical experience as providing clues to the shape of life after death. We will return to this point shortly.

For the present, it suffices to note that the positive experiences described by Moody's interviewees, while uncanny, fall short of mystical betrothal and mystical marriage. They seem to be mediated by specific concepts and therefore seem to transpire within ego-consciousness. Moody's subjects hear noises, experience a variety of feelings, remember specific events, hear specific messages and questions put to them by psychopomps and by the "being of light." Their approach to the limit (of death presumably) is mediated by images. Their habitual beliefs condition their interpretation of their experiences. In other words, Moody's subjects experience their encounter with the "being of light" in ways that contrast sharply with the graces of mystical union.

The presence of benevolent psychopomps and the review of life in the presence of the "being of light" would seem to be thoroughly convergent with three age-old Christian beliefs: belief in the communion of saints, belief in guardian angels, and belief in a personal judgment at the moment of death. The psychopomps who greet the moribund are from among those who have gone before. Their assisting presence at the moment of death suggests that devotion to the saints and belief that the church on earth stands in communion with the blessed of God is a sound one. The psychopomps have an angelic aspect: they come bearing messages, and they seem to have a special care for the person who is dying, in the manner of guardian angels.

Moreover, the description of the review of life in the presence of the "being of light" well accords with the theology of divine judgment articulated in the fourth gospel. In Johannine theology God judges the world by the simple expedient of revealing the full scope of His love and demanding from humankind an appropriate response. Those who encounter the "being of light" are encompassed by a sense of acceptance and are lovingly challenged concerning their stewardship.

Their encounter with the "being of light" falls far short of the Christian mystics' experience of contemplative union with God, a fact suggesting the possibility that the encounter with the "being of light" is only an initial one. Further growth in one's relationship with that noumenal presence once one has crossed to the other side is not, then, out of the question.

The negative experiences of near-death suicides are suggestive in other ways. None of Moody's subjects seem to have experienced the cosmicization of their attitude to the world that Rahner suggests should follow automatically on departure from the body. Perhaps the reason is that none have fully died. Nevertheless, Moody's subjects seem to carry with them the ego-perspective on the world with which they "died." This seems particularly striking in the case of the suicides whose isolation, loneliness, conflict, and pain perdure and are in fact intensified.

But the cosmicization of consent to God and to the world does seem to attend the higher states of mystical prayer. The expansion of one's world perspective to quasi-divine proportions, if it occurs, need not then be the automatic concomitant of physical death and may have to await a deeper, purifying contact with God, not unlike mystical purification.

Heaven, Purgatory, Hell

None of Moody's subjects passed beyond the limit to which they felt drawn. Had they done so, they would not presumably have returned to tell the tale. But had they passed over and returned, what would they have recounted?

If our reflections on these murky subjects have at least an element of initial plausibility, there is a hint of an answer in the experiences of the Christian mystics. For Christian mysticism is full of intimations of immortality. Indeed the mystical exploration into God seems to suggest that the distinction between time and eternity may not be so neat as either Rahner's theology of death or Thomistic and Platonic metaphysics suggest.

And indeed Christian theology has never been altogether easy with a total disjunction between the here and the hereafter. In Pauline theology, death and resurrection with Jesus are a process that is being accomplished even now, even though the consummation of that process must await the second coming of the Lord. Medieval theology speaks of faith in God as a present intimation of the beatific vision. The final dualism that needs to be exorcised from a Christian theology of the human is, then, the dualism of time and eternity.

Both Teresa and John of the Cross felt that their experiences of purgation and of mystical enlightenment were relevant to a theology of the afterlife. John of the Cross believed that the dark nights of sense and especially of spirit were relevant to a theology of purgatory. Official teaching concerning purgatory holds that purification after death awaits those who die in the love of God but have not yet made adequate satisfaction for their sins.[90] Needless to say, the theological term "satisfaction" must be construed in ways that preclude anything that might be interpreted as divine vindictiveness. In *Charism and Sacrament*, I suggested that for the repentant, sin becomes its own punishment. The knowledge that I have rejected and hurt one I love is always painful. The greater my love for that person, the more intense the suffering. Painful too is having to face the present consequences of such a betrayal.[91]

The pain of purification described by the mystics is just such a torment. Once one has known the love of God, confrontation with one's unhealed sinfulness, especially in the knowledge that it stands as an obstacle to perfect union, is an agony. But when it is informed by divine love, it is an agony that brings its own healing.

The pain of the dark night of the spirit is, moreover, the effect of God's action upon the mystic. It results, not from divine vindictiveness (such a thought is an authoritarian blasphemy), but from the lack of faith, hope, and love in the mystic's own heart and from resistance to the divine action. Mystical purification is a rearrangement of the mystic's personality, a pneumatic rolfing, which is an unavoidable precondition to perfect union with God.

Most of us die without having undergone such a purification. The mystics know, however, that without such purification perfect union with God is impossible. They also insist that the highest graces of the mystical marriage lead one to the threshold of the beatific vision. In other words, just as the mystics have explored the meaning of ego-death long before the experience of physical dying, so too they have experienced that the purification of human limitation and sin is the unavoidable prelude to the face-to-face vision of God. To those of us who die without having known such purification, the words of Hamlet would seem to apply: "If it be not now, yet it will come. The readiness is all."

The preceding reflections also cast light on the human descent into hell. For if it is indeed possible, as mystical experience suggests, to know in this life the kind of ego-death that is the prelude to contemplative union, and if in addition contemplative union can lead to the very threshold of the beatific vision, then one would also expect that an *inchoatio damnationis*, or anticipatory descent into hell, ought to be available in the present life as well.

Appreciative insight into the meaning of the descent into hell has been traditionally dominated by a host of interrelated archetypal images: images of the Satanic, the demonic, the diabolical; images of the shadow, of entrapment in the persona; images of despair.

Once again, an adequate Christian interpretation of these images must exclude from them any hint of divine vindictiveness. Ignatius Loyola has, however, provided us with the key. In his rules for the discernment of spirits, he suggests, quite correctly, that God enters appreciative consciousness differently before and after conversion. He writes:

> In the case of those who go from one mortal sin to another, the enemy is ordinarily accustomed to propose apparent pleasures. He fills their imagination with sensual delights and gratifications, the more readily to keep them in their vices and increase the number of their sins.
>
> With such persons the good spirit uses a method which is the reverse of the above. Making use of the light of reason, he will rouse the sting of conscience and fill them with remorse.[92]

Ignatius's concern in the rules for discernment is primarily with primitive, pre-archetypal affective responses. But when one extends the principle he enunciates into the realm of archetypal thinking, it becomes instinct with foundational significance.

Every Jungian archetype has both a positive and a negative aspect. The self is no exception. In its positive aspect, the self is a symbol of integrating wholeness and enlightenment. But the self becomes demonic when it devours rather than sustains ego processes. The dark side of the self presides, as we have already seen, over the process of ego-disintegration described in Chapter III. In other words, as one descends the scale of personality dysfunction, an archetypally mediated confrontation with God will be apt to be dominated by demonic imagery. We are not suggesting, as Jung seems to do at times, that there is a demonic side to the Deity.[92] We are suggesting that the violent and the psychotic are often inclined to project their personal demons onto the Godhead.

If, moreover, Ignatius's suggestion is correct, the more one is oppressed by the untamed dark powers in one's own heart, the more one is possessed by the demons of rage, fear, guilt, shame, and violence, the more will the attempt of God to enter in communion with the sinner be felt as an alien and threatening incursion. For the diabolic, who destroy and counterfeit meaning, and for the demon possessed, God will, then, be most apt to enter appreciative consciousness as a tempting, seemingly Satanic influence. For the tormented heart, therefore, any experience of the God of love is difficult to come by. For the despairing heart, it may well be impossible.

Moreover, as Dante saw clearly, subjection to one's personal demons brings other torments as well: entrapment in the persona and shadow possession. As one descends into hell, the shadow takes possession of larger and larger areas of the personality until one is all but identified with the shadow self. At the same time one becomes increasingly entrapped in the diabolical schemes one has concocted out of the turmoil of one's own crazed heart. Hitler's rise and fall provides a horrifying case study of this aspect of damnation.

There is one final ingredient to add to our witches' brew: despair. John of the Cross likens his experience of the dark night of the spirit to the experience of hell, with this single exception: he never lost hope. The descent into hell is never complete, therefore, until one so closes one's heart to God that transformation in the power of the Holy Breath ceases to be possible. The New Testament and official Church teaching both assures us that such a decision is no theological fiction but a real possibility. For one who has despaired of God, the pain of hell must, then, be twofold: the pain of losing the joy of the beatific vision and the pain of sense, i.e., the suffering that results from living with the tormenting consequences of one's own sinfulness and without hope of redemption. As Karl Rahner has observed:

> The just God is "active" in the punishment of hell only insofar as he does not release man from the reality of the definitive state which man himself has achieved on his own behalf, contradictory though this state be to the world as God's creation.[93]

Only this need be added; if God is indeed the God of love proclaimed by Jesus, He will allow such a state to perdure only if the damned offer no alternative. For God cannot save us without our cooperation, and there is no reason in principle why the human self cannot define its perspective upon reality in such a way as to exclude God permanently. If there is any opening in a person's attitude to the action of the Mother Advocate, we may trust in faith that human hearts that depart this life otherwise tormented will in the next know, not the hell of self-inflicted despair and pain, but the purifying action of divine love that is the prelude to the marriage of the Lamb.

Corrolaries

The preceding analysis of the "last things" differs notably from the theory proposed in W. Norman Pittenger's *The Last Things in a Process Perspective*. Pittenger describes his eschatology as an attempt to represent the "gospel" in "starkly human terms." By "starkly human" Pittenger means a version of the "gospel" that not only demythologizes but "dekerygmatizes" Christian belief in the resurrection. In other words, Pittenger's book really has little or nothing to do with a Christian understanding of the "last things." It offers the reader instead a sterile exercise in philosophical reductionism.[94]

But Pittenger's book is a useful object lesson in what happens when one substitutes Whiteheadean philosophy for the gospel. Pittenger offers his reader a death that is irreducibly solitary. While death is certain, he tells us, personal survival is not. Hence, heaven and hell should be understood as present states of existence. The worst one can do with one's life is to miss the subjective aim that Whitehead's God offers each new occasion of experience. Divine judgment is nothing else than God's attempt to make the best of bad situations.

The emergent problematic here presented rejects philosophical reductionism as methodologically inadequate. It argues that death becomes solitary through despair. It defends personal survival after death, and while it acknowledges that heaven, purgatory, and hell are presently in the making, it affirms them as states beyond the grave. It rejects Whitehead's understanding of "subjective aim" as naturalistic, philosophically questionable, and unable to explain adequately the gracing, charismatic action of the Holy Breath. And it interprets the divine judgment in categories derived primarily from the fourth gospel.

But the preceding analysis is also relevant in its consequences to Christian missiology. The Catholic mission to the Orient has begun to assume an ecumenical aspect, symbolized by books on "Christian Zen" and "Christian Yoga" and by theological efforts to find points of convergence between Christian and Oriental approaches to God. Such dialogue needs to be continued and deserves to be carried on carefully and critically.

But if the preceding analysis is sound, then Christian mysticism has an important redemptive word to speak to the Orient at a crucial period of cultural transition. Bernard Meland has suggested with considerable plausibility that the most serious threat to religion in the far East is secularization.[95] Certainly, capitalism and communism offer the emerging nations a slightly different version of materialistic secularism. Both versions are the death of religious faith.

Secularization is the work of the rampaging and often sinful human ego. A religion whose spontaneous bent lies in the contemplative flight from history and from conscious ego processes can offer no direct opposition to the secularizing incursions of modern technocracy.

But if charismatic piety is the gracing of ego-consciousness in faith, and if the charismatic transformation of ego processes is the sacralization and sacramentalization of human history, then a balanced Christian mysticism can speak directly to the contemporary religious needs of both the Orient and the West. For a balanced charismatic piety freed from pietistic introversion and subjectivism has the power to sacralize the secular ego. And authentic Christian mysticism has the power to establish dynamic continuity between charismatic and contemplative forms of prayer, to correct the soteriological inadequacies in yogic forms of mysticism, and to lead the oriental search for God to fulfillment in the mystical marriage.

Trail's End

We have reached the end of our last set of switchbacks. There is a double pleasure at the completion of any taxing ascent. One can look back over the trail, its windings and its challenges and say: "I know that path. It is not the only way up. But it has been my way. And I have mastered it."

The path of our reflections has been a winding one. It began in autobiography. It has led to our present vantage point. And it still ascends to the dim heights traced by the mystics. Its first challenge was the thicket of methodology. After several false starts, we broke through and began our speculative climb.

Our ascent has spiraled. Again and again we found ourselves standing over the trailhead but at a new elevation. Yet each spiral brought its own surprises. We began to understand that the salvific integration of experience is its transformation in the power of the Holy Breath, that transformation in God is personal and social liberation, that the liberation of experience is its charismatic sacramentalization, and its sacramentalization is the victory of the cross, that the victory of the cross is the dawn of Easter.

But the greatest pleasure of a successful climb is the vista of distant peaks tantalizing and inviting in their beauty. Theology is a mountain range: its summits are all part of a single soaring thrust of the earth into the clouds. The Christian anthropology sketched in these pages is of a piece with the theology of conversion outlined in *Charism and Sacrament*. Beyond both lie the mysteries and winding paths of pneumatology, Christology, ecclesiology, all inviting the mind and heart to further foundational explorations. But the trail we have just completed has been long and challenging enough. We have resisted following many of its branches and detours, but we are tired. And if the good Lord gives the time, if our legs and lungs stay strong, and if our hearts and our vision long for expansion, we may take the trail again one day, not quite knowing where it may lead, but hoping for a vista, a new angle on the universe, a new breath of clean air, a new draught of living water.

Notes

1. Rm. 5:17.

2. Mk. 8:31, 9:31ff., 10:34–38; Jn. 5:24, 8:51, 11:25, 12:33, 18:32; 1 Th. 5:10; Rm. 5:6ff.; He. 2:9, 9:15; Col. 1:18; 1 Co. 15:45.

3. Is. 53:12; cf. Is. 53:7–12; Mk. 8:31, 9:31, 10:34ff.; Mt. 12:40, 26:6, 27:63ff.; Jm. 2:19.

4. 1 Co. 15:5ff.; Ac. 9:1–9.

5. Jm. 20:29–31.

6. Mt. 22: 43ff.; Lk. 1:43, 2:11; 1 Co. 8:5ff., 12:3; Rm. 10:9, 14:9; Col. 2:6–15; Ac. 2:33, 10:42, 36; Ep. 1:20; Phil. 2:10; Rv. 4:1–21. For a sensitive handling of the complex imagery that colors Christian aspiration for the end time, see: Austin Farrer, *A Rebirth of Images* (Glasgow: University Press, 1949).

7. C. G. Jung, *The Structure and Dynamics of the Psyche* (Princeton: Bollingen, 1960), p. 395.

8. *Ibid.*, pp. 395–396; Whitemont, *Symbolic Quest*, pp. 279–281.

9. Jung, *Structure and Dynamics of the Psyche*, p. 407; cf. *The Archetypes of the Collective Unconscious*, trans. R. F. C. Hull (New York: Bollingen, 1959), p. 123.

10. Edinger, *Ego and Archetype*, pp. 131–156.

11. C. G. Jung, *Aion: Researches into the Phenomenology of the Self*, trans. F. C. Hull (New York: Bollingen, 1959), p. 114.

12. *Ibid.*, pp. 55ff.

13. Stanislaus Lyonnet and Leopold Sabourin, *Sin, Redemption, and Sacrifice* (Rome: Biblical Institute, 1970).

14. Gelpi, *Charism and Sacrament*, pp. 125–131.

15. Teresa of Avila, *Interior Castle*, trans. E. Allison Peers (New York: Doubleday, 1944), pp. 28–29.

16. *Ibid.*, pp. 28–43.

17. *Ibid.*, pp. 46–54.

18. *Ibid.*, pp. 56–69.

19. Jung, *Structure and Dynamics of the Psyche*, pp. 388–414.

20. The "mystic scruple" is the fear of selfishness in one's love of God; Felix Marti-Ibañez, "The Heart of Teresa," *MD*, XIX (April, 1975), p. 12. Cf. Teresa of Avila, *Autobiography*, trans. Kieran Kavanaugh, O.C.D., and Otilio Rodriguez, O.C.D. (Washington: I.C.S. Publications, 1976), pp. 38–77.

21. Teresa of Avila, *Interior Castle*, p. 85.

22. *Ibid.*, pp. 87–88.

23. William Johnston, S.J., *The Mysticism of the Cloud of Unknowing* (New York: Desclee, 1967).

24. Gordon Allport, *The Individual and His Religion* (New York: Macmillan, 1950), pp. 31–36.

25. Pierre Babin, *Crisis of Faith* (New York: Macmillan, 1950), pp. 31–36.

25. Pierre Babin, *Crisis of Faith* (New York: Herder and Herder, 1969).

26. Allport, *op. cit.*, pp. 42–43.

27. Babin, *op. cit.*, pp. 56–71.

28. Evelyn Underhill, *Mysticism* (New York: E. P. Dutton, 1961), pp. 44–94, 266–297; Karl Rahner, S.J., "Visions and prophecies," in *Inquiries* (New York: Herder and Herder, 1964).

29. John of the Cross, *Collected Works*, pp. 160–168, 156–157; Teresa of Avila, *Autobiography*, pp. 193–194.

30. John of the Cross, *Collected Works*, pp. 156, 189.

31. *Ibid.*, pp. 187–189.

32. *Ibid.*, p. 194.

33. *Ibid.*, p. 195.

34. *Ibid.*, pp. 196–202.

35. *Ibid.*, p. 204.

36. *Ibid.*, p. 208.

37. *Ibid.*, p. 210.

38. *Ibid.*, pp. 211–213.

39. *Ibid.*, pp. 107–147.

40. Teresa of Avila, *The Way of Perfection*, trans. E. Allison Peers (New York: Doubleday, 1964), p. 185.

41. *Ibid.*, pp. 200–202.

42. DS 2195–2269; Ronald Knox, *Enthusiasm* (New York: Oxford, 1961), pp. 231–355.

43. Teresa of Avila, *Interior Castle*, p. 98.

44. Teresa of Avila, *Autobiography*, pp. 109–110.

45. *Ibid.*, pp. 113–114.

46. Teresa of Avila, *Interior Castle*, p. 101.

47. *Ibid.*, p. 119.

48. Teresa of Avila, *Autobiography*, p. 120.

49. *Ibid.*, p. 129.

50. John of the Cross, *Collected Works*, pp. 410–411.

51. Underhill, *op. cit.*, p. 382.

52. John of the Cross, *Collected Works*, p. 337.

53. *Ibid.*, pp. 329–389, 213–292.

54. *Ibid.*, pp. 462–499.

55. *Ibid.*, p. 497.

56. Teresa of Avila, *Interior Castle*, p. 209.

57. *Ibid.*, pp. 206–235; cf. George Morel, *Le sens de l'existence selon S. Jean de la Croix* (Paris: Aubier, 1960); von Balthasar, *Die Heerlichkeit*, II, pp. 464ff.

58. James, *Varieties of Religious Experience*, pp. 299–301.

59. *Ibid.*, pp. 311–336.

60. Joseph Maréchal, *Studies in the Psychology of the Mystics*, trans. Algar Trorold (New York: Magi, 1964).

61. R. C. Zaehner, *Mysticism, Sacred and Profane* (New York: Oxford, 1961).

62. *Ibid.*, pp. 84–106.

63. *Ibid.*, pp. 101–102.

64. *Ibid.*, pp. 1–29.
65. *Ibid.*, pp. 30–83.
66. Abraham Maslow, *Religions, Values, and Peak Experiences* (New York: Viking, 1964).
67. Zaehner, *op. cit.*, pp. 148–149.
68. Mircea Eliade, *Yoga, Immortality, and Freedom* (Princeton: Bollinger, 1958), p. 3.
69. Eliade, *Cosmos and History*, pp. 3–58.
70. *Ibid.*, pp. 51–92.
71. *Ibid.*, p. 104.
72. *Ibid.*, pp. 95–137.
73. *Ibid.*, p. 99.
74. Karl Rahner, *Theological Investigations*, V, pp. 115–135.
75. Gelpi, *Charism and Sacrament*, pp. 97–109.
76. Eliade, *Yoga, Immortality, and Freedom*, pp. 162–273.
77. Gelpi, *Charism and Sacrament*, pp. 63–65.
78. *Ibid.*, pp. 27–61.
79. Karl Rahner, *On the Theology of Death*, trans. Charles H. Henkey (Freiburg: Herder, 1961), pp. 15–48.
80. Elisabeth Kübler-Ross, *On Death and Dying* (New York: Macmillan, 1969), pp. 38–49.
81. *Ibid.*, pp. 50–81.
82. *Ibid.*, pp. 82–84.
83. *Ibid.*, pp. 85–111.
84. *Ibid.*, pp. 112–137.
85. John of the Cross, *Collected Works*, pp. 591–592.
86. *Ibid.*, p. 578.
87. Raymond A. Moody, *Life After Life* (Atlanta: Mockingbird, 1975), pp. 25–70.
88. *Ibid.*, p. 126.
89. Alfred North Whitehead, *Science and Philosophy* (Patterson: Littlefield, Adams, 1964), pp. 85–104.
90. DS 1304, 1580, 1820.
91. Gelpi, *Charism and Sacrament*, pp. 234–238.
92. C. G. Jung, *The Answer to Job* (Princeton: Bollingen, 1974).
93. Karl Rahner, "Hell" in *Encyclopedia of Theology* (New York: Seabury, 1975), p. 604.
94. W. Norman Pittenger, *The Last Things in a Process Perspective* (London: Epworth, 1970).
95. Bernard E. Meland, *The Realities of Faith: Revolution in Cultural Forms* (New York: Oxford, 1962): *The Secularization of Modern Cultures* (New York: Oxford, 1966); Smith, *Experience and God*, pp. 158–205; Eliade, *The Sacred and the Profane*, pp. 162–213.

Glossary

In the course of the preceding analysis, we have had occasion to apply dialectical and foundational method to a number of different philosophical and theological questions. In the course of our argument we have been forced to employ a number of technical terms derived from process and substance speculation. And we have augmented the list of technical terminology in our own foundational analysis of the dynamics of human emergence. What follows is a list of technical definitions. The terms are, then, derived from three sources: from Whiteheadean philosophy, from a Thomistic philosophy of substance, and from a foundational theology of human emergence. In the far left-hand column there is an indication of the speculative tradition from which the term that follows it is derived. A Whiteheadean term is preceded by the letters: Wh. A term in Thomistic substance philosophy by the letters Th. And a term used in our own foundational theory of human emergence, by the letters: em. When the same term is employed in more than one speculative context, it is preceded by the appropriate designations; and in its subsequent definition, there is an attempt to clarify the different senses in which it is used in each of the frames of reference in which it is employed.

em ABDUCTION: an inference that argues from a rule and a result to a case; the formulation of a hypothesis.

Th ACCIDENT: that which exists in another and not in itself; the modification of a substance.

Th ACT: an intrinsic principle of specification. Act is the metaphysical correlate of potency; together they divide being.

em AFFECTIVE CONTINUUM: the ongoing evaluative transmutation of dative feelings into physical purposes of increasing complexity and consciousness. The affective continuum discloses more or less vaguely the vectoral thrust of experience and eventually yields to the inferential disclosure of the laws operative within experience.

Th AGENT INTELLECT: a spiritual faculty of the human soul that uses the sensible phantasm in the imagination to produce an impressed species on the possible intellect that determines the latter to know one specific object rather than another.

em ALLEGORICAL MEANING: the meaning disclosed by physical purposes and by appreciative consciousness. Allegorical structures of knowing are concrete, imagistic, archetypal. Its laws are not those of logical inference. It follows instead transductive patterns of spontaneous association and of synchronicity.

em ANAGOGICAL MEANING: the meaning disclosed through the inferential explication of the theoretical consequences of explanatory hypothesis.

em APPRECIATIVE CONSCIOUSNESS: conscious physical purposes; a more or less vague affective awareness of the vectors present in any given situation.

em ARCHETYPE: a spontaneous image that recurs in a variety of individuals, epochs, and cultures, that is heavy with affective significance and therefore connotatively rich, and that is endowed with a central core of meaning that is linked by free association with images and attitudes of varying degrees of conscious or unconscious evaluative differentiation. A theology of human emergence brackets Jung's causal explanations of archetypes and is content to note their reality and power within human affectivity.

Th BEING: that which is.

em CASE: a general classification designating an instance of a specific kind of rule. A case functions in experience as an evaluative element in inferential understanding.

Wh CONCRESCENCE: the growing together of contrasted feelings into a concrete satisfaction.

Wh CONFORMAL FEELING: the feeling of an initial fact as limiting
em the possibility for realistic development present in any given process.

em CONVERSION: the decision to assume conscious, personal responsibility for the subsequent development of a distinguishable realm of experiential growth. Realms of experience are distinguished by the kinds of laws that function within them. There are four such realms in human experience.

Affective conversion aspires to the healing and healthy
growth of physical purposes. *Intellectual conversion* aspires
to the critical revision and elaboration of propositional
feelings that are logical, coherent, applicable, and adequate.
Moral conversion aspires to the critical revision and
readjustment of personal decisions in the light of values
that can be legitimately affirmed as ultimate and absolute.
Religious conversion aspires to integral personal growth
before God in response to every authentic instance of
divine self-revelation.

em   DAIMONIC: the unexpected surge of powerful physical purposes
        into consciousness.

em   DATIVE FEELINGS: the initial evaluative presentation of initial
Wh   facts within experience.

em   DECISION: an action that terminates evaluation and reduces a
Wh   given process to concrete satisfaction. A theology of
        emergence distinguishes two kinds of decision: initial
        and final. *Initial decision* terminates conscious evaluative
        processes and prepares the body for final decision. *Final
        decision* is the realm of final fact; it engages bodily
        energies to effect environmental transformations.

em   DEMONIC: the unexpected upsurge of destructive and powerful
        physical purposes into consciousness.

em   DIABOLIC: that which shatters and/or counterfeits meaning and
        purpose.

em   DIALECTICAL THEOLOGY: a functional specialty within the theo-
        logical enterprise that seeks to clarify and evaluate the
        historical issues relevant to the resolution of a controverted
        religious question.

em   EGO-CONSCIOUSNESS: consciousness based on evaluative
        discrimination and evaluative synthesis of discriminated vari-
        ables. Its most basic form is body-consciousness, the
        evaluative discrimination of one's own body from its
        sustaining environment. In its evaluative form, ego-
        consciousness may or may not be loving.

em   ENVIRONMENT: those facts and forces within experience that
        nurture the growth of an emerging self. The human self
        experiences two dynamically interrelated environments.

Its sustained environment is its own physical body. Its
sustaining/disintegrating environment is those forces
that either nurture or inhibit bodily processes.

Th ESSENCE: what a reality is as distinct from the fact that it is.

Wh ETERNAL OBJECT: a pure potential for process.

em ESCHATOLOGICAL: pertaining to the Biblical "end time" when the
full scope of divine salvation will be finally revealed.

em EXPERIENCE: a process in which three kinds of variables function:
factual, qualitative, and legal.

em FACT: the dyadic relationship of action and reaction prescinded
from the evaluative elements that present it within experience
and the legal elements in which it is grounded.

Th FACULTY: the accident of a substance that endows it with the
essential and abiding capacity to act in a certain way.

em FEELING: a relational element within experience. There are
three basic feelings: qualitative, factual, and legal.
More complex feelings combine these basic feelings
into patterns of varying integration and complexity.

Th FORM: an intrinsic principle of essential specification.

Th FORMAL OBJECT: the reality attained by the activity of a
faculty (material object) together with the aspect under
which it is attained. For example, the formal object of
the faculty of sight is extended, material things as
colored.

em FOUNDATIONAL THEOLOGY: a functional theological specialty
that attempts to articulate a normative account of the authentic
conversion experience that grounds a religious tradition.

em FUNCTIONAL SPECIALTY: a field of theological inquiry distinguished by the kind of questions and issues it addresses and
by the operational procedures it employs.

em GRACE: that aspect of the evaluative form of an experience that
is shaped by overt faith-dependence on the Breath of Jesus.

Th IMPRESSED SPECIES: the determination of a faculty prior to action

that determines it to respond in one way rather than in
another.

em INDUCTION: an inference that concludes from a case and a result to a
rule; the verification or falsification of a deductively
clarified hypothesis.

em INEXISTENCE: the relational presence of one entity in another
that it shapes as an experience.

em INFERENCE: the evaluative interrelation of a rule, a case, and
a result.

Wh INITIAL DATUM: the state of the universe at the beginning of a
process.

em LAW: a habitual schematization of the self; a generalized tendency
to evaluate and/or decide in a specific manner.

em LITERAL MEANING: the realm of meaning disclosed through dative
feelings and primitive, imageless physical purposes.

Th MATTER: an intrinsic substantial principle of pure potentiality;
the pure capacity for change. Matter is opposed to spirit.

em MEANING: the evaluative disclosure of relationship.

em METHOD: a normative pattern of operations yielding cumulative
and progressive results.

em NATURE: that aspect of the evaluative form of an experience that
is motivated by response to values that are not opposed
to the historical self-revelation of God but that remain
untouched by overt religious faith.

Wh NEGATIVE PREHENSION: a negative relationship that differentiates
one occasion of experience from another and helps define
its perspective on the universe.

Wh NEXUS: A public matter of fact.

Wh OBJECTIVE IMMORTALITY: the status of an occasion of experience
once it has achieved satisfaction, and with satisfaction
the immutability of a past fact.

em PERSON: a relational reality subsisting in its own right but

not simply in itself and imbued with either a developing
or an abiding capacity for self-understanding as the
basis for decision. To subsist in one's own right is to
function within experience as a relationally distinct center
of evaluation and decision.

Th PHANTASM: the image produced by the organic faculty of the
imagination.

em PHYSICAL PURPOSE: in Whiteheadean theory, the abrupt focusing
Wh of appetition upon an eternal object ingredient in a
physical datum; in an emergent anthropology, the more
or less vague, affective disclosure of vectoral feelings
within experience.

Th POTENCY: the intrinsic capacity for determination by an act;
potency is the metaphysical correlate of act.

Th POSSIBLE INTELLECT: a spiritual faculty of human cognition whose
formal object is finite, sensible reality insofar as it is
capable of being understood as being.

Wh PREHENSION: a concrete fact of relatedness. Every prehension
includes a subject, an initial datum, the subject's
objective datum (or perspective on the universe), its
negative prehensions, and its subjective form (or way
of prehending the universe). An element in the subjective
form of a prehension is its subjective aim.

Wh PRESENTATIONAL IMMEDIACY: that character that accrues to any
em reality conceptually illumined within experience, namely,
that it is presented to a subject for further evaluation
and begins to function as an element in the subject's
temporal present.

Wh PROPOSITIONAL FEELING: in Whiteheadean theory, a matter of
em fact in potential determination, a theoretical feeling; in an
emergent anthropology, the inferential disclosure of the
legal basis of fact and of value.

em PROCESS PHILOSOPHY: a broadly based and pluralistic speculative
movement whose vision of reality is characterized by a
scientific fallibilism, a sensitivity to evolutionary
theory, and a preoccupation with the developmental character
of experience.

em PROCESS THEOLOGY: a broadly based and pluralistic movement of
     thought that attempts to fuse Christian belief and insights
     gleaned from process philosophy.

em QUALITY: a particular instance of suchness; an evaluative
     element within experience.

em RESULT: a fact capable of being grasped inferentially as a
     case, or instance, of a general rule, or law.

em RULE: a law disclosed inferentially.

em SATANIC: the character of those forces in experience disclosed
     to appreciative consciousness by the image of Satan,
     who is the mythic personification of Anti-Christ.

em SATISFACTION: in Whiteheadean theory the reduction of an atomic
     occasion of experience to concreteness through decision
     and the perishing of immediacy; in an emergent anthropology,
     the incremental specification of experience through decision.

em SYNCHRONICITY: the emergence of meaningful coincidences within
     experience that defy strict causal explanation.

Wh SOCIETY: a nexus of actual occasion of experience endowed with
     either a diffused or a dominant principle of order.

em SOTERIOLOGY: a theological account of the meaning, sources,
     conditions, and effects of graced transformation in God.

Th SPIRIT: that which is immaterial, i.e., free from the limitations
     of matter in both its reality and operations.

Wh SUBJECT: in Whiteheadean theory, an actual occasion of experience
em   in which a prehension functions as a concrete element; in
     an emergent anthropology, a complete, developing legal
     entity, the self that emerges from the incremental
     legal schematization of experience.

Wh SUBJECTIVE AIM: that aspect of the evaluative form of experience
em   that endows it with purpose. In an emergent anthropology
     aims are designated as "personal" and "individual" rather
     than as "subjective" and are interpreted as the evaluative
     disclosure of vectoral feelings.

Wh SUBJECTIVE FORM: the way in which a subject prehends its
em   datum. In an emergent anthropology, the form of experience

is called "personal" or "evaluative" rather than subjective
and embraces the entire realm of quality.

Th SUBSTANCE: that which exists in itself and not in anything else.

em SUBSTANCE PHILOSOPHY: a rational account of reality as a whole
which employs the term "substance."

em SYMBOL: that which mediates the evaluative grasp of meaning.
There are two kinds of symbols. An *expressive symbol*
is a fact that renders apparent the law in which it is
grounded. An *interpretative symbol* is an evaluative response
that discloses the relational structure of experience.

em TRANSDUCTIVE THOUGHT: pre-inferential, evaluative responses
that shape the realm of physical purpose. Transductive
thinking is concrete, prelogical, often haphazard,
structured by memory and by the law of synchronicity.

em TRANSMUTATION OF EXPERIENCE: experiential development in
continuity; one experience transmutes another: (1) when it
develops in real continuity with the prior experience; (2) when
it includes a qualitatively distinguishable variable not present
in the prior experience; and (3) when the novel variable is
integrated into the subsequent experience in such a way as to
reduce the latter's constitutive relational structure to a
mutually reinforcing unity.

em TRANSVALUATION: an instance of the conscious, evaluative transformation of experience. A concept is transvalued when
the presuppositions that had formerly governed its use
are reversed in such a way as to create a new interpretative
frame of reference, and when the original concept is employed
within the novel frame of reference in such a way as to
retain some of its original meaning while simultaneously
acquiring novel denotative and/or connotative significance.

em TROPOLOGICAL MEANING: the meaning disclosed through the inferential elucidation of the practical and moral consequences
of explanatory hypotheses.

Wh VECTOR: a definite transmission of energy from one occasion of
experience to another.

em VECTORAL FEELING: a law viewed as orienting an instance of
experience toward a future.

Index